D0122942

The
Onassis Women

The Onassis Women

An Eyewitness Account

Kiki Feroudi Moutsatsos

with Phyllis Karas

G. P. Putnam's Sons

New York

PHOTO CREDITS

Chapters 1 and 9: Archive Photos. Chapter 3: Pop-
perfoto/Archive Photos. Chapter 5: Cecil Beaton/Cam-
era Press/Retna Ltd. Chapter 6: SMP/Globe Photos.
Chapter 8: Tom Blau/Camera Press/Globe Photos.
Chapter 10: Alain Dejean/Sygma. Chapter 12: Studio
Kapa. Chapter 13: APIS/Globe Photos. Chapter 14:
Sygma. Chapter 15: Gaillet/Gamma. Chapters 2, 4, 7,
and 11: Courtesy of the author.

G. P. Putnam's Sons
Publishers Since 1838
a member of
Penguin Putnam Inc.
375 Hudson Street
New York, NY 10014

Library of Congress Cataloging-in-Publication Data
Moutsatsos, Kiki Feroudi.
The Onassis women / by Kiki Feroudi Moutsatsos with
Phyllis Karas.
p. cm.
ISBN 0-399-14443-9
1. Moutsatsos, Kiki Feroudi. 2. Onassis, Jacqueline
Kennedy, 1929–1994. 3. Callas, Maria, 1923–1977.
4. Onassis, Aristotle Socrates, 1906–1975. 5. Women—
Biography. I. Karas, Phyllis. II. Title.
CT3203.M68 1998
387.5′092—dc21   98-17129 CIP
[B]

Printed in the United States of America

1 3 5 7 9 10 8 6 4 2

This book is printed on acid-free paper. ♾

BOOK DESIGN BY JUDITH STAGNITTO ABBATE/ABBATE DESIGN

To the memory of my dear friend and boss, Alexander S. Onassis
—Kiki

For my husband, Jack
—Phyllis Karas

Contents

Acknowledgments

Both KIKI and PHYLLIS would like to thank their capable, energetic, and much adored agent, Helen Rees, for believing in their dream and transforming that dream into a book proposal. They also want to thank their brilliant editor, Nanscy Neiman-Legette, who helped shape that book proposal into a magnum opus of which they will always be enormously proud. And they also send special thanks to Arju Parikh, who read and understood, and was always there to make the road an easy and pleasant one to travel. And to Mary Thomseu and Harold Weintraub, who made it all happen, a lifetime of thanks.

Kiki would like to thank Miltos Yiannacopoulos, Roula Strathis, Yianna Papadakos, Jean-Pierre de Vitry, and Grigoris Kouris for the memories they shared with her. She is also appreciative to the Onassis Establishment for their best wishes and to Vassilis Giannitsiotis for his exceptional generosity. Most important, she is deeply grateful for the love and encouragement her husband, George, and two sons, Alexander and John, along with her mother, Petroula Feroudi, constantly provided.

Phyllis thanks her writers group, Nancy Day, Anne Driscoll, Melissa Lutke, Elizabeth Mehren, Carolyn Toll Oppenheim, and Caryl

Rivers, for their constant support. She is also grateful to her friends, to Sheila Braun, Merilyn Edelman, Barbara Ellerin, Barbara Gilefsky, Chalese Glennon, Sharda Jain, Arlene Leventhal, Karen Madorsky, and Barbara Schectman, who listened, and understood when she couldn't listen to them. To her husband, Jack, and two sons, Adam and Josh, as well as to her sister, Toby, and brother-in-law, Larry Bondy, there are no words to express the love and gratitude she feels for them. There would be no joy without their love. For Hy and Mae, and Edna, Mel, and Julie Karas, and Sheryl Perlow, there are endless kisses, for they too listened and cared at every step of the journey. And to her precious mother, Belle Klasky, who still miraculously remains her biggest fan, there are tears and infinite love.

Foreword

The following foreword is written by Miltos Yiannacopoulos, a major Greek shipowner and Aristotle Onassis' most trusted adviser. He was also the general inspector of all of Mr. Onassis' companies, including Springfield Shipping Company, Olympic Maritime Panama S.A., Financiera Panama S.A., Victory Carriers S.A., Olympic Airways S.A., and Olympic Aviation. Today Mr. Yiannacopolous lives with his wife, Ada, in downtown Athens.

Finally, someone has written an honest and perceptive book about Jackie and Aristotle Onassis and the extraordinary Onassis family. The fact that this person is Kiki Feroudi Moutsatsos, who was without question an intimate of the family, makes the book all the more valuable. I personally have been waiting for years to have someone present an accurate account of what happened to these exceptional people, and Kiki's version of their lives is both fascinating and legitimate.

For the last nine years of Aristotle's life, Kiki was not merely his business secretary, but his invaluable personal assistant, handling everything in his life, from organizing the cleaning of his shirts and suits to paying the bill for a $10,000 piece of jewelry for his wife or mistress. In reality, Kiki not only planned his wedding to Jacqueline Kennedy, she also developed a close and warm relationship with Jackie, with whom she spoke on a daily basis and spent a great deal of time when Mrs. Onassis was in Greece.

All three of Aristotle's sisters adored Kiki and regarded her as part of their family, keeping her at their sides in both the good times the family celebrated as well as during the tragic times they endured. Yet it was her involvement with his oldest sister, Mrs. Artemis Garofalidis, that was the most remarkable. Those of us who saw the two of them together often commented that they appeared like mother and daughter. After Mr. Onassis' death, Kiki continued to remain a valuable employee of Olympic Airways for an additional twenty years, maintaining close relations with his daughter and sisters and widow.

For the Greek people and the world, it is time we opened the door between the man who controlled the world and the two women he loved the most. Kiki's voice is at all times an honest and perceptive one, for she was a family insider whose revealing view of the life beyond that door sustains and enriches this most exceptional story.

Prologue

Lor Jackie and Ari, at the beginning, the world was theirs, to taste its pleasures and revel in its joys. For these two demigods, the sunlight was unfiltered and incessant. But the darkness came. As it always does. But once, before the shadows appeared, oh, what light there was.

On one of those bright, sunny June days, the sounds of laughter from this island ascended into the heavens, where the gods rejoiced, anxious to join the mortals below. For this was an island where both the mortals and the Greek gods played. For when the mortals slept the pure sleep of the blessed, the gods reveled in the treasures of the island. The gods cherished this jewel, content to share it with the unsuspecting mortals. For nowhere was there a more godlike island. Four hundred acres in size, with a view of the mountainous end of Ithaki, in the sinuous shape of a scorpion, the island of Skorpios shone like a flawless jewel in the Ionian Sea.

As the gods watched that June day, the mortals feasted on moussaka, *soupa avgolemono,* ouzo, dolmades, souvlaki, and *octapi,* along with eggs of the sea urchins. And then they rode their stallions and sang songs of love. The gods cherished those sung by one voice so beautiful that when the raven-haired Greek woman opened her mouth and the notes rose to the heavens, all in Olympus grew silent.

And then the gods would watch the mortals revel in the beauty around them—gracious white horses, grass so green it seemed a rich velvet carpet, bougainvilleas of hues no god had ever seen. Magnificent olive and almond trees dotted the landscape, surrounded by groves of slender cypresses. Threaded among these trees, the heady scent of jasmine permeated the island. And no mortal on Skorpios dreamed life could be finer anywhere else.

And then one day the gods grew jealous. For no reason they decided the mortals felt too much joy. The island of Skorpios was too precious to belong to them alone. And so they hurled their thunderbolts and waited impatiently for their sharp arrows to find their marks. And when the gods had thrown their final weapon against the hapless mortals of Skorpios, the land had changed irrevocably. Where charming houses had once stood, filled with exquisite furniture and art, one house remained. And the whitewashed walls of the tiny chapel where Jackie and Ari had vowed their love had turned to ruin. Zebras and rare birds no longer dotted the land, and the green grass was parched. And the luxurious ship, whose bright lights had lit up the island, had disappeared. But, saddest of all, gravestones rose from the earth, each bearing a common last name etched into gray granite: ONASSIS.

Today, the gods no longer gaze down with envy on those who called the island of Skorpios their home. As soon as the island became theirs, the gods realized their fatal error. Without these mortals and their demigod, the island was a piece of land surrounded by the sea. Yet if the gods were to return their gaze to Skorpios, they would see the island is peopled with more than the ghosts of the family who once ruled its land.

For today, perhaps once a year, a helicopter drops noisily from the sky and releases a graceful, slim girl, no more than thirteen, with dark eyes and long black hair. The child, whose name is Athina, never comes alone. Sometimes she brings her French father, Thierry, or her three siblings. She visits the graves that cover the island, and strews white flowers beside each one. First she bends at the grave of her mother, Christina Onassis, who loved her dearly for almost four years. Then she kneels at the grave of her uncle, Alexander Onassis, whose plane was ripped out of the sky by the wrath of the jealous gods. Next she bends at the grave of her great-aunt Artemis, the old woman who died when Athina was an infant. And, lastly, she sits down beside the grave of her grandfather, Aristotle Onassis, part god, part mortal, whom she never met.

And for a while she is silent, a child old beyond her years, touched by the landscape of sorrow beside her. Then, suddenly, she becomes a child again, and her laughter rings through the air as she and her friends enter the fading pink house and are greeted by Olga, the elderly housekeeper, who waits anxiously for the day when the last member of this unlucky family returns. For Athina, a few treasures remain, but mostly all that surround her are the memories of a family the gods denied her the chance to know.

If perchance those gods were to look down upon this scene, they would quickly avert their eyes, perhaps sorry for what they have done, perhaps glad that there is no longer any reason to envy the island of Skorpios below.

Chapter One

Meeting Jackie Kennedy in Glyfada

I T W A S a warm summer evening in early August 1968 when I first met Jackie. It had been more than two years since I had begun to work for Aristotle Onassis as his private secretary. Mr. Onassis had a home next to and nearly identical to his sister's villa, yet it was at Artemis Garofalidis' villa around which the family's social activities in Athens were centered. Mr. Onassis and his two children, Alexander and Christina, not only ate their meals at Artemis' house, but spent most of their leisure time there. To the three of them, in Athens, this was home. A large, elegant, two-story home, more than a hundred years old and with an Old World charm, Vassileos Georgiou 35 in Glyfada exuded the grace and glamour of its mistress.

Yet something was sharply different that August night. From the moment Mrs. Artemis' chauffeur, George Margaritis, delivered me to her door at around seven, I sensed this evening was going to be surprising. The servant who opened the large wooden door of the house appeared nervous and excited as she took my coat and ushered me into the living room. Mrs. Artemis, dressed in a lovely, long evening dress adorned with beautiful and expensive jewelry, a large lace scarf flowing whimsically around her neck and encompassing her small shoulders, greeted me in the living room with her customary kisses on each of my cheeks. A slight woman who weighed no more than ninety pounds, Artemis had large black eyes, which that night were highlighted by a heavy display of eyeliner and mascara. Her thin lips also were accentuated with bright color, artfully and generously applied. I could recognize immediately that my hostess was excited. A romantic woman by nature, Mrs. Artemis loved planning special evenings at her home and would spend an entire day organizing the menu and preparing her wardrobe and home for such an event. That evening, her narrow, dark face was flushed with exuberance, and her long, thin hands were fluttering nervously in front of her chest. She was, I understood, an energetic and excitable woman, but never had I seen her so exhilarated.

"You will meet someone very interesting tonight, Kiki," she informed me as her butler, Panagiotis, handed me a glass of wine. "You will be the only one to meet her tonight. Do not ask me any more questions. Just sip your wine and let me look at you."

As always, I did as she asked, for I was only nineteen and used to Mrs. Artemis' treating me as if she were my mother. While I sipped my wine, however, I wondered who her special guest was.

At that moment, an airplane flew overhead, and the proximity of

Vassileos Georgiou 35 to the Athens airport caused an uproar that reverberated throughout the walls of the elegant home. How could such wealthy people tolerate such a constant and noisy distraction? I wondered. After midnight, the number of planes diminished, although they never disappeared for more than a half hour at a time. No members of the Onassis family found that the sound of the roaring engines disturbed their slumber. Even for the relatively fragile Artemis, this sound, rather than keeping any of them awake, instead lulled them all to sleep. Airplanes were part of their lives. Not just because Mr. Onassis owned Olympic Airways, but perhaps because the excitement of moving speedily, faster than ordinary people, whether by luxury ship or supertanker or elegant car or airplane, was in their blood. For Mr. Onassis' hero, I had already learned, was the mighty Odysseus, whose fabled journey was an inspiration for his own life. Ironically, and tragically, it was that love of ascending, especially on airplanes, that destroyed this family. Yet that is a story to be told much later. This evening in August 1968 was full of promise and vivacity, and the sounds of the indefatigable airplanes overhead intensified that fervor.

The villa, which felt like a fanciful castle to me, was electrified that evening by an aura of excitement. Of one thing, however, I was certain: It was most unusual that I was the only guest at Vassileos Georgiou 35 to be meeting Mrs. Artemis' special visitor. Mr. Onassis was on business in London, and his children, Christina and Alexander, were on holiday with their mother in Switzerland. But Mrs. Artemis never suffered from a lack of dinner guests. Most evenings, she invited her brother's business associates and close friends, Professor Georgakis or Costas Gratsos, or his cousin and associate Costas Konialidis and his wife, Ritsa. Her other guests were varied and always interesting, friends such as Prince Stanislas and Lee Radziwill, or American celebrities such as Greta Garbo or Elizabeth Taylor or Richard Burton. This night, however, there was an air of mystery in the room that captivated my attention.

I had been there nearly an hour, chatting with my hostess about local gossip, when the mystery guest finally appeared on the winding wooden staircase to the right of the living room in which we sat. I knew there were four bedrooms upstairs and that Mrs. Artemis' husband, Professor Theodore Garofalidis, was away on a hunting trip, so I was surprised that anyone was upstairs. My surprise turned to near shock when I recognized the slender, tall, dark-haired woman who was my hostess's mystery guest. She was Jacqueline Kennedy, the widow of the slain American president.

My shock was not totally justified, I reminded myself quickly, for Mrs. Kennedy's name had been frequently discussed in the Olympic Airways offices these past few months. Although I had never spoken to the former First Lady, I had made arrangements for her to visit Skorpios several months earlier, when she had gone on a brief cruise on Mr. Onassis' yacht, the *Christina,* to the Caribbean. I had also arranged for her brother-in-law, Edward Kennedy, to come to Skorpios to visit Mr. Onassis just this past August. I knew that Mr. Onassis had made at least two trips to the United States involving Jackie Kennedy this past summer: one to Hyannisport to visit some of the Kennedys, including Rose Kennedy; and a second one to Newport, Rhode Island, with his daughter, Christina, to spend time with Jacqueline Kennedy's family. Also, just a few months earlier, before the horrific assassination of Robert Kennedy, much office discussion had been centered on Mr. Onassis' generous contributions to Mr. Kennedy's political campaign for the American presidency. For the past two months, it had seemed as if the name of Jacqueline Kennedy had been mentioned every day in our office. But gossip about famous and glamorous women was not unusual in these offices. There was hardly a famous or glamorous woman whose name hadn't been linked with Mr. Onassis, if only for a brief moment. Still . . . Mrs. Kennedy herself. In Glyfada. Wearing a simple, short green sheath dress, adorned with a single strand of pearls, her thick hair styled in a soft flip, revealing tasteful gold earrings, the former First Lady of the United States appeared hesitant as she walked into the room.

Despite the conversations I'd had with Mrs. Artemis and the Olympic Airways personnel about this woman, I was overwhelmed and nearly unable to speak when I saw her approach me. At nineteen, I was easily embarrassed under normal circumstances and, in this most unusual occasion, I felt myself flush with chagrin. What right did I have to be in the same room with such a famous woman? What would I possibly say to her? I thought about averting my eyes with respect, but Jackie was looking directly at me. I swallowed my unease and stared back at her.

My first impression was that she was childlike, innocent and gentle. Yet, even in that first moment, I glimpsed a sense of wisdom, of cleverness that was barely hidden in her simplicity. My first impressions remained unchanged and accurate for the following twenty years.

Mrs. Artemis was on her feet the second she saw Jackie, her hand outstretched to welcome her surprise guest into the living room. Despite her cascading long gown, Mrs. Artemis appeared tiny in comparison with the tall, elegant Mrs. Kennedy. I guessed that our hostess was twenty years older than her guest, but I sensed immediately that these two women, despite their age difference, were already becoming good friends. The way they smiled at each other and held hands revealed a sense of comfort and trust that was obvious even to me. I knew that the two women had met before, at least twice when Jackie had cruised on the *Christina*, but Artemis had never indicated to me that Jackie Kennedy would be visiting her in Glyfada.

"Jackie, this is Kiki," she informed her guest, speaking in French, as I stood there, trying to absorb the scene around me. I knew that Mrs. Artemis spoke no English and could converse only in Greek and French. "She is like a niece to me. But you will find her to be our girl. She does everything for everybody at Olympic Airways. Especially for Aristo. You will love her the way we all do."

"Oh, Kiki, it is so good to meet you," Jackie said warmly, she too responding in perfect French, her large brown eyes staring directly into mine. "I have already heard so many wonderful things about you."

I was amazed at how natural she appeared, so unlike what I imagined a former First Lady of the United States would be. I was still uncomfortable to be in her presence, but her smile and kind words eased my discomfort. I found that smile honest and sincere, yet I later learned that not everyone who met her agreed with my reaction. Many others thought her smile false and insincere. Perhaps I was naive. Or perhaps I saw a different smile.

"So, tell me, Kiki," Jackie Kennedy addressed me again, while I studied her smile and tried to think of a suitable response to her generous remarks, "are you married?"

"Oh, no," I answered, of course, in French, although I spoke English, smiling myself, surprised at her blunt question. "Not yet."

"But you will be soon, I am sure," she informed me in her small, breathless voice.

"Oh, yes, she will," Mrs. Artemis agreed. "As soon as we find her the right man." She and Jackie shared a knowing smile, as if they each could already see my future husband.

For the next hour, the three of us sat in Mrs. Artemis' living room, drinking wine and eating the delicious hors d'oeuvres Panagiotis served us. Jackie tasted all the Greek foods she was given. For a slim woman, she had a healthy appetite as she graciously accepted the carrots prepared in Mrs. Artemis' special sauce, eggplant salad, baked rolls, and mozzarella cheese. She appeared especially to enjoy the small fried zucchini rolls Panagiotis had prepared so perfectly. When she praised him for the delicacies, the usually unflappable Panagiotis blushed with pleasure. This man was accustomed to serving dozens of celebrities in this living room, yet the presence of Jackie Kennedy was unnerving even to him.

I found myself too engrossed in Mrs. Artemis' guest to eat more than a small bite of cheese, but I was delighted to discover that Jackie loved so many things Greek: literature, art, food, history, philosophy. She brightened visibly when she mentioned that when she had been on the *Christina* with Mr. Onassis in August 1963, she had visited the famous outdoor theater at Epidaurus on the north shore of the Peloponnesus in southern Greece. "I saw *Electra* performed at the site of the ancient Greek ruins," she told me, her face animated at the memory. "Your wonderful actress, Anna Synodinou, played the title role and I was so impressed with her acting. I went up to her after her performance and remarked how amazed I was that someone so young as she could play such a role. She told me that she was not so young, but was the same age as Electra. I was amazed."

Jackie also recounted how some employees of the Epidaurus theater had offered her embroidery made by young girls from the village of Ligourio in the Peloponnesus. When I promised that I would ask Professor Yiannis Georgakis to introduce her to Niki Goulandris, the vice president of the most famous museum in Athens, so that she could learn much more about the arts and history of Greece, she squeezed my hand with pleasure.

We talked about so many things that night, but a possible marriage to Mr. Onassis was never discussed. I saw a beautiful ring on Mrs. Kennedy's finger, but I dared not ask about it. I personally knew he had bought an expensive ring in Spain that was supposed to look a great deal like the one she was now wearing. I also knew that Mr. Onassis and Mrs. Kennedy had kept in telephone contact with each other since her first cruise on the *Christina,* in August 1963, three months before her husband's assassination. I had actually heard a great deal about that particular cruise. About how Mrs. Kennedy's sister, Princess Lee Radziwill, had suggested that Jackie join her on the *Christina,* in order to recover from the death of the Kennedys' infant son, who had lived only a few days after his birth. About how Mrs. Lee had danced barefoot around the ship many nights and how she had swum in the nude in the ocean during the cruise. And also about the rumors that Lee Radziwill was having an affair with Aristotle Onassis and that she was anxious to help her sister regain her strength and peace of mind. Many years later, when I also heard other rumors suggesting that Mrs. Kennedy slept with Mr. Onassis on that cruise, I could not help but smile at the absurdity of such an accusation. The seeds for a future love affair between Mrs. Kennedy and Mr. Onassis might have been placed in the soil, but Mrs. Artemis had been adamant in telling me the relationship was not consummated during that particular voyage. No way, she had insisted proudly, would her brother sleep with two sisters during the same cruise.

Nearly five years after that memorable cruise, Mr. Onassis had already been divorced from Tina Onassis for nine years, and, even though he appeared to adore his celebrated mistress, opera diva Maria Callas, there was still incessant talk about him and other women. Jackie, however, did explain that she was in Greece for only four or five days. She missed her two children and would return to them in New York soon. Another time, she assured Mrs. Artemis, she would bring them to Greece to meet all of us. "Caroline and John will be so excited to come here," she said. "I know they will love to get to know you both."

A few minutes before nine, Jackie excused herself and went back upstairs to retire for the night. She was exhausted from her long flight. When she left the room, she kissed both me and Artemis in the customary Greek way. I still felt uneasy to be with this famous woman, but far less so than I had felt a few hours earlier. Yet, even in that short period of time, I had learned a lot. Already there was a rapport between Jackie and Mrs. Artemis that showed promise of a strong and important relationship. Artemis was, I had learned firsthand these past two years, a teacher, a woman who liked to be in charge, to be listened to and respected. Her relationship with her younger and only brother was equally strong and important.

I was not certain if my employer would marry this charming and famous woman, most probably the most desired woman in the world, yet I could not help being awed by such a possibility. Aristotle Onassis had amazed and fascinated me during the two years I had worked for him. Jackie Kennedy, I thought as I sat on the elegant pink sofa and tried to concentrate on Mrs. Artemis' words, would be very fortunate to marry this remarkable man. They would be a couple, I was certain, for whom nothing would be impossible. A couple who would shock and fascinate the world. An extraordinary couple, indeed.

Chapter Two

Entering a New World

TWO YEARS before that August night in 1968 when I was introduced to Jackie Kennedy at the home of her future sister-in-law, I had met the man who would become her second husband. On that day, in the fall of 1966, at the age of seventeen, I had begun a job at

Olympic Airways that would change my life, leading me into a world I would find filled with unimaginable wealth, glamour, excitement, and tragedy.

It was just a secretarial job, my father had warned me when I left our house in Athens for my interview. An editor and writer for two Athens newspapers, the *News* and the *Acropolis,* my father worked closely with a relative of Amalia Hadjiargyris, Aristotle Onassis' personal secretary. A well-known and highly respected newspaper writer, my father, George Feroudi, held connections to many influential Greek families and individuals. He had been told it was possible that Amalia could use an assistant, someone to work in her office. It was not an important position. The work itself might not even be interesting; it could be boring or unimportant. But it was with Olympic Airways and in the office of Mr. Onassis.

Just thinking about Aristotle Onassis made me so nervous I could barely sleep the night before my interview. After all, there wasn't a person living in Greece who didn't know who Onassis was. Every day, the newspapers would be filled with stories about him and his family, his two children, Alexander and Christina, his ex-wife, Tina Livanos Onassis, his three sisters—Artemis, Merope, and Kalliroi—and, of course, his renowned mistress, the world-famous opera singer Maria Callas.

I had read every story that appeared. I knew it all. I knew how he had begun his affair with Callas during a three-week cruise on the *Christina* with Winston Churchill in 1959. After the cruise, Tina Onassis, who had married Aristotle Onassis in 1946 in the Greek Orthodox Church of Saint Trias in New York, followed by a lavish reception in the Grand Ballroom of the Plaza Hotel and a month-and-a-half-long honeymoon to Florida, had filed for divorce, as had Maria's husband, Giovanni Meneghini. For the past eight years, I had seen photographs of the two celebrated Greek lovers, and, like everyone else who was fascinated with them, I wondered if they would ever marry. Tina had married Sonny Blandford five years before. There seemed no reason why these two Greeks would not be joined together forever. He was the richest man in Greece and she was Greece's leading diva. I had heard about their fights and knew that her opera career appeared to diminish as her love for him expanded. I had also read that Maria was a very moral woman and did not want to be responsible for having destroyed another woman's marriage, yet she, like all of us, had to have known that there had been problems in Tina Onassis' marriage before she met and fell in love with Tina's husband.

It was impossible to deny that Maria Callas and Aristotle Onassis belonged together. Most Greeks believed they were two parts of one person, a pair that no one should separate. She was fiery and tall and beautiful. She had made Tosca her own magical part, learning it in an unheard-of twenty-four hours, becoming, at age seventeen, the world's most devastating Tosca, the woman destroyed by hate, jealousy, and pain. He was rich and exciting and unafraid of anyone or anything. If she was Tosca, he was Zeus, controlling the world beneath him with his thunderbolt of money, intelligence, and audacity. Her voice drew her audience to its feet, tears streaming down their faces in appreciation of her God-given talent. His 315-foot yacht *Christina* and his private island of Skorpios were the most desired vacation spots of the world's most intriguing people; his financial acumen won him the respect and fear of businessmen throughout the world.

In 1960, I had heard Maria Callas sing *Norma* in Epidaurus, in the Peloponnesus. I was only eleven at the time and had gone to the concert with my parents. It was a dress rehearsal, and Maria had been noticeably nervous. Her costume had been too tight and she had pulled at it anxiously during her performance. It was obvious that she was a perfectionist and any small detail that was not correct upset her. Still, from the moment she opened her mouth, I had been spellbound. To me, she was like a woman of God, her intense personality matching her magnificent voice. Her talent was of the same magnitude as that surrounding Mr. Onassis' wealth and business success. These were no two ordinary human beings.

And I was going to have an interview to work in the company owned by one of them.

The night before my interview at Olympic Airways, I lay in bed, unable to sleep, remembering one particular photograph of the former Tina Onassis. She had been wearing a long shimmering evening gown, with a white fur coat draped softly over her shoulders. Her hair was a warm honey blond color, but her dark eyes looked sad and tired. Perhaps it was the way the camera had caught her. Or perhaps she was a tired and sad woman since the divorce from Aristotle. She was so much smaller and more delicate than Maria Callas. I could not help but wonder what her life had been like since she had stopped being Mrs. Aristotle Onassis. I had read an article about Mr. Onassis in which he had been quoted as saying he had always been attracted to tall, statuesque women. "I guess I should have been a sculptor," he had told the reporter. There was nothing tall or statuesque about the delicate Tina Livanos Onassis. I wondered how she would have felt if she had read that same article.

I was quite well versed in what Tina's life had been like before and during her marriage to Aristotle Onassis. I knew that Tina Livanos had been the seventeen-year-old daughter of wealthy shipowner, Stavros Livanos, when Aristotle, forty, had married her on December 29, 1946, in the Greek Orthodox Cathedral of Saint Trias in New York. She had been born in 1929 in England and moved with her family to Montreal in 1940 and to New York in 1942. She went to boarding school in Connecticut. She spoke mostly French and English and little Greek. Rumors of her infidelity and unhappiness with her marriage had appeared in dozens of magazines and newspapers, along with attractive pictures of her and Aristotle and their two children, christening ships, traveling on the *Christina,* and vacationing in exotic locations.

Like so many other Greeks, I was intrigued with the concept of this model-slim, blond, beautiful woman, once married to the richest man in the world, displaced by the tall, elegant, raven-haired opera singer, and now seeking love with other, more ordinary men.

But the former Tina Onassis wasn't the only Onassis woman filling my brain that sleepless night. I had seen pictures and heard about Aristotle Onassis' three sisters. The one who appeared most frequently in the press was his older sister, Artemis Garofalidis, the only sister with whom Onassis shared a mother and a father, and with whom he was rumored to be the closest. She was often described as cold, aloof, and forbidding. In her photographs, she appeared to be quite lovely, but painfully thin, adorned with exquisite jewelry, her aristocratic face solemn and unsmiling. I'd seen pictures of her with her niece Christina, and had heard that they, too, were unusually close. Christina, a year or so younger than I was, resembled her aunt Artemis more than her pale and delicate mother Tina, although she was a much larger person than her aunt. Still, in her looks, she was unquestionably Greek.

I also knew that Aristotle had a home beside his older sister's villa in Glyfada, and that his children were more at home there than at any of their other glamorous homes. I could not remember seeing a picture of Artemis with Maria Callas, and I suspected they were not very close to each other, even though they loved the same man. Even if I did obtain a secretarial position at Olympic Airways, I would not expect to meet the mysterious Artemis.

Just the name Christina Onassis excited me. What was her life really like? I had often wondered. What was it like to have all the money you could possibly want? To live on a huge yacht named after you? To go wherever you wanted whenever you wanted? She didn't seem very attractive in the photographs I'd seen, with dark circles under her eyes and her large Greek nose. Her hair was often wild and unflattering. I'd heard rumors of Christina considering plastic surgery to correct her cosmetic shortcomings, but I had not seen any indication that it had happened yet. She had been photographed dancing at tavernas with handsome young men. Several pictures had shown her dancing wild Greek dances on the tops of tables at these tavernas. Often she looked heavy, yet there were times when she appeared thinner. I'd read about her weight problems, and had been embarrassed for her when the newspapers exposed her heavy body in a bathing suit or short dress. It must have been hard for her to have been with her petite mother and thin aunt when she was at her heavier weights. From all I'd read and seen, she seemed an emotional young woman who, despite her grand wealth, did not appear to be going through life easily or happily. The few pictures that showed her smiling were rare.

When I thought of Alexander Onassis, however, I could not help but smile. Despite his thick glasses, he was an extremely handsome young man. I had noted the way his nose now appeared shorter than it had a year or so ago and believed the reports that he had undergone plastic surgery. He was only a year older than I was, but dozens of photographs had appeared in the papers showing him in the company of beautiful women, most much older than he. It was a frequent rumor that he was, despite the fact that he was still a teenager, an excellent and skilled lover. I knew he worked at Olympic Airways and I grew weak at the thought of possibly meeting him the next day.

How would I ever walk through the front door of Olympic Airways? I wondered as sleep eluded me that entire night. Aristotle Onassis and his mistress and his entire family were larger than life. Don't worry, Kiki, I told myself as I watched the sky begin to brighten, you will never even meet the man. Even if you are lucky enough to find a job at Olympic Airways, you will probably never meet Aristotle Onassis or his ex-wife, daughter, son, sisters, or mistress. It simply will not happen.

But it did happen. The next day, I not only met Aristotle Onassis, I began to work for him. And from my first day of employment for Olympic Airways, the work I did there was never boring. Their offices on the fourth floor at 8 Othonos Street in Syntagma Square in Athens were most impressive. There was a doorman on the first floor who ushered visitors to the elevator and another doorman who admitted them to the fourth floor. There were also, I noted somewhat uneasily, several policemen in the building who obviously protected the employees. All four floors of the building belonged to Olympic, and Mr. Onassis' office was on the top floor. The carpets on the fourth floor were blue and gray and very thick. The large glass windows, I soon learned, were covered by a material that allowed those on the inside to look out, but prevented those on the outside from gazing through them.

Somehow, I ended up sitting at a desk at Olympic Airways, waiting for the woman who would interview me for the job, when Mr. Onassis walked into the office. I knew the moment my eyes met his that this was Aristotle Onassis. He was short, yet he appeared much taller than he actually was. His eyes were dark and serious and his hair thick and beginning to gray. Feature by feature, he was certainly not classically handsome, yet there was something unique about his face and the way he moved that I found riveting. When he noticed me sitting at the desk of another employee, he stared at me, nodded briefly, and walked into another office. He spoke not one word to me, yet I had sensed his power, his intelligence, and his charm. Later that evening, I tried to explain what I had felt to my father, but few words could express my feelings. I knew that I had been in the presence of a great man, and that someday he would be one of the most important people in my life.

Amalia Hadjiargyris was this man's personal secretary, and had been working for him since 1956, when Aristotle Onassis began Olympic Airways. She needed some help and decided, as soon as she met me, that I would be her assistant. Not only was I thrilled with my new job but I was also young and enthusiastic and most eager to learn. When Amalia took a vacation one year after I had been working for Olympic Airways, I was able to perform all her duties. With Amalia's patient instruction and my long hours in the office, I assumed added responsibilities and become more invaluable to Megalos, or Big Boss, as most of the employees at Olympic Airways referred to Mr. Onassis, though rarely, if ever, to his face.

Several times in my first year of employment, I was asked to deliver airplane tickets or important papers to Mrs. Artemis in Glyfada. Amalia explained to me how difficult it was to find trustworthy people to do personal errands such as that for the family. Often drivers or messengers ended up taking advantage of the Onassis family, speaking to reporters about their visits or even secretively taking pictures of the house in Glyfada. Amalia was delighted when I suggested I personally deliver the items to Mrs. Artemis. Truthfully, I enjoyed those trips away from the office and found it easy and natural to be kind and considerate to my employer's family.

"You are an angel," Mrs. Artemis would tell me when I arrived with the papers or tickets. "How can I ever thank you, my dear?"

"There is no reason to thank me," I insisted. When I walked into her house with one of her packages, Artemis Garofalidis was always wearing a long flowing dress, even on a hot summer day. Never, in all the years that I knew her, did Mrs. Artemis ever appear in pants. Even when she went for a long walk on the beautiful stretch of beach across the street from her home, she would wear a dress. Perhaps a short dress rather than a long one, but a dress, nevertheless. When I saw her in her home, her makeup was always impeccable and her hair perfectly styled and piled up attractively on top of her head. I also noticed that she favored long, elaborate earrings that could be seen, no matter how her hair was arranged. Even though she was a very small woman, both in height and weight, her feet appeared to be quite large. I learned later that she preferred to wear big, comfortable shoes at all times, always concerned that her feet should have plenty of room and not be squeezed into tightly fitting shoes. By the back door of the house, Artemis always left multiple pairs of large walking shoes for her daily walks to the nearby stretch of beach.

From the first time I walked into the villa, I was enthralled with the elegant old two-storied home, beautifully maintained, and full of original priceless art and aristocratic furnishings. The area carpets were from Persia and Spain, as well as from Greece, and like the furniture and draperies, all bespoke refinement and wealth. It was an honor to be invited into the house even for such a short period of time.

After a year of these telephone calls and visits to the house, Mrs. Artemis decided the way to thank me for my trouble was to invite me to dinner. I found out later that she and her two younger sisters, Merope and Kalliroi, had talked about me before Artemis met me. "We heard from our brother," Artemis told me, "about this clever young woman—this child, really—who was now working in his office. He told each of us all how bright you were and how you could find solutions to problems quickly. I was curious about this little Kiki and I wanted to get to know you better myself."

I have never completely understood what it was that made me the Olympic Airways employee whose relationship with Mr. Onassis did not end at the end of the workday. I knew that one major advantage that I had in my new position was that I was young, much younger than Amalia, and filled with energy and a desire to please my new employer and his family. Artemis, I could tell immediately, liked young people, as did her two younger sisters. Also, it did not hurt my position that I was attractive. Always, I worked very hard, whether on the telephone or in person, to show the proper respect to all members of the family. Perhaps, as a result of my attitude toward them all, within less than a year of my employment, unlike Amalia, who had worked for Mr. Onassis for many years, I was developing personal relationships with the members of his family, including sixteen-year-old Christina and eighteen-year-old Alexander.

Even though I was delighted that my position as a secretary for Olympic Airways now involved meeting other members of the Onassis family, at first my parents were concerned that this was not a good idea. They were worried that my becoming personally involved with the family might jeopardize my job. But they agreed I had no choice but to accept Mrs. Artemis Garofalidis' invitation and be on my best behavior. In truth, I was delighted with the idea of spending an entire evening with Mr. Onassis' sister. I was certain this one dinner invitation would provide me with an experience to remember for a long time. I never expected, nor did my parents, that this dinner invitation would be merely the first in an endless number of dinner invitations that would connect me solidly and forever with the Onassis family.

Why would they want *me* at their dinner table? I wondered as I nervously prepared for my first evening in Glyfada. I understood that I was doing a superior job in my role as secretary to Mr. Onassis, but how was I to act in his sister's luxurious home? Yet Mrs. Artemis made it clear from that first dinner that in her house I was not to be treated as Mr. Onassis' secretary. Why, at Vassileos Georgiou 35, I was not just her prized guest; here I was fast becoming, despite our thirty-year age difference, her treasured friend as well.

Artemis' husband was absent from his home frequently in pursuit of his favorite pastime, hunting. The couple had suffered the loss of their only daughter, Popi, at the age of eighteen as a result of polymytosis, several years before I came into their lives. Artemis talked about her daughter only rarely, unable to speak about her for more than a few minutes without tears. From the first evening I was invited for dinner to her home, Artemis always insisted I sit next to her or across from her during our apertifs, and many times I looked up to find her staring intently at me. Even though she adored both Christina and Alexander, when all of us were together, Artemis spent more time concentrating on me than she did on either of them.

"You remind me of my beautiful Popi," she told me. "Sometimes I glance at you, Kiki, and for one quick moment I think she is back with me. Forgive me, but I cannot stop staring at you tonight." I saw the black-and-white pictures of Popi that graced the walls and furniture of Artemis' home, covering the large antique piano, along with other tastefully framed photographs of the Onassis family, and I did notice a slight resemblance between Popi and me. She seemed to be my height and weight, our eyes were both black and large, and the round shapes of our faces were similar.

It was uncomfortable to have Mrs. Artemis bestow such attention upon me, but I learned early to maintain a distance between her and me like that I had with her brother, never using the familiar "you" when I addressed her. I called her, as I called her two younger sisters and later Jackie, Mrs. Artemis, Mrs. Merope, Mrs. Kalliroi, or Mrs. Jackie.

I kept my gaze downward, never staring directly at any of them unless I was addressed by them, and never speaking to them until I was spoken to. I could understand that my presence reminded Mrs. Artemis of her beloved daughter and that she appeared to be growing fond of me, but I knew my place in all their lives and was careful to do nothing to endanger it.

As I became more involved in the Onassis family, I also allowed Mrs. Artemis some degree of control of my life. For the first year, however, I always returned directly home after work. Since I was so young when I began to work for Olympic Airways, my father insisted on picking me up after work. On the nights when I worked late, sometimes until one or two in the morning, my father was always waiting outside the building. "Tell your father to come upstairs," Mr. Onassis would tell me on those nights. "There is no reason for him to wait down there while we are up here." But my father preferred to wait downstairs, alone, no matter how many hours I was occupied upstairs.

After my first year with Mr. Onassis, however, my father began to relax a bit and allowed Mr. Onassis' driver, George Margaritis, to drive me from the Olympic Airways office on Syngrou Avenue to my home in Athens. While I spent a few minutes talking to my parents about my day and changing my clothes for the upcoming evening, George waited outside my house. When I returned to the black Cadillac, George drove me to Glyfada, about fifteen minutes from my home, where I remained until midnight. One night, knowing I had my driver's license, George asked me if I wanted to drive the Cadillac myself. I said, "Yes, I would like to try," and drove a short distance along the road behind the airport. Although it was exciting to be behind the wheel of that sleek car, I much preferred to be the black Cadillac's passenger rather than its driver.

Nearly every night, after dinner in Glyfada concluded and the other guests prepared to leave, Artemis pleaded with me to spend the night at her home. "It will be like having my Popi back in her bed," she implored me, but no matter how badly I felt, I steadfastly refused. It was difficult enough to return to my parents' home after midnight, full of wine and good food, and rouse myself early the next morning to go to work. If I had stayed in Glyfada, I would never have received enough sleep to perform well at my duties the next day. Still, there were a few nights when Artemis simply would not let me go and I knew I would not be able to walk out her front door. Those nights, I slept in the room that had been Popi's, a bright, warm room decorated with a beautiful pastel satin spread over the bed and matching curtains. The skylights made the room even more open and bright. Still, despite the beauty of the room, I did not sleep as well there as I did in my own bed, for my mind was filled with thoughts of a young girl who had died too young and never had a chance to live her own life.

Still, there was a feeling about being a dinner guest in Glyfada that often made it difficult for me to remember exactly who I was. For that first evening at Glyfada was not to be my last, and with each successive invitation, I was swept away on a cloud, feeling like Cinderella, as the limousine delivered me to the door of the villa and the servants gracefully removed my coat and ushered me into the living room. Each evening I went to Glyfada, I convinced myself it would be the last, that Mrs. Artemis would tire of me and feel as if she had done enough to thank me for whatever I had done for her in the office. But, no, the next day she would call me at the office and make certain I would be returning that evening. "I cannot wait to see you tonight, my darling," she would insist. "George will be waiting for you, no matter what time you are through."

And I would return and, before I understood what was happening, I was no longer treated as a guest or a friend, but rather as a member of the family. As Mrs. Artemis fussed over me and confided in me, my surprise turned to shock. Her eyes sought me out all evening long and her smiles were destined mostly for me. It was my plate and wineglass she insisted be constantly refilled and my hand she touched as she entered or left the room. Some evenings she even led me up the stairs to her boudoir and placed one of her exquisite brooches on my dress or adjusted one of her silk scarves at my neckline.

Each evening, as I sat at her dinner table, mesmerized by the sophistication around me, I reminded myself that, despite the borrowed jewelry on my neck, I was an employee of Olympic Airways, a mere secretary to my hostess's brother; yet each evening I found it more difficult to believe that was true. For each evening was more special than the previous one. Each dinner was more delicious, each conversation more stimulating, each guest more fascinating. And I was as cherished a guest as a visiting princess. It was inconceivable but it was happening. The door to the world of these charming and gracious people had opened to me and it appeared as if there were nothing I could say or do to make them close it.

Chapter Three

Megalos

As CLOSELY as Mr. Onassis would draw me into his family's life, I had to remember that to him, I was an employee, not a friend, not a confidante. My own face, I learned quickly, was an important aspect of my job, for it had to display a distance, a boundary appropriate for someone in my position in the Onassis world. I saw personally how he appeared to act familiarly toward many of his employees, and members of his boards of directors. Yet as soon as this familiarity was returned by his employees, his attitude changed. I witnessed enough firings of these overly familiar employees to understand what type of behavior my employer did not value in his workers. I occupied a status impossible to define, difficult to navigate, but crucial to preserve if I was to continue to work for him. I may never have understood exactly why I was hired by Mr. Onassis, but I learned quickly that my job was varied and never dull. Not only did I handle a myriad of important business affairs for him, I was also in charge of numerous details concerning his personal life.

As his personal secretary, I paid all the bills for the company and decided which letters he received were important and which could be discarded. I replied to nearly all of his letters, many of which I still have in my possession, and also fixed the time of the meetings with all the directors of the company. I took extensive notes of these business meetings and typed them up afterward. I also decided which telephone calls would pass through to Mr. Onassis, his son, Alexander, his colleague and brother-in-law, Professor Garofalidis, his friend and business associate Professor Georgakis, or his cousin and associate Costas Konialidis. Costas Konialidis was the chairman of the board of directors of Olympic Airways, a position Professor Georgakis assumed some years later. Mr. Onassis' mother and Mr. Konialidis' mother were sisters and, I learned early in my employment, the two men were close friends as well as cousins and business associates. Mr. Konialidis, unlike Mr. Onassis, maintained a real office on the sixth floor, one filled with expensive furnishings, including beautiful artwork and comfortable leather couches. Mr. Konialidis had a red light attached to the door of his office. When that red light was on, Costas Konialidis was talking on the telephone and no one was to disturb him. After a year or so of my employment at Olympic Airways, Mr. Konialidis informed me that I need not obey that rule.

One crucial aspect of my job concerned transferring money from one of Mr. Onassis' business accounts to another. For instance, depending on the value of the drachma or dollar or franc or my boss's particular needs, I would write private letters to his various banks, transferring money from a bank in Greece to one in Monte Carlo or Geneva or New York. I would send this particular mail by special car to the airport to be forwarded by company mail to New York or Geneva, often working with a short period of time, finding a way to get it on the plane to Geneva seconds before the pilot took off. These transfers involved large amounts of money, many thousands of dollars at a time, and I had to be well informed about the financial world market, as well as meticulous and, above all, secretive with this responsibility.

There were often complaints about the fact that Mr. Onassis, like most Greek shipowners, did not fly the Greek flag on the hundred or so supertankers he maintained during the years I worked for him. It was not merely the high cost of Greek taxes that caused my employer to fly either the red, white, and blue Liberian flag, with a star on the upper left side of the flag, or the Panamanian flag, with its two blue corners and two red corners, on his ships. It was the excessive Greek red tape that caused him to register his ships with Liberia and Panama. He enforced strict regulations on his own ships and made certain the safety of his crews was never jeopardized, but he also grasped any opportunity to avoid giant piles of what he considered a useless barrage of idiotic rules.

In addition, I kept all of Mr. Onassis' personal files. For instance, rarely a day went by when I did not call people to see if they had completed items Mr. Onassis had ordered, such as suits or shirts; or arrange for and await the arrival of his favorite foods, such as water from Paris, oranges from his Glyfada garden, mozzarella cheese from Rome, bread from Paris, ouzo from the island of Mytilene, cigarettes from Switzerland, cigars from Havana, or vitamins from Switzerland.

Another important aspect of my job was to handle all of Mr. Onassis' travel arrangements. I learned early on that he rarely made plans far in advance and often decided quickly that he would leave on an Olympic flight in a few hours. He had an innate dislike of others' knowing his travel plans and kept them secret until the last possible moment. I would make all the necessary and often last-minute flight arrangements and make certain everything was in place for his arrival at his destination. Because we had Olympic Airways offices all over the world, as soon as I knew Mr. Onassis' schedule I would send a telex to the manager of the Olympic office at his place of destination. It would be the immediate responsibility of that manager to meet Mr. Onassis' plane and make certain that his hotel or apartment was prepared for his arrival.

In Athens, I would call his bellman and ask him to deliver a fresh suit to the office or to take care of some personal need for Mr. Onassis. I would make his dinner reservations and call his friends or business executives concerning his luncheon appointments.

All of these duties would have been simpler to execute had my employer been a man of typical mentality, who made his arrangements several weeks, or even days, in advance. Mr. Onassis, however, was no such man. Of all the things that he hated the most, schedules were at the top of his list. Never would he look at a calendar and map out his plans for the coming month. Instead, he preferred to decide at the last minute. And merely depart the moment he was ready. This mentality wreaked havoc on many of us who tried to keep him on some sort of a schedule. However, I learned early that the only way to deal with his attitude was to be prepared for anything at any moment. If he decided at ten o'clock in the morning that he and Professor Georgakis would be leaving for Paris in two hours, then I simply made a few calls and, if necessary, bumped a few passengers, and he and the professor were off to Paris.

Unfortunately, not only did Mr. Onassis refuse to make plans in advance, he often broke the few he did make. If he told me he was leaving the office for lunch at Glyfada, I would hurriedly call Panagiotis and tell him to prepare lunch for the boss in fifteen minutes. Panagiotis would have his staff running around wildly, to prepare Megalos' favorite foods in such a short period of time. A half hour later, invariably, I would receive a frantic call from Panagiotis. "'Uncle' is not here," he would complain. "Lunch is ready, the bread has been cut, the meat and vegetables and cheese set out, and there is no 'Uncle.' Where is he, Kiki?"

I would call his driver and find out that Mr. Onassis had changed his mind a few minutes before they arrived in Glyfada, had telephoned Professor Georgakis from his car, and was meeting him at the Antonopoulos fish restaurant in Athens in ten minutes. I had no choice but to call Panagiotis and deliver the frustrating news.

Dealing with my boss's lack of adherence to a schedule was not as big a challenge as handling his ever-changing and unpredictable moods. For it was crucial that I relate information about his disposition to his most trusted advisers and his lawyers, who would call me to see when it would be an advantageous time for them to see "Thios," as many of them called him. If they needed to ask a favor or to deliver bad news, we tried to find the moment when Mr. Onassis would be best able to handle such information. Unfortunately, his moods shifted so rapidly that even in the ten or fifteen minutes it might take for someone in the building to reach Thios' office, by the time his adviser was at his door, Thios' mood had changed. For the others who were not so important to Mr. Onassis' business, I would decide if and when they could meet with him or speak to him on the telephone. My boss, I came to understand, was a man who preferred to listen rather than to speak. He concentrated on other people's words and, although he did not always respond, I would learn later that he had not missed one. When he was not in a meeting listening to others, he was on the telephone, either talking very softly or roaring in anger.

Because my employer did not like to speak more than was necessary, and because he could often be moody and difficult to deal with, I often adjusted my own personality to deal more effectively with his. For me, this was a surprisingly easy task. For instance, I soon learned that Mr. Onassis' face did not often reveal his thoughts. If he was sad or concerned, his face did not register those emotions. It was almost impossible for people with whom he was doing business to guess what Mr. Onassis was thinking during their meetings. I was convinced that the reason he always wore his thick dark glasses was so that no one could see his eyes and get an idea about what was going on in his mind. For all his outgoing personality traits, he was an intensely private man who kept his feelings and plans to himself as long as possible.

I also came to see that Mr. Onassis was a perfectionist who demanded the same high standards from those who worked for him as he did from himself. For instance, before he left for any cruise on his *Christina,* whether it was a one-day excursion or a three-week trip, he made a full inspection of his ship. If he found some small problem with the ship, even something as minor as a brass knob that was not perfectly polished, he could erupt into a fit of fury, swearing at the offending personnel with an array of curse words I could never repeat, never mind translate. Whenever I witnessed Mr. Onassis losing his temper at one of his workers, whether on his *Christina* or in the office, I shuddered at his exhaustive and ugly supply of swear words.

There were times, however, when he was wrong and falsely accused his workers of committing an offense for which they were not responsible. When he learned of his mistake, Mr. Onassis would merely shake his head and stop yelling or reinstate the fired personnel. But never would he apologize. The words "I am sorry," unlike horrific swear words, did not belong in his vocabulary.

I was particularly impressed, however, with his ability to decide who was speaking the truth and who was lying to him. Occasionally, although quite rarely, he did make mistakes and believed people whose words were untrue. When that happened, he was furious, mostly at himself, and immediately rectified the problem, firing those who had betrayed him or refusing to deal with that particular person again. Yet even at those times he would not apologize for his actions.

I learned quickly how to sense when he was worried and managed to alleviate his concerns speedily and without instruction. If he was informing me about a complicated letter he wanted me to write, I would tell him not to worry about it. "I know what you want to say," I would tell him. "Just leave and I will have it ready for you when you return." And when he returned, he would read the letter and smile broadly.

"You are so smart, *pedimou* [my child]," he would say. "That is exactly what I meant."

Sometimes, after a meeting with Costas Konialidis, he would walk into my office with a certain look on his face and I would immediately dial the telephone and hand it to him. "Mr. Zambelas [from the financial department of the Onassis Establishment] is on the phone," I would say, and he would shake his head in surprise.

"You are like a witch, Kiki," he would tell me. "You knew who I wanted to speak to before I did."

And I did. Other times, I would walk into his office with a cup of coffee, and he would say, "I was just about to ask you to make me a cup of coffee." This man who didn't like to talk unnecessarily did not have to do so with me. I could understand him without his explaining things to me. I could read it in his face or hear it in his voice.

There were times, however, when I was far from perfect in my employer's eyes. For example, sometimes when he came into my office to ask me the time of his appointment with one of his associates, things did not go as well as I expected. "Oh, no, Mr. Onassis," I would tell him, "that appointment is for next week."

Furious, he would stand in front of me, his eyes, I could see despite his dark glasses, glaring at me. "I am certain that appointment is for today," he would insist. "You have made an error."

Even when I showed him his date book and the date of the appointment marked in for a week later, he would shake his head in anger. "No, Kiki," he would repeat, "you have made an error."

For the rest of the day and a good part of the next day, he would not talk to me except when he absolutely had to, and even then it would be without looking at me. I would try everything I could think of to win back his favor. "Can I get you a cup of coffee or a cheese roll, Mr. Onassis?" I would ask him, and he would barely look up at me as he shook his head. "You look very handsome today, Mr. Onassis," I would say later, but again all I received for my efforts was a curt nod of his head as he walked quickly away from me. Whenever he had to walk by my desk, he would keep his head down and act as if I were not there. All day and night, I worried that Miltos Yiannacopoulos would come over to my desk to dismiss me, having received his directions from Mr. Onassis. However, I soon understood this was just my boss's way and, eventually, he would come around. Even though he would never admit that I had not made an error, he would finally stop being angry.

"Good morning, Kiki," he would simply greet me the next day as if nothing had happened between the two of us. "How are you this morning?" And I would breathe a sigh of relief, safe, until the next time I disappointed him.

There were other aspects of his personality that could be difficult for me to deal with; in particular, the fact that he frequently did not arrive at the office when he was expected. "Where is Aristo, Kiki?" Costas Konialidis would ask me. "He should have been here an hour ago."

In truth, Mr. Onassis rarely stayed in the Olympic Airways office for a long period of time. He would appear only when there was a meeting or a problem that had to be solved. Yet when he was expected and did not appear, I would call his houses in Glyfada and speak to his butler Panagiotis, "Where is Megalos?" I would ask, and Panagiotis would inform me that Mr. Onassis had left the house over an hour before. There was nothing we could do but wait for his black Cadillac to show up. However, even that could be misleading, for often when we saw the familiar black Cadillac parked outside the office building, Mr. Onassis was still nowhere to be found. One of his drivers, either George Margaritis or Andreas or Stavros, would insist that Mr. Onassis had entered the building at least an hour before, but none of us had seen him. When he did finally show up for the meeting, everyone's nerves were frazzled, but Mr. Onassis was calm as could be. Sometimes, I suspected, he went through this routine just to give himself the upper hand in the upcoming meeting.

I never objected to any of these duties and did everything within my power to make certain that every necessary detail was performed perfectly to make my employer's professional and personal life run smoothly.

Many times, Mr. Onassis made my job very easy. For, despite his wealth and power and mercurial temperament, he was, in many respects, a simple man. Most days, unless I asked him what he wanted for lunch, he would not think to ask me to get it for him. "Would you like me to get you some lunch, Mr. Onassis?" I would ask him after one o'clock had passed and he was still in the office.

"Oh, that would be good, Kiki," he would answer me, looking up from the paper he was reading.

"What would you like, Mr. Onassis?" I would ask.

"Whatever you want to bring me," he would answer.

"Perhaps some cheese and a roll?" I would suggest, and he would nod his approval and return to his work. He was grateful when I brought him the light lunch and ate it right away, but I knew that if I had not reminded him it was lunchtime, he would never have asked me for anything for lunch.

One afternoon, however, he arrived at the office and asked me to get him some coffee. I prepared it and opened the door to his office and brought it over to his desk. "Here is your coffee, Mr. Onassis," I said, and then turned around to leave.

"Just one second, Kiki," he said. "Where is the sugar?"

"Oh, dear, I forgot it," I said, and immediately brought him some sugar.

I was halfway out of the room when he asked, "Kiki, where is the spoon?"

"Oh," I said, embarrassed, "I am sorry. I will bring it right in to you."

"That is okay," he said, laughing. "Can you lend me your pencil?" I took the pencil out of my hand and watched, amazed, as he used the pencil like a spoon to mix the sugar into his coffee. I felt ashamed to watch my employer use my pencil to stir his coffee, but it did not appear to bother him at all.

The way Mr. Onassis ate certain foods was yet another example of how simple a man he could be. Unlike most Greeks, he did not eat fruit on a plate with a knife and fork. "Eat it this way," he would suggest to me when I brought some fruit into my office for our lunch. I would watch, smiling, as he bit into a juicy piece of fruit and let the juice run down his fingers. When he was through with the fruit, he would lick his fingers clean with his tongue. Although I much preferred to eat my fruit with a knife and a fork, I did try it his way a few times.

Three years after I went to work for Mr. Onassis, he asked me why I thought he had hired me to be his personal secretary. "After all," he said, "you were a young, inexperienced, seventeen-year-old girl. What possible reason would I have had for hiring you?"

"I don't know," I said, blushing.

"Take a guess," he insisted. "Why would I hire you? Surely you can think of at least one reason."

"Because you thought I might be smart?" I finally answered, wishing he had never brought up such an embarrassing subject.

"Oh, no," he said, laughing now. "Not because of that. Take another guess. There has to be another reason I would have hired you."

"Because I was a little bit pretty," I said, blushing deeply now.

"Oh, no," he said again. "Not because of that. But don't worry, I will tell you why. It's so simple. The value of the drachma went up the day I met you. I knew you were good luck. And I was right."

Mr. Onassis might have been right about my being good luck for him; for many years, that was how I felt. But I also knew that he was good luck for me, exposing me to a fascinating world I would never have known. There was no doubt that to me, the most exciting part of my job was working with Mr. Onassis himself. His personality was so grand, so large and fascinating, that I was never bored with my job.

From the beginning of my employment at Olympic Airways, I viewed Mr. Onassis as a completely Greek man. Many people who knew him well called him "El Greco" or "The Greek," and I understood why. When it came to women, in particular, he could not have been more El Greco. One of his closest friends and business associates was Costas Gratsos, who was the director of Mr. Onassis' New York operations and the vice president of Victory Carriers, his shipowning division. Costas and Aristo had been friends since they were small boys growing up in Smyrna, which was part of Turkey, and their affection for one another never faded. Costas was one of the few people who could look Mr. Onassis directly in the face and tell him he was wrong. The two men not only loved each other, they respected each other.

One day, Costas came into our office, and in front of me and Amalia, he began to talk to Aristo about women. "A Greek man should never be bothered with sad thoughts of women," he insisted. "He should date only beautiful women, with very beautiful legs, and he should buy them everything they want. He should take them to expensive restaurants and have long lunches with them and take them to exciting concerts. He should show the woman that he is interested in her as a person and cares about everything she does. But a Greek man does not need to marry this woman. He just needs to love her. With all his heart and all his money."

"Women love you because you are a real Greek man, Aristo," Costas continued. "You take very good care of all the women in your life. I have never met a woman who would not love you. Just do not marry her or she will cause you grief."

Aristo, who had not yet become seriously involved with Jackie Kennedy, but was having an affair with Maria Callas, laughed and said that was excellent advice. But, although he was a real Greek man who loved interesting, beautiful women who often appeared out of his reach but never were, Aristo did not always follow his friend's advice. With Maria Callas, he did; however, with Jackie Kennedy, he did not. For this beautiful woman he did indeed marry.

But these two women were not the only people he took care of. Although Mr. Onassis did not make significant contributions to charitable organizations in Greece, he was exceptionally generous to the thousands of Greek citizens who, when they needed something, determined they should get it from Mr. Onassis himself. Like so many rich men, Mr. Onassis rarely carried money in his pocket. Whenever he went into nightclubs in Athens, the patrons always asked him for money for their children's operations or for employment for their children. He'd tell them to come to the office the next day, and I'd keep a list of all of them and what they needed. He'd always remember having seen each one who came into the office and many times prepared me for a request I would be receiving from someone he'd met the night before.

So many times, he told me, it was no problem to help those in need. The hard part, he explained, was to give them this help without insulting them. I remember once when he was ready to untie his small Chris-Craft from beside the *Christina*, he noticed a boy holding the small boat for him. "Who are you and what are you doing here?" he yelled at the boy. "No one can see you here. Don't you understand that it is dangerous for a boy like you to be here alone beside my ship?"

"The only thing I understand," the boy, whose name was Georgakis and who was fifteen years old, replied, "is that I want to live, I need to work, and I need money."

Mr. Onassis was deeply touched by Georgakis' earnestness and asked him what kind of job he thought he could do. "Any job you can find for me," the boy said. "Please take me on your boat."

When Mr. Onassis determined that the boy was telling the truth and had no family to take care of him, he found him a job on the *Christina*. Several years later, Georgakis was employed by Olympic Airways, where he remained deeply devoted to his employer for the rest of Mr. Onassis' life.

In our office on Syngrou Avenue, where we moved from the offices on Othonos Street in 1968, one man kept coming in and telling me how ill his children were and how little money he had. Mr. Onassis told me to give him some money, but I overdid it and kept giving him more money every time he came. I felt so bad for this man who seemed so lost. One day, he came into my office with his face covered with blood. I screamed and Mr. Onassis came in while I was handing him money. He looked carefully at the man and put his fingers on the man's face.

His face, Mr. Onassis discovered, was not covered with blood; it was covered with tomato juice. Mr. Onassis laughed and said, "Oh, Kiki, you are just so good, too good," and sent the man away. But he never forgot that story and laughed about it many times afterward.

We never laughed about Christo, however. Christo was a little boy with leukemia whose father asked Mr. Onassis for money for his son's treatment. Every year, Mr. Onassis paid so that Christo and his parents could go to Paris where the little boy would undergo treatment for his disease. When he was thirteen, Christo died of complications from his disease. One day when Mr. Onassis asked me if I had taken care of Christo's ticket for Paris, I told him, "Mr. Onassis, it is not necessary for us to do that this year."

"Why not, Kiki?" he asked me.

I said, "He doesn't exist anymore. Christo died."

He put his face in his hands and cried. "Oh, no," he kept repeating through his tears. This was before his own son, Alexander, died, and the first time I had ever seen Mr. Onassis cry. Men from Smyrna, legend said, did not cry. Mr. Onassis was from Smyrna, but his reaction to the death of a young boy he hardly knew proved that Mr. Onassis was creating his own legend. Christo's mother had sent me a picture of her son and I took it out of my desk and showed it to Mr. Onassis. He looked at the picture for a long time and then asked me if he could have it.

"Of course," I answered, and watched him put the small picture into the pocket of his pants.

One other hardworking man was rewarded for his ambition by my employer. This man owned a small shop where Mr. Onassis liked to buy cheese pies. One day when he went into the shop, he approached the owner and told him he wanted to buy fifty cheese pies. "I am sorry," the man told him, "but you will have to wait your turn. There are other people ahead of you."

So Aristo waited his turn, and he bought his fifty cheese pies. Several days later, Mr. Onassis returned to the store and told the owner, "I am Onassis. Can you give me fifty cheese pies now?"

"You have to wait again," the man told him. So Aristo waited again, and after he bought his fifty cheese pies, he asked the owner of the small shop for his name and address. The next day Aristo sent him a check for $1,500.

When the man called him, shocked, and asked him why he had sent him such a large check, Mr. Onassis explained. "I saw whenever I came into your shop that you know how to make and keep money. You treat all your customers fairly and that is the way to be a success." The man was able to open four new shops to sell his delicious cheese pies and he became a big success. But when Mr. Onassis came into his shop to buy cheese pies, he still made him wait in line.

Yet the real Aristo could also be ruthless and cruel when someone did something he considered inappropriate, or far worse, stupid, in regard to his business dealings. He spoke Greek, English, and Turkish fluently, but when he and his cousins and business associates, Costas and Nicos Konialidis, who was married to Mr. Onassis' younger sister, Merope, were discussing business details they wished no one else to hear, they conversed in fluent Spanish. Sometimes Mr. Onassis used English words in an amusing way to insult those who had offended him. For instance, often he would say to me, "Pay no attention to him because he has no afternoon." I knew what he meant by that, since the Greek word for "brains" was similar to that for "noon"; thus, he was telling me, in his sly way, that the man was without brains and, therefore, stupid, and I should ignore everything that "stupid" man said to me.

I had heard him scream and rant at employees or managers or other businessmen, calling them words far worse than "stupid." While I was grateful that this vocal rage had never been directed at me, once I did cause it to be directed at someone close to me. At the age of twenty-two, when I had been working for Mr. Onassis for almost five years, I was involved in an unhappy romance. Mr. Onassis learned how badly a certain young man was treating me and confronted me with what he knew. "Is all this true, Kiki?" he asked me and I nodded. "Call him on this phone now," he ordered, and I did as he asked.

"If you hurt her in any way," Mr. Onassis told the young man during the brief phone call, as I sat at my desk, listening and unable to move, "I will destroy you financially for the rest of your life. You will leave her alone and never call her again and do nothing to make her life difficult or unpleasant. Do you understand?" I do not know for certain what the young man answered, but I do believe it was "Yes." Of course, I never heard from him again.

Sometimes I witnessed Mr. Onassis using his enormous personal wealth to try to gain advantage in his business dealings. In 1969, when he was trying to iron out the details of his $400 million Omega Project with military dictator George Papadopoulos, Mr. Onassis (over the protests of advisers) made available to the ruler his $300,000 seaside villa in Lagonissi for as little as 20,000 drachmas (about $660) a month. He was also excessively generous to other officials in the junta government. I personally delivered or arranged for the delivery of cash, expensive watches, and crosses from Lalaounis and Zolotas jewelers, and once, even, an expensive set of furniture imported from Singapore.

Even though he was an astute businessman, Mr. Onassis was not always careful with his money. One day, Mr. Onassis arranged for a large amount of cash to be delivered to my office. At the end of the day, Mr. Onassis asked for the money in packets of one million each. After I handed him ten packets, he put the money in the pockets of his pants and announced, "I'll take you home now, Kiki."

In the elevator, he began talking about other things with me and became so distracted that two packets fell out. Without his noticing what I was doing, I picked them up and said nothing. When we went to the car, he was still talking about other business concerns, and I asked him if he had all the money. "Of course, I do," he answered, and then proceeded to count them.

It didn't take him long to realize that two packets were missing. When I pulled those two packets out of my pocketbook, he laughed loudly and began to hit me jokingly in the arm. While George was driving us home, Mr. Onassis leaned over and kissed me on the cheek, and said, this time without laughing, "Thank you, my child."

That time, as always, when Mr. Onassis had George drive me home, he acted protectively toward me. No matter how much of a rush he was in, Mr. Onassis always insisted that his driver drive the Cadillac to my door and wait until I was inside my house before he drove off. Many times, I was embarrassed to be sitting in this big Cadillac that was slowly driving down the narrow street on which I lived. Neighbors could not help but notice this large car and wonder whose it was. Still, there was no way that Mr. Onassis would allow me to walk the short distance from the beginning of my street to my house. "Wait until the child is safe before you leave," Mr. Onassis ordered George. "Even if I am not here, you will wait until you can no longer see her before you drive away."

On important business decisions, Mr. Onassis consulted with Miltos Yiannacopoulos, who was the general inspector of all Mr. Onassis' companies, including Olympic Maritime, Springfield Shipping, Olympic Airways, Olympic Aviation, Victory Carriers, and Financiera Panama and was also a wealthy ship owner in his own right. At Olympic Airways, it was always Miltos, Mr. Onassis' most powerful adviser, who advised on what employee would be promoted or dismissed, who was the proper person to be the general manager, and who should become a director. And, when Mr. Onassis made a decision that someone should be fired, it was Miltos who performed that unpleasant job for him. Whenever I received a salary increase, the decision was made by Miltos, who handled most of the financial concerns of Mr. Onassis' companies. It was also Miltos who was sent to Singapore to inspect the ships Mr. Onassis was building. And Miltos who was the intermediary between the Onassis enterprises and the government, whether it was the democratic government or Papadopoulos' junta government. For instance, before Mr. Onassis would set up a refinery or enlarge or improve his Airways, Miltos would make the presentation to the government. A tall, serious man who was never without his eyeglasses, Mr. Yiannacopoulos had studied economics and was considered infallible in most aspects of finance. There were many business associates who fell out of favor with Mr. Onassis during the years I worked for him; however, his overriding trust in Miltos Yiannacopoulos remained steadfast.

Yet that didn't mean that Mr. Onassis was ever afraid to deal with his employees by himself. When the Olympic workers were on strike, I was afraid, and asked Mr. Onassis if I should go to work. "I don't think it's necessary," he said, but I could tell by the look on his face that he wanted me to go to work.

When he asked me what the climate among the strikers was, I told him, "They're crying about Jackie and saying that you spent all your money on her and now you have none left for them."

"The pilots and all the personnel are getting enough," he told me. "If they insist on striking, there will be a lockout." I did go to work that day and was greatly relieved that the strike was settled very quickly.

The Olympic Airways pilots always seemed to be outsmarted by my employer, for he knew just how to handle them. Whenever they requested a meeting with him to demand a raise in their salaries or discuss some grievance, Mr. Onassis never refused such a meeting. He would order me to speak to the head of their group and find out exactly what their concerns were. Then he would decide on the day and time of the meeting and tell me to inform them of the upcoming meeting, which would always be set for the late afternoon. The meeting was held in the office Mr. Onassis shared with Mr. Costas Konialidis, which was beyond my office, making it necessary for any of their visitors to pass through my office.

During the meeting, I would offer the pilots drinks, pistachios, bread, cheese, coffee, sandwiches, and cakes. After several hours had passed, all the pilots were getting full and tired, and they would request that Mr. Onassis stop the meeting and begin it again first thing the next morning. But he refused, telling them, "No, your requests are very important to me and we will continue today until we have finished every one of them." Amazingly, the more exhausted the pilots became, the stronger and more alert he grew. Finally, the weary pilots accepted whatever terms he offered them and practically crawled out of the meeting, wanting nothing except to go home and to bed. Mr. Onassis was full of smiles as the pilots staggered through my office. The men understood that this was all part of their boss's system, but there was nothing they could do about it.

I always found it fascinating that this powerful man had no office of his own. Of course, he did not come into the office for long periods of time, usually just to settle a problem or attend an important meeting. It never seemed to bother him that he had only a simple desk, at which he rarely sat, in Costas Konialidis' large office. Yet Mr. Konialidis was a completely different type of worker than Aristo. He came to work very early and stayed very late, always maintaining a steady, calm disposition and an organized work style. He was a wonderful man to work for, but he was the complete opposite of his more dramatic and mercurial cousin.

However, one most upsetting time for all of us in the Syngrou Avenue offices occurred when Mr. Konialidis and Mr. Onassis had a particularly severe argument. We were used to the two of them disagreeing loudly and often, yet their arguments were always resolved by the end of the workday. This time, however, the argument grew worse as the day went on and continued into the following few days. Finally, in complete exasperation, Mr. Konialidis announced to his cousin, "It is obvious you do not like the kind of person I am and that we can no longer work together. I have no choice but to leave the company."

I waited for Mr. Onassis to say something to make him change his mind, but he simply nodded and ordered me to make an unrelated telephone call for him. I watched, silent and in despair, as Mr. Konialidis packed a pile of his papers into a small box and left the office without another word.

For two years, Costas Konialidis did not reappear at the Syngrou Avenue offices. Instead, he worked in his tobacco company in Montevideo, Uruguay. Once during that two-year period, I was at the Athens airport with Mr. Onassis when the two men accidentally met. Mr. Konialidis looked as if he wanted to speak to his cousin, but Mr. Onassis refused to look at him and turned around to walk in another direction. Before I turned around to follow my employer, I could see the tears forming in Mr. Konialidis' eyes as he stood there, watching Mr. Onassis walk away.

Suddenly, however, one day when I least expected it, Mr. Onassis casually asked me to call Mr. Konialidis in Montevideo. I did as he requested, and, two days later, Mr. Konialidis was back in his office, and the two men were talking and joking and yelling at one another as if they had never been apart.

I had learned before that incident with Mr. Costas Konialidis that my employer never thought with his heart when it came to business deals. A deal was a deal with him, and his only thoughts for these deals were to gain money. He had no trouble, as he exhibited with his cousin, in separating personal friends and deals. Members of the board of directors at Olympic Airways often said that Mr. Onassis used his employees, especially his directors, as if they were lemons. "He will suck the juice out of us," one particular director complained to me. "And then he will throw away the rind, for we will no longer be of any use to him."

I had noticed that when it came to those who would become directors, Mr. Onassis always trusted his instincts. He did not particularly care if a man was well educated, but he was often impressed by clever, good-looking directors. Still, none of these men was immune to falling out of favor with him. While all his top men would bang their heads around him, yessing him, flattering him constantly and speaking to him respectfully, if one of them made a mistake or if someone else he trusted more spoke poorly of one particular director, then the director would be quickly fired, most often by Miltos Yiannacopoulos. Sometimes, however, he didn't fire that person directly. Instead, he would inform me that he did not want to receive phone calls from him and would prefer to speak to the person under that director. It didn't take long for that director to realize that his effectiveness and his job were over. It seemed as if these men would all work hard to get to a top position, yet there was a great danger that they would fall quickly from that lofty point.

Repeatedly during the nine years I worked directly for Mr. Onassis, I never questioned that business was the most important aspect of his life. Nothing mattered more to him than being successful in business. He had told me once that "Business is business and friends are friends," and I understood exactly what he meant. While he involved many of his closest friends in his business, the bottom line was that when they were all involved in a business deal, the friendship mattered not at all. Miltos Yiannacopoulos always called him Mr. Onassis when they were in the office or even when they were away from the business, never addressing him as Aristo, no matter where they were. Professor Georgakis, like Costas Gratsos and his other close business associates, called him Aristo when they were alone or in a social setting, but in front of other business associates, they all called him Mr. Onassis.

"It is not so good to be a friend of Mr. Onassis," Miltos told me once. "My friend does not like to mix the two, business and friendship. It might be easier just to be a business associate and not a friend." But Miltos had obviously made a decision to be both, a decision from which, as Mr. Onassis' most trusted adviser, he never wavered.

For the most part, none of the Olympic Airways pilots ever became Mr. Onassis' friends. Still, even though the pilots were often frustrated by Mr. Onassis' tactics in dealing with their strikes, they were always relieved when he personally appeared at their important meetings. For they knew that he would make decisions quickly and spare them weeks of unnecessary waiting.

When it came to making other decisions concerning his business, he made them equally as fast. In 1971, he decided that his project for an oil refinery in Greece, the Omega Project, was not going well. Even though a lot of his employees were involved, he halted the project. Once that decision was made, he moved onward, refusing to consider it again. "It is enough," he said simply to me one day. "I do not want to think about it anymore."

As hard as he worked, my boss could play with the same amount of energy. Mr. Onassis could easily work a full day and spend the next twelve hours drinking and partying in Athens. His favorite bouzoukia was the Neraida, in Palaion Phaleron, a seaside suburb ten miles outside of Athens, where he would listen to traditional music and dance and drink ouzo all night long, most often with Professor Georgakis. When he was in an especially spirited mood, he and the professor would hurl pottery at the walls and on the floor of the nightclub, smashing dozens and dozens of plates in a single night.

I was also impressed when, after one of these all-night escapades in the bouzoukia, he would return to the office at around eight, shower, change his clothes and put in a full day's work before returning to Glyfada that evening. Those days, I would study him carefully, certain that he would fall asleep the minute he sat down at his desk, but he rarely exhibited any sign of fatigue.

Another one of my employer's talents, I also learned, was that he was a bit of an actor who could switch roles quickly. For instance, in the middle of a meeting with his pilots, arguing fiercely with them about their wages or demands, he could be shouting, banging on the table with his fists, yelling horrible swear words, and turning red in the face. I would be sitting in my office, hearing the ugly sounds emanating from the meeting, when, after their marriage, Jackie happened to call. "Could you check, Kiki dear," she would ask me, "if it is all right with Aristo for me to take the helicopter from Skorpios to Athens this afternoon?"

"Oh, I am certain it is all right, Mrs. Jackie," I would answer her as her husband's loud shouting from the room beside me made it difficult for me to hear her soft words. "You can ask him yourself."

"Oh, no, Kiki," she would insist in her breathless, little girl voice. She was, I learned soon, smart like a cat. She knew how to handle her husband like few other people ever did. There was little she could not get from this man, if she just handled him correctly. "I do not want to bother him. Could you please ask him for me?"

"Of course, Mrs. Jackie," I would say, and would take a deep breath and knock on the door of Mr. Konialidis' office. "I am sorry to bother you, Mr. Onassis," I would say to my red-faced employer, "but Mrs. Jackie would like to use the helicopter, if it is all right with you."

And, in a flash, his face would lose the redness and he would tell the pilots he would be right back and walk out of the office to take the call at my desk. "Of course, honey," he would say to her in a perfectly calm voice, "you can take the helicopter from Skorpios. Is there anything else you might like me to arrange while you are in Athens, my darling?" Yet the moment that phone call was over, he would be back in front of the pilots, continuing his latest tirade, his face redder than before.

It was also not the least bit unusual for Mr. Onassis to appear at my desk one morning and tell me to cancel a meeting with one of his business associates. "That man is a liar and a thief!" he would shout at me. "I never want to deal with him again. Never!"

And an hour later, he would ask me again if I had canceled the appointment. "Oh, I have tried, Mr. Onassis," I would lie, "but his phone is busy. Do not worry. I will reach him in time to give him your message."

And he would nod his head and walk away. That scene was repeated two or three more times, until an hour before the meeting, when he would calmly ask me the exact time the man was coming to his office. "He will be here in a an hour," I would tell him and he would nod amiably and return to his work. The meeting between the two men always passed smoothly and uneventfully. There were, however, other times when Mr. Onassis made such a request and I followed it immediately. It was all part of my job to learn to decipher which fury was sincere and which one would disappear in the wind.

It was also, I must admit, part of my job to become what some might call a snoop. For instance, I needed to resort to somewhat sneaky tactics to determine exactly how my employer spent his nights in order to plan his days properly. And so I did what I had to do. Each morning, as soon as I arrived in my Syngrou Avenue office, I would call Mr. Onassis' residence and ask Panagiotis, "How passed the night, the Megalos?" And he would tell me what I needed to know. If there had been an argument with Maria during dinner and she had spent the night sulking in her Santorini suite on the *Christina,* some other personnel from the ship would report it to me. Or, after his marriage to Jackie, perhaps, the server who delivered dinner to Jackie and Aristo in the dining room of the *Christina* had overheard unpleasant words as he placed the soup in front of his employer. Or maybe a maid in the pink house had seen the two newlyweds embrace warmly in the garden of the house and retire to their room much earlier than usual. Or Mr. Onassis' helicopter pilot might report that Mr. Onassis had asked for the helicopter to take him to an island Maria was visiting while Jackie was in New York.

All of us who were employed by the Onassis family understood that Mr. Onassis' moods affected each one of us. If I knew that he had a bad night and a serious argument with either Maria or Jackie, then I would rearrange his business schedule, postponing an important meeting until later in the afternoon, when he would most likely have calmed down or rectified the unpleasant domestic situation. There was no detail about Mr. Onassis' personal life that his staff considered too unimportant or trivial to share with me. I was grateful for this unwavering access to the moods and circumstances of my boss, and I used each piece of information I received to make the life of our employer run as smoothly as possible. It was as if we were all collaborators, struggling to understand and please the man who joined us all together. For when that man was both happy and productive, every one of us who worked for him could be happy and productive as well.

Unlike Mr. Onassis, however, Mr. Konialidis never brought his personal problems to the office. It was never necessary to check with his staff to see how his night had gone. No matter what happened between him and his wife Ritsa, his disposition was the same, day after day. But Mr. Onassis was a different story. I would not say that his life was more interesting than Mr. Konialidis', but his personal life did impact on his business life far more strongly than his cousin's did.

For instance, there were times when Mr. Onassis would return to Glyfada from his heavy partying and I was informed that he would most likely be sleeping until noon, therefore missing an important morning meeting that I had arranged. Those days, I would have to lie to the visitors and tell them Mr. Onassis had been called away on urgent business. Then, I would call his butler, Panagiotis, a second time and tell him to wake Mr. Onassis before noon and let him know what was going on. Eventually, usually just before noon, Mr. Onassis would call and say, "I'm coming, Kiki. Just hold everything together until I get there."

And I would lie a little bit more and pace nervously until he finally arrived, always greeting me, "Bravo, my child," before he met his visitors. The meeting, miraculously, always went well and no one seemed to suffer as a result of my boss's carousing the night before.

There were other times when Mr. Onassis did not want to meet with visitors who appeared in my office and requested a meeting with him. At those times, we had a system worked out whereby I would usher the unwanted visitors into another office and Mr. Onassis would sneak out of my office while we were gone. He enjoyed these little ploys, but I was exhausted at the end of each one of them, grateful that, at least for that day, the neglected visitor did not understand he was being rejected. Unfortunately, some of these visitors never did get to meet Mr. Onassis, and I would eventually have to explain to them that my employer would respond to their request by a letter, not with a personal meeting. Other visitors were more fortunate, and I was able to convince Mr. Onassis to make a future appointment with them and, this time, to meet them face-to-face.

Whenever Mr. Onassis was with Professor Georgakis, whether at business meetings at Olympic Airways or in the bouzoukia, he enjoyed himself thoroughly. Although Mr. Onassis had a wonderful sense of humor, I do not remember his joking with anyone the way he did with the professor. One day, I was at a luncheon meeting at the airport with Mr. Onassis and the members of the board of directors. Mr. Onassis was enjoying his favorite fish, *tsiros*, and drinking ouzo, as all of them discussed important business matters. When the business details were settled, the professor began telling the group how much money he had gained from a deal he had recently completed on his own. "Oh, really," Mr. Onassis said, laughing as he drank some more ouzo. "Is that so?

So tell us all exactly how much money you stole, my friend." Of course, he was joking and the professor laughed right along with all the directors. If anyone else had said such a thing to the professor, he would have been insulted, but he and Aristo kidded each other all the time and never got angry with one another.

Mr. Onassis' unique sense of humor was evident to many other people besides the professor. So often, he would tell me jokes that would embarrass but still delight me. He often told me little stories about women and their power over men. One story he told me more than once was how women were similar to the sea. "Do you know how they are similar, Kiki?" he asked me. As always when he told me these types of stories, I merely shook my head. "Ah, let me tell you," he would continue, savoring his role of storyteller. "A woman can make a man relax in her arms the way a man can be soothed by the peaceful embrace of the sea moving gently over his body, lulled into tranquillity by the ocean's calm strength. But at other times a woman can make a man roll out of control, rocked wildly on her giant swells. Then there is nothing a man can do but surrender to the sea and let her do to him whatever she chooses. Man thinks he is in charge of the sea. He builds his giant ships and uses the strength of the sea to bring them wherever he chooses. But, deep down, he always knows that against her rages, he is powerless. You agree, Kiki?" I nodded. And went back to work, smiling, not the least bit certain that anything, even the sea, could render my boss powerless.

My boss's superstitious nature was evident in more ways than the one he exhibited when he hired me because the value of the drachma increased the day we met. Once, he planned a trip to Dallas, Texas, with his personal pilot, Jean-Pierre de Vitry, to visit the aerospace industry headquarters. I arranged for the flights of the two men on Olympic Airways, with a routing from Athens to Paris to New York and then on to Dallas. Mr. Onassis was over forty-five minutes late for the flight, and Jean-Pierre sat on board the plane with the other irritated passengers who were complaining loudly about the unexplained delay that might force them to miss their connections in Paris. Finally, to the stewardesses' and pilots' relief, Mr. Onassis' black Cadillac appeared on the runway, and Mr. Onassis emerged from the car. It seemed to take forever for him to walk into the first-class section and be seated beside

Jean-Pierre. "What day of the week is it today?" he asked the pretty stewardess as she handed him a drink.

"It is Tuesday, Mr. Onassis," she informed him, and before she could say another word, he had unbuckled his seat belt and was out of his seat, heading back toward the door, which another stewardess was just beginning to lock.

"Don't lock the door," he told the startled stewardess. "I'm leaving. Tuesday is not a good day for me. I never fly on Tuesdays."

Mr. Onassis headed back to his black Cadillac, but poor Jean-Pierre headed up to the sky with a plane full of infuriated passengers.

I could easily imagine the look of amazement and fury on the faces of all those passengers. It was a look I saw often on the faces of the businessmen who came to our office during the nine years that Mr. Onassis was my employer. Those men might have wanted to kill him, but they marveled at his determination. No one made Aristotle Onassis do anything he did not want to do. Not even the women he loved.

Chapter Four

Artemis: The First
Onassis Woman

IN ORDER to comprehend Mr. Onassis' relationships to all the important women in his life, it is necessary to understand his relationship with the most
influential of his sisters. Because their mother,

Penelope, died when Artemis was eight and Aristo was six, Artemis became more in his life than merely an older sister. The eldest of Mr. Onassis' three sisters, and the only one with whom he shared both a mother and a father, Mrs. Artemis would always hold an important position in his life. After his divorce from Tina, not only did he live next door to Artemis in Glyfada, but his children spent the majority of their time living with her, and when he was not with Maria, he ate many of his meals at her home.

I learned quickly during my employment for Mr. Onassis that Artemis was a key figure in his life. When she called the office, which was usually two or three times a day, I was unerringly polite, and it didn't take long for the two of us to develop a warm telephone relationship. "How is my brother today, Kiki?" she would ask me each day during her first telephone call.

There was little doubt what she meant by that question. She wanted to know her brother's mood. A true Greek woman, she maintained considerable involvement in her younger brother's life. It was a role that surprised few other Greeks. In most Greek homes, a son is highly prized by his mother. The adoration of the male Greek child is undisputed, and his sisters are often left feeling inferior to their brother. If the mother were to die, as happened when Aristotle Onassis was six years old, his older sister might well accept their mother's role and shower her brother with the affection their mother once had shown him.

From my initial days at Olympic Airways, I came to see that Artemis Garofalidis adored her younger brother and considered him the most important person in her life, even more important than her own husband. She also maintained considerable power over his life, but she was smart enough to use that power carefully. It was a game, I learned, the two of them would play constantly, a game that often included me as an unsuspecting player. "Oh, he is fine, Mrs. Artemis," I would answer my employer's older sister each morning. "A bit angry at a few directors, but otherwise he is doing fine."

"Oh, that is good, Kiki," she would say. "So, he didn't have any upsetting personal calls today from any women?"

"Oh, no," I told her. "No women called at all."

"Well, I guess that is good news. Do you think, maybe, you could find out if he intends to come to Glyfada for dinner tonight? Or if he has other plans with someone else for the evening."

I knew exactly who that "someone else" might be. But if Maria had not called that day and he had not requested the helicopter for a quick trip to visit her on another island, I was quite certain he would be dining at Glyfada that evening. "I am pretty certain he will be coming to Glyfada tonight," I would answer, and his sister's voice turned unmistakably cheerful. "But is there something else I can do for you, Mrs. Artemis? Anything at all?"

"Oh, no, Kiki, you are very busy, I am certain. But perhaps if you find out when Mr. Onassis will be leaving the office, you could let me know so I can plan our dinner accordingly."

There was no doubt that my job with the Onassis family had elevated me in an unprecedented manner in my own family's eyes. The oldest of two children, I had a brother, John, who was eight years younger than I was. As in most Greek families, my brother was my parents' prized possession and, despite my age seniority, I often felt inferior to him. Yet as soon as I began to work for Aristotle Onassis, my parents regarded me in a new light. My mother was especially curious about the Onassis family and eagerly awaited whatever information I provided about them. Also, after I had been working at Olympic Airways for a few months, I began to receive requests from some of my parents' friends or relatives seeking favors. For some of these people, I arranged job interviews at Olympic Airways or in other Onassis-owned businesses. For especially close friends, I provided free or reduced-fare Olympic Airways tickets. For others, I made arrangements with renowned doctors who were connected to the Onassis family but were difficult for the average Greek citizen to reach. For my own brother, I was able to secure summer employment at Olympic Airways, whereby he earned money during the months when school was not in session. When my parents saw how easily I was able to do favors for their friends and our relatives, they were impressed and, for the first time that I could remember, praised me greatly. "You are so lucky that your daughter works for Onassis," so many of their friends told them, and they agreed proudly.

At first, when they saw that I had to work long hours, however, my parents became concerned about my health and safety. Many nights when I was working on an important project that needed to be completed as soon as possible, I did not return home at all. Those nights, the only sleep I would get would be one or two hours' sleep on the couch in my office. One such night, after I had collapsed on the couch, Mr. Onassis surprised me by walking into the office. Since I am a very light sleeper, I awoke the second the door to the office opened. Mr. Onassis laughed when he saw how he had startled me. "You go back to sleep," he insisted when he saw me getting off the couch. "I promise you I will be quiet and not bother you." At first, I was amazed that he would just walk into the office at three or four o'clock in the morning, but I soon learned that his sleeping hours were erratic and that he would think nothing of waking his driver to drive him to the office at any hour of the night. Although my parents were initially horrified that my hours were so long, when they saw how happy I was and how much pride they personally received from my position, they no longer objected. Also, after my mother personally met Mr. Onassis and all three of his sisters at Vassileos Georgiou 35, she and my father stopped worrying about my safety.

Dinner at Artemis Onassis' home in Glyfada was an experience that charmed and delighted my mother as much as it fascinated me. There were even times when Mrs. Artemis invited my younger brother, John, to come to dinner in Glyfada with me and my mother. Even though John was only eleven or twelve years old at the time, he thoroughly enjoyed coming to Glyfada. Artemis fussed over him and had Panagiotis prepare foods that he especially enjoyed. If John did not appear to be eating the foods on the table, she would send Panagiotis into the kitchen to make something else for John. If, however, my brother ate the foods he was served, she would insist that more of each dish be brought to him immediately. Sometimes, she also invited my girlfriends or my dates to dinner at her home, and treated each one of them as if he or she were the most important person in the world. She was, without question, the perfect hostess and always eager to meet anyone who was important to me.

Although I enjoyed having my mother or brother or friends at the table during these dinners, as my relationship with Mrs. Artemis grew stronger, I noticed that she did not invite my family or friends as often as she had done initially. For when they were not present, I found that

Mrs. Artemis was more relaxed and anxious to talk to me about more private family matters. I was quickly becoming a confidante to Mrs. Artemis, and it was a role I enjoyed and treated seriously. I did not repeat our private conversations to my mother and made certain I was always available when Mrs. Artemis needed someone to listen to her problems. When she was unable to reach her brother, she would talk to me about the problem she intended to discuss with him. If she was afraid she might anger her brother with her request, she would ask my opinion about it before she mentioned it to him. She talked to me about subjects she did not discuss with anyone else and listened carefully to whatever suggestions I might offer. I knew she was considerably older than I was, but when she requested my opinion, I told her what I thought, and I was surprised and pleased that she began to accept my words as important and worthwhile.

As Mrs. Artemis drew me closer and I became more tightly entwined in her family, my own family never appeared jealous or angry over the amount of time I spent with her. When my mother saw the two of us seated side by side in Mrs. Artemis's home, she smiled proudly and, later, just as proudly described the scene to her friends and relatives. Both my parents understood that this socializing with the Onassis family was part of my new life and they encouraged me to enjoy this aspect of my job. As for Artemis herself, she appeared to know from the very beginning of our relationship that the two of us would become unusually close.

I also soon learned that, when it came to those involved with Artemis' brother, her curiosity was always satisfied. In Aristo's room on the *Christina,* I later saw for myself, a large picture of his older sister presided over his bed. In the painting, Artemis looked sad and forbidding, but in real life, she was anything but that. An energetic, outgoing woman, she always let her presence be felt in his life. Although she weighed no more than ninety-five pounds, anyone who judged her strength by her slight build was committing a serious error in judgment.

"Ah, Aristo," she might say when we were all together, "how is my darling brother tonight? You look so tired. You must be careful to get some rest. You know how much I love you and how I worry about you. You must promise to take good care of yourself. And you, Kiki, must make sure he does that, too. And you must tell me, Aristo, is there anything at all I can do to make you feel better tonight? Just tell me what you want and I will get it for you."

With each successive evening that I spent in Glyfada, I watched Artemis fuss endlessly about the foods her brother was eating. "My darling," she would say to Mr. Onassis, "please do not eat too many of those fried foods. I made you some special meatballs instead. They are so much better for you to eat tonight. Please, my dearest, do not take so much of the hot sauces. I am so afraid they will make you sick."

Whenever she hovered over him, I noted she was careful to judge his mood and make certain that it was the right moment to be so intrusive. If she judged incorrectly, he would lose his temper with her and, no matter who else was there, he would scream at her for meddling in his personal life. There was no doubt Mrs. Artemis was afraid of her brother and that she constantly struggled not to antagonize him. She hesitated to make any decision concerning her finances or personal life without consulting her brother. If he told her to do something and she did not follow his instructions completely, he would berate her cruelly. If he refused her phone calls or did not show up at her home for dinner as planned, she was inconsolable. Often she would call me up, crying on the telephone and begging me to tell her what she had done to make her brother so angry with her. Yet she understood that even with my help, there were times when no one could predict his moods and that she would be unable to reach or please him. Yet there were far more times when he returned her affection and appeared pleased with her concern. Also, no matter where he was or how angry he might be at her, he rarely let a day go by without speaking to her. He loved his sister Artemis as much as she loved him. Of that, I was certain.

Still, although his older sister knew she might anger her brother by interfering in his personal life, she continually did exactly that. Maria Callas was one subject, I learned early, about which Mrs. Artemis had strong feelings. From the beginning of her brother's relationship with Maria, Mrs. Artemis did not approve of their marrying. Maria came from peasant stock. She was heavy. She was a world-famous opera singer, but never would she be a suitable wife for Artemis' only brother. She was, quite simply, not good enough for him. Never would Mrs. Artemis criticize her brother and his relationship with Maria in front of others. Yet when Mrs. Artemis drew me closer to her, she would repeat her private conversations with her brother to me. "Oh, my darling Aristo," she had said to him, "you must be careful with that woman. She is not right for you. Perhaps you could find another woman who is more suitable for you if you did not see her so often."

Many times Aristo would lash out severely at Artemis when she expressed those feelings, yet her sentiments strongly affected his actions. He would resist her suggestions and openly defy her, yet the fact that he never married Maria Callas may well have reflected his sister's opinion of such a marriage. He was a strong man, seemingly undaunted by anything or anyone, yet Artemis' power over her younger brother could not be denied.

While Mrs. Artemis might well have been Maria's enemy, her younger sisters, Merope and Kalliroi, were softer toward their brother's mistress. They thought they should love any woman whom their brother loved. Also, because both of them lived a distance from Glyfada and their brother, Merope Konialidis in Monte Carlo with her husband and two sons, and Kalliroi Patronikolas in Lagonissi with her husband and daughter, they were less strongly affected by the women in his life.

Both Merope and Kalliroi were different from their older sister in many ways. Although the three women spoke to each other nearly every day, the two younger sisters were closer with each other than they were with Artemis. Since Merope spent most of her time in Monte Carlo, she did not come to Glyfada as often as her younger sister, Kalliroi, who lived in Greece, in nearby Lagonissi, did. Kalliroi, in particular, loved to party and have a good time and spent many of her evenings in the bouzoukia, dancing and enjoying herself immensely after her divorce. Dressed in strikingly pretty dresses in bright colors and rich fabrics, Kalliroi looked quite chic as she danced the night away with her good-looking, energetic partners. Photographers often took pictures of the youthful, dynamic Kalliroi, indulging her passion for music and dancing in the Neraida club.

When I first met Kalliroi, she was fifty years old, but most of her friends were at least ten years younger than she was. Her only daughter, Marilena, was my age and slightly resembled her cousin Christina physically, although there was nothing similar in their temperaments. Yet I noticed from the first moment that I met this woman that Kalliroi had a vitality and a joie de vivre that was unrivaled by her two sisters.

Her winning smile and contagious laugh, her dark, sensual, beauty, and her generous, loving nature made her a sheer delight to be with.

After I had been working for her brother for about a year, Kalliroi invited my mother, my brother, John, and me to Lagonissi for a weekend visit. We had all been together at dinner in Glyfada, and my mother had enjoyed Mrs. Patronikolas' company. The weekend in her ocean-side home was a delight for my family. John and I swam for hours in the pool, which was just a few meters from the ocean, and shared a large room in the luxurious house. We also took long walks along the beach with Marilena, who was excellent company for both me and John. Each evening, Kalliroi, who loved to cook, prepared delicious and unusual dinners for all of us and entertained us for hours with her amusing stories and clever jokes. When I thanked her for such an enjoyable weekend, she invited us to join her for another weekend in the near future, an invitation we readily accepted.

Even though Kalliroi always invited Artemis to join us on the weekend, Artemis rarely came to Lagonissi for dinner and would never consider staying there for an overnight visit. The few times that she did join us for dinner at her youngest sister's home, Artemis was accompanied by Panagiotis, who carried a huge bag filled with her special foods. I understood that Mrs. Artemis was a bit jealous of the time I spent with Kalliroi, so I was careful not to tell Artemis how much I enjoyed my visits to Lagonissi. However, I could not help but enjoy my summer weekend visits to Lagonissi and found it difficult to refuse Mrs. Kalliroi's frequent and enthusiastic invitations. It was equally as difficult for me when Mrs. Artemis asked me to come to Glyfada for dinner on a Saturday night when I had already accepted Kalliroi's invitation. Then I would have no choice but to be honest with Artemis and promise that I would return early on Sunday so that we could dine together that evening. In the wintertime, this was not a problem, since I never went to Lagonissi during those months. At the end of the summer, Mrs. Kalliroi closed up her seaside home for the winter and moved into her elegant apartment at 12 Rigillis Street in downtown Athens, near the stadium, where she usually remained through January, when she headed to her villa in Switzerland. Although Mrs. Kalliroi constantly invited me to visit her in Switzerland, I regretted that my busy work schedule prevented me from

accepting those sincere invitations. I was, however, always very dili-
gent in making all of her plane reservations when she traveled back
and forth from Switzerland, accompanied by her rather large group of
servants and excessive amounts of luggage.

Merope, who is two years older than Kalliroi, was a more serious
woman than her younger sister. A dedicated businesswoman, Merope
was involved in her husband's business ventures and completely devoted to her two sons. While both younger sisters called Artemis every day
to receive family news, in particular about their brother and niece and
nephew, the two of them usually agreed with one another about most
issues, not always seeing things the way Artemis did. In particular, they
did not understand their sister's aversion to Maria Callas. However, on
one thing Merope and Kalliroi completely agreed: It was never a good
idea to disagree openly with their older sister.

In addition, they always understood that their older sister's influence over Aristo outweighed theirs. They knew she was a clever woman
and she would continually find other more circumspect ways to express
her dislike for Maria Callas and prevent Maria from becoming their
brother's wife. The entrance of Jackie Kennedy into their brother's life,
they both agreed, afforded Artemis the most effective weapon with
which to wage her successful battle of permanently thwarting his marriage to Maria Callas.

Still, as I became more involved with the Onassis family, I was
continually surprised by the power Artemis held over her brother's life.
I understood it was the Greek way for Artemis to wield such power, yet
at times it did appear strange to me. Her frequent calls to me at
Olympic Airways to attempt to determine her brother's every mood
were not annoying since I accepted them as part of my job, yet I often
wondered how she had managed before I came to work for her brother.
Amalia was always courteous to her employer's older sister, but her
responses to Artemis' calls were brisk and less revealing than mine.
Still, I have no doubt Artemis had other means to receive her information, for nothing could prevent her from interfering in her brother's life.
While Mr. Onassis made deals that involved millions of dollars and
continued relationships with some of the most famous and desired
women in the world, his older sister remained an unyielding and
powerful force in his personal life. To alienate or fail to win over

Artemis Onassis Garofalidis was a grave error for any woman who desired to be a part of that life. For Maria, the error was fatal.

There was no one Mrs. Artemis would prefer to discuss more than her brother, and in me, she had a most receptive audience. Her list of stories about him was endless. In one story, her brother was still a teenager living in their native Smyrna. Their father, Socrates Onassis, was a wealthy tobacco exporter, and he wanted his only son to be as well educated and cultured as possible. Unfortunately, Aristo was a terrible student who disappointed his father with his poor scholastic accomplishments. When Socrates hired a private tutor to teach his teenage son French, Aristo suddenly became an enthusiastic student.

"His French teacher was very beautiful," Artemis explained to me. "Not only did my brother learn to speak French beautifully, but he experienced the first love affair of his life with the French teacher. He continued to improve his mastery of both those subjects, speaking French and making love to beautiful women, for the rest of his life."

In yet another story that she related to me many times, her brother was eighteen and traveling from Greece to Argentina to make his fortune. In 1922, when the Turks invaded Smyrna, Socrates Onassis had lost his considerable fortune and many members of his extended family had been killed or expelled by the Turks. Socrates had been thrown into prison, but eventually he was released and his family settled in Athens. Unable to find a decent opportunity for work anywhere in Greece, Aristotle headed for Buenos Aires. When Aristo was passing though San Remo, near Monte Carlo, he saw the millions of lights that lit up Monte Carlo. "Someday," he wrote his sister, who was living in Greece, "I will have one of the most beautiful houses in that small paradise."

"He meant it then," Mrs. Artemis told me. "And, as always, he did exactly what he said he was going to do."

Shortly after Aristo arrived in Argentina, Artemis further related to me, their grandmother Gesthsemane traveled from an evacuation camp in Samos to Piraeus by ship. Although she survived life in the camp, in Piraeus, when a thief tried to steal her money she fell to the deck of the ship and died instantly. Artemis and Aristo adored their grandmother and became even closer after her death. Without a mother or a grandmother in his life, Aristo became even more dependent on and devoted to his older sister.

It wasn't difficult to see how tied Mrs. Artemis was to her brother, both by economic as well as emotional ties. Her own husband, Dr. Theodore Garofalidis, was an orthopedic surgeon and chairman of the board of directors of Olympic Airways, but her brother provided fabulous cruises on his yacht with celebrity guests and luxurious dinner parties, along with gifts of great material worth. Her brother was, unquestionably, not only one of the most important men in Greece but also the most important person in her life.

Mrs. Artemis' personality was not an easy one for me to understand, yet I never stopped trying to do so. I saw, from the beginning of my nightly dinners in Glyfada, that her treatment of her servants could be erratic. A perfectionist, she was often hard to satisfy and could be a most demanding employer. For the most part, she ran her household with the help of five servants, as well as three drivers and one gardener. The gardener was in charge of the large garden surrounding the house, with its varied types of trees, including succulent orange trees, the lush green grass that Mr. Onassis had imported for Skorpios from South Africa, the lavish flower beds, especially the stunning roses, and the large, elegant pool. The five servants, including her treasured butler Panagiotis, who was unquestionably the boss of all the servants, lived at Vassileos Georgiou 35 in separate quarters attached to the house. When any one of them committed an error, perhaps spilling a dish while taking it out of the oven or breaking a glass, Mrs. Artemis could become furious. Even if guests were nearby, Mrs. Artemis did not hesitate to scream at the poor servant, embarrassing both the guest and the servant with her outburst. Yet her fury, unlike her brother's anger, usually lasted but for a brief moment. As quickly as it had appeared, it was gone, replaced with smiles and apologies.

"Oh, you must forgive me," she would say to the tearful servant. "You know how much I adore you and how happy you make me with your excellent work. Who cares about a stupid dish? So long as you are not hurt." And the servant would immediately forgive her employer, insisting it was her fault and that she would be much more careful in the future.

When it came to payment for her servants, Mrs. Artemis was

unquestionably cheap. "I cannot give any of them raises," she would try to explain to me. "For if I do, then that will set a bad example for my friends and neighbors who have servants. I wish I could be more generous, but there is nothing I can do about the situation."

Amazingly, despite Mrs. Artemis' sharp tongue and stingy pockets, during the twenty years that she was my dear friend, I rarely if ever saw any of her servants leave her. They all seemed perfectly content to work in her home for barely sufficient pay and the constant threat of her explosive temper. I sincerely believed they all loved her and forgave her faults because of the affection she showed them. It is also possible that the excitement of her home and the kindnesses showed to them by Mr. Onassis kept them linked to Vassileos Georgiou 35.

I would not have surrendered one moment of those wonderful evenings at Vassileos Georgiou 35. While Mrs. Artemis' capable butler, Panagiotis, dressed in his impeccable black pants and white jacket and black bow tie, or "papillon," as Mrs. Artemis called it, moved expertly through her spacious home instructing all of the maids in their tasks, she regaled each of her nightly guests with the finest of food, wine, and music.

Most evenings began with Mrs. Artemis' making her grand entrance on the winding, elegant staircase, her evening dress long and billowing behind her, her makeup impeccable, and her smile genuine. One of her favorite fabrics was organza, often embroidered with delicate pink flowers, yet she also favored vivid prints and shades of blue. Her preferred dressmaker, Roula, designed all Artemis' dresses, working closely with her client on every aspect of the creation. Rarely, if ever, would Artemis buy her clothes in a regular store, far preferring to have them custom-designed by the ever-talented Roula. Roula also made certain that her elegant client had an endless supply of long silk or lace scarves, which Artemis wrapped dramatically around her shoulders and neck, and sometimes even swept around her legs, so that she never failed to effect a memorable entry from the staircase into the living room to signal the official start to her dinner party.

"Oh, how beautiful you look tonight, Artemis," all of her guests would declare when they greeted her in her living room. "You are positively radiant."

"Oh, thank you," she would respond graciously. "And how exquisite you look," she told her female guests. "And I had almost forgotten how handsome you were," she informed her male visitors. Many evenings I was invited up to her bedroom to help her fix her hair or to decide between two gowns. I was always amazed at the way she arranged her bedroom. The two large beds were close to one another and elegant, with their engraved headboards and pink satin bedspreads. However, it was what was on Mrs. Artemis' bed that was the most remarkable. For, here, scattered over the rich pink fabric, lay all her jewelry, every exquisite piece stretched out for her constant inspection. Although her servant put the jewelry away before Mrs. Artemis went to bed each night, during the day and early evening, the jewelry remained open to her view. Like a small child playing with her favorite toys, Mrs. Artemis would receive great satisfaction from viewing or touching each and every ring or bracelet or necklace or earring or brooch that covered her satin bedspread. Sometimes it seemed as if the light offered by that vast supply of gold and diamonds and rubies and silver illuminated the entire bed, as much as did the skylights above it.

In Mrs. Artemis' boudoir, I admired the vast collection of creams and perfumes with which she adorned her skin. She spent a great deal of time, in front of her mirror, applying creams and makeup and fixing her eyes and lips so that they were exactly the way she wanted them to appear. Most of the creams I ordered for her arrived from Switzerland, while her perfumes came from Paris. Her favorite perfume was Gabochard, which she sprayed heavily on her body. Her sister Kalliroi favored a man's eau de toilette, named for the actor Alain Delon, yet when she wore it, the fragrance was surprisingly pleasant on her. Many of Artemis' creams had dates on them that stated they were expired, so I was careful to check them over for her and discard the ones that were not longer usable. Her fingernails, however, never received the type of attention she paid to her face, and she rarely covered them with polish, preferring to leave them, unlike her skin and hair, natural and unadorned.

"You must try this cream, Kiki," she would insist when I was seated there, watching her prepare her makeup. "It would be just perfect for your skin."

If I appeared to like the cream, she never hesitated to give it to me, so I was careful not to sound too enthusiastic about the various jars and tubes she placed in front of me.

Downstairs in the living room, however, seated on one of the graceful couches, usually beside Mrs. Artemis, I spent these long, exciting evenings talking with Christina and Alexander and Mr. Onassis, as well as with Mrs. Merope and Mrs. Kalliroi. Sometimes I even sat in the small cozy space behind the stairs where a small sofa and table were arranged for a more intimate discussion between two guests.

Every evening when I walked into that living room, its thick wooden floor was polished to its usual glow and beautiful bouquets of roses were placed creatively in large crystal vases and scattered effectively around the spacious room. The two sofas on which I usually sat, each covered with an identical rich pink fabric, accentuated with small delicate flowers, faced each other at opposite sides of the spacious room, allowing perfect views of the paintings by Picasso, Tsarouhis, and Thalassinos, illuminated by soft lights, which graced the walls. Many evenings I stared at the famous painting *The Navy* by Tsarouhis, for I adored looking at the boy in the painting dressed in his navy uniform, who often appeared to be smiling directly at me.

Every winter evening, a lovely fire enhanced the handsome marble fireplace, and the sour-cherry curtains, flecked with strands of gold, were drawn tightly, obscuring the ocean views beyond their windows. A large assortment of family photographs, even including several pictures of Tina, as well as many of Merope and Kalliroi and their husbands and families, and of Alexander and Christina, each encased in a silver or gold frame, covered the rich wooden top of the large, antique piano, which was, as always, the focal point of the room.

Although I was never certain exactly whom I would meet when I walked through the front door, I knew the food served on the long, antique wooden dining room table, in the center of which rested the grand silver candelabra filled with softly glowing candles, would be delectable, and the guests charming and charmed.

Many nights, the gatherings were small and intimate, perhaps involving just Artemis, her longtime friends from Smyrna, Roula and Letta, her cousin Tiamkaris, and me. Yet frequently, when her brother was in attendance, the house was filled with other guests, all interesting and carefully chosen by both Mr. Onassis and his sister. One of Mr. Onassis' closest friends, the ever-brilliant Professor Georgakis, at one time the chairman of the board of directors of Olympic Airways, was a frequent visitor, entertaining us with amusing stories about people or politics. Educated in Germany, the professor was the author of many books about Germany, which were widely read by university students in Greece. He spoke a multitude of languages, but he also possessed a sense of humor that delighted all of the guests at Glyfada. Celebrities such as Rudolf Nureyev or Elizabeth Taylor and Richard Burton, or Prince and Lee Radziwill, dined at Vassileos Georgiou 35. Unfortunately, I never had the pleasure of personally meeting Miss Taylor or Mr. Burton; however, Kalliroi entertained them one evening at her villa in Lagonissi. "They were both utterly charming," she told me the next day. "And Elizabeth was quite beautiful and elegant. Her husband drank an enormous amount, yet he never appeared drunk. It was quite amazing to watch him consume so much liquor." Most of the celebrities who came to Athens, however, were quickly spirited away by helicopter to the nearby island of Skorpios, where they were escorted on board the *Christina*. But that was a different story.

Dinner in Glyfada had a charm of its own, certainly not as opulent as dinner on board the *Christina*, but an evening of great fun and sophistication. As the official "First Lady" of the villa, Mrs. Artemis oversaw every little detail of the evening. She spent a great deal of time each day instructing her handmaids in the preparation of the dishes she chose for that evening's meal. The foods she served, she always explained to her guests, were light and of the best quality. When a guest complimented her on a particular dish, she would blush with pleasure, then painstakingly describe every ingredient that had been placed in it. Whenever we finished one of her dishes, she was quick to send Panagiotis to our side to refill our empty plate. The pleasure she received from others eating her food was so genuine that each guest had a difficult time refusing a second helping. No matter how full he was.

As young as I was then, I was never bored by those evenings, nor did I feel out of place or inappropriate. Perhaps I should have, but I never did. Besides, many of these evenings were too special to waste one moment feeling overwhelmed or insecure. There was too much else to concentrate on. The food was always served graciously by Panagiotis at the long dining room table, which was covered with handmade tablecloths and decorated with silver candles set in the elaborate candelabra, and exquisite silver spoons, knives, and forks. She had more than one set of dishes, yet the one she favored was white china, with delicate blue flowers along its gilded edges. Often Mrs. Artemis served her special meatballs with chili that her brother and both his children adored, using one of several sets of hand-painted china or pottery. Of course there was red roe caviar and Greek ouzo for Mr. Onassis. But there was also *kourabiedes* (white candy with sugar), souvlaki, chicken with potatoes done in a special Smyrna way, fried zucchini in rolls, baklava, *galaktoboureko* (similar to crème caramel), Greek coffee, cheese from Italy, bread from France, and water from Paris. The seating arrangements were carefully orchestrated by our hostess, who made certain not only that she sat next to her brother and across from me, but also that every woman was sitting between two men.

Whenever Christina ate with us, unlike her aunt, she dressed simply, preferring to wear a black skirt and white shirt and flat-heeled shoes. She wore little makeup and put her thick black hair behind her ears in a casual style. It was always obvious when she or her brother joined us that they were anxious to eat and leave, heading to a bouzoukia, where they could enjoy the rest of their evening. Before she left for the taverna, Christina often changed to a designer dress, usually by Dior or Chanel, and fussed for a long while with her hair. "I wish she would let me help her more with her clothes," Artemis remarked to me many nights when Christina left us. I smiled at Artemis and nodded my head in agreement, but I knew Christina would never be found in a gown like the type her aunt wore every evening.

Christina's father was also not in attendance at Artemis' house every evening. And many evenings, especially before he married Jackie, he ate quickly and then left with Professor Georgakis to visit his favorite bouzoukia. After his marriage to Jackie, Aristo went out with the professor only when Jackie was in New York, or when she would accompany him to a nightclub, where she often enjoyed herself immensely. It was very rare, however, that he would he leave her home alone in Greece and go out without her. Yet when it was just the two men, they could stay at the bouzoukia until dawn, drinking and cavorting with the beautiful women who graced their table. Nearly every day, following their visits to these clubs, I was handed a bill from the owner of the restaurant or club where they had spent the evening, detailing a large sum for all the dishes the two of them had hurled at the walls or fireplaces. It was a Greek custom to break these dishes, one Mr. Onassis followed diligently and excessively. Some days, I would pay as much as a thousand dollars for his dish-throwing custom.

During the dinners at his sister's home, however, I was surprised to learn that Mr. Onassis believed strongly in "kismet," or fate, and could be as superstitious as the rest of us. However, one practice that this oldest sister enjoyed, which he did not support, was the reading of the coffee remnants. Thus, on the evenings when her brother was absent from Glyfada, Mrs. Artemis often instructed one of her frequent guests, Letta Kiosseoglou, to read our coffee remnants from our cups. Letta had known Mr. Onassis and his three sisters many years earlier when they were all children in Smyrna. Her husband had been a wealthy man and had helped the Onassis family when they needed assistance. However, when her husband sadly lost all his money and property in Smyrna, Aristo had given him a large sum of money with which to support his family. A widow living near Glyfada when I began to work for the Onassis family, Letta was the same age as Artemis and a close friend. Mrs. Artemis was very fond of Letta and frequently sent her driver to Letta's home to bring her to Glyfada for dinner. Letta was a quiet woman who spoke only when someone spoke to her, but she was also kind and gentle and very adept at reading coffee remnants. Thus, when the three of us were having dinner alone at Glyfada, the minute we finished our meal, Letta would read our cups. Sometimes she would tell us true things, but often the three of us just laughed and enjoyed ourselves, not worrying about the exact words Letta spoke.

Often during those evenings when her brother was not in attendance and when she had drunk too much vodka, Mrs. Artemis would turn on me, and, disgusted with something I had said or something I had done wrong, talk to me in a cruel manner, using much the same tone she might direct at an offending servant. "You are a very silly girl, Kiki," she would lash out at me. "What is wrong with you? Do you not have a brain in your head? I cannot understand how anyone could be so stupid." The first time she acted that way toward me, I was shocked and deeply hurt. I wanted to turn and run out of the house, but I was too paralyzed with surprise to move. It did not seem possible that someone who treated me so kindly could suddenly become so mean.

Other times her insults were even worse as she accused me of having affairs with certain men. If I was one minute late and she was in one of those abusive moods, she would berate me for my tardiness. "Never will I allow you back in this house again!" she would scream at me. "You are the rudest person I have ever met."

When I started to cry in front of Letta, she soothed me, saying, "Kikitsa, don't worry. Artemis is like your mother. She thinks she has the right to be your teacher. She doesn't realize how much she is hurting you. She really likes you so very much." And I would stop crying and be grateful for Letta's kindness. And, no matter how much I was hurt, I would forgive my teacher and friend for her unkind behavior, certain it was the vodka, not her heart, speaking.

When Mr. Onassis was present, the meals were never followed by Letta's readings. Instead, music continued long after the meal was finished, as some guest played the piano, a beautiful antique piano that Mr. Onassis had bought years earlier in Spain, which was covered with the pictures of the entire family. I loved to study these photographs, not just because they were filled with celebrities, but because everyone in them, family and friends, was always smiling and looking both beautiful and contented. When it was my turn at the piano, Mr. Onassis insisted I play "*Me Ena Oneiro Trelo*" ("With a Dream Crazy"). Often another guest would play the same song on the bouzouki, a Greek instrument similar to a guitar, and Mr. Onassis would sip his ouzo and smile the faraway smile that covered his face whenever he heard that song.

I studied my employer's face often those memorable, delicious evenings as I basked in the affection and warmth his family afforded me. I observed the way he looked at his daughter, Christina. I cannot say his face emitted love and kindness as he stared at her. Instead, I noted the annoyance that face exhibited, as the strangeness, the moodiness, and the sadness that were always such a part of his daughter came to light. When Christina ate large amounts of chocolate or other foods, disgust would cover his face, and if she said something that annoyed him, he would rant and scream at her, no matter who else was in the house. Other times, his mood was disinterest, as he appeared unconcerned with whatever his daughter was saying or doing. There were rarer moments when he was grasped by a warm affection that delighted his daughter like no other extravagant gift which he might bestow upon her. Then she was *"chryso mou,"* "my golden one," and could do no harm in his eyes.

There had been rumors that Tina did not intend to have a second child, and would have preferred to end her second pregnancy. After all, like most Greek women, she felt she had her one son, so why should she have another child? Sons are so highly prized in Greek families that a daughter's worth is often minimal by comparison. Artemis believed that it was her brother who convinced Tina to proceed with the pregnancy. Whatever Tina's true feelings were about being pregnant again, Christina was raised in a family that appeared to value her less than her brother.

I noted that when I first came to work for Mr. Onassis, he treated his daughter more kindly than he did as she grew up. It seemed that when she was just sixteen, she was more obedient and more apt to follow her father's instructions. Then he was delighted to give her whatever she wanted and buy her expensive presents. However, as she grew up, she developed more of a mind of her own and often did things that angered her father, particularly in regard to some of the men with whom she became involved. Then her father turned against her and berated her for her poor judgment and impetuous decisions. When, at an older age, she did not follow his suggestions, he knew he could no longer beat her as he could before she turned eighteen, so, instead, frustrated by his lack of control over her, he could often act less generous and colder to her.

With Alexander, Mr. Onassis was noticeably more loving. As with his daughter, however, he often lost his temper at his son and belittled him in front of others. But that was typical of the relationship between Greek fathers and sons. The fathers, like Mr. Onassis, fiercely adored their sons, but they demanded a great deal from them and were enraged when their sons did not live up to their expectations. But this particular Greek father's rage was easily displaced by an intense pride and love that I never saw him bestow upon his daughter. He could laugh loudly with Alexander, but minutes later he would be angry enough to throw something at him. One minute his arm was draped around his son's shoulder as if he could not get close enough to him. Yet without much warning that same arm could be poised to strike his son's face. Like all who knew and loved Mr. Onassis, Alexander struggled to learn to take these mood changes in stride.

As Alexander and Christina learned to deal with their father's mood changes, I adjusted to their aunt's vodka-induced personality. Mrs. Artemis was my friend and my protector, as well as my tormentor. But, without her, I would never have become privy to the life my employer and his family lived beyond the office walls of Syngrou Avenue. Neither Mrs. Artemis nor her brother were easy people to understand, yet I never stopped trying to accomplish such a feat. For Mr. Onassis, I had a job to perform and I strove to do that as capably as possible. For Mrs. Artemis, the lines were cloudier. I was to be her adoring friend, her treasured but occasionally disobedient daughter, and her brother's trusted private secretary. I was to listen to her problems and help her solve them. I was to help her reach her brother whenever she needed his advice or presence. The rewards, to me, for performing all those roles in these two Onassises' lives were large. Not only was I given large sums of money from my employer, as well as gifts of jewelry and clothing from his older sister, but I was made to feel important and valued in their lives. If I had not come to work for Mr. Onassis, I would never have received access to the exciting, luxurious lives these people lived and into which they drew me. For many years, I saw mostly joy and glamour in these lives, only occasionally marred by sorrow. Yet the more I came to know these Onassises, the more I came to understand that this joy and glamour was laced with pain, which, while often hidden, was never completely absent.

Chapter Five

Maria: A Grand Passion

T HERE IS no doubt that Mr. Onassis' marriage to
Jackie Kennedy strongly affected the life of every member of his family. Yet none of his relatives—neither his
sisters, nor his daughter or son or ex-wife—was as
irrevocably affected by this marriage as was Maria

Callas. Her life, especially after she fell in love with Aristotle Onassis, played like a Greek tragedy. She came into his life amid high drama and exited surrounded by even more theatrics. Aristotle, the ancient Greek philosopher, not the twentieth-century shipowner, defined tragedy as "an imitation of an action that is serious, complete in itself, and of a certain magnitude." He suggested that catastrophe results from a flaw in the character of the hero. Others contend that it results from events beyond the hero's control. Tragic heroes, Aristotle said, "are men of high estate who enjoy great reputation or prosperity."

Adultery, which brought these two lovers together, might well be considered a serious action, and few would deny that these two modern Greeks, the opera singer and the shipowner, were "of high estate" and enjoyed "great reputation or prosperity." Yet as the secretary to one of these characters while the drama was unfolding around them, I wondered if the looming tragedy could be averted and their lives could be sweet and filled with joyful love. The answer, I learned sadly, was no.

Yet the view I was offered of the two of them, while often intrusive, was clear and impossible from which to avert my eyes. Maria Callas had been a legend to me before I began to work for Mr. Onassis, but no matter how many times I heard her voice over the telephone or met her in person, I could never quite believe I was speaking to the diva.

During all my dinners at Glyfada, I never once met Maria there. It was not merely that Artemis did not want her there, it was that Maria did not want to be there. There were occasional times when Aristo and Maria would dine at Artemis' home in Glyfada, but their meals there were usually for just the two of them, sitting in Artemis' elegant dining room, eating a simple meal together.

After those meals, I would often hear from the staff of Glyfada, who would report on the meal. "*Afentiko* [boss] and Mrs. Maria were most unhappy during their lunch together," Panagiotis might warn me before Mr. Onassis returned to the office. "He will not be in a good mood for the rest of the day."

Or one of the family drivers would call me to tell me that he had taken the couple to lunch at the Asteria restaurant in Athens. During the ride to the Asteria, Mr. Onassis had held Maria's hand tightly and called her "Maritsa," the way her name would have been spoken in his homeland of Smyrna. On the way back from the restaurant, there had been so much kissing and laughing in his car that the driver was certain *Afentiko* would not be coming back to work until much later that afternoon. If at all. I was grateful for these calls and planned the rest of the day accordingly.

From the moment that Aristo and Maria became lovers, however, I had been told, the *Christina* was the place where both of them felt the most comfortable together. "She feels protected there," Artemis explained to me. "There are no crowds begging for her autograph or photographers pursuing her with their cameras, and no fans asking when she will perform next. She is safe there. My brother makes sure of that. Besides, she is a very private person and it suits her to be only with him. She felt her mother and her older sister, Jackie, took advantage of her. Jackie was always prettier than Maria and their mother's favorite. Maria also believed her own husband Meneghini mistreated her, using her terribly and making a fortune off her talent. My brother would never do that to her. He is taking care of her now. The rest of us she does not need. Only him."

I understood what she was saying. That famous voice was always soft and hesitant as she spoke to me on the telephone in the office. "Please, Kiki, may I speak to Mr. Onassis?" she would ask me. "If he is not too busy."

"Of course, Mrs. Maria," I would answer her. "I will get him right away for you."

Although Mr. Onassis was not the type to become enthusiastic and excited over a phone call, when he heard who was on the phone, he did appear satisfied. I would close the door to his office when he began speaking to her, and although there were times his voice was louder than normal and I heard a few words that he might shout, I did not listen to these private conversations. I went about my work, ignoring the drama about me.

Many Greeks insisted that part of the tragedy between these two lovers was the fact that Maria gave up her career for Aristo. That is not entirely true. By the time she met him, Maria had already had an exhausting operatic career and was experiencing problems with her voice. In moments of anger, Aristo referred to that voice as "a whistle that no longer works." His words were cruel and usually retracted, but

Maria had been sadly booed during a few of her concerts and had been experiencing more stage fright than usual when she met Aristo.

Artemis loved to tell me one particular story about Maria, which took place in 1957, well before the diva and her brother became lovers. At that time, Maria postponed a performance of *Norma* in Italy because she perceived an unpleasant attitude in her waiting audience. She was certain that they were a cold and unfriendly audience and that they would be hoping for her voice to fail, even for one second, so that they could boo her. Adamant about not performing in front of such a hostile crowd, Maria simply stated she did not feel well and canceled her performance.

"The best part of the whole scene," Artemis explained to me, "was that when all the men and women who had traveled to the opera returned to their homes hours earlier than expected, many of them discovered their wives or husbands in bed with their lovers or mistresses. All those people who wanted to hurt Maria with their coldness and lack of respect were now hurt by her. And they deserved it, don't you think?"

Artemis was also fond of repeating the story of Maria's first performance as Tosca at the Athens Opera. In 1941, at the age of eighteen, she had been called to the stage as a replacement for an elderly soprano who violently opposed Maria's appointment to her opera company. When the soprano sent her husband to prevent Maria from reaching the stage, Maria tore at his face with her nails, drawing blood. He responded with a punch to her face that delivered her to the stage with a black eye, yet her reputation as the Tigress had been created. The fire in her heart escaped through her lips, from that night and forever afterward. "Can you imagine a young unknown acting like that?" Artemis asked me after she related the story, her own head shaking in amazement at Maria's determination. "My brother had better be careful. The woman will always be the Tigress."

Artemis was clearly proud of Maria's behavior and admired her strength in refusing to be treated poorly. She might not have wanted the opera singer to have married her brother, but she never failed to recognize Maria's talent and spirit.

I was always a willing audience for any stories that Artemis wanted to relate about her brother and Maria. I knew many of the details before I went to work for Mr. Onassis, but hearing them from his sister, who had been a witness to so much of what had gone on and who adamantly opposed a marriage between the two of them, made it even more dramatic than it already was.

Aristo had fallen in love with Maria when she sang *Medea* at Covent Garden in London, after having pursued her for months in Paris and Venice. On a cruise on the *Christina* that departed from Monte Carlo to Istanbul and Venice on July 22, 1959, with Artemis and her husband, Dr. Theodore Garofalidis, Sir Winston and Lady Churchill, Tina, and Maria's husband, Giovanni Meneghini, on board, Maria and Aristo officially began a love affair that shocked the world and destroyed both their marriages.

"I could see it happening before my eyes," Artemis told me. "And there was nothing anyone could do to stop it. All his life, my brother loved meeting and making love to famous women. The more important or well known the woman, the more he loved to love her. Maria was the most famous Greek woman of our time. It was inevitable he would love her."

At the end of the three-week cruise, Maria announced to her husband that she loved Aristo and, Artemis told me, shaking her head with amazement and despair, left the ship with a bracelet engraved with *TMWL* (To Maria With Love) from her new lover. Ironically, Tina already owned a bracelet with the initials *TTWL*, and Jackie would receive her *TJWL* a few years later.

This bracelet was just one example of the couple's intentions not to hide their love for each other. On September 10, with Artemis and Dr. Garofalidis, Maria boarded the *Christina* in Venice and set off with Mr. Onassis for a two-week cruise. When the couple disembarked in Greece, amid much fanfare, their life together in their country officially began. "There was nothing I could do about it," Artemis explained to me. "It was a fait accompli that they would be lovers. But they were not rushing to become man and wife."

Artemis always insisted that Maria did not give up her career for Aristo, preferring to believe that when she met Aristotle Onassis, Maria had simply had enough of her demanding lifestyle as the world's greatest living opera singer. "Aristo told her that she needed to sing for only him," Artemis told me. "And she never complained when he said that in front of others." Still, there are those who insist that Maria's voice became richer, with a new depth of expression, once she began her relationship with Mr. Onassis. Yet all who have followed her career agree that once she fell in love with him, nothing in her life was ever the same.

In 1958, she gave twenty-eight performances of seven operas in six cities around the world. Yet in 1960 she gave seven performances of two operas in two cities; in 1961, she gave five performances, two of them *Medea*, two in Epidaurus and three at La Scala; in 1962, she gave two performances of *Medea* at La Scala; and in 1963, she sang no opera onstage at all. She did perform concerts and made some recordings, but in 1964, when her relationship with Aristo was beginning to deteriorate, she returned to opera for her last stage performances ever. But during those five years, it has also been well documented that she was losing her voice, as well as her ability and desire to perform in front of thousands of adoring fans. The stage fright that she had always held at bay was beginning to paralyze her, and it seemed obvious that her desire to live a life outside the fictional characters whose voices she assumed was beginning to propel her.

Artemis also insisted that Maria was a perfectionist, and when she could no longer perform according to the high standards she had set for herself, she did not want to sing any longer. Artemis said it was obvious to anyone who saw the two of them together that Aristo offered Maria a new life that she had never before contemplated. He took all the passion that she poured into her voice and provided another outlet for such energy and ardor: him. Instead of standing on the stages of the great opera houses of the world, facing an impassioned and demanding audience, Maria now stood beneath the cypresses of Skorpios and faced only one adoring fan. While he did not offer her sixteen curtain calls and tumultuous applause, he redirected the sensuality she had previously poured into her music. She was no longer merely a diva; now she was a woman. The sun and the ocean and the flowers and trees at Skorpios replaced the lights of the stage, and, like a flower that had been denied the light of the sun, she suddenly blossomed into a luscious exotic rose.

There is little doubt that an exhausted Maria welcomed with open arms this chance to live a real life with a real man. But Artemis understood that Maria expected even more than her brother gave her. The security and protection from all the people who used her, always ready to find a way to profit from her talents, was an immense gift that no one else could award her. But, in addition to all these incomparable gifts, Maria expected a never-ending love affair and the respectability of marriage. That was not to happen.

Also, as Artemis explained to me, years of living with Meneghini had made Maria deeply insecure. No matter how much Aristo loved her, she could never become secure in his love. "A woman who is adored by her fans but mistreated by her husband will never be secure," Artemis insisted. "I do not know if my brother can ever make up for what Meneghini did to her."

Although Maria and Meneghini divorced on November 14, 1959, and, eleven days later, after nearly thirteen years of marriage, Tina sued Aristo for divorce on the grounds of adultery, Aristo still never married Maria. And he played games of war with her already-damaged nerves that she most often lost, even further reducing her chances of returning to the stage. Yet for the nine years they were together before he took another wife, Aristo appeared to replace singing in her life and, according to the personnel in Skorpios who saw the two of them together, despite her enduring insecurity, he unleashed a sexuality few could imagine she possessed.

For these years, however, there were as many highs and lows in Maria's life as in the musical scale. There were moments when it appeared as if Maria could have it all: Aristo and her career. On August 6, 1961, she performed *Medea* in Epidaurus and received seventeen curtain calls. But in 1964, during a performance of *Poliuto* at La Scala, she nearly collapsed from stage fright. Offstage, there were beautiful cruises together, as well as rumors of an affair between Aristo and Lee Radziwill. There were expensive gifts of jewelry that enthralled her and verbal insults in front of others that humiliated her.

And there was a sister who could not accept the fact that this woman might someday be her brother's wife. "She will never make him happy," Artemis told me many times. "They are too much alike. They are both big bosses. How can they ever live together without killing each other?" I knew what she meant, for both Mr. Onassis and Maria were strong-minded people who did what they wanted when they wanted. Neither of them knew how to give in to the other.

The staff in Paris who saw them together before and after his marriage to Jackie affirmed that they seemed even more connected after that marriage than they were before. They had been lovers before, but after his wedding to Jackie, Maria and Aristo were like twins who could never be separated. It was as if his marriage had unearthed an even stronger passion in Aristo for Maria. As if the new American woman in his life, while beautiful and unique, could never, no matter what he had originally imagined, completely replace Maria.

"If they really wanted to get married, they would have done so," Artemis told me. "It could not have been just because of me that they did not marry. It had to be because of the two of them." There were frequent rumors that the two of them were going to get married, but it never did happen. Shortly after I came to work for Mr. Onassis, one of the drivers told me that *Afentiko* was going to get married in London within a week. He had heard Maria and Mr. Onassis discussing such a wedding when he drove them to dinner in the Psaropoulos restaurant in Athens one night. The week, and several more, passed and no such wedding occurred. Another time, one of the personnel from the *Christina* insisted that there was going to be a wedding ceremony on the boat for the two of them, but again no such wedding materialized. Yet another time, one of the maids in Mr. Onassis' Avenue Foch apartment in Paris warned us that a wedding was imminent. Again, it never happened. At least not between Mr. Onassis and Maria Callas.

Artemis had yet one more theory about why they would never wed. "My brother is a real Greek man," she told me. "Real Greek men like to be the one to ask a woman to marry them. Maria asked Aristo to marry her. Now he will never be the first to ask. And he will never marry her."

Yet those who saw them together on the *Christina* and in Paris insisted that it was as if they were already wed. With Maria, Aristo was natural and talkative and totally alive. The two of them could talk for hours, discussing a problem he could not solve without her advice. I personally saw later, after his marriage to Jackie, that Mr. Onassis could never get as angry with his second wife as he did with Maria. Nor did he seem to display the same passion with her that Maria brought out in him. It was not just that Maria and Aristo were both Greeks; it was that they were both, in so many ways, the same person.

But Maria was certainly the most celebrated Greek woman in our country. I thought she was beautiful, almost godlike. A big woman who had always struggled with her weight, Maria had huge black eyes, lustrous black hair, porcelain skin, and a prominent patrician nose that gave her face a noble beauty. She was also a deeply religious woman who believed that whatever happened to her was God's will. She prayed to God often and found much strength in her religious convictions.

There was no doubt, however, that her relationship with Mr. Onassis, while the great love affair of both their lives, was a stormy one. I had always heard from employees of the *Christina* that the two of them fought often and viciously, and frequently in public. If she pressed him too hard, he might even strike her. In that respect, they were no different from other Greek couples with larger-than-life personalities who were always dealing with each other about emotional issues. Both of them had strong opinions about everything that they would not hold inside.

Panaghis Vergottis, a Greek shipowner and close friend of Aristo who later became a close friend to Maria and an intermediary between the two lovers, repeatedly described the two of them as fire and dynamite. One moment they could be quarreling with such intensity that one might think they would kill each other. Minutes later, they were kissing passionately and struggling to find the nearest cabin where they could make love. For, always, no matter how viciously they fought, they made up and continued to love each other. I also learned soon after I began to work for Mr. Onassis that Maria adored flowers and could be made happier with a beautiful bouquet of flowers than she would be with a gift of jewelry. When I received reports from the personnel on the *Christina* or in the Paris apartment that there had been a fight between Mr. Onassis and Maria, I knew that I would be instructed to send flowers to that location. As I had learned quickly myself, Mr. Onassis almost never apologized to anyone for his bad behavior. Maria was no exception to that rule. Sometimes, however, he sent notes with his flowers to express his regret, but usually he preferred to let the exquisite flower arrangements speak his words of apology.

The staff on the *Christina* told me how silent and worried Maria was when she was alone on the *Christina* awaiting Aristo's arrival. Sometimes she would not speak at all, but would spend an entire day standing inside the ship, looking far away at the sea. No matter what they offered her, she would not eat or drink, but maintained her vigil, looking out at the ocean. The personnel would have taken her anywhere she wanted to go, but, as always, she was most content on the *Christina*, removed from crowds of people, enjoying her solitary peace amid such luxurious surroundings. But without Aristo, this peace sometimes turned painful. "She is like the wife of a fisherman waiting for her husband to return from a day out at sea," one of the employees on the *Christina* joked to me. "I think she believes he is not coming back." Yet the moment Maria spotted the Chris-Craft coming from the Piaggio, she came back to life. Suddenly she was laughing again, running as fast as she could to meet her precious Aristo.

There were, indeed, many wonderful moments between Maria and Aristo on the *Christina* before Mr. Onassis married Jackie. Maria was always very comfortable on the boat and had her own suite there, the Santorini suite. The suite was decorated to resemble a typical Santorini home. Decorated primarily in blue and white, the room contained a double bed, covered with a sea blue bedspread that was adorned with small white flowers, delicate blue sconces on its whitewashed walls, and paintings of the volcanic island by its artists. Maria kept many of her clothes in the closet in the room and covered the top of the bureau with her bottles and jars of perfumes and creams. Occasionally, she would visit the largest guest house on the island, but it was only on the *Christina* where she felt truly at home.

Maria called Mr. Onassis "*passa mou*," or "my boss," in an affectionate and good-natured tone. For the most part, he was indeed her boss. Especially in regard to her incomparable voice. She sang often for company and was the center of attention whenever she was on board for parties. Once, he urged her to sing at a special concert for the people of Levkas, a neighboring island from which Skorpios received some of its water. Maria kept refusing, insisting that she was no longer able to sing in front of a large group of people, but finally she agreed. The night of the concert, nearly everyone of the island of Levkas attended and was enthralled with her exquisite rendition of *Cavaleria Rusticana.*

Many people asked Maria for her autograph that evening, but as she did often, she hesitated, feeling too shy to write her name. Instead, she took a long list of all who wanted her autograph and, in the privacy of her suite on the *Christina,* meticulously wrote her name on separate slips of paper and mailed them to everyone who had requested her autograph.

During the first few years of Aristo's relationship with Maria, he often insisted that his entire family accompany him to Maria's performances. Even if Artemis or Kalliroi or Merope or their husbands did not want to attend, they would go. No one wanted to make Aristo angry, and a refusal to hear Maria sing *Medea* or *Tosca* would never be forgiven.

Although Maria was often uncomfortable in large groups, she enjoyed small parties on board the *Christina* with Mr. Onassis' friends. She appeared very relaxed with two frequent guests of Mr. Onassis, Greta Garbo and Bette Davis. The two American actresses arrived in Skorpios on private airplanes that I arranged for them and were lovingly welcomed by Mr. Onassis and Maria. Mr. Onassis enjoyed inviting those two American actresses to come at the same time and even planned a special cruise to the Caribbean on the *Christina* for the four of them. I also knew personally that my employer was exceptionally generous to Miss Garbo, in ways other than merely inviting her as his guest on the *Christina.* Whenever the actress was experiencing financial difficulties, which could be frequent, he never hesitated to send her a large check.

When Miss Davis and Miss Garbo were in Skorpios, the two actresses spent a lot of time swimming at the beautiful beaches of Skorpios or in the pool on the *Christina.* Both of them wore dark sunglasses and covered their heads with full scarves. Unlike Maria, they always moved as if they knew they were beautiful and that everyone would be staring at them. Maria had an appealing simplicity to her demeanor that contrasted sharply to the way Miss Garbo and Miss Davis handled themselves. This Greek woman with the most beautiful voice in the world was, above all else, a lady, a tall, elegant, unaffected lady.

Whenever the American actresses visited Skorpios, either alone or together, the chefs on the *Christina* tried to prepare foods that they might especially enjoy. One time when Bette Davis came alone to Skorpios, the three of them enjoyed spaghetti with a special red sauce with garlic, pepper, and green vegetables that the chef on the *Christina* made just for the American actress.

Maria was more relaxed and cheerful with those two women than she was with many of the other guests on the *Christina*. So often when Mr. Onassis would tell her whom he had invited to join them on the *Christina*, she would complain bitterly. "But, Aristo, don't you think we would be so much better alone?" she would plead. "We would have such a wonderful trip, the two of us. We do not need anyone else with us to have a perfect time." Time after time, however, Mr. Onassis convinced her he had made the right decision in inviting the guests to join them. For some of those guests, she would follow Mr. Onassis' request to play the beautiful antique piano on the *Christina* and sing along to her own accompaniment. Mr. Onassis adored music and had also purchased magnificent pianos for his home in Glyfada and for Artemis' house there. Although Maria's hands never graced the keys of the pianos in Glyfada, when she played her magic on the piano on the *Christina* the personnel on the ship felt as if they were in La Scala, and had to hold themselves back from racing to their feet amid thunderous applause when the last note was sung. It was difficult, several of them told me, for them to go about their duties when the diva was singing a mere few feet from them.

When the guest was Greta Garbo or Bette Davis, however, Mr. Onassis never had to convince Maria to welcome her warmly. Still, whenever the two American actresses visited Skorpios, he could not keep himself from flirting with them, holding their hands, staring into their eyes and telling them how beautiful they were. Whenever Maria witnessed this behavior, her face grew dark with sadness and she dissolved into tears. "Oh, Maria," he would then say, turning his attention away from Greta Garbo and Bette Davis and concentrating only on Maria. "Everyone knows that you are the most beautiful woman in the world. I love everything about the way you look. And everyone knows that." He would cover her face with kisses, while the actresses looked on. Like a small child, Maria would blush and smile and be filled with happiness once again.

Maria's jealous nature was only temporarily eased by Mr. Onassis' compliments. He could not seem to help flirting with pretty women, especially with Greta Garbo. One evening in 1967, before Mr. Onassis married Jackie, I was having dinner on the *Christina* with Maria and Miss Garbo. Maria was especially quiet that evening and hardly ate at all. Things had begun to deteriorate for Maria and Aristo, and arguments and separations were common for the two of them. That night, however, when my napkin fell off my lap and I bent down to retrieve it from the floor, I saw my employer's leg happily and skillfully entwined with Greta Garbo's leg. I blushed deeply, greatly embarrassed, and caught Mr. Onassis' eye. He laughed lightly and offered me a look that I read easily. "Please don't say anything to Maria," was his silent entreaty, and of course I obeyed.

One other guest that Maria especially enjoyed was Winston Churchill. Considering how fond he was of Tina Onassis, it was an accomplishment of Maria's that she won his affection, too. Although Mr. Churchill died in 1965, a year before I came to work for Mr. Onassis, Artemis had told me about all eight cruises he had taken on the *Christina*. She also described how, for Mr. Churchill, Maria had eagerly played the piano and sung whatever songs he requested. Maria laughed at his jokes and asked him to tell her amusing stories. One night, he told her and Aristo a story about struggling to find a taxi driver to drive him to his radio show. The only driver he could flag down refused to take him, explaining that he had to race home to listen to Winston Churchill's address in peace and quiet. "He simply would not believe I was that man," Churchill told her, and Maria laughed and laughed at his amusing story.

"If you decide to leave politics," Aristo told his famous British guest that night, "I can always get you a job as a comedian."

It also impressed Maria that Mr. Churchill's face was always serious, even when he was kidding her with a joke. She praised the formal attire he wore on the *Christina* and would frequently chastise Aristo for his appearance. "Look at how elegant Mr. Churchill looks at lunch today," she would say to Mr. Onassis. "He is dressed in such a handsome suit. And look at you. You are dressed too casually. Why do you not put a tie on for lunch?"

Mr. Onassis would laugh and appear in his casual clothes. He was happiest wearing a pair of loose-fitting cotton pants and a short-sleeved shirt, often with a sweater draped across his shoulders. "Since I own the boat," he told Maria and Mr. Churchill, "I get to wear whatever I want." And the two of them would laugh and agree.

Two other guests who were favorites of Maria were Elizabeth Taylor and Richard Burton. In comparison to Miss Taylor, Maria Callas looked especially tall and large. But the two women possessed remarkable but opposing styles of beauty. Miss Taylor was small and delicate and her purple eyes were ravishing and exquisite, almost as if they were a precious gift she graciously and temporarily bestowed upon her viewer. Yet, Maria Callas' elegance was dark and piercing, part of a strong and powerful appearance that could fill any room she entered. One night when the four of them were on the *Christina* together, Maria was laughing and joking and having a wonderful time with her lover's guests. Several of the personnel on the ship remarked to me about what a good mood she was in that evening. So many days and nights, there was such an air of melancholy around her that there seemed nothing could make her truly happy. Yet that night she laughed delightedly at Mr. Onassis' and Mr. Burton's jokes and her eyes were alive and sparkling. She sat down at the piano and graciously played every song Mr. Onassis or the Burtons requested. Except for the fact that Mr. Burton appeared to drink far too much, that night was perfect.

Often when Maria was on Skorpios, she found plenty of other things to do to keep her melancholy at bay. She enjoyed walking with Aristo or strolling alone among the small, narrow streets of the island. Having a daily massage on the *Christina* was a frequent part of her routine. So was her Swedish exercise regime. Every morning, she would exercise, walking and stretching and doing whatever she could to lose weight. She took these exercises very seriously and concentrated on each one of the exercises until she did it perfectly. She especially enjoyed swimming, and frequently walked around the ship or through the streets of the island in her swimming clothes, looking nothing like the glamorous opera singer who appeared on the stage in magnificent gowns. The thinner she was in these casual clothes, the happier she was. And when things were going well between her and Aristo, she would be very slim and very happy.

She was also satisfied to spend time on the beach or on the *Christina*. Once, she even tried her hand at embroidering, decorating pillows and tablecloths and napkins, working carefully and meticulously on each design. Some of the employees on the *Christina* were surprised that she was as skilled at that type of project as she was. Most of the time, however, she was content to swim by herself or to lie under the sun, enjoying the trees, plants, flowers, small animals, horses, and birds that filled the island. Skorpios, at those times, was her home, and it seemed hard to believe she had lived another life so filled with hard work, devotion, and fame.

All the staff on the *Christina* tried hard to please Maria, but she was not an easy person to please. The fact that she was an insecure woman who, despite her great talent and fame, did not have total confidence in herself did not make their job simple. Maria once told Artemis that when she was singing, she felt as if she were in a glass box where nobody could hurt her. The minute she stopped singing, however, the box shattered and she felt exposed and unprotected. Unfortunately, some of the staff on the *Christina* did not seem able to help her step out of this glass box easily. And, while they were always polite and respectful to her, many of them did not genuinely like her. One reason for their lack of affection for her might have been that Maria never offered compliments to them. Before many dinners, she and Aristo walked into the kitchen and sampled the food the chef was to serve, praising it loudly and excitedly with each mouthful. However, when she was alone, Maria never continued this habit of expressing her gratefulness for whatever was done for her. This neglectful attitude often frustrated them and made it difficult for the employees to feel affection for her. It seemed such an easy thing to tell someone what a nice job he had done, but Maria had trouble uttering those simple words.

Yet Aristo never seemed bothered by Maria's inability to make his staff feel they were pleasing her. Unfortunately, there were also times when, no matter how much time and attention he offered her, he, too, was unable to please her. She wanted him always to be next to her and nowhere else. Whenever he had to return to Athens on business, Maria complained bitterly and showed her insecurity. She would cry and doubt his love and create a great scene. "If you leave me here alone, I will not be here when you return," she would threaten as he prepared for his departure from the island. "You will regret what you are doing to me."

Despite her dramatic scene, he always left, and when he returned, he would say to her, "See, my darling, I came back to you. You are the only woman I love." Although she never completely believed him, she was always there waiting for him.

It was true that Maria did not trust people. Once she told Mrs. Artemis that, like her husband Meneghini, her own mother and sister had taken advantage of her singing talent and wanted only her money. Her best friends, like her husband and family, had also treated her badly. "Everyone in my life has used me," she complained bitterly. "Aristo is the only person I have ever met who does not take something from me. Instead, he offers me everything. Everything I could ever want."

"She is right," Artemis said to me. "She will never find another man who will treat her as well as Aristo. But I wish she would."

When Maria gained weight, Artemis disliked her even more. She knew that Maria, long before she became involved with Aristo, had once weighed over 200 pounds, and she feared that, at any time, she could become fat again. Yet Mr. Onassis sometimes did not appear concerned if Maria's weight rose a small amount. In fact, there were times when he seemed to ignore the fact that she was exercising and trying to lose weight and encouraged her to be heavy. Perhaps, subconsciously, Artemis thought, it was his way of being certain she could never return to the stage. Frequently, at meals on the *Christina,* when Maria was attempting to stay slim and eat only small amounts of food, Mr. Onassis acted upset. "You are not giving satisfaction to the cook," he would rebuke her. "He will be unhappy when he sees all this food left on your plate. You cannot return such a plate to the kitchen." And Maria would smile sadly, shake her head and finish every delicious morsel on her plate, including the fattening foods from Smyrna, such as pastourma, meatballs, and small fries, which she, like her lover, adored.

It was not just Maria's weight or her voice that Mr. Onassis controlled. It was her complete appearance. Eye makeup, lipstick, and rouge on her face displeased him, so Maria wore little if any makeup. "You are beautiful when you are completely natural," he reminded her anytime she used mascara or eyeliner. "Take that off and show me the face I love." And, of course, she did as he asked. Even her taste in clothing he dictated, urging her to dress in the simple classic style she adopted. One night when I was at dinner with them on the *Christina,* Maria left the table to change her dress. The personnel there told me that was something she did frequently when the one she was wearing did not please her companion. There was little if anything she would not do for that man.

However, Mrs. Artemis never ran out of reasons to tell me why her brother and Maria were not well suited for marriage. One such reason I knew was Maria's inability to offer other people a compliment. Maria never made a great effort to win Mrs. Artemis' approval, which did not go unnoticed by Mr. Onassis' oldest sister. The few times I saw the two of them together on the *Christina*, I never saw Maria treat Artemis with the deep respect that she required. While she was polite and courteous to her lover's sister, Maria did not seem that interested in Artemis. At first, I thought she might be afraid of Artemis and then I realized that she was not that concerned with anyone at the table, except for her lover.

"They are both big bosses," Mrs. Artemis seemed to enjoy repeating to me. "They both know everything and neither one knows how to give in." Several times, she described to me one evening she'd spent on the *Christina* with the two of them. Mr. Onassis adored classical music as much as Maria did and the three of them were having a quiet evening, listening to beautiful music. Mr. Onassis began to identify each piece of music, easily recognizing a work by Beethoven, Mozart, or Verdi. Maria, however, argued over each concerto and insisted he had made several mistakes. The two of them fought nearly all evening, until finally Maria gave in and admitted he had been correct. Mrs. Artemis said her evening had been ruined by Maria, who, she insisted, did not know as much about music as her brother.

Often, I purchased beautiful jewels for Mr. Onassis to give to Maria. She especially liked rings. One, for which I paid the bill, cost, as Mr. Onassis put it, "the same amount of money as a ship." Unlike Jackie, Maria came from a poor family and had lived with her mother until she got famous and married Meneghini, the man who managed her career, and although she was often satisfied with flowers, she was still thrilled to receive beautiful jewels from her lover.

One of the things I considered the saddest about Maria's relationship with Mr. Onassis concerned these jewels. I knew exactly what jewels Mr. Onassis purchased for Maria during the two years before he married Jackie. Naturally, I was surprised to see Jackie wearing some of those same jewels after their marriage. "You should not be surprised," Artemis told me when I shared my observations with her. "When Aristo told Maria their relationship was over, she left behind many of her jewels that he kept in a special place on the *Christina* for her. So he gave them to Jackie. What does it matter? So long as someone is enjoying the jewelry, who cares whom he bought it for?" We were both certain, however, that Jackie did not suspect that those particular pieces of her jewelry had been worn first by her husband's mistress.

Although there was no doubt that Mr. Onassis' relationship with Maria was experiencing much difficulty when I went to work for him, many of the employees on Skorpios and in the office talked about her frequently. I had personally heard and read about rumors insisting that Maria had two abortions during her love affair with Mr. Onassis. One supposed abortion in 1966, when she was forty-three, was rumored to have been especially crushing for her since she wanted this baby very badly and was heartbroken that her lover wanted no part of it. Although the personnel on the *Christina* discussed many personal matters about Aristo and Maria with me, this was one subject that was never raised. Perhaps there was an unwritten rule that the subject was taboo. Or perhaps they were rumors. I tend to believe the former explanation. However, I cannot speak for certain about something that I did not ever discuss with either the Onassis family or their staff.

There was, however, one woman who worked for Olympic Airways who shared a close mutual friend with Maria who often talked to me about her. "All Maria really wants is to get married and have children," this woman told me. "She never wanted to spend her life as an opera singer. Her family forced her to sing when she was young and Meneghini never let her stop. When she told him she wanted a child, he wouldn't even think of it. He told her she would miss a whole year of her career and would never regain her stature. She always believed Aristotle Onassis would give her a husband and children, but he did neither.

"In 1965, when they were making a film of *Tosca*, he wanted her to play the role Irini Pappa played opposite Anthony Quinn, but she refused. She did not want to be in the movie. I don't think Aristotle forgave her for that. But she didn't want to see her face on the screen. She always thinks her face is ugly and her body is fat. She would tell me that some people would love her and some would hate her, but there was nothing in between. She was tired of trying to make all her fans happy at every performance she gave. Her fame was too much to bear, and she didn't want it anymore. She loves living in luxury with Aristotle, but now she's too alone too much.

"She believes in God and prays a lot that He will give her the strength to do what she has to do. She really believes He sent her Aristotle and he will be the man to give her a new life and a family and be there forever for her. And she never stops hoping that will happen."

There were times, I came to see personally, when Maria's trust in Mr. Onassis had to be wounded deeply. I could see what was happening when I received the bills from Zolotas, the jeweler. Sometimes, Mr. Onassis gave Maria beautiful jewelry for specific reasons. And these reasons were not just that it was her birthday or name day or he wanted to tell her he loved her. Sometimes he had no choice. For instance, sometimes he went far beyond simple flirting and cheated on Maria with other women. One particular night, he left her on Skorpios, claiming he had to return to Athens for an important business meeting. When Maria saw his picture in the newspaper the next day, his arm around Lee Radziwill in an Athens nightclub, she went crazy. Mr. Onassis had met Lee Radziwill in 1963 and invited her onto the *Christina*. Maria disliked Mrs. Radziwill immediately and asked Aristo to send her away. When he refused, Maria went into her suite, gathered all her personal belongings, left the ship, and headed to Paris. Mr. Onassis was not terribly serious about Lee, and after a few days, he sent flowers to Maria, asking her to return. By the time Maria returned to the ship, Lee Radziwill was gone. Months later, when Maria saw the new picture of Lee and Aristo in the newspaper, she called him in his Olympic Airways office, screaming hysterically, and threatening to jump off the ship. Mr. Onassis made a hasty return to Skorpios, this time carrying an exquisite necklace, worth $1 million. Apparently, that gift was enough to calm his furious lover, but Aristo liked that necklace, which was put in a safe-deposit box on board the *Christina*, so much that he gave it to Jackie several years later. The truth was that when Mr. Onassis liked a particular piece of jewelry he would think nothing of buying two of them. When I saw Mrs. Jackie wearing that necklace, I thought at first that it might have been one of those pieces he bought in duplicate; however, Artemis insisted this necklace was one of a kind.

Along with her incessant jealousy, Maria also maintained a deep fear of journalists and was always alerting Aristo concerning strangers approaching the island of Skorpios, so that he could send them away immediately. One afternoon while the two of them were relaxing on the beach, Maria spotted several water-skiers and yelled to Mr. Onassis to get them away. "Oh, Maria," he answered her, laughing, "let the young lady do her waterskiing. She is so pretty and thin. It is nice to look at her."

Maria became furious over his remark and started to storm away from him. He grabbed her arm and pulled her back beside him. "But you know I prefer women who are tall and a little bit fat like you, my darling," he said lovingly. It only took Maria a few minutes to smile again and continue to enjoy herself on the beach again.

Yet one more source of contention between Mr. Onassis and Maria Callas was her two small dogs. Maria adored her poodles, the white Pixie and the brown Jeddah, and always asked if she could bring them onto the *Christina*. For some reason, Mr. Onassis disliked her dogs and rarely permitted her to bring them onto the boat. Maria would beg him, crying, to let her take them with her, but he repeatedly told her they were not welcome.

Maria rarely entertained her own company while she was on Skorpios and saw little of her mother or sister while she was there. Mrs. Artemis told me that Maria resented the fact that her mother favored her older sister, Jackie, and never felt appreciated by her mother. Still, despite Maria's displeasure with her mother and sister, Mr. Onassis kept in touch with them and often gave them large sums of money for their living expenses. Maria, however, once told him that she would much rather have him be kind to her dogs, which she loved, than cater to the relatives she disliked. It was one wish, however, that he did not grant her.

Maria relished being on the *Christina* and spent a little time in the simple house on Skorpios, yet she never made any changes to either place. Once when she made a simple suggestion about rearranging some furniture in her suite, Mr. Onassis turned nasty. "Never forget, my darling," he informed her coldly, "you are not the housewife here. You are only a guest." Once again, Maria became terribly upset and began screaming and crying at his words, but he appeared not to hear her as he walked quickly away from her. The personnel on the *Chris-*

tina understood that Maria was not their boss. They followed her instructions when she asked them for something but they never went out of their way to please her the way they did for other guests. I did not understand how little they did for Maria, until I saw firsthand the way they treated their boss's second wife. For Mrs. Jackie, there was never a task too unimportant to perform. Her needs they anticipated and delighted in satisfying. Maria was, as her lover and their boss made clear, just another guest.

There was no doubt that Jackie's success in winning not just the affections of the staff of the *Christina* but Mr. Onassis' love and name broke Maria's heart. Many of us worried about how she would survive such a shock. But we soon learned that marriage did not mean their love affair was over. One month after his marriage to Jackie, Mr. Onassis was in Paris seeing Maria. If anything, their love appeared to grow stronger. Maria, however, never returned to her beautiful Santorini suite on the *Christina* after that marriage. Mr. Onassis never permitted that. He also worked hard to make certain the two women never met. And the two women might well have done the same thing. The rare times that Maria was in Greece, Jackie was in New York. Since Maria spent most of her time in her apartment in Paris, Jackie was careful not to visit that city when Maria was there.

Mr. Onassis owned a luxurious apartment on 88 Avenue Foch in Paris, just a brief distance from Maria's apartment on 36 Avenue Georges Mandel, and where he spent a great deal of time. Although Maria did occasionally come to Avenue Foch, they met more frequently in her home. So many times when I called Paris to speak to Mr. Onassis about business, his aides would tell me in a funny way, "Oh, you cannot speak to Megalos now, Kiki. He is busy doing Greek business." I knew exactly what that meant. He had headed down the short flight of stairs from his apartment en route to 36 Avenue Georges Mandel.

Many Greek people, unlike Mr. Onassis' three sisters, were disappointed that Mr. Onassis did not marry Maria. They would have much preferred to see him marry Greece's most exalted opera singer than Jackie Kennedy. Even though many of the personnel on Skorpios did not particularly like Maria, they remained committed to the belief that she was the right wife for their employer and constantly told me that Afentiko was making a giant error in not marrying her. "She is the only woman in the world for him," many of them affirmed. "They belong together forever." When all the tragedies befell the Onassis family after his marriage to the American Jackie, some of these people insisted that had happened because he had not married the Greek love of his life, Maria Callas. He had tempted the fates by marrying a woman so far out of his reach. That was the flaw in his character that permitted the tragedy to occur.

Costas Gratsos, Mr. Onassis' dear friend and business associate, tried to convince Aristo to marry Maria. Costas was fond of Maria and believed the two of them would be much happier if they married. This was one of the rare instances in which Mr. Onassis did not take Costas Gratsos' advice.

Christina and Alexander Onassis were not disappointed that their father did not marry Maria. They did not want him to marry anyone, except their mother. It was sad that Maria never had any children of her own, but she did not win the affections of Mr. Onassis' children. Christina and Alexander did their best to avoid having to be near the woman they considered responsible for the dissolution of their parents' marriage in 1959, yet when they were forced to be in her company, they always called her "*Kyria*" or "*Madame,*" a word they spoke sarcastically and without respect. Ironically, after Aristo married Jackie, Christina changed her mind about Maria and her father. But by then it was too late.

The summer of 1967 was Maria's last complete summer on Skorpios, and it was filled with the pain of knowing that the life she had experienced with him for nine years was about to end. The following year brought to light all her worst nightmares. Aristo was involved seriously with another woman, the most famous woman in the United States. Maria knew that Aristo had entertained Jackie Kennedy alone in his Paris apartment. She knew he had been having frequent telephone conversations with her since 1963. She knew he took Jackie on a cruise to the Caribbean in May 1968. She knew he went to Jackie's side when Robert Kennedy was killed on June 6, 1968. And she knew in August 1968 that he wanted her to leave so that he could marry Jackie. "He doesn't love Jackie," Maria told Costas Gratsos. "He just likes to be admired by very important women. So he will change me for another, more important woman. But I am certain he does not love her at all."

There is no doubt that Mr. Onassis' marriage to Jackie nearly destroyed Maria. By then, her singing career was over and she was forty-five years old. For nine years, she had given this man everything he wanted and now he was leaving her alone. She had no marriage and no child, no career and no voice. "I have lived the most beautiful years of my life next to Aristo," she told Costas Gratsos before she left the *Christina.* "And I have lived the worst."

But the woman who walked off the *Christina* in August 1968 was different from the woman who had boarded it in 1959. Onassis had made her more than an opera singer; he had made her an opera. She wasn't just singing her role; she was living it. There had been much pain as well as joy in these past nine years, but every bit of it had been real. Still, even with that knowledge, Maria was a defeated woman. Aristo had left Tina for her. Now he was leaving her for Jackie. All the pain she had felt when she had sung of the agony of the heroines whose lives she had portrayed on the stage was hers. Her world had never been more real. Or more painful.

"I am beginning the final performance of my life," Maria told Professor Georgakis shortly before she packed her clothes and perfumes and creams and left her adored Santorini suite on the *Christina* for the final time. "It is one I am playing all by myself and it will be the saddest one I have ever performed." And indeed it was.

After Mr. Onassis' marriage to Jackie, Maria never asked me to do her favors or to make whatever travel arrangements she needed to fly to Paris or to London or Italy. Never once after that marriage did she call his office in Athens to speak to him. Nor did Mr. Onassis ever ask me to arrange for his trips to visit her. He always took care of those details himself. Many times Miltos Yiannacopoulos acted as his intermediary, telephoning Maria himself and organizing the next rendezvous between her and Aristo. But I knew, as did everyone who was involved with Mr. Onassis, that Maria was an important part of his life during his six-and-a-half-year marriage to Jackie. Perhaps, so many of us thought, he knew that he could have both of these women in his life. Perhaps he knew that Jackie would never leave him because of his continued affair with Maria, no more than Maria would leave him because of his marriage to Jackie. He could have both of them, the woman he married and tried to love, and the woman he didn't marry and always loved. It is also possible that the separation caused by his marriage to Jackie fanned his ardor for Maria and made their passion, now more inaccessible, stronger. Maria understood on her first cruise on the *Christina* that she could not live without Aristo, but it took him a little longer, and a second marriage, to realize that he could not live without her.

Chapter Six

Jackie: The Second Mrs. Onassis

O N T H E rainy early evening of October 20, 1968, Aristotle Onassis married Jackie Kennedy, ending any dreams Maria Callas might have had of becoming his wife and the mother of his children. Yet he believed, on that day and for many days afterward, that he was marrying the one woman who could bring him happiness for the rest of his life.

Two weeks earlier, he had walked into my office, wearing his customary dark suit minus his jacket, his silk shirt rolled up to his elbows, his face filled with unaccustomed smiles and pleasure, and made his announcement to me. "Please, Kiki," he told me as he leaned across my desk, "you will call Zolotas and ask them to bring here some of the best jewelry, including gold crosses, that they have strung."

I was used to such a request from my employer. Dozens of times in the past year, he had asked me to have Zolotas, whose shop was located at 6 University Place in Athens, send over five or ten gold crosses or necklaces or rings or bracelets or pins or earrings, from which he would choose one, most often for Maria, but occasionally for one of his sisters or even yet another female. The jeweler would send one of his personnel to deliver the costly jewelry in a large sack or a suitcase and leave it with me until my boss had a chance to make his selection. Mr. Onassis never took a long time to make his final decision, occasionally asking me to put on a necklace or pair of earrings, and I was always impressed with the tastefulness of his final choice.

Two weeks before his wedding to Jackie, I agreed to call Zolotas immediately. "You must know why I want them," he told me as he picked up a telephone. I nodded. I did not need him to tell me what I now knew for certain. Artemis had just told me the week before that Jackie had visited her brother in Paris and he had served her an elegant dinner himself at his Avenue Foch apartment. Artemis had carefully described to me how Aristo had personally selected all the foods and wines and flowers for the dinner. After the servants had prepared everything according to his specific orders, he had dismissed them and handled the dinner presentation himself. Never before, at least according to Artemis' memory, had her brother done such a thing for a woman. He was, Artemis had told me many times since I'd met Jackie at her home in August, very much in love with Jackie Kennedy. Now, I was as certain as she had been: Mr. Onassis was going to marry the former First Lady of the United States, and his bride would receive, among many other gifts, an exquisite gold cross.

The day of the wedding was overcast and rainy, but that meant the marriage would be filled with good luck. Mr. Onassis and Mrs. Jackie were nervous but happy. His two children, Christina, eighteen, and Alexander, twenty, however, showed no signs of happiness. Their bags were packed the moment their father's bride's feet touched Greek soil. "I will never sleep in the same house as that American woman," Alexander told me before the wedding. True to his word, the moment she arrived in Glyfada, he checked into the Hilton, where he sent most of his belongings. The day of the wedding, he was so melancholic that I worried he would begin to cry at any moment. When one of the personnel of the *Christina* asked him a simple question after the wedding ceremony, Alexander could not even look at him. With his head lowered, in a soft voice, he muttered, "I do not know. Ask the bridegroom. He knows everything." Christina was even more miserable and had exhibited frequent fits of rage in front of both me and Mrs. Artemis during the weekdays before the wedding. Nothing either one of us said to her could convince her that what was happening that October day was anything other than a disaster.

I was so exhausted the day of the wedding I could barely stand up. The two weeks leading up to it had been hectic for me. I had been so busy with the arrangements for the wedding that I could not pay any attention to Christina's furious face or Alexander's sad eyes. While Mrs. Amalia Hadjiargyris tried to help with many of the details, as did Professor Georgakis and Miltos Yiannacopoulos, much of the responsibility for the wedding was mine. Although Artemis offered her suggestions whenever I asked her advice, most of her concentration concerning the wedding was directed toward designing her own dress with Roula. Never had Roula had to create such an important dress for Artemis in such a short time. Aristo and Jackie had selected her as their *koumbara*, or witness, and she wanted to look almost as beautiful as the bride on October 20.

While Artemis worked hard with Roula, Amalia and I wrote and sent out approximately seventy-five invitations. Although most of the press knew what was happening, we tried to keep as many of the details as private as possible. Certainly, we wanted the guest list to be kept out of the newspapers.

The invitations, simple white cards with gold lettering, were sent to approximately seventy-five people, mostly directors from Mr. Onassis' companies and their wives, who were invited to the reception to be held on the *Christina*. Only a very small number of people, including the immediate family and closest friends, would be invited to the ceremony itself. Because we had so little time with which to work, we did not mail the wedding invitations. Instead, we placed them on Olympic flights and sent them through company mail to all the Onassis companies throughout the world, including Paris, Monte Carlo, the United States, Switzerland, Argentina, and Uruguay. With the help of Professor Georgakis and Miltos Yiannacopoulos, Amalia and I worked out the details for a Greek Orthodox service in the small chapel of Panayitsa ("Little Virgin") on Skorpios. Next, we hired photographers for the ceremony, and selected white *koufeta*, white candies filled with pistachios, and white flowers to decorate the church. It had been my personal task, however, to arrange for all the flights and hotel arrangements of the few guests of Mrs. Kennedy who would attend the ceremony and reception. This group included Mrs. Jackie's two children, mother, stepfather, and sister and brother-in-law and their two children, along with two Kennedy sisters, Jean Smith and Patricia Lawford, and Mrs. Lawford's daughter, Sydney, who was also a close friend of Caroline Kennedy. Mr. Edward Kennedy, it was explained to me, unfortunately, would be unable to attend because the U.S. Senate was in session and there were urgent political matters he needed to attend to in Washington, which could not be rescheduled on such short notice.

The day before the wedding, I wrote and distributed to the members of the press the statement of Mrs. Jacqueline Kennedy. It stated, "We wish our wedding to be a private moment in the little chapel among the cypresses of Skorpios with only members of the family present, five of them little children. If you will give us those moments, we will so gladly give you all cooperation possible for you to take the photographs you need. We will do everything we can to make tomorrow a pleasant day for you. And we hope that when the day is over, and your work has been completed, you will think about it all, and wish us happiness and peace."

Jackie and her family had spent the day of the wedding on Skorpios, both on the *Christina* and in the small house on the island. Jackie and her children dressed on the ship and were driven in a jeep with Aristo the short distance in the rain to the small wedding chapel. When I first saw Jackie moments before the ceremony, I thought she looked radiant and far more well rested than she had the night I met her in Glyfada. Her Valentino two-piece dress was an ivory color, with long sleeves, a high neck, and a skirt that met the tops of her knees. It was simple and elegant, as were the white ribbons and flowers she had placed in her long, dark hair. I was delighted that she remembered my name and told me she was happy to see me again. I could see that she was more nervous than she had been the first time I had met her, but who could blame her? All day long, an army of photographers and journalists had been attempting to invade Skorpios. None of the photographers would be allowed to take pictures during the service, but that did not stop them from positioning themselves as close to the shores of the island as possible. So far, Mr. Onassis' large band of security men in patrol boats, aided by helicopters and more boats from the Greek navy, had held them all at bay. Still, it was quite alarming to look at the waters around the island and see dozens of boats filled with the press, and even more so to look around the chapel and see the smaller group that had somehow made it to land. Obviously, Mrs. Kennedy's gentle request to the press to give her family privacy on this special day had been ignored.

Despite the scene around him, Mr. Onassis greeted me warmly, looking quite handsome and calm in his dark navy suit and a red tie, with a small white rose in his upper left pocket. He and Jackie were holding hands and talking softly to one another before the ceremony, managing to ignore the hubbub around them.

When I walked into the tiny chapel of Panayitsa, I forgot all the chaos outside. Everything looked exactly the way Amalia and I had planned it. The inside of the chapel was covered with pink and white roses, sending a heady perfume to all corners of the small structure. White candles were everywhere, adding a warm gentle glow to the chapel. When I thought of all the hundreds of journalists hoping to get inside the chapel with their notebooks and cameras, I could not help but gasp. The walls of the delicate structure would surely burst if even half of them made their way inside the chapel.

The chapel was filled mostly with family members. Mrs. Kennedy's stepfather, Mr. Hugh D. Auchincloss, escorted Jackie into the church. Aristo's three sisters were dressed beautifully and, accompanied by their husbands, all of them had warm, excited smiles on their faces. Kalliroi's daughter, Marilena, who was my age, was looking especially pleased with the choice of her uncle's bride. Only a few executives from Mr. Onassis' companies were in the chapel, although many others would be at the reception. Christina and Alexander stood out from the rest of their crowd with their unhappy, angry faces. They stood very close to each other, whispering occasionally, looking even more embarrassed than enraged. I also noticed that Panagiotis was nowhere to be seen on the island. Then I remembered that Mrs. Artemis had requested that he stay at the house in Glyfada to prepare food for visitors they might need to entertain the day after the wedding.

The ceremony itself was Greek Orthodox, which meant that there would be no music. However, the priest, Polikarpos Athanassiou, from a church in Athens, who had a long black beard and was wearing a gold robe, and had been personally selected by Professor Georgakis, was singing throughout the forty-five minute service, as were the twenty or so guests who were huddled together inside the small white church. Caroline and John held tall, white candles on the left and the right of the couple during the ceremony. The flames of the candles eerily lit up their serious and nervous faces. I could imagine how scary all this was to them. All the words spoken around them were in a language they had never heard before. Except for a few of their aunts and uncles and their grandparents, nearly all of the people around them were strangers. In addition, young as they were at ages almost eleven and eight, Caroline and John had to be worried about what would happen to them now that their mother was marrying a man they hardly knew. I wished I could run over to them and assure them that we were all kind, warm people, even if we spoke a language different from theirs, and that they were going to love their new lives in Greece, but of course I did no such thing during the service.

After the priest completed the religious portion of the ceremony, speaking and singing only in Greek, the bride and groom exchanged gold rings and then drank red wine from a silver goblet. Jackie, who I realized did not speak one word during the ceremony, accepted a delicate sip of the wine, while Mr. Onassis enjoyed a more generous drink. Next, the priest placed the delicate wreathes of *stefana* flowers on the heads of the bride and groom. Artemis, the official *koumbara*, moved the wreaths three times, back and forth from one head to another. As Artemis positioned the wreathes, which symbolized the couple's joining together in a wedding union, above their heads, the bride and groom, their hands joined and heads bowed, danced the special Greek wedding dance, the *issaia*. They moved slowly around a small table on which the priest had placed some white bonbons, finally arriving back in the same spot where they had begun. While Jackie and Aristo danced carefully around the table, the guests threw white flower petals on them. Once the dance was complete, the wedding couple faced the priest, and standing beside the *koumbara*, they listened carefully and seriously as the priest offered his best wishes. Then the priest removed the wreaths of flowers from their heads, placed them carefully in a box, and handed it ceremoniously to the new Mrs. Onassis. Finally he blew out the candles closest to where he stood, and after white rice and more white flower petals were showered on the couple, the wedding ceremony was officially complete.

Immediately after the service ended, the newly married couple walked, hand in hand, out of the tiny chapel. It was raining more heavily now, as the new husband and wife climbed into a gold jeep, which drove the two of them, and Caroline and John, a mile or so to the *Christina*. The chilly wet weather seemed to bother no one as more jeeps delivered the rest of the guests the short distance to the *Christina*. The huge ship was lit up with hundreds of white lights, which sparkled cheerfully, despite the black skies. Even the inside of the Piaggio, which Jackie and Aristo used to fly back and forth from Athens, was decorated with white and pink roses.

From six o'clock that afternoon until five or six the next morning, the guests enjoyed the wedding festivities on the *Christina*, drinking, eating, dancing, and celebrating this most special of all marriages. The most spirited dance of the evening was the famous Greek dance, the *syrtaki*, made famous by Anthony Quinn in *Zorba the Greek*, which Jackie appeared to enjoy for the first time. I also noticed that Jackie was now wearing an exquisite new ring, a heart-shaped ruby set among a circle of diamonds, for which I later paid a bill of $1.25 million.

That particular ring caused a bit of drama that evening when Jackie first appeared wearing the exquisite piece of jewelry. After Jackie showed the ring to her mother, Janet Auchincloss, Mrs. Auchincloss showed it to Caroline Kennedy, who tossed it excitedly into the air. I thought I would faint until the ring was safely back on Jackie's finger. That was not the last time that ring would cause me discomfort. A few weeks after the wedding, the same ring again caused mild hysteria when Jackie discovered it was missing. Mr. Onassis instructed the crew of the *Christina* to conduct a massive search of every inch of the ship and of the island of Skorpios. While all the personnel were frantically searching for the ring, Mrs. Onassis was taking apart all the drawers in the suite she shared with her new husband and every other suite she had entered. Finally, at least two hours later, the ring was discovered under a rug by a maid on the *Christina*.

However, the night of the wedding, the ring looked perfect on Mrs. Onassis' hand. Actually, everyone on the *Christina,* with the exception of Christina and Alexander, with their long, sad faces, looked perfect, including all the male personnel, who were in their finest attire, dressed smartly in their black-and-white dress suits. The head chef on the ship had outdone himself, preparing his most spectacular Greek specialties for the evening meal. All varieties of fishes and meats covered the tables, surrounded by special salads with fresh vegetables; caviar; octopus; shrimps; lobsters; and Aristo's favorite meatballs, cooked in the Smyrna sauce with pepper, garlic, and basil. Each table was covered with a new, expensive, hand-embroidered tablecloth, created especially for the evening. Bouzoukia instruments were playing beautiful music, especially Mr. Onassis' favorite song, *"Me Ena Oniro Trello"* ("One Foolish Dream"). The words of the song seemed especially meaningful that night, for our host of the evening was indeed living what was once "one foolish dream." It was a lavish feast for which Mr. Onassis had spared no expense in order to make the evening memorable for his new bride and her family.

I read after the wedding that some newspaper writers insisted that the bride looked sad and worried. I do not know which bride they were looking at, for the bride I saw looked radiant and happy. There were, of course, moments when Jackie looked nervous, especially when she lost sight of her children for a moment or so, but she smiled warmly at all the guests who congratulated her and looked eager and excited over the new life she was about to begin in Greece as Mrs. Aristotle Onassis.

Jackie's children appeared to relax a bit once the religious service ended and the festivities began. Martha Sgubin, their loyal and capable governess, was with them at all moments of the evening. At one point during the dinner, I approached them and chatted with them for a few minutes. "My name is Kiki and I work for Mr. Onassis," I told them. "You look like such nice children, and I am certain you are going to love spending time in Greece. I promise you it will not always rain like this, and you will love the island of Skorpios when the sun is shining."

They both smiled at me and said "Thank you" in unison. There was no doubt the children were overwhelmed by what was going on around them, yet it was also obvious that they were polite, well-brought-up, adored children.

There are those who also insist that there was no love in this marriage—that Jackie married Mr. Onassis for money and security, and that he married her for her name and status. These same people assume there was a prenuptial agreement concerning Mr. Onassis' money. I disagree with all of those assumptions. I saw firsthand the way the married couple acted, not just on their wedding day, but in the six and a half years to follow. This was a marriage that included many moments of love and affection. I will not say that this love was strong enough to overwhelm catastrophic obstacles later placed in its path by the sad fates that ruled their lives. Yet it was their own unique brand of love that joined this couple and held them together for many of the years of their marriage.

There were, however, countless times during that memorable wedding day when I found myself thinking of Maria Callas. And I knew I was not alone in my thoughts in that chapel or on the *Christina*. I knew the personnel from the island, and some of the guests as well, were concerned about her welfare. What was Maria doing that day? I wondered. Whom was she with? What was she feeling? Even as we stood in the chapel, I visualized Maria sitting beside the chapel, in a spot where I had been told she loved to sit and read. The next day I heard that Maria had spent that evening in Paris, celebrating the seventy-fifth anniversary of Maxim's restaurant. Those who saw her there said she looked radiant. She was, I understood, a wonderful actress and performer. I also read in another newspaper that Maria said that Jackie had given her children a grandfather. No matter what she said or how she looked, I knew Maria's heart had to have been broken beyond repair on that rainy October day.

For Mr. Onassis' three sisters, however, there was no sorrow that day. His younger sisters, Merope and Kalliroi, had both learned in the few short months since Mrs. Jackie had been in their family's life that Artemis would resent any of their attempts to become deeply involved with their new sister-in-law. Yet in the short period of time they had to meet their new sister-in-law, both of them already felt a connection to Mrs. Jackie.

I was certain Jackie would like both of these women once she got a chance to know them. Merope Konialidis was an upbeat, outgoing woman who maintained a small apartment in Phaliron, not too far from Glyfada, yet her primary residence, with her husband, Nicolas, and two sons, was a beautiful home in Monte Carlo, to which they were frequently inviting me. When I was able to accept their invitations, I especially enjoyed going to the casinos with them.

Kalliroi Patronikolas, the youngest child in the family, lived near the ocean, in Lagonissi, about thirty-five minutes from Athens. Her home was a mere fifty yards from the ocean, a large two-level house with a living room with a fireplace, a private dining room, two bedrooms, and three guest rooms, and magnificent views of the ocean from all the rooms. Her gardens boasted the same lush grass that covered the garden in Artemis' home and the island of Skorpios. It was her pool that was often the center of activity in her ocean-side home, for it was here that Kalliroi preferred to do her frequent and lavish entertaining. Even though she was divorced from her husband several years after Jackie's marriage to her brother, Mrs. Kalliroi was the most vivacious of the three sisters. Physically, Merope and Kalliroi resembled each other more than they resembled Artemis, however; Merope and Artemis shared identical large, expressive black eyes.

It hadn't taken me long to understand many of the dynamics of this unique family, a major one of which was the fact that all three of Mr. Onassis' sisters were afraid of him. Although he took good care of them and brought them expensive presents, each of them knew that he could explode into a fit of rage if she did not follow his orders or do exactly as he said. Each one of his sisters asked his opinion in every important aspect of her life and tried diligently to follow his advice. Even though he often complained bitterly of their constant questions, he rebuked them for making decisions without his input. Any failure to follow the advice he offered inevitably resulted in unpleasant scenes they all struggled to avoid.

The day of the wedding, Mrs. Artemis could not have found one reason to disagree with her brother or incur his wrath. She was as happy as he was with his choice of a second wife. At the end of her brother's honeymoon cruise aboard the *Christina*, I shared a secret plan with her I knew she would approve of. When I made the arrangements for Mr. and Mrs. Onassis to fly to New York on an Olympic Airways flight, I enlisted Mrs. Artemis' help in planning a special surprise for the newlyweds.

Unbeknownst to them, we had all the seats of the first-class flight removed and replaced by a large and comfortable bed. We also ordered specially designed curtains, bedspread, and sheets to decorate the bridal suite. I do not know how Mr. and Mrs. Onassis felt the first time they saw the renovated first-class area, but I do know how one steward, who had not been informed of our plan, felt. When, shortly after takeoff, he unsuspectingly separated the curtains to the honeymoon suite, he was greeted with the sight of the owner of Olympic Airways and his new bride, lost in each other's naked body, arms and legs wrapped around each other, flying through not just the sky but a passion that seemed, to his shocked eyes, unearthly. When he realized exactly what he was viewing, he pushed the curtains back together and staggered out of the first-class section. "I could not believe what I was seeing," he told me when he called me from New York the next day. "But the fact that the two of them never even knew I was standing there, openmouthed, dumbfounded, and staring at them, amazed me even more."

For those who think this was a marriage of mere convenience, I only wish that steward had held a camera in his hands. For those who think this marriage was blessed by the gods, I only wish they had been right.

Chapter Seven

Alexander: The Love of His Life

WHEN ARISTOTLE Onassis married Jackie Kennedy on October 20, 1968, he believed that his life would now be complete. His business was flourishing, his health was as strong as ever, and his two children were with him and proceeding in the right direction. Christina, at eighteen, was, he understood, a difficult child, but Alexander, at twenty, was his treasure, his future. As in all Greek families, the son had merit far beyond that of his sister. Conversations were more serious around him; passions were stronger; arguments were more extreme. In his own family, even though all three of his sisters were married to men who could care for them financially, Mr. Onassis was the central figure in his oldest sister's life and a vitally important figure in his two younger sisters' lives. Alexander grew up watching his aunts defer to his father's wishes as he protected and governed their lives. This was how a brother and a sister were to get along with each other.

Alexander was far from perfect in his father's eyes, but with time he just might become so. His father was so busy that weeks might go by without Alexander seeing him. Yet, no matter how far away he was, his father was rarely completely absent from Alexander's life. Even when his son was twenty years old, Mr. Onassis nearly always knew where he was and what he was doing. And he never hesitated to let his son know if Alexander's actions did not please him. Alexander was his son, his only son, and the power he held over him was infinite. When Mr. Onassis' two children were with him, he never ignored his daughter. But his eyes were on his son, and it was his son's words he heard first, and his son's face he noticed the minute he walked into a room. In that respect, he was no different from the typical Greek father.

Aristo knew both his son and daughter had not been delighted with his marriage to the former First Lady of the United States, but they would adjust. Jackie would figure out a way to win their affections. Jackie and her two children and he and his two children would become an extended happy family. Christina might present a bit of a challenge to his plan. But Alexander, his son, Mr. Onassis told me after the wedding, would be won over more easily and would make the merging of the two families an easier feat. "You know my son, do you not, Kiki?" he asked me. "He will do fine with my marriage, will he not?"

"Oh, yes," I answered both his questions, but in regard to the second question, we could not have been more wrong.

As for the first question, I was getting to know his son. The first thing I learned was that Alexander Onassis asked everyone to call him "Alexandros." The last thing he wanted to be called was "Mr. Onassis." Although I never wanted to disobey Alexandros, I explained to him that I was more comfortable calling him Mr. Onassis. He tried to convince me otherwise, but I held my ground and never, not even when we were together outside the office, called him anything besides Mr. Onassis. Even though I could not express my real feelings to him, in truth, I was afraid to get too close to him. The last thing I wanted was to fall in love with my employer and I understood, from the very beginning, that it was more than possible that could happen. With Alexandros, as with all members of the Onassis family, I was cautious not to become overly familiar, for I loved my position at Olympic Airways and could never jeopardize my job. But with Alexandros, far more than with Mr. Onassis or Mrs. Artemis or Christina or Mrs. Kalliroi, it was most difficult for me to maintain that distance.

When we first met, Alexandros was eighteen, just a year older than I was. I liked him immediately, drawn to his gentle, unassuming manner. I thought he was especially handsome, even before he had his nose fixed. Sometimes, when we were working together, I would look at him and think he was growing even more handsome with each day. His thick, dark hair; his warm black eyes; his polite yet masculine manner—he could be quite irresistible without even trying. He wasn't a tall man, though he was taller than his father, and he managed to appear both slim and solid. Yet there was an air of sadness around him that, strangely enough, made him even more appealing. I always struggled to dispel that sadness, even if for just a few moments.

Most often, when we were together, Alexandros was so shy that he had trouble looking me directly in the eye. Yet I worked hard to make him more comfortable with me. It took me a year or so before I became Alexandros' main secretary. When I came to work for Olympic Airways, Amalia handled his calls and letters, yet within a short period of time, she handed some of that responsibility to me. I was pleased to work for Alexander and gladly accepted the extra work. Each time I wrote a letter for him or performed some task he needed done, he was grateful. "This is wonderful, Kiki," he would tell me. "Bravo. You knew just what needed to be done." After a few times, whenever I told him not to worry, that I would do what needed to be done, he smiled and said, "I do not worry about anything you do, Kiki."

Because I was much younger than Amalia, Alexandros seemed

more comfortable with me. Soon he arranged for our phones to be connected so that I could answer all his calls and decide whom he should speak to and whom he should ignore. When he first informed me that he wanted me, not Amalia, to come into his office when he needed a secretary, I was hesitant to hurt Amalia's feelings. But Alexander was insistent. "You are the one I want to talk to, Kiki," he told me. "When I ring, you are to come into my office." I knew that Amalia was jealous of my position with Alexandros, but she never made it difficult for me to follow his instructions.

From the beginning, I never had any problem deciding which of his incoming calls were important and which were a waste of time. It got so that I was with him nearly every moment he was in the office, and I was able to understand his different moods. I knew when he was in a good mood and would want to work on certain projects or when his mood was lower and it was better not to ask him so many questions. He began to depend on me for many things, but I didn't mind that at all. Soon he was asking my opinion about business decisions, and when I told him not to do something, he listened to me. The other secretaries in the office, besides Amalia, also noticed that after I came to work, Alexander rarely asked them for any help. They also remarked often that it was only when he was with me that Alexander smiled.

In order to understand, however, what it was that made Alexander smile or frown, it is necessary to understand the relationship between a Greek mother and her son. There are few Greek mothers who do not adore their sons and consider them the most important people in their lives. As much as a Greek mother might love her daughter, it is her son around whom the world revolves. Alexander's mother, Tina Livanos Onassis, was sadly one of those rare Greek women who did not appear to adore her son, and who barely tolerated her daughter. Perhaps because she was so young when she became a mother or perhaps because she had been overly privileged from the day she was born, but whatever the reason, she did not provide Alexander with the type of loving mother most Greek sons possess. Fourteen when she first met Alexander's father, seventeen when she married him, and nineteen when Alexander was born, Tina remained childlike all her life. Instead of drawing her firstborn son close to her and treasuring him above all others, she was too busy with her own pleasures to adore him. As a result, Alexander grew up quiet and unappreciated, often ignored, but always gentle and kind, aware that something important was missing from his life but helpless as to how to restore this missing link. Whenever he met someone for the first time, he was shy, and it was never easy for him to make new friends. It was perhaps this vulnerability that made so many women want to mother him, as well as to love him.

Still, despite his own mother's failings, Alexander never stopped loving her and hoping that she and his father would remarry. He had been heartbroken over his parents' divorce in 1959 and equally depressed over his mother's subsequent two remarriages in 1961 and 1970. For years after his parents' divorce, Alexandros tried everything he could to bring his parents back together. He would never accept the fact that they were going to live separate lives. One day, three years after the divorce from Aristo, Tina came to visit Skorpios unexpectedly, and the thirteen-year-old Alexandros was convinced his parents were finally going to get back together again. After they all had lunch and dinner together on the *Christina,* he waited for his parents to tell them of their reconciliation. However, when Tina left without making such an announcement, he was crushed.

Several days later, he learned about her plans to marry Lord Blandford and was even more heartbroken. The moment he heard the news, he ran into his small Chris-Craft and drove it at such high speed that he crashed into another boat and badly damaged both boats. That was the second time that Alexandros had been involved in a boating accident. The second boat was driven by George Tzafferos, who later became Mr. Onassis' New York driver. George risked his life to save Alexandros and suffered permanent scarring on his face as a result of the accident. Although both boats were ruined, thanks to George Tzafferos' bravery Alexandros escaped serious injury. However, from that day on, Alexander was convinced that the *Christina* was a curse, that somehow the yacht was unlucky and the root of all his parents' problems. After all, it was on the *Christina* that his father had consummated his love with Maria Callas, the woman who had ruined their marriage in the first place. And it was on the *Christina* that his parents were unable to fall in love again and attempt to give their marriage another try. "When I inherit the *Christina,*" he told a friend shortly after that accident, "the very first thing I will do is burn it into ashes."

Still, despite this pain in his life, Alexandros found much to love; in particular, anything that moved, especially automobiles and airplanes. Mr. Onassis kept urging his best friend, the brilliant Professor Georgakis, to do anything he could to interest his son in academics, yet there appeared to be nothing the professor could do to turn Alexandros into a scholar. Even though school mattered little to him, Alexander taught himself everything he could about planes. His office at Olympic Airways was filled with planes, pictures of planes, replicas of planes, miniature planes hanging from the ceiling. Mr. Onassis told me many times that if it had not been for his son's love of planes, he would have sold Olympic Airways years earlier than he did. Alexander was a careful pilot and always checked and rechecked his airplane before he took off. His aunt Artemis was proud of her nephew's fastidiousness, bragging to me about how neatly he kept his clothes and belongings in her house in Glyfada. She was certain he was just as careful with the instruments of each plane he flew.

Alexander felt it was irresponsible to fly just for pleasure. But helping those in need was another story. Countless times he sought out assignments to fly missions of mercy wherein he transported ill children or adults from remote Greek islands to hospitals in Athens. Once, the grateful father of one ill little boy handed Alexandros a small tip after the flight to Athens. "I didn't have the heart to tell him who I was," Alexandros later told me. "Without his realizing what I had done, I did manage to return the money to his pocket."

That little boy was certainly not the only person to benefit from Alexander's generosity. So often I would hear him on the telephone, making plans to transport someone in need of medical care to an Athens hospital. One particular morning, the weather was awful and the Olympic planes were not flying. When Alexandros passed by my desk, he told me he was on the way to Levkas to pick up a small boy named Pedros and fly him to Athens for emergency surgery. "But the winds are furious and the rain is nonstop," I warned him. "It is not safe to fly today."

"It is not safe for Pedros to wait another day for his operation," Alexandros told me. Before I could offer another warning, he was out of the office. I waited until late that evening for Alexandros to return to the office. He was beaming as he walked in. "Were you waiting for the rain to stop before you dared to go home?" he joked when he saw me at my desk.

"Tell me how Pedros is, Mr. Alexandros," I said, and he laughed gently.

"Pedros is as happy as any five-year-old who has just had his appendix out can be," Alexandros told me. "But I can assure you, he is completely safe."

Often Alexander would receive calls from people in Santorini who needed his help. One February evening in 1971, he was notified about a man whose motorcycle had crashed into a house. The man was near death and would not survive more than a few hours unless he was transported to a hospital in Athens. Once again, the weather was treacherous and unfit for flights, but Alexander decided to risk his life and try to save this man's life. While I sat in the office and watched nervously as the winds whipped furiously along Syngrou Avenue, Alexandros flew back and forth to Santorini and saved the injured man's life. Only two weeks later, he returned to Santorini to transport yet another man involved in a near-fatal car accident when he tried to avoid hitting an animal. This time, luckily, I did not learn of this flight until Alexandros and his passenger were safely back in Athens.

Yet another time, Alexander flew with his friend and flying instructor, Dimitris Kouris, to an outer island to transport the daughter of a Soviet ambassador back to Athens. The little girl was sick, close to death, but Alexander and Dimitris saved her life with their heroic flight.

Time after time, I saw Alexandros display an almost intemperate need to help those who were less fortunate than he was. When I saw him risking his life, flying in dangerous weather conditions to save the life of a small child or a pregnant woman or an injured adult, I worried about him. Who would save Alexandros? I wondered as I watched him race off on his missions of mercy.

On ordinary days, there was a look about him, an old-man look, that saddened me deeply and made me forget my friend was in his early twenties and had barely experienced life himself. Yet it was during those moments of his life, when he was risking his life to save the life of someone else, that he looked alive. I hated to see him take such chances with his life, but I hated even more to see him looking so serious and sad, so old that life seemed to have passed him by, aging him beyond his years.

Although his father owned the Airways, where he was employed, Alexander was serious about his job, which involved controlling many important aspects of airport management. He was always on time and never shirked his responsibilities at Olympic Airways. Even though his office on Syngrou Avenue, which was beside mine, was small, he was satisfied with it. He also maintained a private office at the airport. If he knew of any employees in need, he asked me to give them an extra check or rearrange their schedules. All the employees of Olympic Airways liked Alexander and no one seemed jealous of his wealth and position. So often, he told me as I handed him his monthly paycheck of 45,000 drachmas, or $1,000, "I want to be paid like everyone else here, only for what I do. I don't want any special favor because of who I am. I want to be as independent as possible." Besides his monthly allowance, I always received a monthly bill from the Hilton Hotel in Athens where he maintained a suite after his father's marriage to Jackie. I sent the bill to Miltos Yiannacopoulos, who promptly paid Alexandros' rent. However, before Alexandros put the monthly check for his allowance in his pocket, he would often hesitate. "Kiki," he would ask, his eyes looking away from my face, "do you have an economic need?"

"No, Mr. Alexander. I am fine," I would reply.

"Do not hesitate if you need something," he would tell me in his most serious tone, forcing himself to look at me as he spoke. "Whatever you need, you must let me know."

Of course, I never asked him for anything, but when people sent him presents for Easter or Christmas or on his name day or birthday, he urged me to take them. Once when I asked him why he wouldn't just keep these gifts for himself, he told me, "Since my father married, I have no home. I live in the Hilton Hotel. I have no room for these things."

Every day, Alexandros gave me the personal letters and cards that were sent to him and told me to read them and inform him as to which of these pieces of correspondence were important. He never asked me to answer the letters for him. Instead, he took care of those matters himself. Yet he trusted me to tell him which letters should be answered and which could be discarded. He also asked me to arrange for his personal trips. I made all the arrangements whenever he needed to fly out of Greece on a personal or business trip. Yet, no matter what personal or official matter I handled for him, he never seemed comfortable giving orders and was both courteous in his requests and grateful for my help.

For such an enormously wealthy man, his needs were simple. He didn't care to go to expensive restaurants or to shop for new clothes or jewelry. Like his father, who always claimed he was a simple man with no money in his pockets, Alexander did not like to spend money on himself. Once when his friend George Kouris, who along with his brother Dimitris was one of Mr. Onassis' two personal pilots, told him that he had brought a pair of pants to a specialist to get them repaired, Alexander was impressed with his friend's cleverness. When George told him the name of the man who repaired his pants, Alexander immediately brought three pairs of pants to the same man. "Fix these the way you fixed George Kouris' pants," he ordered the tailor.

When the tailor found out whose pants he was repairing, he was amazed. "If the son of Onassis is repairing his pants," he said to George Kouris, "what will the rest of us do?"

There were other times when Alexander balked at spending money unnecessarily. Once when he and his girlfriend and Dimitris Kouris were planning a trip to Switzerland, he asked Dimitris to make the hotel reservations for the three of them. When they arrived in Switzerland, Alexander was dismayed to see that Dimitris was staying in a simple room and he and his girlfriend were booked in an expensive suite. "This is not necessary," he complained to Dimitris. "Next time, make sure you make me a reservation in a simple room, too."

When he wasn't working, Alexander liked only to eat a light lunch or dinner and fly. At work, he dressed every day in a dark blue or gray suit and acted as serious as he looked. Although he spent most of his time working at Olympic Airways, he did enjoy being with his two closest friends, Roger Loubry, an excellent airplane technician, and Jean-Pierre de Vitry, his flying instructor, both of whom shared Alexandros' passion for planes. Jean-Pierre, like Roger and all of Alexander's other friends, was older than Alexandros.

Another friend of Alexander who was much older than Alexander was the former King Constantine of Greece. Before 1967 and the dictatorship of Papadopoulos, King Constantine was the ruling figure in

Greece. After the 1967 coup d'état, Constantine was sent away to Rome with his family. Alexander and Constantine remained friends, and Alexander insisted on keeping in touch with him after he was deposed. Concerned that he should not insult Papadopoulos with his devotion to the former ruler, Alexander sent me to Italy with gifts for the former royal family several times. He was always anxious to hear everything I could tell him about Constantine and his wife Anna Marie, and especially their youngest child, Pablo, when I returned to Greece. "Tell me exactly what the children said and how they looked," he would ask me as soon as I returned to the office. "Don't leave out any details about any of the family." Like me, Alexandros seemed to be more comfortable with older people. I often realized that, except for each other, Alexandros and I had few friends our own age.

Alexandros, however, did spend some time with someone besides me who was close to his own age, Panagiotis Konidaris, the Onassis family butler. The two men were not friends, since Panagiotis was a servant of the Onassis family and always appropriately respectful to his employer, but they did enjoy each other's company. Panagiotis was fifteen when he started working for the Onassis family in 1964, two years before I came to work for Olympic Airways. Barely a year younger than Alexandros, he lived in Glyfada in Mr. Onassis' house and worked for him and his family. A friendly, capable young man, Panagiotis served the food and performed a multitude of chores for the family, including, of course, Christina and Jackie, as well as Alexandros. It did not take long for the young, intelligent Panagiotis to become the boss of all the Onassis servants. When I needed information about Mr. Onassis' frame of mind, it was always Panagiotis to whom I first spoke.

Whenever Alexandros was setting out on his boat, a blue Chris-Craft named *Bertman,* sixty feet long with a speed of about forty miles per hour, Panagiotis was a great help to him. Together, they would prepare the foods that Alexandros wanted to take with him on his journey from Athens to the outer islands, pack all the food and gear on Alexandros' motorcycle, a small Honda, and drive, always too fast, to the small port in Glyfada where Alexandros kept the *Bertman.* Once they stowed everything on the boat, Panagiotis would drive the motorcycle back to the Onassis home in Glyfada. Often, before he headed back to Glyfada, Panagiotis would take a quick boat trip with Alexandros to an outer island or go for a fun motorcycle drive with him. Of course, neither one of them ever forgot that Alexandros was the boss and Panagiotis was the servant, but sometimes when I saw the two of them together, they looked like two good-looking young men simply enjoying each other's company.

In 1969, when Panagiotis went into the military for two years, Mr. Onassis became emotional and worried about his servant's safety. He handed Panagiotis 9,000 drachmas, or about $300, which Panagiotis reluctantly accepted. During the two years he served in the military, Panagiotis returned to Glyfada on every one of his free days. Both Aristo and Alexandros were delighted whenever they found Panagiotis working there on those days.

No matter whom he was with, Alexandros always seemed happy in his *Bertman.* He used it to travel to many of the nearby Greek islands for the day, but also frequently took the boat to Skorpios. His father often drove in the boat with him, looking relaxed and content when Alexandros was driving him around Skorpios in the *Bertman.* Mr. Onassis usually wore a hat to protect his head from the sun, but Alexandros never wore a hat. He preferred to drive his boat as fast as he could, with his thick black hair flying in the wind, his father standing beside him, enjoying the sun and the wind and the pleasure of being out on the beautiful bright blue ocean.

One day, an employee on the *Christina* told me, when Alexander was just fifteen, someone from the ship had taken him in a Chris-Craft to nearby Preveza. While Alexander was there, he met a pretty girl who lived there. A few days later, he took his own *Bertman* to visit the girl. Mr. Onassis was sitting on the deck of the *Christina,* having a lunch of bread, cheese, olives, and a little wine, when he asked where Alexander had gone. When he was told that his son had returned to Preveza to see a young lady, he became so angry he could no longer eat his lunch. "No one should have introduced him to that silly simple girl in the first place!" he yelled. When Alexander returned to the Skorpios several hours later, his father was pacing the beach waiting for him, and immediately put his arm around his son and led him off for a walk. The employee from the *Christina* told me that Alexander never returned to Preveza again after that day.

As Alexander grew older, however, there were other young women whose company Alexander did enjoy and of whom his father did approve, in particular, the actresses Liza Minnelli and Julie Christie. These two celebrities came often to Greece to visit Alexandros. Each time either of them desired to see Alexandros, I made all the arrangements for their flights and accommodations, always providing rooms for them in the Hilton as guests of Alexandros. When Alexandros was with one of the young women, the two of them would go out to fine restaurants for lunch or dinner or travel to Skorpios for fun and relaxation. Whenever they visited Skorpios, it was only for the day and they would return to their suites at the Hilton in Athens that evening. There were a few times that the two young women traveled together to be with Alexandros, but most frequently they came separately.

It is safe to say that Alexander Onassis never suffered from a loss of female companionship. Some of his appeal obviously came from who he was, as well as from his dark good looks and smooth manners. However, it was often said by those who knew him better than I did that Alexandros was an especially good lover. In that respect, he was indeed his father's son. Unlike his father, however, Alexander did not seem to have the need for many affairs with different women. There were many girls who approached Alexandros because he was Alexander Onassis, but they never succeeded in winning his attention. According to the other employees in the office, in Glyfada, and on Skorpios, who knew far more about these things than I did, however, those who won Alexander's attention were amply rewarded. For, these same voices said, part of his appeal was his superior body structure. Making love with Alexander, these women reported, was a giant and prolonged thrill.

There was only one woman, however, who was the real thrill of Alexander's life. She was Fiona Campbell von Thyssen, a Scottish-born model and the ex-wife of a wealthy European businessman, sixteen years older than Alexander and the mother of two teenagers. Alexandros was only eighteen when he met and fell in love with the tall, beautiful, dark blonde Fiona at a party in St. Moritz given by Alexandros' mother, Tina, who was divorced from his father at that time.

One night when Alexander and I were having dinner together, he talked to me about Fiona. "She fills me up like my sister, my mother, and my woman," he told me. After that, I often suspected that Alexandros' love for this woman might be the result of his negligible relationship with his mother. Perhaps it was Fiona's age and maturity that attracted Alexandros and provided him some sense of maternal affection.

Yet none of those factors mattered to Alexandros' father, who was bitterly opposed to his son marrying such an older woman. "My son is crazy, Kiki," he told me. "He could have any woman he wants and he chooses one who should be his mother, not his wife."

"Why does he not marry Fiona's daughter Francesca?" he asked me another time. "She will make him a far better wife than her mother will."

"But she is only seventeen years old," I reminded him. "She is too young to get married."

"She is the perfect age to marry my son," he insisted. "But he is too stupid to realize that."

I do not know whether Mr. Onassis repeated his suggestion to his son, but, for Alexandros, Fiona, whether she was his sister, his mother, or his mistress, was the only woman whom he appeared to love. Although they spent a great deal of time together in her London apartment, they met each other regularly everywhere they had the chance, in Europe and on the Greek islands. They especially enjoyed visiting the islands of Skiathos, Santorini, Hydra, and Mykonos. Fiona appeared to love Greece, as well as Greek bouzoukia and Greek food. The two of them never asked me to make any travel arrangements for them. They preferred to do it themselves, often taking off without any definite schedule to follow.

Frequently Jean-Pierre de Vitry would fly Alexander by helicopter to the small island of Spetsai, near Piraeus. Jean-Pierre would leave Alexander there very early in the morning and pick him up late in the evening. Fiona would always be waiting for Alexander, and the two of them would spend their day and evening in an old and beautiful house they rented there. In Spetsai, they could be together without the fear of photographers or tourists disturbing their hard-earned privacy.

Alexander and Fiona also loved spending time together in Porto-Rafti, another small island also close to Athens. Alexander told Jean-Pierre many times that if he and Fiona were ever to get married, this is where they would want to live. They knew exactly where they would build their dream house on the island. The house, Alexander insisted, would include two separate flats: one for him and Fiona, and the second for his close friend Dimitris Kouris, who was divorced, and Roula, the woman Dimitris planned to marry someday.

One of Fiona and Alexander's other favorite places to escape to was the island of Porto-Heli. Here, they always stayed at the house of Bird Smith, the director of BP oil company. One particular time that Fiona and Alexander were in Porto-Heli, however, did not turn out to be paradise for either of them. The trip started out happily. Alexander informed Jean-Pierre that Fiona had invited him and his girlfriend to join the two of them for a visit to their favorite retreat. Fiona was staying in Bird Smith's beautiful house and thought the four of them could have a wonderful time together. At four o'clock in the afternoon, Jean-Pierre flew the helicopter, *Alouette III*, from Athens to Porto-Heli. A delighted Fiona met her three guests at the airport, hugging all of them and expressing her happiness at their arrival. After a particularly delicious dinner, Alexander, Jean-Pierre, and his girlfriend decided to spend the night with Fiona in Porto-Heli.

The next morning, at around seven o'clock, Jean-Pierre could not find the helicopter in the spot where he had left it the afternoon before. However, he did find a message at the airport from Alexander. Alexander and Fiona had quarreled bitterly during the night, and at three o'clock in the morning Alexander had flown the helicopter back to Athens. He would return at nine o'clock in the morning to pick up Jean-Pierre and his girlfriend. Back at the house, a furious Fiona confirmed the story and remained in her room until the helicopter carrying her three guests had left Porto-Heli, shortly after nine o'clock that morning.

There were sadly other times when Fiona and Alexander would quarrel and treat each other unfairly. Sometimes, when Alexander was angry with Fiona, he would call his two beautiful friends, Elsa Martinelli and Odile Rubirosa, or the Greek actress Patricia Viterbo, and invite them out for a night on the town. Rubirosa was a widow and at least five years older than Alexander, yet although his father disapproved of his son falling in love with Fiona, he approved of Alexander's relationship with this older woman. "Alexandros needs a mature woman and that woman is good for him," he told Artemis. "Besides, she is not old enough to be his mother."

Aware that he was making Fiona jealous every time he went out with Elsa Martinelli, Odile Rubirosa, or Patricia Viterbo, Alexandros would insist that they visit one of the more popular tavernas in Athens, where they would break a hundred dishes and dance the *syrtaki*. Invariably, Alexander and one of his three attractive companions would be photographed, and he delighted in the fact that Fiona would inevitably see these pictures in the London newspapers. I, of course, paid the bill for the hundred dishes the next morning.

For a day or so after such an evening, there would be no phone calls from Fiona. Although Alexandros did not spend a great deal of time on the telephone and frequently asked me to screen his calls and talk to his callers for him, he was adamant about receiving Fiona's calls. Always, he would say to me, "If Mrs. Princess Fiona calls me, please find me wherever I am." When she did call again, I made certain I found him immediately.

Some days, he would come into my office and say, "Kiki, today I have much work to do and I do not want to be disturbed with phone calls. Please take all my calls for me."

"But what if Mrs. Princess Fiona calls?" I would ask, laughing slightly.

"Even if she calls, I do not want to be disturbed," he would answer me in his serious manner. But the moment she called, I would go into his office and tell him she was on the telephone. He would look up at me and smile, embarrassed. Then he would pick up his phone and close the door the minute I left his office. There were other times, when he would come into my office and ask me if she had called, and I would assure him she had not. Those days, he would appear nervous and anxious and did not leave his office all day long. Out of respect to his father, Alexandros appeared to have decided he could not marry Fiona, but it made him an even sadder man than he already was that the love of his life might never become his wife.

Defying his father by marrying Fiona would have been the most difficult thing Alexander had ever done. Despite their frequent disagreements and Aristo's moments of rage and disrespect toward his son, I witnessed many moments that convinced me Alexandros was the person Mr. Onassis loved the most in the entire world. Even during their day-to-day activities at Olympic Airways and Olympic Aviation,

I could see the affection Mr. Onassis held for his son. Although I rarely saw him kiss his son with outward tenderness, the love was evident. Mr. Onassis' eyes were always bright when he was with his son. He was looking at him, touching his sleeve or shoulder, his feelings of pride for his son evident in all his movements. Most times when the two of them were together, I would see their bodies touching, the son's arm flung across his father's shoulder, Alexander whispering something in his father's ear, Mr. Onassis concentrating intently on his son's words. Most days they spoke constantly on the telephone to each other, sometimes calling as often as twenty times a day to discuss business and personal problems. I knew that Alexandros wanted his father's approval for whatever he was planning to do. Whenever Alexandros had to leave for Monte Carlo or anywhere else on business, he was always making certain his father approved of those plans. Alexandros did not need to ask his father what he thought, for Mr. Onassis was always offering Alexandros his opinion. He was also urging him to be careful, to do what he liked, but to protect himself as much as possible. Alexandros never appeared to take his father's concerns for his safety seriously and simply nodded his head, barely listening to his father's words.

I especially enjoyed seeing the two of them joke together. For instance, Alexandros was never comfortable acting as if he were the big boss. That was a position he did not mind allowing his father to possess. But sometimes he exaggerated his lack of importance in Olympics Airways. One night, after dinner in Glyfada, he asked his father, half-seriously and half-jokingly, "My boss, would you mind very much to give me some days on vacation?"

"You need a rest, Alexandros, my son?" Mr. Onassis answered him in the same tone.

"A small rest," Alexandros replied.

"Well, then," Mr. Onassis answered his son, putting his arm around him and caressing him like a child, "you can take twenty days' vacation this year."

Even when Alexander had been a little boy, Mr. Onassis had taken pride in his son's accomplishments. When Alexandros was twelve, he mysteriously disappeared on the island of Skorpios. No one knew where he was for several hours. Mr. Onassis was just about to panic when the captain of the *Christina* called to tell him he had located the missing twelve-year-old in the parking lot for the *Christina*. When the captain had asked him what he was doing there, staring silently at the cars, Alexandros answered, "I will show you how to park the cars better so that they can all fit together in a smaller amount of space." He then took a piece of paper and sketched the captain a much more methodical and space-saving plan for parking the cars.

When his father heard the story from the captain, he smiled broadly and said, "He is as clever as his father."

There were, of course, other times when the two of them argued with each other. Alexander's typical reaction when his father was angry with him was to lower his head and remain silent until his father's anger began to fade. During those times, Mr. Onassis' face blackened with rage and, for a few moments, it would seem as if he might lash out and strike his son. But he rarely did. Alexandros knew enough to wait out the storm, and later, when his father became calm again, he would bring up the subject again, this time with more success.

There was no doubt, however, that Mr. Onassis felt much fear for his son's safety and tried hard to protect him. Even though Mr. Onassis never worried about his own personal safety, he obsessed about Alexandros'. "Alexandros," he was always telling him, "you must be careful. Before you fly, please ask the technicians to check the airplane." Alexander was both too innocent and too self-confident to pay much attention to his father's concerns, and he mostly ignored his father's fears. Flying was his reason for living, and he was serious and competent every time he stepped into his plane. Being afraid in a plane was beyond his comprehension.

When Mr. Onassis asked Alexander to take over the management of Olympic Airways or to assume an important role in the shipping business, Alexander was not interested in either position. However, when his father gave him Olympic Aviation, a small fleet of planes which provided scheduled service to the smaller Greek islands, an air taxi, and local charter service, Alexandros was delighted. He dreamed that this company, under his control, would grow bigger and bigger.

Before the company began its operations, Alexander invited a group of journalists to visit him at the airport, where he made the announcement of this new Onassis venture. As Alexandros walked to the podium to deliver his message, he noticed Miltos Yiannacopoulos walking in back of him. "Please come and walk in front of me to the stage," Alexandros insisted.

"Oh, no," Mr. Miltos responded. "Today you are leading all of us."

Alexandros blushed and then shook his head firmly. "No, Mr. Yiannacopoulos," he repeated. "I will always walk in back of you and my father; never in front."

Mr. Onassis, who overheard that discussion, was beaming with pride at his son's behavior that day. Alexandros' speech only added to that pride. "Our fathers are constructing the bases of the building, but we will make it head right into the sky," Alexandros told the journalists. "There will be no limit to how high we can go." It was an even greater source of pride to both Mr. Onassis and Alexander that Olympic Aviation became a strong financial success under Alexander's control.

However, Alexander's dislike of Jackie brought no pride to his father and only expanded during the marriage. One day when Artemis, Aristo, Jackie, and I were having lunch at Glyfada, Alexandros refused to come downstairs and join us at the table. Mr. Onassis left the table several times to try to convince his son to have lunch with him and Jackie, but each time he returned to the table, he was alone and angrier. Finally, when we were midway through the meal, Alexandros joined us. But he didn't say one word during the rest of the lunch. Nor did he do more than merely pick at his food. Jackie continued to smile and eat her meal, as if she were not aware of the hostility her stepson felt toward her. Mr. Onassis, however, did not smile once.

Usually, the moment Jackie arrived in Glyfada or Skorpios, Alexandros left those places, preferring to live in his suite in the Hilton in Athens, frequently spending much time there with Fiona when she visited him in Athens. One day, when he was arranging for some of his belongings to be sent from Glyfada to the Hilton, he handed me a huge box filled with all his tapes, including those by Frank Sinatra, Joan Baez, Nat King Cole, Louis Armstrong, and Paul Mauriat. "I know you will enjoy these, Kiki," he said shyly as he put the box on my desk. "And I will be pleased that they will have a good home." Since Alexandros and I shared the same tastes in music, I was delighted to receive such a present. Today, more than twenty-five years later, I still play and treasure every one of those tapes.

Although planes were the great love in Alexandros' life, he also knew as much about the mechanics of cars as he did about airplanes. Once when he was driving his own car, he noticed an elderly couple who had pulled over to the side of the road and were trying to find out what was wrong with their car. He stopped his car and immediately began to fix theirs. Within fifteen minutes, their car was operating perfectly again. When the woman recognized their mechanic as Alexander Onassis, she was shocked and overwhelmed with gratitude. Embarrassed by their thanks, Alexander insisted they had done him a favor by letting him fool around with their car.

There was no doubt, however, that Alexander's love for cars was equaled by his love for driving them at dangerously high speeds. With airplanes, he was infinitely careful, even when he undertook dangerous missions of mercy, always checking the controls and flying at safe speeds. With cars, however, the more reckless side of Alexandros emerged. It was Fiona's fear for his life that convinced him to listen to her and trade in his Ferrari for a more conservative navy Mercedes 500. There was no doubt the Mercedes was a heavier and safer car than the Ferrari; however, whenever I was a passenger in that Mercedes, I cannot say that I felt safe with Alexandros behind the wheel. I was grateful that I was not with him the first day he drove another of his new cars, an Alfa Romeo that he had imported from Italy. He had driven the beautiful new car from Italy only a few meters when he crashed into a tree. Alexandros survived the accident without any injuries, but the car was not so fortunate. Still, he managed to drive the car back to the shop where he had purchased it just a few minutes earlier and bought himself a brand-new car.

Of all his cars, however, it was his navy Mercedes that Alexander cherished the most. He always tried to park it in such a way that it took up four parking spaces, so that no one could park near him. When he entered our office one afternoon after lunch, he was shaking with a rage he rarely exhibited. Someone had scratched the driver's door of his car, and he was inconsolable. I went down to the parking spaces to look at his car with him and was careful to exhibit the proper concern for his car and to avoid mentioning the way he had treated his new Alfa Romeo several months earlier. Together, we made the arrangements to have the Mercedes car restored to its perfect condition.

Since Alexandros' office was next to mine, we saw each other every time he came into the Olympic Airways office on Syngrou Avenue. Often we had lunch together, and many times he overcame his initial shyness and invited me out for dinner. Anxious not to start any rumors about our relationship, I was hesitant to go out with him. However, some nights, he found a remote restaurant where he would not be recognized and where we could enjoy a relaxing evening together. Those nights, we would talk about everything, from business to planes to his family. Most of the time, he would ask me my opinion about his father or sister or a business transaction and would listen seriously to my response, as if what I said was of great importance to him. Over and over, he would ask me the same question, until he was satisfied I had told him all my thoughts about that particular subject. He made me feel important and intelligent, as if my thoughts were a significant consideration to him. When I was able to get him to talk about something that mattered to him, like a mission of mercy he had just completed or a pilot or airplane he admired, he became animated and enthusiastic and could talk for hours, gesticulating with his arms and raising his usually soft voice for emphasis. When he was through expressing his thoughts, he'd lean back in his chair, smile warmly at me, and touch my arm gently.

One particular night, we ended up having dinner together at the Hilton Hotel. He looked particularly handsome that night in his dark navy suit and his black necktie and light blue shirt. But he was also especially sad that evening, and I tried very hard to lift his spirits. "You are so lucky to be able to live with both your parents," he told me as he began to eat his main course of fish. "I have no house and no mother. I cannot think about her getting married again. It embarrasses me to think about her with another man who is not my father."

"You have no reason to be embarrassed, Mr. Alexander," I told him. "Not about your mother. Not about anything."

He was quiet for a moment, his eyes looking down at the table. Then he looked up at me and smiled gratefully. I will never know for certain if what I felt for that special, sensitive young man was love, but I do know that I treasured every moment we spent together, just the two of us.

Alexandros was two years older than his sister, Christina, and the two of them were not particularly close when they were growing up. I know that Alexandros was sometimes resentful of the fact that his sister did not work and was given larger sums of money than he was. He often thought she was spoiled and irresponsible and he paid little attention to her when they were together with their father. He seemed unaware of the favoritism his father most often displayed toward him. Whenever I saw Mr. Onassis with both his children, I noticed that his arm was usually around Alexandros' shoulders, rather than around his daughter's body. It was Alexandros to whom he directed his comments and on whom his eyes rested. It was only when he was alone with Christina, and Alexandros was not present, that Mr. Onassis appeared affectionate to his daughter, holding her then in his arms.

Christina looked like she could have used a mother to talk to, yet, although Artemis was always nearby, I sensed that it was her father whose attention Christina craved. When he was away from the office, he always called and asked to speak to his son. Often, he ended up yelling at Alexandros, but even if he hung up on his son, he called back a few minutes later to continue the conversation. When he was in the office and Christina called him, Mr. Onassis always spoke to her, but the calls were brief and to the point, and he never gave that call the energy or attention he afforded his son's conversations.

As in many typical brother-sister relationships, Christina and Alexander frequently fought and were sarcastic and nasty with each other. Yet when their father became involved with Jackie Kennedy, their mutual dislike for her drew them closer. For the two weeks before the wedding, Christina called her brother at the office far more frequently than normal. Instead of their usual short phone calls, these calls were much longer.

A few days before Aristo's marriage to Jackie Kennedy, Artemis called me at work and asked what I was doing that evening. "Oh, nothing special, Mrs. Artemis," I answered her. "I will probably just finish up my work here and go home."

"Would it be all right if I have my driver pick you up and bring you right here for dinner?" she asked, her voice sadder and softer than usual.

"That would be fine," I said, "but I will have to go home and change my clothes first."

"Oh, you do not need to do that, Kiki," she assured me. "It will just be the two of us. You are the only one I need to talk to."

As soon as I arrived at Glyfada that night, Artemis began to tell me why she was so sad. "Last night, I had my brother and my niece and nephew here for dinner. Aristo tried to talk to his children to tell them about him and Jackie. He told them how important it was that they grow to like Jackie. That she was very much like their grandmother, Penelope. He even told them that they physically resembled each other, since both women had expressive black eyes, which were large and wide apart. He told them Jackie was nice and polite and honest and that they would like her if they gave her a chance. But no matter what he said, they would not listen. Finally, looking defeated by his two children, he left the house.

"I talked to Alexandros and Christina all night long. I told them that they had to understand that their father was still relatively young and that he needed a woman who would satisfy his needs and take care of him. I told them no man should live alone without a woman beside him. I told them that Jackie was a serious and strict woman who loved her own children very much and she would love them, too, if they gave her a chance to do that. But they wouldn't listen to me. They said all I cared about was a foreign woman and her children, and I should care more for my own niece and nephew. They said that if I truly loved them, I would not love this woman. They became angry and disappointed with me. I do not know what I can do to help my brother's children love his new wife."

"You are doing everything you can," I assured Mrs. Artemis. "The children love and respect you and they will do what you ask of them. Maybe not right away, but within time."

Mrs. Artemis shook her head in disagreement. "I do not think they heard one word I said," she told me, sad and crying. "For the first time, they seem only to listen to each other. And for the first time that does not make me pleased."

Their father's marriage to Jackie might indeed have provided the first step Christina and Alexander made toward forming a stronger relationship. As their father grew closer with his new wife, he seemed more distant to them. It was this distance that connected his two children to each other. Many times after the wedding, I would see the two of them together, sitting side by side, listening carefully to each other as if they were discussing something serious. Yet, ironically, it was another marriage that drew them even closer. When Christina married her first husband, Joe Bolker, Alexandros was not happy with her choice. "He is too old for her," he told me. "When he is an old man, she will still be young. What kind of life is that for her? She will never have children and a family with that man. I cannot think what she was doing when she married him."

After her wedding, when Christina kept insisting to Alexandros that she was happy, he finally changed his mind about her husband. "If he is making her happy, then I must be wrong about him," he told me one day. "What else is important except that the person you marry makes you happy?"

Three months after his sister married Joseph Bolker, there was another wedding in Alexander's family that upset him far more than Christina's marriage. On October 22, 1971, Tina Onassis Blandford married her former brother-in-law Stavros Niarchos. Niarchos had been married to Tina's sister Eugenie, whose death on May 3, 1970, had been originally deemed suspicious enough to have warranted a judicial inquiry involving her husband. The post-mortem examination indicated Eugenie had suffered bruises or bleeding on numerous parts of her body, but her injuries were explained as the result of attempts to revive her from an overdose of barbiturates. Ultimately, the evidence presented to the Greek court was found insufficient to charge Niarchos with any wrongdoing in connection with Eugenie's death. Yet suspicion hung over his head for many years to come. Alexandros was devastated by the news that his mother had married this man. Not only did this marriage crush his hopes that his mother would remarry his father, but her choice of a third husband was a man beyond contempt. When Alexander returned to Athens from London after he'd heard the news about his mother, he looked ill. Alexander's voice was barely audible for weeks after that wedding and he lost almost twenty pounds in a short period of time. There was nothing anyone, not even Fiona, could do to restore his spirits. "I will never forgive my mother," he told me. "She has embarrassed me more than I ever thought possible." Eventually, however, he began once again to accept his mother's phone calls. Yet after that wedding, a light in his eyes went out and never returned.

Christina was equally as distraught as her brother over their mother's third marriage. She became suicidal when she heard the news, but Bolker stayed by her side and helped her regain her desire to live. She and her brother spoke several times a day, no matter where they were, trying to understand what had happened to their mother and how they could deal with such a calamity in their lives.

Unfortunately, Alexander's sister's marriage did not last for more than a few months after the bombshell about her mother and Niarchos hit her. Yet, despite his own despair over their mother's marriage, Alexandros was at his sister's side, trying hard to cheer her up after her divorce. Christina called the office even more often then, asking only for her brother, and he would spend a long time talking to her and trying to make her feel better. Sometimes I would hear him telling her stories about a problem between Jackie and their father, and I, too, knew that was what would make Christina feel better. Also, they began to spend many evenings together, just the two of them. Christina was always eager to be with her brother and managed to forget all her problems when they were together. At a local taverna, she would talk loudly and dance rather wildly, sometimes by herself, while Alexandros watched and smiled. They were as different as a brother and sister could possibly be, but it seemed as if the despair over their mother's third husband and Christina's failed marriage was drawing them closer. It was obvious now to anyone who saw them together that they had begun to love each other.

In 1971, however, long before I met my future husband, George Moutsatsos, I loved someone else in a special way. His name was George Kouris, and he was one of Mr. Onassis' personal pilots. Even though I was only twenty-three and George Kouris was nearly forty, we had an affair and I expected to be engaged to him shortly. Unfortunately, he was very attached to his mother, who favored him above his two brothers and was not anxious for him to marry me. Still, we planned to be married someday, either after his mother was no longer living or after we waited a few more years. George and his brother Dimitris always flew Mr. Onassis' Learjet for him and were daring and responsible pilots, who were rarely afraid, and were close friends to both Mr. Onassis and Alexandros. Alexandros knew about my relationship with George Kouris and would sometimes joke that he was too old for me.

But he was very close with George and also said that he thought we would be very happy together. Mr. Onassis' sisters, especially Artemis, were delighted that George and I were going to become engaged. Many times, Artemis had chastised me for having an affair with George and she was glad I was finally going to end the affair and make plans to marry him.

On a February evening in 1972, I was at the Athens airport taking pictures of Mr. Onassis' new Learjet, which George and Dimitris Kouris were about to take on its maiden voyage. George suggested I accompany him on a short flight from Athens to Nice, where he and Dimitris were scheduled to pick up Alexandros and fly him to Paris and then home to Athens. George knew I enjoyed Alexandros' company and thought it would be a fun venture for the four of us. I thought about George's offer for a few minutes, especially since I loved shopping in Monte Carlo, where I often purchased unusual swimwear and original crafts from the nearest villages, such as cups, plates, and paintings. However, when George told me that it was going to be a quick round trip just to pick up Alexandros and bring him to Paris and then immediately back to Athens, I declined. George was disappointed but understanding and we made plans to see each other when they came back to Athens.

Because of bad weather, the flight was delayed from leaving Athens for almost half an hour. Five minutes before they were due to land in Nice, the plane crashed into the sea. Neither of the two Kouris brothers' bodies was ever retrieved from the sea off Cap d'Antibes, where the plane disappeared.

Mr. Onassis and Alexandros, along with George's remaining brother, Grigoris, launched a full investigation into the crash, an investigation led by Miltos Yiannacopoulos. The crash appeared suspicious, but no definite conclusions were ever reached. Alexandros' guilt that two Greek brothers died in that suspicious crash en route to pick him up haunted him. He was part of the wide search along the coastline for traces of the plane but no one never discovered so much as a piece of metal from the downed plane.

Personally, I was heartbroken that the man I had loved and planned to marry had died such a tragic death, and for many months, I could not remove myself from the state of shock into which I had slipped. I tried to go about my work and my daily routine, but it was as if I were never quite awake. My friends kept telling me that I was lucky to be alive and that it was a miracle I had not been in that plane. I understood what they were saying, but it was a long time before I could snap out of the depressing sadness that enveloped me.

Still, there were times when I believed that Alexandros' pain was even stronger than mine. I knew he had been a devoted friend to both George and Dimitris, but his despair over their deaths was incessant. Not only did he mourn the pilots' deaths deeply, but he also generously supported their mother for the rest of her life. One night, several weeks after the accident, when he went to visit Mrs. Kouris, Alexandros smoked so many cigarettes that a huge ashtray was filled with the butts of his cigarettes. This ashtray was not only covered with his cigarette remains, but its entire surface was soaking wet with his tears. That evening, there seemed no way Alexandros could control his crying.

Several weeks later, when the investigation appeared to be ending, Grigoris Kouris urged Alexandros to continue to help him retrieve a piece of the plane that he was certain he could find in the ocean. Kouris believed that there had been an explosion in the plane, and that if they could locate this one piece of the plane, they would find the holes that would prove his theory that a crime had been committed.

Alexandros agreed to continue this investigation and asked Stelios Papadimitriou to intercede on his behalf and hire the famous underwater diver Jacques Cousteau to assist them in their renewed search. However, after Alexandros unexpectedly traveled to London and refused to return Grigoris' phone calls, Kouris became concerned. When Kouris caught up with Alexandros in London, Alexander finally explained what had happened. "I cannot help you any longer," he regretfully admitted to his friend. "I am deeply sorry but my father is making it impossible for me to continue to investigate this crash."

When Stelios Papadimitriou later asked Mr. Onassis why he had made his son stop the investigation, Aristo did not answer him right away. "Was it because of the money?" Stelios asked him.

"Of course not!" Mr. Onassis shouted. "Are you crazy to think such a thing? I will not risk my son's life for anything. Do not ask any further questions. This matter is closed."

Afterward, when I discussed this matter on separate occasions with both Grigoris and Alexander, as well as with others who had been involved in the investigation, it was evident that Aristo had become afraid of something. We all understood that Aristo feared no one and that the only thing that could have frightened him would have been telephone calls threatening his son's life. To this day, Grigoris is convinced that his brothers were not killed in an accident, but rather it was a crime intended to include the murder of Alexander Onassis which caused that Learjet to crash into the ocean over Nice.

So often, when the two of us were together, Alexandros told me how sorry he was, and that he considered himself responsible for George's death. No matter how many times I tried to assure him he was not to blame, he never listened to me. "If I had not gone to Monte Carlo, they would both be alive," he insisted repeatedly.

One evening, several months after the crash, I found him sitting in his office, with the lights off, staring at the wall. He seemed startled to see me at his barely closed door, looking to me almost as if he were sleeping with his eyes open. "I think about that crash all the time," he told me in a hushed voice. "Do you?"

"Yes, Mr. Alexander," I admitted.

"Everyone says we were lucky not to be on that plane," he said softly. "I am grateful you were not on that plane. But I do not feel lucky. I feel guilty."

I could not find my voice to answer him, so I silently nodded and left him alone, closing the door behind me as I walked away from him. I wanted to tell him that I too felt guilty because, as heartbroken as I was to have lost my wonderful George, I was grateful Alexander had not been in that plane. But I knew it was neither proper nor necessary to tell him that. Tragically, another crash followed two years later, and this time, the gods were not so generous with my dear friend, my darling Alexandros.

Chapter Eight

"Christina, *Chrysso Mou*"

ALTHOUGH ALEXANDER was an easier person to deal with than his younger sister, Christina and I did not take long to form our own special relationship. I was almost two years older than she, and in many ways I became a big sister to her. I felt an affection as well as a sympathy for her, but most of all, like few people who dealt with her in her family and in the office of Olympic Airways, I believed I understood this complicated teenager. During all of Christina's troubled life, I never lost any of those feelings for this perplexing woman.

The most defining aspect of Christina's life was unquestionably whose daughter she was. It might not have been easy to be a child of Aristotle Onassis, but for Christina, it was often an insurmountable hardship. Alexander struggled with this burden all his life, but in most aspects it was a battle he won. Christina did not win many battles easily or soundly. She went through life sadly, one of the few people I have ever met about whom I could say, "She did not have one completely happy moment in her entire life." Even years later, when her first and only child was born, she could not savor that moment because fear over her daughter's safety had already begun to plague her. Although there were certainly many times, especially when she was a teenager, when Christina appeared carefree and full of life, her leaden veil of misery was poised and ready to cover her face at a moment's notice.

Life, I saw firsthand, was not kind to Christina. It did not help that she was the daughter of one of the richest men in the world, for she was also, or perhaps because of that, miserable. Alexander was the son of the same man, and while he may have been sad, he was rarely miserable. Perhaps the reason for this was because he had the greater portion of the one gift that eluded his sister: their father's love. Oh, Aristo loved his daughter the way many fathers did, but Alexander was the greater prize, and neither Aristo nor Christina ever forgot that. Just one moment with the three of them and anyone could see which of the two children the father preferred. The look in Aristo's eyes, the movement of his arm around their shoulders, the tone of his voice, the kiss on the cheek, the turn of his head—all the messages were there. Alexandros was his son; Christina was his second child.

No matter how close I became with Christina, I never forgot that I was her father's employee. As with all my relations with the Onassis family, I maintained my distance. It was important, above all else, that I protect myself and my job. But Christina demanded the most from me of any of the Onassis family. I worked long hours for Mr. Onassis and

Alexander, but Christina's demands were different. She wanted to be my friend. And to be a friend to Christina would take more effort than to work for her father.

I had heard the stories that Christina's mother, Tina, had not been anxious to have a second child and that she was never pleased with the daughter she was convinced by her husband not to abort. Christina did not look like Tina, and her often heavy figure, the stories continued, could repel her slim, elegant mother. There was something about Christina that made me want to believe those rumors, for despite her vast material possessions, she possessed no self-confidence. I had also heard how, after her parents' divorce in 1959 when she was nine years old, Christina was shuttled back and forth between her parents, but spent most of her time living in her aunt Artemis' beautiful villa in Glyfada. One day, her aunt told me, a little girl who was playing with Christina admired an exquisite doll that Christina's father had given her. "I would love that doll," Christina's friend sighed as she lovingly touched the beautiful doll.

"I would gladly give it to you," Christina told her friend, "if I could have something you have."

"Oh, you can have anything I have," her friend answered immediately, hugging the doll tightly.

"Oh, no, this is something you cannot give me," Christina said sadly.

"Oh, yes, I can," the little friend insisted. "Just tell me what you want and I will give it to you right now."

"I want two parents just like yours," Christina told her firmly. "Two parents who will love each other and live in my house with me until I grow old."

Christina's little friend handed her back her doll and started playing with another toy.

When I first met Christina in 1966, she was sixteen years old and still living in Glyfada with her aunt Artemis. She did spend some time with her mother in London and her mother's mother, her grandmother Livanos, in Greece, but the villa in Glyfada was her primary residence. Her aunt tried to take good care of her, but Christina was very much on her own. Despite all the gifts her father bought her, the one thing she desired the most from him was his attention. Although I never heard him say no to one of her material requests, he rarely came close to satisfying her incessant desire to be with him.

In 1967, Mr. Onassis decided that his seventeen-year-old daughter should begin to work in the Olympic Airways office. Since she had not been much of a student and had no desire to continue her education, he felt it was time she learn about his business.

Before then, the only contact I had with Christina was when she called the office and asked me to handle her travel arrangements. If she were traveling to Paris to buy some clothes or to New York to visit a friend, I would book her flight on Olympic Airways, arrange for the driver to pick her up in Glyfada at the appropriate time, and alert the staff at the Paris apartment or at the New York hotel suite when she would be arriving. She would also call every day to speak to her father or check on his whereabouts. She was always polite and grateful for my assistance and usually excited about her upcoming travel plans.

Once she began to work for Olympic Airways, it became my responsibility to find work for her to do while she was there. We knew almost from the first day, however, that this arrangement was not going to work. Christina was not the least bit interested in working for Olympic Airways. She didn't want or need an office and was most comfortable sitting on the carpet near my desk. Although many journalists did not write complimentary articles about Christina's looks, and unflattering photographs of her appeared in many publications, I always thought she was very attractive. I did think her nose was a bit too large and I noticed the dark circles that always appeared under her eyes, but she was still a pretty girl. Her best feature was her eyes, which were very large and a rich, deep tone of black. Her hair, whether she wore it up or long, was as black as her eyes and wonderfully thick and lustrous. When she came to work at Olympic Airways, she dressed simply, like a student, in a white T-shirt and black skirt, with flat-heeled shoes, giving little care to her personal appearance. For the most part, she would spend whatever time she was there talking on the phone to her friends or talking to me. I tried to give her whatever attention I could, but my days were too busy for me to spend much of them with her. She was always happy and talkative and laughing over some story she wanted to share. If her father asked her to do an errand for him, she always refused. She did not mean to be difficult, but her fear of the journalists who usually hung around our office building in Syntagma Square prevented her from walking outside the building by herself.

Christina's mother, Tina, who, at that time was still married to her second husband, Sonny Blandford, the Duke of Marlborough, did call the office frequently to speak to her daughter. Although they did not see one another often, Tina kept in close telephone contact with both her children. Christina was delighted to speak to her mother and was usually in a good mood when they hung up. I also knew that Tina would call Mr. Onassis regularly to discuss their children's problems and concerns with him. I sensed that he enjoyed speaking to her and still felt much affection for her.

As pleased as Christina was with her mother's frequent calls, Christina had two other great loves at that time, and for the rest of her life as well: in particular, Coca-Cola and chocolate. "Please, Kiki," she would ask me almost every day, "come with me to Papaspyros, so I can buy some chocolate."

Whenever I agreed, she was delighted, for I managed to prevent the journalists from bothering her while we walked to the nearby pastry shop. Ever since she was a young girl, she had been afraid of paparazzi snapping her picture and journalists asking her questions. There was little I could do to stop any of them from taking her picture, but whenever they approached us, I told them firmly to leave us alone. Sometimes they listened to me and left us alone, although there were many times they ignored me and snapped away. Still, Christina always marveled at how boldly I spoke to them and begged me to teach her how to act the same way. I tried, but Christina froze when a journalist came near us and never got one of our rehearsed words out of her mouth.

As soon as we walked into the pâtisserie, however, Christina found her tongue and bought at least a dozen large pieces of her favorite chocolate, as well as several cups of Coca-Cola, and two or three small, round cakes with Gruyère cheese in them. The cakes were for her father, who loved them but tried to convince Christina to let someone else go out and buy them for him. "It is my pleasure, Baba," she always told him sweetly, and he shook his head, half smiling, half angry, as he ate his delicious cakes.

I tried to have lunch with her whenever I could, and again I would escort her through the line of waiting journalists to the little restaurant we chose for lunch. While we ate our lunch, we would talk the way most young girls would, about our boyfriends or plans for the future. Whenever we were in the office or with other people, I always addressed her as Mrs. Christina, but when we were alone, just the two of us, it was acceptable for me to call her simply Christina. When we were alone, we discussed our own personal problems and how a woman or a man could be happy, and what a normal person must have in order to be satisfied. We always reached the conclusion that money did not bring happiness. We also agreed what a real friend should be like and what would make a perfect family. To Christina, a perfect family meant a mother and father who loved their three or four children and stayed with them forever. She talked about her father and how much she loved him and wanted to be with him. She always repeated her one major conviction to me: To love was nothing, to be loved was something, and to love and be loved was everything.

Christina talked about all the things in her life that made her unhappy, and I tried to convince her that there was a solution to every problem, except sickness and death. "Oh, you are the great solution finder," she would kid me. "Whenever there is a problem, Kiki can fix it." Anyone seeing the two of us together at our lunches or during our breaks in the office would have assumed we were two friends, relating our innermost secrets to each other. I never forgot that I was her father's employee, yet I could not help seeing her as a young girl who needed tenderness, love, and serenity. Most of all, she needed a real friend.

Much of the time, however, she sat cross-legged on the carpet beside my office desk and ate some chocolate and a roll with cheese and drank her Coca-Cola while I tried to do my work. She usually had some story to tell me about her latest boyfriend, for there would always be one male in her life. Her aunt Artemis had told me how much Christina hated to be alone, and I saw firsthand how true that was. It didn't matter who the boy was; Christina wanted one with her at all times.

When her father came by and saw her on the carpet beside my desk, he would frequently laugh, and she would jump up to kiss him. But he got nervous when he saw her eating. Sometimes he would just smile at her and walk out of the room without saying anything mean about her eating habits. Other times, he would make nasty remarks to her about what she was eating and how she looked, and she would get very upset and storm out of the room.

One day, when she was sitting in my office, stuffing one piece of chocolate after another into her mouth, he walked in and stood in front of her, his face filled with disgust. "What are you doing to yourself!" he screamed at her. "You will lose your teeth from all that candy. You will get too fat and ugly. I am sure you will feel miserable but it will be too late for you. You will have destroyed your beauty. And no one will want you." Then he turned away from her and stormed out of my office.

Christina immediately began to cry and dropped the box of chocolates she was holding. For the next week, I could see that she was making a great effort not to eat candy, but her attempt to give up chocolate did not last long. But she did try to put away the candy when her father was present.

Her father also would get frustrated with the way she handled her personal life and never stopped giving her advice about how she should act and what people she should spend her time with. Once when the three of us were in the car together, he was in the front seat with George Margaritis, and Christina and I were in the back. When Christina tried secretly to pop a diet pill into her mouth, Mr. Onassis suddenly turned around and began to scream at his daughter. "What are you doing!" he shrieked. "You are crazy with those pills! Give me the bottle now or I will throw you out of this car." Frightened by her father's rage, Christina nearly choked on the pill in her mouth. Although she obediently handed the container of diet pills to her father, she did manage to swallow the one pill in her mouth.

Neither one of us could believe that he had known what was happening in the backseat, but somehow, perhaps by looking in the rearview mirror, he'd been able to see exactly what Christina was doing. As frightened as she was by her father's rage, once he had settled back into his seat, Christina remarked to me, "That man is amazing, is he not?" I nodded in agreement, but I understood that Christina would have another vial of diet pills in her pocketbook. What I wasn't certain about was whether or not he would have thrown her out of the car had she not given him one of those containers. I knew that, like most Greek fathers, until his daughter was eighteen, he would beat her if he felt it was necessary. But Artemis often told me that he felt he was losing control of his daughter and was often helpless to stop her from doing what he considered wrong.

Still, whenever the two of them were together, no matter where they were, Mr. Onassis could never have a conversation with his daughter without telling her what to do. Even though Christina appeared to listen to him, she still did whatever she wanted to do. It didn't take long for Mr. Onassis to know that his daughter was not going to follow his advice and become a part of his business. At least, not then.

Finally, after less than six months with us, Christina left Olympic Airways. She wanted to travel and to do other things with her life. The first thing she did, however, was to travel to London, where she had her nose shortened and the black circles removed from under her eyes. The result was wonderful. Some people who saw Christina after the surgery did not realize that she had undergone plastic surgery. They thought she looked prettier and more well rested than before. With her thick black hair and large, expressive black eyes, however, Christina was now becoming an attractive woman. But even then she continued to have a problem with her weight. Even after the surgery, she drank countless glasses of Coke and consumed excessive amounts of rich chocolate and could easily gain a lot of weight.

For all the years that I knew Christina, this weight problem plagued her. It was scary the way her weight could fluctuate. For months, she would be at a good normal weight, which for her was around 140 pounds, neither too thin nor too heavy, and then, suddenly, almost overnight, her weight would begin to balloon, and she would gain thirty or forty pounds in a few weeks. There was no doubt that her weight problems were tied to her mood swings. When she was in a happy mood, her weight was low. Yet as soon as her moods darkened, the weight came on. It was a vicious cycle, one she never managed to break.

Yet one more problem in Christina's life was her relationship with her friends. It was so hard to be her friend. Not only was she overly demanding, needing my complete attention every moment we were together, but I never knew how she was going to act. Sometimes when we were together, she would be acting fine and then, all of a sudden, she would start to scream about something, ranting and raving like a wild woman. She did not care who else was around. She would just go on and on until she had completely exhausted herself. And everyone around her.

She also changed her mind so frequently that it was almost impossible to count on her. Even if she decided to go out with her friends, there was a strong chance she would change her mind before she left the house. So many times, just when she was about to go out the door, she would decide she didn't want to leave. She'd return to her room, change out of her beautiful party clothes, often a Dior or Chanel dress, and stay home, usually depressed and unhappy all evening long. Sometimes, she would calm down a bit and read for most of the evening, but many nights she would sit with the servants and talk to them and eat with them until they retired for the night, leaving her alone and sad.

Christina did have a few close friends, especially Marina Tchomlekdjoglou, but all of them told me how hard it was to be her friend. Marina was a polite young woman, very beautiful and delicate looking, with large black eyes and a warm, friendly smile. Her father did business with Mr. Konialidis in Buenos Aires and in Montevideo, and her family knew the Onassis family well. Christina liked her very much and they appeared to enjoy each other's company whenever they were together. Still, Christina told me more than once, "Kiki, I have no friends except you. You are the only one who does not want something from me. You do wonderful things for me, like help me escape the journalists. And you are always there to listen to me. You are a wonderful friend."

Her temperamental moods were as unpredictable as they were unpleasant. Sometimes she would walk into the house in Glyfada with only smiles and kind words, satisfied with her day's activities or excited about her evening plans. Mrs. Artemis and I would listen to her cheerful conversation and wish her a happy evening as she left with her friends. Yet it was not uncommon for her to return to the house a half hour later, depressed and moody, refusing to talk to either of us as she headed up to her room. Her intense dislike of being alone always brought her downstairs after a brief period of time, but her crying and unhappiness made everyone else's evening as miserable as hers. Still, there were many days and evenings when she was all smiles and good nature and a sheer delight to be around. Sadly, those moments were rarer than her hours of misery.

As hard as her relationships were with females, they were far more difficult with males. Christina wanted a boyfriend more than anyone else I knew. And she didn't care what she had to do to get one. "I want someone to love just me," she told me many times. "Someone who will be good to me and stay with me all the time." I watched, unable to help her while she went from one bad man to another.

There were many unhappy relationships with men that Christina shared with me. One that was especially unpleasant involved a young man whom Christina had been dating for almost three months. "He is very special to me," she confided gaily one day. "I think he will be the one I love forever."

We were working together in our office the day a small, rather clumsily wrapped package arrived for her from him. When I handed her the package, her whole face lit up. "Oh, Kiki," she told me excitedly as she ripped open the package. "I can't believe he really did this. He told me he was sending me something very special. Something that would prove how he felt about me." While I watched, sick at heart for her, she pulled out two pairs of her own underpants from the box. She looked confused and dazed as she held up the two pairs of soiled underwear in front of her face. Finally, she dropped them to the floor and rummaged madly in the box for a note. There was none. I tried to speak to her, but she would not listen to me.

"I will call him and find out what he means," she told me as she stormed into an empty office to make the call, leaving the offensive package and its contents sprawled all over my desk. When a half hour had passed and she still had not come out of the other office, I knocked softly on her door and went in. She was sitting on the floor, staring at the wall. "He did not answer my calls," she told me dully, and we both understood what he had meant by sending her the offensive package. It killed me to see her so humiliated by a man, but, unfortunately, this was neither the first nor the last time she was treated in such a degrading manner by a man.

One other person that Christina was convinced did not love her was her stepmother, whom she sarcastically referred to as *"Kyria"* or *"Madame."* From the moment her father brought Jackie Kennedy into their lives, Christina was determined to hate her. Despite the fact that her mother appeared happily remarried to Sonny Blandford, neither

Christina nor her brother ever abandoned the hope that their parents would remarry. Considering how much she disliked Maria Callas, Christina was grateful that Maria and Aristo never married. When, suddenly, her father married Jackie Kennedy, Christina was devastated. There was not one thing about Jackie that appealed to Christina. She hated the way Jackie talked, dressed, walked, and even the way she ate her food. She made fun of her stepmother behind her back to everyone, except her father. She found it difficult to talk to Jackie and did everything she could to avoid being in the same room with her.

She constantly called me to check on Jackie's plans so she would not inadvertently bump into her. She wanted to know Jackie's exact flight arrangements, so she would never be in Paris when Jackie was there or run into her at the Athens airport. Every time she called the office or stopped in to see me or Alexander or her father, she was asking me a million questions about Jackie. "When is *Kyria* coming?" she would ask me. "Is *Madame* in New York or Paris? What has my father bought for *Madame* today? Where will *Kyria* be eating dinner tonight? What are *Madame*'s plans for tomorrow? Are any of *Madame*'s friends coming to Skorpios? Are her children coming back soon? Have you heard one word from *Kyria* today?"

No matter how hard I tried to convince Christina that Jackie was a lovely woman who could become her friend, as well as her stepmother, she refused to listen to me. Jackie sensed Christina's dislike immediately and seemed to realize it would be a losing battle to try and win her stepdaughter's affections. Yet, unlike Christina, Jackie was not a real Greek woman in the sense that she did not openly exhibit her feelings. A true Greek woman, like Artemis or Christina, would not hesitate to let someone know she didn't like her. Many times, Jackie would try to be sweet to Christina, even though she could not help but dislike her. To Christina, this was phony, and it only irritated her more when Jackie acted that way toward her.

Almost from the beginning of the marriage, however, both women made concerted and successful efforts to avoid each other so that they were rarely in each other's company. Unless Mr. Onassis forced them to be together for a specific event at which his entire family would need to be in attendance, they kept their distance from one another. When it was necessary, for birthdays or special holidays, each woman usually resorted to sending flowers to the other. Rarely did they give each other personal gifts that they had thoughtfully selected. Unlike Jackie with her proper behavior, Christina made no secret of her hatred for her new stepmother. There was no one in her life who did not know how she felt about Madame.

When Christina called to speak to Alexander or went into his office to speak to him, the two of them always spoke about their father, discussing his moods and his plans. They liked to know exactly where he was and with whom and for how long. But when the two of them started to discuss Jackie, their voices changed. They were no longer concerned, loving children; they were scheming, unhappy stepchildren. If anything, their dislike for Jackie drew them closer together, as she was the one common enemy they both wanted to defeat. So often, they spoke of the time when Jackie and their father would separate, always keeping that hope alive in each other.

Artemis often talked to me about Jackie and her brother's children. She wished that they would be closer and discussed with me why they were not. It was easy to blame Christina for her problems with Jackie, for she could be a selfish, spoiled teenager. Yet Artemis wondered if there could have been more that Jackie could have done to win over her stepdaughter. Artemis fretted that it often seemed as if her sister-in-law didn't care at all about either of Aristo's two children, and that she was too involved with her own life to find time to worry about whether they liked her or not. Whenever she brought up the subject with me, Artemis inevitably became upset, for it seemed as if there was no solution to the problem.

For my part, I worked hard to keep any information I knew about Jackie away from Christina. It was simply easier for me to do that. One day, in the Athens office, however, I received a telex from New York informing me that a fur coat Jackie had ordered would be arriving in a day. When Christina walked by and found the telex on my desk before I had a chance to hide it, she went crazy, screaming and yelling about Jackie and ripping the piece of paper to shreds. Every employee on the sixth floor of the Olympic Airways building on Syngrou Avenue came out of his office to see what the terrible hubbub was about. A few days later, when the actual fur coat arrived, I was careful to make certain Christina did not see it, for I had no doubt that Christina would attack the expensive fur in the same manner she had savaged the telex.

The scene concerning that fur coat was not the only occasion when Christina exhibited her feelings about my relationship with her stepmother. Whenever Christina heard me talking to Jackie on the telephone or making plans to meet her somewhere, she became jealous and made my life miserable. As with so many of my dealings with Christina, I learned to hide my actions from her and avoid these unpleasant scenes.

When Christina married her first husband, an American, Joseph Bolker, in Las Vegas on July 27, 1971, I was surprised. Yet from all that Christina told me, Mr. Bolker seemed like a decent man, and she appeared to be in love with him. Her father, who was busy celebrating Jackie's forty-second birthday on Skorpios at that time, nearly went wild with fury when he heard the news.

Ironically, neither Jackie nor Tina believed the marriage was catastrophic. Jackie thought Mr. Bolker reminded Christina of her father and could provide her with the stability she needed. Tina, who was seven years younger than her new son-in-law, was pleased that her daughter was happy and wanted to give her the opportunity to try and make her marriage work. At that time, however, Tina was planning to marry her former brother-in-law Stavros Niarchos, whom she did marry on October 22, 1971, a marriage of which neither her children nor her first husband approved. Artemis was certain Tina appreciated the fact that her daughter's unexpected marriage might move some of the spotlight away from her own personal affairs.

Artemis was genuinely delighted that her niece had found a man who was making her happy. "I think it is good that she has married an older man," she told me, for Artemis believed a woman should marry a man at least ten years older than she. "He will give her the love and tenderness and security she needs to grow up into a mature woman."

However, Mr. Onassis disagreed with his sister, and both his present wife and his ex-wife. Mr. Bolker was forty-eight and Christina not even twenty-one, and he had four daughters, one of whom was Christina's age. Mr. Onassis had understood that Christina often formed strong friendships with older men, such as with his business associate Costas Gratsos, so he assumed this would be that type of relationship. He never expected his daughter to marry this older man. And when she did, he was certain Bolker was only after his daughter's money. "If you stay married to this man," he screamed at his daughter over the telephone, "I will take away all of your money and all of your property!"

Christina was not bothered by her father's ranting. "Should I ask you what I should do with my life?" she answered him far more boldly than usual. "If so, then I would have to ask Madame as well. And I do not care to do that."

"I am very happy," Christina insisted when she called me from Los Angeles shortly after the wedding. "This is a man who really loves me. I am so lucky to have found him." Of course, I did not go to the wedding, but I did send her beautiful flowers for which she called to thank me the day they arrived in California. Her voice was so filled with excitement that I wanted to tell her father how happy she sounded, but I knew better than to discuss Christina's marriage with him.

When Christina and Joseph Bolker were divorced a year later, I was disappointed for her but not surprised. I had witnessed the phone calls from my office when Mr. Onassis would call Christina and scream at her about her marriage. "If you do not leave him and come back to Greece," he shouted at her many times, "I will stop thinking of you as my daughter!" He would turn to me after those phone calls, his face black with anger, and shake his head back and forth. I had witnessed the fury he exhibited over a business associate's action or an employee's stupidity, but this was a different, more powerful rage. I could not imagine any human being withstanding that unbroken wrath. Christina had been uncharacteristically strong to defy her father with that marriage, but to stay married to Joseph Bolker for more than a year would require more strength than she possessed.

Christina's relationship with her father was more complex and intense than her relationship with any other man. There was no question that she adored her "Baba" more than any other person in her world and hungered for his attention. No matter how much time she spent with him, she desired more. When they were together, she behaved like a young girl, embarrassing him with her constant kisses and loud laughs. She was almost giddy with pleasure when she was with him. Even when he was angry with her.

I never doubted that her father loved her dearly and often looked at her with pride and affection, yet he was both baffled and infuriated by her constantly changing moods. One evening at around six P.M., shortly after Christina's divorce from Bolker, I received a phone call in our office from London, informing me that she had attempted suicide in London. She was in a hospital in London, and no one knew if she would live or die. I called Glyfada and asked for Mr. Onassis, but was informed that he was on his way back to the office. When he arrived several minutes later, I struggled to find the right words to tell him what had happened to his daughter. "Mr. Onassis," I began hesitantly, "there has been a bad accident in London. Christina is very ill."

Before I could finish my sentence, he interrupted me. "I can imagine what she has done to herself this time," he said coldly. "Let her go to the devil. I do not care if she dies. Now, let us get some work done around there." It made me want to cry to see the lack of love in his eyes as he spoke those words, but I understood that he was responding emotionally and without thinking to the situation, and that later he would see things differently. I also understood that there was nothing I could do to make him love his flawed daughter at that moment when she needed him so much. Even more sadly, like all those who knew Christina well, I also understood it was not the first time his daughter attempted suicide, nor would it be her last.

Several months after Christina's divorce from Joe Bolker, during a cold, damp November, she convinced me to spend some time with her in the Onassis Avenue Foch apartment in Paris. Both Mr. Onassis and Artemis had also urged me to go, and he found some important company work for me to do while I was there. During that visit, as in previous visits, I was awed at the spaciousness and beauty of the Onassises' Paris apartment. The apartment, at 88 Avenue Foch, was in a very old and well-respected building and had been part of Mr. Onassis' life since his marriage to Tina. The furniture was antique and elegant, some of it dating from the seventeenth or eighteenth centuries, with many of its pieces vintage Louis XIV or Louis XVI. The walls were all covered with tapestries, which were arranged in such a way as to diminish the noise from the outside entering the apartment's walls. The wooden floors were covered with Oriental carpets, and costly original paintings adorned these walls, all of which were equipped with alarms to prevent their theft. Because Mr. Onassis and his children did not spend a considerable amount of time in this apartment, it was maintained by a small staff of servants, which always included George and Eleni Syros.

I always found it amusing that Mr. Onassis rarely sat in the antique furniture that adorned the apartment, each piece being worth thousands of dollars. Instead, he preferred to relax in a long, wooden chaise lounge type of chair. "Why are you sitting there, Mr. Onassis?" I asked him once when I was visiting there. "You have so many beautiful chairs and sofas to sit in, yet you choose this plain wooden chair. Why?"

"Because it is far more comfortable and I can rest better here," he told me. "Besides, I do not like to sit in furniture from before the French Revolution. It makes me uncomfortable, in more than one way."

Christina always made a point to tell me not to touch the paintings because they were very expensive and reminded me about their alarms. When I thought of all the different friends that Christina invited to this expensive apartment, I thought it was an excellent idea that there were alarms attached to these original paintings.

During that November visit, it was bitterly cold in Paris, but Christina and I still managed to go out and walk each day. Mostly, however, as soon as I finished my work for Olympic Airways, the two of us stayed in the apartment, and she talked about her problems. It was as if we were back in the Olympic Airways office on Syngrou Avenue, discussing our hopes and dreams over our lunches. As always, Christina detested being alone and was grateful that I was sleeping in her apartment. She bought me designer clothes and expensive dinners and tried hard to control her tantrums during that visit. One of the most pleasant evenings we had during that visit was when Christina regaled me with a lavish dinner at Maxim's. As always, the service and food at the elegant Paris restaurant were excellent, and we were treated graciously from the minute we entered the dining room. Even though many people recognized Christina and heads often turned wherever she walked, she was unusually amiable the entire evening, and even smiled pleasantly at a photographer who snapped her picture as we left the restaurant. I accompanied Christina to the Onassis Paris apartment many other times, but that was one of my most enjoyable visits.

The day I was leaving to return to Athens, however, Christina became very sad and pleaded with me to stay a few more days. "When you leave, I will be all alone," she complained as she sat on the bed in the guest bedroom while I packed my suitcase. "You don't want me to be alone, without anyone who loves me, do you?"

"But you have plenty of people who care about you," I told her.

"Nobody loves me," Christina insisted that November afternoon in Paris. "No one takes care of me." And I knew she was right.

There were many drastic changes to occur in Christina's life after November 1972. She, who hated above all things to be left alone, would be left, in a short period of time, by all the family members she adored. No one would expect this temperamental, difficult woman to have survived such losses, but she did. For more years than any of us could have predicted.

There was no doubt that Christina changed in many ways after these heartbreaking losses. Yet, despite these changes, she and I always remained good friends. While I detested her endless moods and frequent tantrums, I did understand that she was, in many ways, her father's daughter. She was clever, and she was never dull or boring. Yet, sadly, happiness was even more elusive for her than it was for her brother, mother, and father. Their deaths made this happiness not just elusive, but impossible.

Chapter Nine

The Pink House

I T W A S sad, but not a surprise, to Artemis and her two sisters that their brother's two children resented his new marriage. However, they were delighted to witness the loving and enthusiastic manner in which the newly married couple began their married life. Still, Mr. Onassis' entire family soon understood that his two children were not the only hindrance to his perfect marriage. For it was obvious shortly after his wedding to Jackie, perhaps within as soon as one week, that Maria was back in Mr. Onassis' life. It was as if she had never left.

It was true that after Aristo's marriage to Jackie, Maria never called the office again, nor did she visit Skorpios or Athens; however, there was rarely any difficulty in her seeing Aristo in other locations. It was in Paris, however, where they most frequently met. In 1967, Maria moved into a luxurious apartment there, on the second floor of 36 Avenue Georges Mandel. It was close to the Onassis apartment on the fifth floor at 88 Avenue Foch, and according to the staff at both Avenue Foch and Avenue Georges Mandel, the two of them often appeared closer and happier in both those homes than they had been before Mr. Onassis' wedding.

Many times when Mr. Onassis wanted to meet with Maria, he would have Miltos Yiannacopoulos call her for him. Maria often used Miltos in the same manner, relaying a message to Aristo through him. It seemed as if both Maria and Aristo were not anxious to speak directly to each other on the telephone and preferred to have an intermediary make their arrangements for them. Miltos was often in Monte Carlo or Paris or London or Rome, but wherever he was, neither Aristo nor Maria had any difficulty reaching him.

Whenever Aristo visited Maria in her Paris home, he made sure she was informed to switch off the lights at the entrance to her apartment, so that no one could see him entering her home. Artemis insisted that her brother was doing whatever he could not to embarrass his wife. "He may not be faithful," she told me one night, "but he is considerate and discreet."

While it was apparent that Mr. Onassis and Jackie appeared to love each other, obviously something was missing, from the very beginning, from their marriage. Even Artemis, who wanted nothing more than for Maria to disappear from her brother's life, admitted that she was still very much a part of it. Neither one of us, nor any of the employees who saw them at close view, believed that Aristo was with Maria only to make love. Their relationship went beyond sex. He needed her to discuss his problems, his innermost thoughts and feelings. Had Jackie been able to assume that role, perhaps he would not have craved Maria. I do not know exactly why he went to Maria so often. All I know for certain is that he went.

Mrs. Artemis told me that she suspected her sister-in-law knew about her husband's indiscretions with Maria. Although the two women never spoke about it directly, Artemis sensed Jackie's discomfort one time when a guest at Glyfada inadvertently mentioned Maria's name during a discussion of the opera. For the rest of the evening, Jackie appeared unusually quiet.

"I smiled at her when we said good night," Artemis told me. "I kissed her and told her that my brother loved her with all his heart. She nodded at me in such a way that I am certain the unspoken words about Maria lay between us. She is not a stupid woman. She has to know. But she is smart enough to know also that she is the woman my brother married and the woman he wants to spend the rest of his life with. And she has to know that Maria will rarely, if ever, come to Greece now. Jackie need not fear being embarrassed by her appearance."

Still, as all of us knew, almost immediately after their wedding, Aristo was not going to be faithful to Jackie, and there were nights when she was alone in Skorpios while her husband flew to Paris or London or Monte Carlo for business or pleasure. There were, of course, many times when Jackie left Greece and traveled to Switzerland or London or New York or Palm Beach or Hyannisport without her husband. The Onassises were not a typical married couple who had dinner together every night in their one home. Still, at least at the beginning of their marriage, Jackie did spend a sufficient amount of time in her new husband's homeland. When she was there, Jackie rarely complained to her sisters-in-law about her husband's activities, and kept busy, either with them, with her Greek friends, or with her American family or visitors. Her favorite visitor appeared to be her sister Lee, for whom I was frequently arranging flights to and from Athens. Many times, Lee arrived with her son and daughter and her husband, but most often she arrived alone, and she and Jackie would spend sun-filled days sitting together on the beaches of Skorpios or enjoying the shops and sights in Athens.

Jackie's days in Glyfada and on Skorpios may not have been always totally idyllic, yet when I read the salacious and untrue stories about what other authors claim happened to her during her six-and-a-half-year marriage to Aristo, I am stunned. And deeply angry. To read that Aristo hit Jackie and caused bruises on her face that were disguised only by her trademark oversized sunglasses is not merely preposterous, but a gross lie. There is no way that Jackie could have hidden such a bruise from those of us who were part of her daily life in Greece. While I might not have personally seen her every day, I was in constant touch with family members and personnel who did. Artemis and Panagiotis saw Mrs. Jackie every day and night she was in Glyfada. If Jackie had a bruise on her face, one of them would have told me about it. Stefanos Daroussos, the chief communication expert on the *Christina,* and George Parissis, the chief engineer of the ship, knew every move and every phone call that Jackie and Aristo made on the ship. What they did not personally see or hear, their staff reported to them. Maids, both in Glyfada and on Skorpios, took care of all of Mrs. Onassis' needs and saw her countless times each day. Servants brought her food and organized her activities. If Mr. Onassis raised his voice at his wife, I was informed, either immediately or the next morning. Nothing concerning this couple around whose affairs all our lives revolved escaped our careful scrutiny. Therefore, when I hear that someone wrote that Aristo hit Jackie and bragged to his friends about it, I am able to say, without the slightest hesitation, that did not happen.

As for the false stories that Mrs. Jackie had an eating disorder and vomited after many of her meals she ate on the *Christina,* I must almost smile at the absurdity of that suggestion. Certainly, Jackie and I often complained about our weight, but unlike me, she was far better at controlling the amounts of food she ate each day. If she had a big lunch, that evening, she would eat a very small dinner. If she knew she was planning to eat a lavish dinner, she was very careful about everything she ate during the day. She also exercised every day and appeared to have a perfect understanding of exactly how much she could eat before she began to gain weight. Although she was especially partial to baklava and Panagiotis' lemon mousse, she did have a fair amount of self-control and would never ask for a second helping of those fattening desserts.

Jackie and I frequently discussed Artemis' eating habits and how little she ate and how thin she was. Jackie often tried to tempt Mrs. Artemis to eat a fattening food by raving about how good a dessert or main course tasted, but Artemis never indulged herself with rich foods. Artemis always told Jackie that the best way to stay thin was not to eat the moment food was placed in front of you. Instead, Artemis suggested, you should simply stare at the food for at least five minutes and then proceed to eat as slowly as you can. That way, she promised, you will eat only a small amount of the food on your plate. I did notice that Jackie tried Artemis' way of eating a few times, but it didn't seem to work for her the way it did for Artemis. For unlike Artemis, when Jackie was hungry, she ate whatever was on her plate.

The idea that Jackie could have thrown up frequently after her meals on the *Christina* or in Glyfada without the servants remarking on such an occurrence is impossible to contemplate. She was watched too carefully for such a habit to have gone unnoticed in Greece. Yes, she was careful about how much food she ate each day, but to say that she was anorexic during her marriage to Aristo and her weight became dangerously low because of such an eating disorder is an outright lie.

And other lies must also be put to rest. Was Mr. Onassis a cross dresser, a man who liked to dress in women's clothes? Yes. During a carnival time when all Greeks celebrated in the streets with parades and at private parties, donning the clothes of the opposite sex, as did the other revelers. However, if the question is, Was Mr. Onassis frequently donning bras and nylons and skirts and blouses and enjoying a secret life dressed as a female named Arianna, the answer, once again, is a resounding no. There is no way such an occurrence could have happened without my knowing about it.

The stories about Mr. Onassis having sexual escapades with young men is yet one more example of authors taking great liberties with the truth. These outrageous stories insist that Aristo used two Italian boys in Rome for his sexual pleasure. They even go on to say that his employees were alarmed at the violence Mr. Onassis displayed toward these boys during their sexual encounters. The truth is, Mr. Onassis spent very little time in Rome. When he had business at the Olympic office in Rome, he would far prefer to take care of it during the day and, often, even after dinner, fly to Nice or Paris to spend the night at his homes there. When he needed to go to Rome, I would either send a telex or telephone Mr. Gogos, who was the manager of the Olympic Airways office there, and alert him of Mr. Onassis' impending arrival. Mr. Gogos would arrange for Mr. Onassis to be picked up at the airport and, if it was one of the rare days when he would spend the night there, he would make the necessary hotel reservations in

Rome. Mr. Gogos, to whom I spoke at least once a week to arrange for Mr. Onassis' mozzarella cheese to be flown from Rome to Athens, would make certain that all the other foods Mr. Onassis usually ate were available for him in case he desired his particular breads or ouzo or other specialties while he was there and that the suits he left at the Olympic office in Rome were ready for his use.

What happened to Mr. Onassis in Rome affected everyone who worked for him in Athens, or Paris, or Monte Carlo, or the United States. Thus, the same avenues that filtered information about his whereabouts to us in Greece operated, with different names and faces, in Rome. Never could such scandalous behavior with young men have occurred without Mr. Gogos or our office hearing about it. While Mr. Onassis was not offended by homosexual behavior between others, it had no appeal to him. Women, we all knew for certain, were his only objects of sexual desire.

Reports that Mr. Onassis was drunk on the day of his wedding to Jackie offend me almost as much as the above stories. Standing beside him several times during that late-afternoon ceremony, I personally would have known if he were drunk. I would have seen that he was walking unsteadily or slurring his words the way he might if he had drunk too much. However, that day he was in complete control of himself and all the activities surrounding him. The next day in our office, everyone was calling me to discuss the wedding, and not one person who was there mentioned anything about Afentiko being the least bit drunk. When, in the past he had drunk too much, we would all laugh about it, but the day after the wedding, there were no such jokes about Megalos. While he certainly drank enough at the celebration following the ceremony to have reached a state of inebriation, in the church he was unequivocally and happily sober.

Jackie was involved in many projects on Skorpios and, always, above all else, she shopped, whether with her sister, her sister-in-law, or Niki Goulandris, or even alone, perhaps, as Artemis once suggested to me, finding revenge in her excessive spending habits, charging great bills to Mr. Onassis while he was with Maria. Yet never did she appear to sit alone in Greece, either in the pink house she redecorated on Skorpios or on the *Christina* or in Glyfada, and fume over her husband's infidelity; it was as if it did not happen.

Besides, at least for the first three years of Mrs. Jackie's marriage to Aristo, their love for each other appeared strong enough to overcome his marital infidelities with his former mistress. Jackie had confessed several times to Artemis that she and her first husband did not spend a large number of hours together during his presidency. Jackie explained that the president had been busy with important affairs of the state and she had learned how to keep herself occupied with her own important projects. As for her second husband, she made it clear she was satisfied with the number of hours she and Aristo spent together. She did not need to be with him twenty-four hours a day. Still, the attention with which Aristo showered her the first year of their marriage, she assured Artemis, delighted and contented her.

Artemis was convinced that Jackie's love for her new husband and their life together surpassed her love for New York. It wasn't merely that Jackie was eager to embrace this new culture, but also because Aristo worked hard to make certain she was given everything she needed to fall in love with his country. Everyone was told to give Jackie whatever she wanted and to help her in any way he could. It was as if Mr. Onassis had married an injured creature and we were all responsible for helping her wounds to heal.

When Maria had first come to Skorpios in 1963, the employees told me they all did whatever they could to make a difficult woman happy. Yet there was a difference in the way they treated the two women. In 1968, they understood that their boss wanted every effort made to satisfy his new wife and keep her secure in all his homes. Never, like Maria, was Jackie considered a guest. Jackie was the wife, the woman in charge. They were not only to fulfill her requests but to anticipate her needs. It was a task every employee initially and uncomplainingly accepted and worked hard to accomplish.

It was not so much a chore, but rather a delight for all of us to watch the way Jackie adapted to her husband's country. Whether she was in Glyfada or on Skorpios or in downtown Athens, she seemed at ease in Greece. She had been married to Mr. Onassis for only a few months when she began to study the Greek language. She bought several different books, which she studied carefully, and also took some lessons with Professor Georgakis. Every time she called me on the telephone, she would say *"Ti kanis, Kiki?"*, which meant "How are

you?" I would ask her the same thing and she would answer, *"Kala,
epharisto poli, Kiki,"* or "Good, thank you very much." I knew she
was proficient in several languages, including French, but I was
amazed at how easily she learned many words in our difficult language.

When Mrs. Jackie and I conversed, however, we often spoke in
French. If she had been previously speaking to someone in English
or French, when we talked, she continued our conversation in that
language. However, most frequently our conversations were in
English. When she spoke to Mr. Onassis' sisters, who had been educated in French schools and spoke the language fluently, she conversed in French. When Mrs. Jackie conversed with the employees
on the *Christina* or in Glyfada, she spoke both in Greek and in
English. When she talked to her husband, it was primarily in English, although Aristo spoke French, Spanish, Turkish, and Italian, as
well as Greek and English. No matter what language Jackie spoke,
however, her voice was always delicate, soft, and pleasing, and the
person with whom she was conversing nearly always offered his full
attention to whatever she was asking for or discussing. Still, we all
found it exciting that she was trying to learn our language and, whenever possible, used Greek words in her conversations with us. The
best part of her learning to speak Greek, however, was the pleasure
it provided her husband. "Are you the one who is teaching her?" he
would ask me jokingly, as she carried on a brief, but accurate, conversation in Greek with Artemis or with me or even with a waiter in
a restaurant. "Now I cannot talk behind her back in Greek. This
woman understands every word I speak."

Not only did Jackie enjoy learning the language of her new country, but she also introduced it to her children. "They are at a perfect
age to learn new words," she told me when she asked me to help order
Greek tapes for them. "For them, it will be easier to learn than it is for
me." I was delighted to help her find cassettes of popular Greek songs
that she and the children enjoyed listening to together. Carolyn was
especially facile at learning a new language, but both she and John
were bright and enthusiastic and easily picked up Greek words and
phrases.

Jackie also made many new friends in Greece, who helped satisfy her thirst for knowledge about her adopted country. She purposefully sought out people who could teach her what she wanted to know. Professor Georgakis would spend long hours discussing Greek litera- ture with her and searched for books about both ancient and modern Greek writers. He often remarked on how fast she read and how much material she absorbed. "She is the most curious student I have ever met," he told me. "No writer is too obscure to escape her notice."

Niki Goulandris, who was the vice president of Goulandris Natural History Museum in Athens, furthered Jackie's strong interest in classical Greek art, making certain Jackie never missed an exhibit or a new addition to the museum. Niki and Jackie often walked together through Monastiraki, an old section of Athens, where Niki would explain the artifacts they came across and where Jackie found many antiques she was anxious to purchase. Whenever Jackie saw something that appealed to her, whether an artifact or a painting or a piece of antique jewelry, she would consult with Niki before purchasing it. She listened closely when Niki would relate a story about the article's ori- gin and would excitedly repeat each detail to Artemis as soon as she saw her. "You have already learned more than I know," Artemis told her one night during our dinner together. "Are you sure you were not born here?"

"Sometimes I think I might have been," Jackie answered her thoughtfully.

One of Jackie's major undertakings in Greece was the refurbish- ing of the white house in Skorpios that Aristo had painted pink for her. She hired a Spanish architect and decorator, Julio Lafuente, to help her with her project and spent countless hours and a vast amount of money to make this small house beautiful. Although Maria Callas had spent a little time in the house before Mr. Onassis' marriage to Jackie, she was unquestionably more comfortable in her Santorini suite on the *Christina*, which she considered her home. Yet, Jackie viewed the pink house, the largest of the eight guest houses on the island, as a perfect project on which she could lavish her attention and considerable dec- orating skills.

When Jackie was finished with her first project as Mrs. Onassis, the house, which was a mere fifteen-minute walk from where the *Christina* was moored, was still simple and traditional, like a typical

Mykonos house, but unquestionably charming and unique. While she was involved with the redecoration of the house, Jackie read many books about the Greek islands and tried to remain faithful to the design of a Mykonos home. The house, of stucco painted pink, with white trim around its multiple windows, had views of the ocean from most of these windows. Although the house was constructed on two levels, it was not large. On the level at which one entered was a spacious bedroom for Jackie and Ari, with a large, comfortable bed, which could be covered, if necessary, with a canopy of white netting to protect its owners from nasty mosquitoes that occasionally found their way inside the house. The worst time for mosquitoes on the island was during the summer time, so Jackie and Aristo usually slept on the *Christina* during those months, for bugs were never a problem at any time on that ship. Still, Jackie found it rather romantic to sleep beneath the umbrella of soft gauze fabric in the pink house, which she said reminded her of the desert, of Saudi Arabia, where the beds were routinely enshrouded in this white netting. "My prince and I will be settled happily under our rustic canopy tonight," she joked with Artemis and me one day. "Nothing, not even a voracious mosquito, can disturb us there."

On the same level as that romantic hideaway were another large bathroom, a living room, and a kitchen. On the second floor, which was reached by a small staircase, were one other bedroom and bathroom, which could be used by guests or even by Mr. and Mrs. Onassis. Guests, however, usually stayed in the small guest houses, which were near the Hill House, a house similar to the pink house but closer to the beach. The Hill House was on a higher spot than the pink house and boasted more spectacular views of the ocean, but the pink house was infinitely more charming. The floors throughout this house were terra cotta tiles, covered with thick flokata area rugs in white and beige tones. The main living room featured a fireplace, surrounded by decorative tiles. It had been Mr. Onassis' one request that the large, comfortable sofa be placed in front of the fireplace, where he could lie down and fall asleep, enjoying the flames of the fire. Truthfully, I never heard that he actually did such a thing, but the sofa, covered in fabric printed with small flowers, was positioned there, just in case such an event might happen.

Outside the pink house grew lush vegetation and trees, which, along with air conditioning, kept all rooms of the house cool and shaded. The lavish gardens offered complete privacy, as well as delicious respite from the sun.

When Jackie completed her work on the house itself, her island home boasted an unrivaled elegance, complete with expensive paintings, Greek furnishings, hand-designed pillows, and charming, peasant-styled curtains. In the library section of the living room stood a bookcase filled with books that Jackie had personally selected. Some of the books, I noticed, were by famous authors, but many were by writers that Jackie explained to me were not as well known, but excellent and worth reading. Lovely artwork, most by Greek artists and featuring island scenes, and again painstakingly chosen by Jackie, graced the walls in all the rooms of the house.

Jackie selected new pottery and dishes and silverware and stemware for the house, mostly blue and white, always favoring pieces with a traditional Greek flavor. She adored fresh flowers and kept her beautiful vases filled with bouquets of flowers, especially orchids and roses that she asked me to have delivered, as well as with wildflowers that she personally collected throughout the island. Pots, overflowing with hardy plants, sat in every room of the house, while, in front of all the doors of these rooms, additional plants loomed, often resembling small trees. Because Mr. and Mrs. Onassis did not spend much time in the pink house, a staff of servants did not live there. Instead, housekeepers from the *Christina* or the island were assigned to the house and kept it in perfect order. Still, the house was a treasure for Mrs. Onassis, one she loved to show off to all her visitors to the island.

Every time a bill for Jackie's redecorating the pink house or flower purchases or new artwork came across my desk, Mr. Onassis uncomplainingly paid it. Much of the decorations for the house, including some of the furniture, slip covers, and curtains, came from expensive stores in London, but Mr. Onassis never objected to the weighty bills. "It is good for Jackie to have something to do here," he told me once. "Let her buy whatever she wants for the house. This is a good project to keep her busy."

So many days Jackie would call the office and apologize for bothering me. "Oh, no, Mrs. Onassis," I would insist, "it is no bother. What can I do for you?"

"There is a bill I would like for you to pay," she would explain.

"There is no problem," I would tell her. "Just tell me what it is and I will pay it."

"It is from Martino's for some furniture for the house. Would you mind very much to take care of it for me now, Kiki?"

I knew that Martino's was a lovely antique store in Athens where Jackie often bought expensive items for the pink house. "Of course, I will take care of it," I promised her. The next day when I spoke to her she would remind me about the bill. "Oh, it was paid yesterday, Mrs. Jackie," I assured her.

"Thank you so much, Kiki," she would say gratefully before she asked me about her husband's plans for the day or what time I thought he might be home in the evening. Never did I check with her husband about the bills she asked me to pay. If they were exceptionally large, I forwarded them to Miltos Yiannacopoulos, who dealt with them, often calling the merchants and discussing the prices with them, many times managing to reduce them. But whether they were small bills, which I paid personally, or whether they were larger and given to Miltos, I made sure that they were dealt with quickly, knowing that was what my employer would want.

Yet this refurbishing often seemed to be more than a mere project to keep Jackie busy. It became almost an obsession. Once she finished the pink house, she turned her eye to the entire island and, literally, would leave no stone unturned in her effort to transform Skorpios into her vision of splendor. It was not that the island was not beautiful before she married Mr. Onassis, but there was still a raw beauty to it that she was determined to refine. First, she changed all the stones leading from the streets to the sea, handpicking all the hundreds of stones that would replace the former stones, selecting only natural stones, discarding anything that appeared artificial. Then she decided that it would be both more practical and more lush to cover sections between the stones with grass. She also concentrated a great deal of her energy on the area around the pink house itself, finally deciding to replace the plain high walls around her new gardens, where she grew orchids and tulips and roses, with a small delicate wall. At various times of the day, Jackie could be seen driving around the island in her red jeep, inspecting the work in which she was involved and seeking out more improvements that she could consider.

Not everyone in Skorpios was delighted with Jackie's renovations. One of the gardeners in Skorpios who was constantly receiving orders from Jackie grew frustrated with her never-ending demands on his time. "She is a new boss, trying to change the whole island," he complained to me one day when I was visiting the island. "These stones have been here for many years. They have stories to tell, these stones. Maybe Mrs. Jackie does not like the stories they have to tell and that is why she throws them away."

There were a few workers on the island who had been close to Maria who agreed with the gardener. They felt that Jackie was trying to throw away all the memories of Maria and Aristo that had filled the island before she arrived as Mr. Onassis' new wife. They told me that she acted as if she were the First Lady of the island and did not want any of them to remember the remarkable past history of Skorpios. It was as if she were removing all the traces of the scores of famous people who had once stepped on the soil of the island and enjoyed its beauty. Some of the workers actually cried to me as they bemoaned the changes that she made in Skorpios. "Look at these stones," one of the gardeners protested as he filled his wheelbarrow with large stones. "I remember the day Winston Churchill's feet touched these stones. Should I take them and throw them into the ocean just because Mrs. Jackie doesn't think they're good enough for her feet to touch? Nothing is good enough for her. Soon not even Mr. Onassis will be good enough for her." There was nothing I could say to make him feel better. A few other workers on Skorpios, who were especially loyal to Mr. Onassis, also found it impossible to get along with his new wife. After a few months of his marriage, either they were dismissed or they left on their own. I will not say that Jackie was jealous of these workers, but she acted as if she, not these people, wanted to be the one who looked after Aristo and his homes.

There were, however, many employees who had no problem with allowing Mrs. Onassis to assume that role. They had come to work for Onassis in 1963, when, already divorced from Tina, he had purchased the island for $110,000. They had seen firsthand that Maria had taken no interest in improving or feminizing it. Now a woman with exquisite taste was concentrating all her energy on the place where these people lived and worked, and that energized and delighted many of them.

I heard many stories from these people whose hearts Jackie won quickly. One of these workers was Achilleas, a simple employee on the *Christina*. A few days after their wedding, Aristo and Jackie were sitting in the garden of the pink house in Skorpios, discussing future trips with Jean-Pierre de Vitry, Mr. Onassis' personal helicopter pilot. Jackie was telling Jean-Pierre how much she loved Greece and its islands and how excited she was about having a chance to see as many of the islands as possible. Jean-Pierre was a tall, handsome, interesting man with whom Jackie enjoyed conversing in French. Jean-Pierre was describing some of the islands to Jackie, who was listening intently when Achilleas, accompanied by several other workers from the ship, stopped by to offer their congratulations to the newly married couple.

Mr. Onassis was delighted to see his employees and greeted them warmly, as did Jackie, who kissed each one of them. After the employees left, Jean-Pierre continued his descriptions. Suddenly, Achilleas reappeared, asking to speak to Mr. Onassis for just a brief moment about a personal matter. Aristo insisted he join the three of them for a drink first. While the four of them were relaxing with their drinks, Mr. Onassis convinced Achilleas to ask his question. "I was going to ask you for a raise," Achilleas finally admitted. "Your employees were hoping that your new happiness might convince you to raise their salaries."

"Oh, so that is it," Mr. Onassis said, smiling. "But now that I am a married man, where would I ever find the money to give you all raises?"

Jackie laughed and reached over to touch her husband's hand. "Oh, Aristo," she said sweetly, "what are you talking about? If you do not have enough money to give them their raises, then you could borrow some of mine." Then all of them laughed and Aristo happily agreed to Achilleas' request.

Achilleas was not the only person on Skorpios to become indebted to Aristo's wife. Gina, one of Jackie's housekeepers in the pink house, considered it a privilege to help Mrs. Jackie rearrange the furniture and furnishings in the house. Frequently, Jackie would decide that she wanted to get rid of something that she did not like in the house and would give it to Gina. In truth, Jackie was never completely satisfied with the way the house looked and was constantly redecorating it, rearranging the furniture and replacing furnishings with newer ones. It was a passion of hers that no matter how lovely a room looked, she thought about making it look even lovelier. One afternoon when Jackie and I were sitting together in the living room of the pink house, she was telling me about her plan to change the fabric on the couch. "Why do you like to change things so much, Mrs. Onassis?" I asked her. "Are you that way in your New York home, too?"

"I suppose I am," she answered me thoughtfully. "But the truth is I love to decorate and change things. I want my homes to express my personality in everything I use there. There are so many things in this world that I cannot change, but when it comes to furniture and draperies and flowers and even the roads in Skorpios, I can make the changes I want. That brings me enormous satisfaction and pleasure."

I understood what she was saying, and I saw firsthand how animated she became when she was discussing changes in the pink house and on the island. Her taste was always impeccable and I found it fascinating to watch the way her touch, and Mr. Onassis' money, could transform a plain and unremarkable room into a place of rare beauty and warmth.

One day, Jackie offered Gina an expensive vase that Artemis had given her, but which she had never liked. Gina was a particularly honest person and had refused many offers of money from photographers who wanted to take pictures of the pink house, and she was hesitant to accept such a costly vase. "Oh, you must take it," Jackie insisted. "I know you will take better care of it than I will." Gina always worried that Artemis would notice it was missing from the living room when she came to visit, but if she did, I never heard a word about it.

Yet when it came to the *Christina*, the personnel on the ship were relieved to see that Mr. Onassis permitted no such renovations. However, before she married Mr. Onassis, Jackie had already made one change to his adored *Christina*. A week before their wedding, she asked him to remove the painting of Tina that adorned the wall of the main living room of the ship. Jackie later told Artemis that she understood that in many ways Aristo still loved his first wife. "Seeing her beautiful face in that painting grieves me," she told Artemis, who agreed with her that she should ask Aristo to remove it.

However, Artemis did mention to me that Maria never made such a request to Aristo. "Perhaps Maria was stronger than Jackie," Artemis suggested to me. "Or else she never looked up."

Except for removing that painting and allowing his bride to redecorate the small foyer in the master suite the two of them shared, Aristo was adamant about keeping the *Christina* the way it was. Jackie seemed satisfied to change the furniture in the foyer and order new mirrors and other accessories for this small room. Although Jackie was more comfortable in the pink house since she had furnished it completely to her taste, Mr. Onassis considered the *Christina* his real home and preferred to eat his meals and sleep there, as often as possible. He did not mind spending a few hours in the pink house or in its gardens, but Aristo was always anxious to get Jackie back on the *Christina*. There is no doubt Mr. Onassis and Jackie traveled a great deal, and because her children lived primarily in New York, except for vacations spent on Skorpios, they were in no way a typical married couple or family. Yet, at least for the first few years of their marriage, they did attempt to create as normal a life as was possible for the four of them. But normal for an Onassis had a different meaning than for ordinary people. For Aristo, at least, the only home he had and the one he wanted to share with his new family was the *Christina*. And what a home it was. It was here that the real Aristo emerged, for there was no place on earth where he was more relaxed, yet more in control, than on this boat.

Yet it was when the boat was moored in Skorpios that he seemed the most satisfied, for if *Christina* was his most prized jewel, then Skorpios was his crown. To understand Mr. Onassis, one would have to see him in Skorpios, the kingdom he created, adored, and ruled. The island, which was sinuous, shaped like a scorpion, was four hundred acres in size and had a view of the mountainous north end of Ithaki, his favorite Greek island. Surrounded in its spot in the Ionian Sea by the smaller islands of Levkas, Ithaki, and Madouri, where the popular Greek poet Valaoritis was born, Skorpios was the closest thing to a real home that Mr. Onassis ever found. And, unquestionably, his most prized possession.

However, when he bought the island for $110,000 in the summer of 1963, Skorpios was rocky and barren, except for its olive trees, which two semi-permanent residents harvested and from which they produced 15,000 kilos of prime olive oil a year. Yet Aristo had a dream to make this island his paradise, and in the twelve years that he owned it, that is what he did.

The first thing he did was build a harbor there for his 315-foot *Christina,* the Canadian frigate *Stormont* he had purchased in 1954 for $50,000, when he was still married to Tina, and spent $4 million to transform into his luxurious yacht. After he settled the *Christina* into the harbor in Skorpios, he built roads to service the trucks and cars that would come to his new home. Then he set about making his desolate island bountiful. What he needed most were forests of trees, so, accompanied frequently by his lover Maria Callas, he traveled to other islands and other countries to select the trees that were right for his island. He selected mostly cypresses, his favorite tree, which reminded him of his native Smyrna, to transform his island from brown to green. He was like a small child as he chose each tree, exclaiming, "This is the one! No, this one is better!" Next, he found almond and walnut trees and transported all his trees back to Skorpios on tankers. Once the trees were safely delivered to his island, he supervised their planting with the same eagerness with which he had chosen each one of them. He would not hesitate to get down on his knees, grab a shovel, and help plant the tree himself. Because there was no water available on Skorpios, he had navigation facilities constructed to import water from the nearby port of Nydri. Bougainvillea and roses and wildflowers and jasmine were then planted and took root quickly, imparting vibrant hues to his now blooming island.

However, while the island itself was his paradise, with its forest of bountiful trees, luxurious green grass imported from South Africa, white ponies from Switzerland, and sparkling pool, the *Christina* was the giant playhouse of the man who owned paradise. No home could have served him better. For here, every day when he rose, he could swim in his pool, dine in his luxurious stateroom, and walk into his office, where the sounds of the waves lapping against the sides of the boat mingled with those of his ringing telephones. When he was tired of working in one spot, he could order his crew to prepare his boat for a cruise and head off to Italy or Monte Carlo. And never leave his office. Or his telephones.

If he wanted company, he could send his Piaggio, his hydroplane, to Athens to pick up Winston Churchill or Greta Garbo or Elizabeth Taylor and transport his guests to his vast home on the sea, where they would be ensconced in a suite guaranteed to satisfy any desire for opulence. Of all these guests, Winston Churchill was Mr. Onassis' most coveted visitor. The two men had first met in 1957 in Monte Carlo, and Mr. Onassis had continued his friendship with the British statesman until Mr. Churchill's death in 1965, inviting him on the *Christina* many times during those eight years. Alexander Onassis had always been fond of Mr. Churchill and had nicknamed him "Grandfather of the Victory." Because he adored Mr. Churchill, Aristo did for him what he did for no other guest: He allowed Mr. Churchill to sleep in his own private quarters. Each time Mr. Churchill visited the *Christina*, Aristo slept in one of the nine other suites on the ship, pleased that his special suite was being occupied by his most treasured guest. The first time I was on the *Christina*, when George Parissis, the chief of telecommunications on the ship, gave me a tour of all the suites, I could not keep myself from lying down, for a quick moment, on Mr. Onassis' bed. Just lying on the bed where Mr. Churchill had slept sent chills throughout my body.

Despite his generosity to his most special guest, Aristo never had any difficulty finding an elegant room in which he would spend the night while Winston Churchill slept in his bed. Each of the nine suites on his boat was named for a Greek island and contained its own elegant marble bathroom. The names of Ithaki, Mykonos, Lesbos, Andros, Chios, Santorini, Crete, Rhodes, and Corfu hung proudly above the door to each stateroom. Inside each room, the specific wood or stone indigenous to each island filled the room, transporting its guest vicariously to the shores of the island. All the bathrooms to the suites were filled with marble and boasted ornate gold fixtures, yet comfort was a key consideration in each room.

While *Christina*'s personal suite was Ithaki and Alexandros' was Chios, which was an island near Turkey, Maria Callas had occupied the Santorini suite whenever she was on the ship. When Artemis arrived on the *Christina*, always carrying her own special supply of foods that she brought whenever she left Glyfada, she was settled in either Alexander's or Christina's suite. If her niece and nephew were there at the same time as their aunt, one of them uncomplainingly moved into a different suite.

Whenever I went to Skorpios, I stayed in the Lesbos room, which was decorated with blue-and-white flowered curtains and a sofa in matching fabric. Expensive lamps and decorations representing Lesbos filled the room, and from the moment I opened the door bearing the insignia of the island, I was enveloped in the beauty of that island.

When I was on the *Christina*, I preferred to walk up the staircase with the marble balustrades to the main deck of the boat, rather than ride in the elevator. No matter how many times I was there, I was never able to walk through the massive sea green living room without a small gasp. There was simply too much to take in with one glance. So I gazed silently at the antique piano, the working fireplace inlaid with lapis lazuli, and the enchanting mural of the four seasons by Marcel Vertes. This painting featured Aristo's family in scenes such as Tina ice-skating and Alexander and Christina picnicking on a summer's lawn, and also included a dark-haired, mysterious woman in her bathing suit. That woman could have been Jackie or Maria or some other dark beauty. Then I'd gaze at the two original paintings by El Greco, as well as a painting of Christina when she was five, and finally the exquisite, highly prized jade Buddha.

The first time I was on the boat, Artemis had given me a tour of her brother's bathroom, pointing out the secret door that no one else could see which led directly to the captain's deck. I marveled at the thick gold faucets and the round sunken blue marble bathtub surrounded by mosaics depicting multiple scenes of fishes, a reproduction of the one in King Minos' lost Palace of Knossos, all accented by eighteenth-century Venetian mirrors. It was hard to believe that this was the bathroom of the same simple man for whom I worked, a man who never needed his own desk or his own office. But it most certainly was.

The bedroom of that same man was a spacious four-room suite on the bridge deck, a room he always shared with Jackie. In the main bedroom of the suite was a white couch, multiple mirrors, and a large bed beside which rested four saints' pictures, as well as a photograph of his sister Artemis.

The bar, on the main deck, where everyone gathered for cocktails at sunset, however, was all Aristo. Here he exhibited a fascinating collection of miniature ships and seated his guests on barstools covered with the foreskin of a giant whale and boasting whales' teeth as footrests. Along the bar were engraved scenes from Aristo's most treasured story, Homer's *Odyssey*.

There was also a hospital on the boat with an operating room and X-ray machine, and multiple decks and staircases that seemed endless. There was a movie theater, and a swimming pool whose bottom could be raised electronically and transformed into a dance floor. There was a playroom, originally designed for Christina and Alexander Onassis, with tapestries on the walls that depicted vivid scenes from fairy tales, and dozens of fascinating and costly toys designed specifically for them. Later, Caroline and John, along with their friends and cousins, inherited and were charmed by this enchanting room. There were dozens of telephones on the ship and the communication expert, George Parissis, made certain Aristo could talk to whomever he wanted, whenever or wherever he wanted. Although the *Christina* traveled to the United States as well as to Italy, France, the Middle East, the Caribbean, or anywhere its owner instructed his captain to navigate it, Mr. Onassis most preferred to cruise to the Greek islands, where he could personally show his guests the wonders of his country. Although I was repeatedly asked to take one of his cruises, because of the demands of my job, sadly, I refused each invitation.

However, I never refused an opportunity to spend a few days on the *Christina* when it was in its port in Skorpios. For, no matter where the boat was, even more incredible than its furnishings were its amenities, in particular, its food. With two excellent chefs always in attendance, the meals on the *Christina* were equal to those served in the world's finest restaurants. Breakfast was a simple meal presented wherever the guest desired, on the deck or in the stateroom or dining room. Lunch was most often a beautiful buffet of foods flown in from other countries, offering choices of fishes or meats, lush vegetables, and salads and fruits. Dinner was more formal, served in the dining room, with its one long table and stunningly perfect gold carpet, but again there were expensive wines, imported caviar, choices of main courses, and luscious desserts that were prepared at each table.

As much as I personally enjoyed those meals myself, I also loved to watch the way Artemis and Jackie ate at all of them. Both women tasted nearly all the dishes, eating small amounts of many different foods. Sometimes, especially for Artemis, it was just a tiny taste of each specialty, whereas with Jackie, the amounts were slightly larger. I never heard Jackie complain on the *Christina* or anywhere else about gaining weight or eating too many fattening foods. She displayed excellent self-control at mealtimes and rarely let up with her exercise regime. Swimming in the *Christina*'s pool or the waters of the ocean meant more than a mere dip in the water for Jackie. It meant a long, serious swim, guaranteed to devour many calories. She also enjoyed waterskiing off the shore of Skorpios, managing to stand up on top of the water for much longer periods of time than most guests. Aristo, too, enjoyed swimming, usually in the ocean, to which a special slide from the *Christina* delivered him for his swim, which often lasted an hour and a half.

Aristo's favorite spot on the *Christina* was on the main deck, sitting in a comfortable chair by the pool, staring out at the sea. To watch him on his magnificent yacht, a relatively small man dressed usually in the simplest of clothes, a short-sleeved shirt and baggy pants, smoking his Havana cigar and drinking his ouzo, surrounded by vast opulence, made me smile. It was a contrast I never completely understood. My boss was at home on this yacht, but, in some strange way, he didn't seem to belong there. He loved to show off his splendid home to his famous visitors and cherished each piece of art or miniature boat, yet he was a simple man, equally at home in a small taverna, his pockets empty as he mingled contentedly with the common Greeks and enjoyed his plain dinner. Yet here, in his real home on the *Christina,* he had an office worthy of a major shipowner and the proprietor of Olympic Airways. Here, in his ocean home, he had every luxury money could buy. He adored and craved this luxury, yet the simple life charmed and rejuvenated him. The man who walked through the doors of the small taverna looked no different from the man who stood on the deck of his 315-foot yacht, for he cherished and needed both worlds.

Mr. Onassis' appreciation for the simple life was as evident on the island of Skorpios as it was in the tavernas of Athens. In Skorpios, when he wasn't dining on his yacht, he might be found eating a simple meal with one of the residents of the island. While most of Mr. Onassis' staff of approximately forty for the *Christina* lived on the ship, most of the people who tended to his land and property on Skorpios lived in small houses that he built for them there. These were the men and women who harvested the olives on the island or worked on the fishing boats or cleaned and cooked in his houses. Their employer would think nothing of dropping in unexpectedly on some of those workers, knocking on their doors during one of his afternoon or evening walks throughout the island.

"What are you eating today?" he would ask them, and before long, he was sitting at their unadorned table, sharing their meal of bread and olives and cheese and wine or ouzo, enjoying and praising every mouthful he ate in their company. He was totally comfortable sitting at those tables, sharing the food with his workers in their simple homes, listening to their stories and sharing some of his own, totally intent on these conversations, looking and acting no different from the relatives and friends of these workers. This same man who could play host to the head of the junta government in his Glyfada home was every bit at ease dining with his peasant workers as he was with a king or president. He knew how to behave. No matter whom he was with.

His personnel in Skorpios appeared to enjoy their life on the island. In no way were they ever treated like slaves. Of course, they were free to come and go as they liked. Usually, however, there was not a lot of activity on the island. The closest port was Nydri, on the island of Levkas, a ten-minute boat ride from Skorpios. In Nydri, unlike in Skorpios, there were a few tavernas and some small shops and places to buy groceries. Yet most of those who worked for Mr. Onassis on Skorpios were relatively self-sufficient. They grew their own vegetables and baked their own bread and made their own cheese and wine. It was a good life for most of them, even if it was relatively quiet. And they never knew when they would be personally visited by the man who owned their island.

Even those who traveled the waters surrounding this island could also, at any moment, be personally involved with this same man. For instance, one day when Mr. Onassis was in one of his Chris-Crafts, heading to the neighboring port of Nydri, he came across a fisherman whose boat was becoming swamped with water. When the driver of the Chris-Craft continued toward Nydri, Mr. Onassis shouted at him, "Stop! Do you not see that man in trouble? Give him our pump right away."

The driver followed Mr. Onassis' orders and handed the weary fisherman a pump to clear the water out of his small boat. When Mr.

Onassis was satisfied the fisherman's boat was again seaworthy, he allowed his driver to head off to Nydri. But he did not stop criticizing his own driver for the rest of the day, reprimanding him for ignoring someone in danger.

Mrs. Jackie, however, did not share her husband's desire to spend time in the homes of those who worked for him. Still, while she luxuriated in the cruises on the *Christina,* unlike Maria, she could be even more content in the pink house than on Aristo's ornate ship. Much of the opulent splendor on the boat might not have been to Jackie's taste, yet she learned quickly that he loved every artifact, small and large, on the *Christina.* Plus, like every visitor to the ship, she could not help but be awed by its luxury.

Mrs. Artemis told me that one night at dinner on the *Christina,* Jackie mentioned to Aristo that she thought the seats that covered the barstools should be replaced with a more comfortable leather. We all knew that Jackie did not enjoy sitting on a stool that was covered with the foreskin of a whale, or resting her feet on the foot stools that were made from polished whale's teeth. Jackie was always so clever when she talked to Aristo, playing with him as if she were a cat stalking a mouse, complimenting him when she wanted something, and making it seem as if her request was his idea. Mr. Onassis was a shrewd businessman and prided himself on knowing how to get anything he wanted from his opponents in a business struggle. Yet with Mrs. Jackie, I felt he was often outmaneuvered. She knew his moods so well. And when he was not in the mood to give her something, she never wasted her time asking. If he was in a bad mood, she accepted his crankiness stoically, never providing him with any reason to be angry at her. Unlike his sisters, who dissolved into tears when Aristo lost his temper with them, or Maria, who shouted back, angering him so much that he might strike her, Jackie calmly repeated, "Yes, Ari," while he ranted, and waited patiently for the fury to subside. Not surprisingly, this anger subsided more quickly when facing Jackie than with any other person in his life.

That night when Jackie commented on the barstools, however, Artemis told me her brother had been unusually affectionate toward his wife and was so sweet and gentle, it seemed as if nothing could make him sad or angry. She had chosen the moment for her request carefully.

"You do not like the way the barstools feel when you sit on them, my darling?" he quietly asked his wife after she commented on their lack of total comfort. "They are not suitable for your body?"

"It is not that they are uncomfortable for me," Jackie answered him. Mrs. Artemis could see the subtle signs that her brother's mood was changing. And there was no doubt Jackie saw them as well. "Actually, they are too comfortable."

"Ah," he said, smiling sarcastically now. "So, you do like sitting on a giant penis? You find that very comfortable?"

"Well, they are a bit slippery," she said. "I guess it just takes some getting used to."

"Well, you will get used to them, my dearest," he said, lighting up a fresh cigar, the nastiness almost gone from his tone now. "Trust me, you will."

Jackie did not flinch. "Yes, I will," she agreed. Later that evening, when Aristo went to make an important business call, Jackie told Artemis that she regretted ever bringing up the subject.

"Aristo loves everything on the *Christina*," Artemis told her. "He is proud of every piece of artwork and every piece of china that he bought for it. It is not a good idea for you to criticize anything here. You understand that, don't you?"

As always, Jackie listened to his sister-in-law. And she changed nothing on the *Christina*.

Mr. Onassis was also not eager to allow his wife to change his personal appearance. When Jackie complained that his ties were too dark and that he should wear lighter ties, he was not pleased. Most of the time, he refused to allow her to buy him new clothes, but occasionally he gave in and wore a tie and shirt that she had personally selected for him. One day he came into the office wearing a white tie with a soft yellow print on it. "Do you like this tie, Kiki?" he asked me as he walked by my desk.

"It makes you look very handsome, Mr. Onassis," I answered him.

He held up the end of the tie and examined it for a minute before putting it back inside his jacket. An hour later, I noticed that he was wearing his usual navy tie.

Although he tolerated few changes on his precious *Christina* and did not surrender his mistress, Mr. Onassis did much else to ensure that his wife would be happy and well occupied wherever she went in his country. Despite his busy business schedule, he made a conscious effort to be in Greece whenever she arrived there from New York. However, there was no doubt his business schedule could be an exhausting one. From the very beginning of their marriage, Jackie understood that his business needs occupied a large segment of his attention.

Only four days after his wedding to Jackie, Mr. Onassis was back in Athens, meeting with the dictator George Papadopoulos, whose junta government had ousted the democratic government of Greece with a military coup d'état in April 1967, working out a ten-point agreement in which Onassis would begin a ten-year $400 million investment project in Greece, known as Project Omega. On November 1, Mr. Onassis again interrupted his honeymoon to return to Athens and disclose Project Omega to a press conference. At that conference, he announced that Project Omega would include an oil refinery which would be capable of producing seven million tons of crude oil within three years, as well as an aluminum plant, shipyards, an air terminal, and possibly even some tourism projects that would revolutionize Greece, as well as make him the wealthiest man in the world. For the next three years, Mr. Onassis concentrated enormous amounts of his energy, time, and resources to this project. For a brief time, he even teamed up with his arch rival, Stavros Niarchos, and attempted, unsuccessfully, to work out an agreement in which the two of them could be partners in this project.

Also, against the advice of some of his own advisers, Mr. Onassis made one of his own personal villas in Lagonissi available to the Greek military dictator and his family. For many years, Papadopoulos and his wife, Despina, lived in the luxurious villa, paying a mere pittance for their rent. In addition, Mr. Onassis managed to find a job in the Athens office of Olympic Airways for a member of Papadopoulos' entourage. There appeared little Mr. Onassis would not do to strengthen his personal relationship with Papadopoulos.

There were even some in the Olympic Airways office who expressed the opinion that Mr. Onassis thought his marriage to the former Mrs. John Kennedy would elevate his status in the eyes of the military government and facilitate the success of his newest project. Within a month of his marriage to Jackie Kennedy, Mr. Onassis did arrange for a dinner in Glyfada whereby George Papadopoulos could personally meet his famous American wife.

The evening of that dinner, the staff in Glyfada was especially frenetic. It was not that they were unaccustomed to serving celebrities at Vasilleos Georgiou 35. However, a Greek president had never before walked through the front door of the villa. Preparing a meal for the Greek military dictator and his wife, Despina, was a daunting challenge for each one of them.

The evening of the dinner, however, everything went smoothly. The colonel and his wife looked glamorous as they walked into the villa. Despina Papadopoulos, an attractive woman of medium height with short brown hair and dark eyes, was elegant that night in a fashionable colorful dress of midlength. Her husband, who was a bit taller than Mr. Onassis and who sported a full mustache and thinning hair, was not an especially handsome man. However, he, too, was dressed in formal dinner wear and seemed both relaxed and pleased to be a guest in the Onassis home.

Panagiotis was in his finest dark blue jacket with white pants and a bow tie, and each of the maids wore a smart pink and white uniform. The food and wines were perfect, as were the flower arrangements and the table setting. However, it was Jackie who was the pièce de résistance for the evening. Looking chic in a form-fitting long black dress, with a diamond necklace as her only ornament, she was a gracious hostess all evening long. Earlier in the day, as she helped Artemis plan the evening's menu, she had told her sister-in-law how proud she was that President Papadopoulos wanted personally to meet her. "I am so glad that I can be a help to Aristo in his business matters," she told Artemis. "Nothing could make me happier than to be an asset to him."

Although the dinner was flawless and George and Despina Papadopoulos appeared enthralled with their host's new wife, in the long run Jackie Kennedy Onassis' celebrity did not influence her husband's success in this particular business matter. Unfortunately, all this effort was for naught and, three years later, neither Aristotle Onassis nor Stavros Niarchos could come to any terms of agreement with the existing military government. In November 1971, Mr. Onassis was forced to abandon the project entirely. It was a great disappointment to him, but he understood the impossibility of Project Omega's ever becoming a reality.

Several years later, in September 1971, Jackie again tried to become involved with her husband's business ventures, this time accompanying Mr. Onassis and Miltos Yiannacopoulos to Belfast, Ireland, where they had been considering buying a shipyard. This venture, however, like Project Omega, did not reach fruition, and the two men ultimately decided that it would not be in Mr. Onassis' best interests to follow through with their initial plans to take over this shipyard.

Still, despite the pressures of these projects, and many other important business deals, when he began his second marriage, Mr. Onassis attempted to make this marriage a crucial part of his life. The last thing he wanted was for Jackie to be concerned or involved in his business worries. He was adamant about her not using her influence with American businessmen to facilitate his transactions in her country and preferred that she not know about any business problems he might be experiencing. If he needed to discuss business with one of his guests, he would suggest that Jackie go upstairs and read or relax for a few minutes. "This will bore you, honey," he would tell her. "I promise to finish the business matter as soon as possible so it will not disturb your evening."

Initially, he rearranged his business meetings so that he could enjoy dinner with his new wife as many nights as possible. He was always searching for new or interesting restaurants at which I would make reservations for the two of them for dinner. And he was always thinking about presents he could bestow upon her that would make her happy. His originality in presenting these gifts to his wife amazed and impressed the personnel on the *Christina* and in Glyfada. One of his favorite ways of delighting Jackie would be to leave a surprise on her breakfast tray, which would be the first thing she would see when she opened her eyes in the morning. Most often, the surprise was a piece of jewelry, a gold bracelet or ruby necklace or antique pendant, which he would have one of the personnel hide in a bouquet of her favorite flowers. Her cries of excitement when she discovered her surprise could sometimes be heard beyond the walls of her suite on the *Christina*. Since Mr. Onassis often went to bed later than Mrs. Jackie and was usually sleeping when she had her breakfast, he was often awakened by his wife's squeals of delight. Sometimes he preferred to put her present under her napkin at dinner, and would act as surprised as Mrs. Onassis when she shook out her napkin and a sparkling diamond bracelet fell onto her lap.

One time when he was in Tokyo on business, he worked out an elaborate plan whereby he had an exquisite strand of pearls sent to our Athens office that we had delivered to the *Christina*, where it was wrapped gracefully around a breakfast roll and placed on Mrs. Jackie's breakfast tray. Jackie may have owned other strands of pearls when she was married to John Kennedy, but when she became Mrs. Onassis, the pearls she wore were not just perfect originals, they were presented to her in a perfectly original manner.

Giving Jackie expensive gifts was not the only method Aristo employed in trying to create a warm and loving marriage. Several times I saw the handwritten or printed notes he had delivered to his wife inviting her to accompany him to another island for a day of lunch and shopping. Once he even sent her a note requesting her pleasure for dancing on the deck of the *Christina*. That note was beautifully printed and read: "My Fair Lady, Mr. Aristotle Onassis requests the presence of your company for an evening of dancing on the *Christina*, beginning at 11 P.M., immediately following dinner."

Mr. Onassis loved to dance and had always been especially fond of the tango since his days as a youth in Argentina after he fled Smyrna. The staff told me that he and Mrs. Jackie had danced that evening on the outside deck of the ship, near the pool, under the stars, just the two of them, their arms tightly wrapped around each other's bodies as they waltzed and tangoed until the sun rose the next morning.

So many times, this powerful, short-tempered man could act like a love-struck little boy who would do anything to win his beloved's attentions or earn a smile from her face. And he easily learned that the biggest smiles from that face came when he surprised his new wife with unique, one-of-a-kind pieces of jewelry. His favorite designer at Zolotas, Ilias Lalaounis, who later opened up his own jewelry shop in Athens, could always be called upon to create something original, exquisite, and costly for Mrs. Onassis.

For Mrs. Jackie's fortieth birthday, the first one they celebrated as man and wife, Mr. Onassis had Lalounis create a special set of earrings for his new wife, commemorating the Apollo 11 space landing on the moon, with which her first husband had been involved. The earrings, with their eighteen-karat gold clasp, included a sapphire and diamond-studded earth and a large ruby moon and cost him over $500,000. Mr. Onassis' favorite stone was ruby and he had a hard time resisting any piece of jewelry Zolotas or Lalounis showed him which included one. Mr. Onassis took great pride in this particular set of earrings, however, which he worked closely with Mr. Lalounis to design.

For that same birthday, however, his wife's most memorable present was a forty-carat diamond ring Mr. Onassis bought, not from Zolotas, but from Cartier in Paris. Actually, Mr. Onassis purchased most of his jewelry selections from stores in Paris, Greece, and New York, occasionally doing business in Rome, but never buying jewelry from London. In his typical manner, Mr. Onassis stopped in at the jewelry store in Paris and selected the ring for his wife, neither bothering to inquire about its price nor to pay for it. Instead, he called Miltos Yiannacopoulos and told him to handle the payment. When Miltos called Cartier to inquire about the price of the ring, knowing that Mr. Onassis always received a 30 percent discount there, he was told it would cost Mr. Onassis $850,000. However, Miltos talked with the owner of the store for a while, and then instructed me to tell the Olympic Airways office in Paris to send a check for $740,000 to Cartier within the hour. As always, Mr. Onassis had not used a credit card or check to pay for his purchase, nor did he know the price of his purchase when he left the store. Working out a fair price and paying the bill was Miltos' responsibility.

Jackie appeared to adore both the ring and the earrings, as well as a beautiful gold belt adorned with her astrological sign, the head of a lion, which her husband presented to her that evening. Jackie was able to show off these three magnificent presents at the party Mr. Onassis threw for her at his favorite bouzoukia, the Neraida nightclub, outside of Athens. Yet I did notice, several days after the party, that Mrs. Jackie had trouble bending her finger when she was fixing her hair and had to remove the ring until her hairstyle was completed. The night of her birthday, however, Mrs. Onassis did not complain about anything.

After that birthday celebration, there were many other jewelry presents guaranteed to make his wife smile and to impress whoever glanced at them. Another set of diamond-and-ruby earrings which he gave her from Zolotas came with a bill for $300,000, which Miltos gave to me and which I promptly paid. I also remember paying the bill for an expensive gold bracelet with a serpent's head studded with diamonds that Aristo presented to Rose Kennedy during a cruise she enjoyed aboard the *Christina*.

Although Mr. Onassis was overly generous to his wife, he was not always so generous with his daughter. One day, I received a call from Zolotas informing me that Christina had just purchased a new bracelet there. Miltos called the jeweler and was told that the bracelet would cost Mr. Onassis $9,000. Unlike with Jackie's purchases, Miltos knew he had to inform Aristo of his daughter's acquisition. Mr. Onassis was furious that Christina would buy something that expensive without asking him first. He called her up and screamed at her that she would have to pay for the bracelet herself. As soon as he hung up from Christina, however, he called Miltos back and told Miltos him to get that price reduced. "Miltos," he told him, "I might not pay that bill at all."

"I understand, Mr. Onassis," Miltos answered him.

When Miltos called him back an hour later and told him the price of the bracelet was now $7,000, Mr. Onassis grunted, "All right then," and hung up. Miltos called me immediately to tell me to prepare the check for $7,000 for Zolotas.

A few weeks later, Miltos received another call from Zolotas informing him that Christina had bought $5,000 worth of jewelry that afternoon. Miltos called Christina and reminded her what her father had said about her excessive spending habits. Furious, Christina yelled at him, "Don't even bother to tell my father about this bill. I don't want you or my father to be in charge of my life. I will pay the bill myself." Mr. Miltos waited a few days and then called Zolotas back and had the bill reduced. Then, he called Mr. Onassis, who screamed again. Then I paid the bill.

Both Christina's jewelry and Mrs. Onassis' jewelry were heavily insured, as was Mrs. Artemis', and all their jewels were kept in a safe place. Mr. Onassis stored most of the jewelry belonging to his wife, his sister Artemis, and his daughter in a safe in the villa in Glyfada, whose location I never knew nor would I have wanted to know.

Aside from Mr. Onassis' generous and considerate presents to his wife, he was also attentive to her children, Caroline and John, and frequently canceled business plans so that he could spend time in Skorpios with them. Both children spent their vacations on the island and often brought a friend with them for some of their visit. Mrs. Onassis' New York secretary, Nancy Tuckerman, always informed Amalia or me or someone else in our office of the travel plans for Mrs. Onassis and her family and guests, and we immediately arranged for their flights on Olympic Airways. Mr. Onassis was delighted each time his stepchildren arrived in Greece, and always acted as if there were no other place he would rather be than with them. Their laughing and loud voices and excited racing throughout the island and the *Christina* never angered or frustrated him. On the contrary, it seemed to delight him. And he did everything he could to entertain them and make them want to spend time with him and their mother in his home. He took long walks with the children through the wooded area of the island, holding their hands tightly, taking time to show them the special animals and birds and vegetation that prospered there. He never failed to answer their incessant questions and laughed loudly and without self-consciousness at their comments and stories. He would eagerly take them fishing or for rides in one of his speedboats, relating long, amusing stories about his youth when they were together. He concentrated on figuring out what would make them happy on Skorpios and buying it to surprise them. He was as excited as the children when one of his presents, such as the beautiful white pony he bought for Caroline, brought smiles and yelps of joy from his stepchildren. When he had business in Athens, he frequently brought John with him, depositing him and a couple of security guards at the movie theater while he conducted his business. He always made it a point to conclude his business meetings early so that he could be there to spend some time with John in the city before they returned to Skorpios.

When Mr. Onassis was not present, he made certain that the personnel on the *Christina* never let his stepchildren out of their sight. There were American Secret Service men who came to Greece with the children and who protected them at all times, but Mr. Onassis assigned his own loyal people, such as George Parissis and Stephanos Daroussos, as well as Costas Anastassiadis, the captain of the *Christina*, to be responsible for the children's safety. While he ignored Jackie's constant reminders that he needed to protect himself, in regard to her children's safety he was incessantly vigilant.

One day, however, he had a particularly tough time protecting John. Jackie had left for New York and entrusted John to Aristo's care. The two of them planned a fun trip to some neighboring islands on the Chris-Craft, but from the moment Jackie left Skorpios, an army of photographers had descended on the island, most of them in small boats. For several hours, Aristo held John like a prisoner inside the boat, refusing to allow him to come onto the outside deck of the boat. "Your mother will kill me if I let them photograph us," he told the young boy, but John was impatient to get off the boat and begin their fun day on the island together. Finally, totally exasperated, Aristo called upon his trusted employee Achilleas to settle the situation. Achilleas boarded a Chris-Craft and drove wildly among the boats around the *Christina*, managing to dump every photographer out of his boat into the relatively shallow water. There were terrible screams and vivid cursing as expensive equipment hit the water, but Achilleas saw to it that every photographer and journalist made it safely to shore. Then Aristo and John appeared on the deck of the boat, throwing towels to the drenched press. "If you want to take a picture now, we are ready," Mr. Onassis told them cheerfully before he and his stepson boarded a Chris-Craft and sped away. It was a most unusual day, for not one picture of Aristo and John appeared on my desk or in a newspaper the next day.

Although Christina and Alexander were not happy with their father's choice of a second wife and held her responsible for the fact that now their parents would never remarry each other, they liked both of his stepchildren. The occasional times when the four of them would be together, Christina and Alexander looked out for the two younger Kennedy children, protecting them and making sure they did not get hurt or lost. Those times, they would actually all play together, despite the difference in their ages, nine years between Caroline and Alexander, seven years between Caroline and Christina, and twelve years between Alexander and John. Christina and Alexander would answer the younger children's endless questions of "What is the name of this?" and "How does this work?" with infinite patience, like their father, never appearing bored or angry with their stepsister or stepbrother.

Once when Alexander took Caroline and John out in his speed-boat, the children's laughter could be heard far from shore, as he raced the boat against the waves. The children returned to shore, wet and excited, as Christina handed them towels and laughed and joked with them as they headed back to the *Christina*.

Although Alexander and Christina preferred to avoid Jackie, when John and Caroline were present, they would consider making a rare appearance for dinners on the island, ignoring their stepmother but enjoying the company of her two children as the six of them ate souvlaki, Greek salads, specially cooked meatballs, spaghetti with cheese, and a wide array of Greek sweets. All the conversations at those meals revolved around the children's questions, and Aristo answered each one patiently. After a while, Alexander and Christina returned to their rooms to make their own plans for the rest of the evening, but were in no rush to end their time with their stepsister and stepbrother.

Despite Alexander's affection for Jackie's children, his dislike for his stepmother grew with each day of her marriage to his father. Aristo tried to make things better between the two of them, but with no success. One day when he and Jackie were preparing to leave Athens from New York, I was waiting at the airport with them and going over some last-minute business details with Mr. Onassis. Suddenly, Mr. Onassis told me and Jackie to wait where we were so that he could find Alexander and have him say good-bye to Jackie. Jackie, who was wearing a simple beige dress and a black jacket, said nothing to me about Alexander while her husband was gone, but after fifteen minutes had passed, I could see she was getting nervous that Aristo was spending such a long time in his son's office. Finally, she told me to get Mr. Onassis and tell him they were going to miss their flight if he did not come right away.

Before I knocked on Alexander's door, I could hear Mr. Onassis pleading with Alexander to come out and say good-bye to Jackie. "I will not do that," Alexander kept repeating. Finally, when he heard my voice, Mr. Onassis walked out of the office, alone, looking very sad.

I was surprised when Mrs. Jackie said, "I do not know why your children are so rude to me." Usually she was so careful in the way she treated her husband. But she, too, was angry now. "I have done nothing to deserve such rude treatment."

"Worry only about your own children, not mine, my dear," he told her nastily as he walked so fast to the plane that there was no way she could keep up with his pace.

There was no doubt that Mrs. Jackie felt no differently about Alexander than he felt about her. One evening, I was on the *Christina* with Jackie, Aristo, and Miltos Yiannacopoulos. The four of us were on the deck, but while Jackie and I were sitting down, Mr. Onassis was exhibiting his usual behavior and, instead of standing still or sitting down, he was pacing briskly across the deck. Mr. Miltos was walking very fast so that he could keep up with Aristo. Jackie and I could hear much of their conversation as they repeatedly passed by the spot where the two of us were sitting. "You know, Miltos," Mr. Onassis was saying, "I have been giving much thought as to who will manage my property after my death. Have you thought about that subject at all?"

"Certainly, Mr. Onassis," Miltos answered him, as always addressing him formally. "That is an important subject for you to consider."

"Well, I have thought about it a great deal and I want to believe that Alexandros will be the one who can manage all my property. He is a smart boy and I think he will be able to do it."

Jackie kept looking up at her husband and tried to get his attention, but he refused to look at her. It was obvious to anyone who saw her face that she was not pleased with what he was saying. However, her husband continued walking and talking as if she were not there. "Yes, Miltos, I am sure my son will be able to follow me. I know Alexandros will not disappoint me."

Finally Jackie got up from her seat, looking quite angry now, and left the deck. Mr. Onassis never even glanced over to where she was sitting.

For his part, Alexander did not actively seek out ways to humiliate his stepmother, but to Jackie it often seemed that way. One day Jackie was in Glyfada, awaiting the arrival of her sister Lee and her two children, who were going to be spending a week in Skorpios. When Jackie found out their flight had been delayed for several hours, she decided to fly back to Skorpios alone and make certain all the arrangements had been completed for her guests' arrival on the *Christina*.

Unfortunately, there was no one available at that moment to take her to the airport to catch a helicopter to Skorpios. When Alexander's driver, Stavros, arrived at the house, she asked him to take her to the airport immediately. Stavros knew that Alexander would not want him to do such a favor for his stepmother, so he hesitated. Finally Jackie began to get angry and insisted that he drive her that very moment. Stavros felt he had no choice but to agree.

When Alexander returned to the house later that evening, Stavros told him, "You know, my boss, I had to take Mrs. Jackie to the airport today. She had to leave right away and there was nobody else to drive her."

Alexander was furious. "No matter what happens," he told his driver, "you will never drive her anywhere again in my car. Do you understand?"

Stavros understood.

Stavros was not the only employee of Alexander who had problems with Jackie's requests. One night when Senator Edward Kennedy was visiting Skorpios, he received an emergency phone call, urging him to return to Washington as soon as possible. Mr. Onassis was very fond of Edward Kennedy and the two of them enjoyed talking about politics and Greek history and philosophy. That particular evening, however, both Jackie and Aristo were out for the evening and Edward was alone. When he suddenly decided to catch the last flight leaving for New York that evening, he asked Alexander's private pilot, Dimitris Kouris, to fly him to the Athens airport in the Piaggio.

"I am sorry," Dimitris told Edward, "but I cannot take you now. You should have told me earlier. It is too late and the weather is getting too bad."

When Edward banged his fist on the table, infuriated with Dimitris' refusal, Dimitris said, "Don't act that way with me. I am not afraid of anyone. Even if you were the President of the United States, I would not take you on the Piaggio tonight."

After Jackie returned to the ship, Edward told her what happened and she was furious with Dimitris. Immediately, she repeated the incident to Aristo, telling him that she would never forgive Dimitris for his rudeness to her brother-in-law. The next day, Aristo spoke to Dimitris and asked him why he had refused to help Edward. "Mr. Onassis,"

Dimitris explained, "it was late and the weather was bad. How could I put Mr. Kennedy's life in danger like that?"

Mr. Onassis listened to Dimitris' explanation and then he said, "Thank you. I know what kind of a pilot you are. I trust you with my son's life every time you fly with him. My wife and her brother-in-law may not be grateful to you today, but I am."

Senator Kennedy was certainly not the only visitor Jackie welcomed to her new home. Her most frequent guests were certainly her family members, for whom she asked me to make arrangements, yet many of her friends, male and female, also came to visit her on Skorpios. "Kiki," she would ask me in a soft voice when she telephoned me at the office, "I am so sorry to bother you, but do you mind very much making a reservation for my sister and her children?" Or for Rose and Edward Kennedy. Or for other friends from the United States. But no matter whose arrangements I handled, she always called me afterward to thank me. Sometimes we spoke in French, rather than in English or Greek, yet no matter what language in which we conversed, her voice was always sweet and slightly breathless.

Her mother-in-law, Rose Kennedy, was one of both Jackie's and Aristo's favorite guests. During the first year of Jackie's marriage to Mr. Onassis, Mrs. Kennedy visited her former daughter-in-law at least three times. Before each visit, Jackie was delighted when she asked me to arrange Mrs. Kennedy's flights. Mrs. Rose Kennedy was a sweet, pleasant, slight woman, but she had a mind of her own. On one flight from New York to Athens, she was accompanied by Edward Kennedy. A few minutes after the Piaggio delivered her to Skorpios, she discovered that her hat was missing. She was inconsolable and could talk of nothing but her straw hat with the plastic fruits. Mr. Onassis felt terrible that Mrs. Kennedy was upset and offered to buy her any hat she wanted in his country. He had his staff locate several beautiful straw hats, which he personally handed to her, but she wanted only the hat she had brought with her from Hyannisport. I sent a dozen telexes all over the world before we finally located her hat in Bulgaria. It took a few days, but Mrs. Kennedy had her hat back and everyone was happy. Truthfully, when I finally saw the hat, I thought it was the ugliest hat I had ever seen and could not begin to comprehend why Mrs. Kennedy had made such a fuss about it. As relieved as Mrs. Kennedy was to get her hat back, Mr. Onassis was even happier. Openly affectionate to his wife's former mother-in-law, he showed his respect for her in many ways, but retrieving her hat for her was just one of them. Not only did he understand how important she was to Jackie and his two stepchildren, but he also genuinely enjoyed her company. Jackie told Artemis that Aristo's kindnesses toward Mrs. Kennedy meant a great deal to her and that she was especially happy that the two of them were so fond of each other.

Although Jackie and Aristo were often surrounded by friends and family on the *Christina* during the first few years of their marriage, the two of them seemed equally content when they were the only guests on the ship. Alone, they would often travel to neighboring islands, especially to nearby Ithaki, the legendary home of Odysseus, Mr. Onassis' ideal hero. Ithaki, a small, quiet island near Skorpios, was a favorite place for Mr. Onassis to spend a day and, in many ways, seemed his adopted homeland. Sometimes he would quote lines from the *Odyssey* as he surveyed the island with his wife, accurately recounting the travels of the indestructible wanderer with whom he strongly identified.

On the deck of the *Christina*, dressed in a pair of simple pants and a T-shirt, Jackie would sit beside her husband, sketching a picture of him as he paced across the deck, talking on the telephone, or sat in his chair, listening to music and the sounds of the sea. He was always delighted with her humorous sketches of him and would study them carefully, commenting on every small detail after she handed them to him. One day, when I was relaxing with them on the deck, he stood over her shoulder and watched silently as she sketched a picture of the sea. "I did not know I married a great painter," he said as he walked back to his chair.

Jackie put down her sketchbook and went over to kiss him before he sat down. "And I did not know that I married a man with such a perfect appreciation for great art," she said, laughing.

Mrs. Onassis also showed her creative side with her camera. Often, as she walked through the woods or along the beaches of Skorpios, she was armed with her camera, which she used to capture images of Aristo and her children, as well as of her three sisters-in-law, or of the natural scenery or sites that filled the island. It was fascinating to watch the way she concentrated so intensely as she kneeled down in the grass or on the deck of the boat or climbed on a rock or a ledge or even lay down on the sand in order to take the photograph she desired. Mr. Onassis often remarked that his wife had far more talent than the idiots who spent their lives trying to take pictures of her.

It would be wonderful to be able to say that all their moments together those first few years were idyllic; however, there were times, of course, when the two of them did not act like honeymooners. Their personalities were so very different that disagreements would be inevitable. Often Mr. Onassis' idea of a perfect day would be to do the same thing he had done many times before. He would be content to eat in the same restaurant he dined in nearly every day, to sit in the same chair in that restaurant, and order the same meal he usually ate. If he was on the *Christina*, he liked to swim in the pool, eat his dinner in his favorite chair, and spend the evening smoking his cigar, listening to classical music, staring at the moon and drinking his ouzo. After such a day and night, he was a contented man.

Jackie, however, craved changes. She was rarely content to sit in one place and do the same thing over and over. Soon after she finished decorating the pink house, she was ready to make more changes in the house. A new lamp, additional pillows, fresh flowers, a different fabric for the couch—all these changes energized her and gave her day a purpose. "Come, Aristo," she would say to her husband when they were finishing dinner on the *Christina*. "Let's go into the house and watch a new film I just received."

He saw that she was restless, but he had no intention of watching a boring film inside the house for the rest of the lovely evening. "Come, my darling," he would suggest sweetly. "Why don't you come sit beside me for a while and look at the beautiful sky?"

"But I want us to see the movie," she would insist, beginning to get angry over his refusal to do what she wanted. "I don't want to just sit here and look at the stars all night."

"Oh, we will not do that," he assured her, and he would suggest something else, perhaps playing the piano, and she would give in, thinking that she had won the battle by not doing merely what he had originally wanted them to do. But, in truth, the victory had been his, for he had escaped going into the pink house to watch her movie and was instead on his boat, doing something he loved, watching the stars and listening to music.

Jackie, however, was not a stupid woman who was easily fooled. She knew that she had married a strong man and his strength pleased her. She had married a man who had the first word, not the second word, and she understood and appreciated that. I also noticed early in their marriage that she was a woman who enjoyed the company of men, even if they were not as strong as her husband, more than that of women. She was a flatterer, who never hesitated to hold the hand of a man to whom she was talking. She especially liked to talk to men who were intelligent and humorous, men like Professor Georgakis, who had something to offer her curious mind.

Mr. Onassis never appeared to be jealous when Jackie became involved in a lengthy, animated conversation with another man. It was as if he knew that he was the only man she was really interested in. American men, such as Peter Beard and Pete Hamill, came to visit Jackie on Skorpios, yet her husband never objected to the time she spent alone with them. "My brother is a real man," Artemis would tell me, "and Jackie knows and loves him." Artemis loved to dwell on the similarities and differences between Jackie's two husbands. For the second time in Jackie's life, Artemis explained to me, she had married a very powerful man, but she was much freer now. Freer to do whatever she liked. Jackie might have been involved in some of the matters of her first husband's presidency, but with Aristo's business she was able to remain uninvolved. Rarely did he come home and discuss his day's work with her. Here no one would bother her to do anything; all everyone wanted from her was for her to be happy. In her new husband's country, she could do exactly as she pleased. Her worries had disappeared. Security was tight, for her and her children. At all times. In Greece, no one was judging her by the clothes she wore or by the speeches she gave. She never had to give a tour of the 315-foot *Christina* in front of television cameras or shake hands with endless diplomats. Here she could read and learn and listen for as many hours as she wanted. She could buy anything she desired and go anywhere she wanted. The freedom was exhilarating.

And the sex was very good, too. One morning an employee from the *Christina* could hardly wait to tell me what he had witnessed the night before. "Megalos will be in a wonderful mood today," he told me. "Although maybe a bit tired."

"Just get to the point," I urged him as the telephones in the office began to ring.

"I was walking along the water's edge very late last night, unable to sleep," he finally continued, thoroughly enjoying himself. "Suddenly, I noticed that one of the small rowboats resting on the shore was moving. When I went closer to get a better look, I saw the naked back of a man. I was startled to see it was Mr. Onassis. And underneath him, equally naked, was Mrs. Jackie. That boat was really rocking. Like it was caught in a storm. I moved away quickly, but I could not help standing at a distance for a while. When I finally left the beach, the boat was still rocking. And the sounds of the waves could not be heard above the sounds in the boat."

One of Mr. Onassis' personal pilots also delighted in relating another story to me about our employer's sex life with his new wife. This one occurred in Mr. Onassis' private eighteen-passenger Learjet en route from Paris to Athens. We all understood how much Mr. Onassis liked to argue, yet this pilot had discovered exactly why Aristo thoroughly enjoyed quarreling. "Megalos and Mrs. Jackie began to have a terrible fight the minute we left the runway in Paris," the pilot informed me when he returned to Athens. "We were barely in the air when they began to shout at each other, calling each other terrible names and swearing they would divorce each other the minute they returned to Athens. At one point, Mr. Onassis told us to land the plane immediately but we were over the ocean so I told him I could not do that. I couldn't understand exactly what the fight was about, but I think it had something to do with Christina. It was quite horrible to hear.

"Suddenly, after a half hour of this vicious shouting, there was silence. My engineer and I both turned around and saw that the curtain separating us from the Onassises' cabin had been tightly closed. However, we heard the sounds. We didn't need any more explanation of what was happening. For the rest of the flight the two of them made noisy love together, calling each other endearing names, and both of them crying out in delight. At one point, he even sang a few lines of a Greek song to her. We had to wait almost an hour in Athens before the two of them were ready to disembark the plane. They both looked exhausted but very happy. And the hat Mrs. Onassis was wearing when she got on the plane in Athens was no longer on her head. I found it later, underneath the cushions that had been scattered over the floor of the rear cabin."

Both of these stories, as well told as they were, were not unusual. Many of the employees of Skorpios had similar tales to tell, all of which proved that Mrs. Jackie was satisfied with her real Greek man. The staff at Glyfada had their own stories also, one of which revolved around Jackie's and Aristo's bed. Soon after they were married, Jackie had personally selected an extremely large bed, which was placed on a platform, for their bedroom in their house in Glyfada. One of the staff said she thought it was strange that Mrs. Onassis replaced a bed in Glyfada where Maria rarely slept, yet continued to sleep in the same bed on the *Christina* where Maria and Aristo had shared many nights together for nine years. Still, despite this lack of logic, Jackie adored her new bed, for which she had a beautiful pink satin coverlet designed. She and Aristo would often retire to their room early in the evening, not just to admire the lovely coverlet. Indeed, they far preferred to spend many hours making love beneath that pink spread.

Whenever Jackie was in Glyfada without Aristo, she would not sleep in that bed. "It is too lonely without Aristo," she told Artemis, who beamed to hear such words from her brother's wife. Aristo, also, would not sleep in that bed without his mate. When Jackie was not in Glyfada, he opted to spend the night in Alexander's former room, obviously sharing his wife's belief that their big bed was just for the two of them.

Several nights when I was dining with Artemis, Jackie and Aristo excused themselves early in the evening and retired to their own home, which adjoined Artemis'. As we watched them disappear, arms around each other, Artemis and I knew the big bed was not going to be empty that evening. If there was a lot of company, however, Aristo would never leave his guests and race off to make love to his wife. While it was obvious he and Jackie maintained a most enjoyable sex life, he was always able to control himself and wait until his guests had left before he indulged himself with his wife.

"The bed is big enough for all my staff to sleep there, along with the two of them, " Artemis joked to me one night, however, when Aristo and Jackie had chosen the bed's company over ours. "But neither one of them wants to sleep in it alone. That is good, is it not?"

It was good, I agreed. But there were many other instances of "good" those first years. One "good" evening when we were all enjoying a relaxing, pleasant evening in Glyfada, Jackie and Aristo seemed particularly pleased with each other and exchanged repeated warm looks during the dinner. At one point in the evening, however, the sounds of the planes flying overhead appeared even louder than usual. Because Glyfada was a mere five minutes from the Athens airport, we were all used to the nearly constant sounds of planes flying above the house as they arrived or departed. No one was ever bothered by the sounds, for they were as much a part of the house as the candles on the table and the flowers in the garden and the beautiful music emanating from the stereo.

That evening, however, even Aristo's voice was drowned out by the sounds of the planes. When he left the room for a moment, Jackie remarked how happy her husband was that night. "He adores the roar of those engines," she said. "The louder they are, the happier he is. I honestly believe he thinks he is up there, flying on each and every one of those Olympic airplanes that flies above us. No sound could make him happier."

That was not quite true. I personally knew of one other sound that could make her husband even happier than the roar of the airplanes: the sound of his wife's voice. Although I had heard some people complain about Mrs. Jackie's voice and describe it as childish and breathless and silly, her husband was not one of those people. To him, her voice was one of her strongest assets, a soft, sexy voice that, even on the telephone, could change his mood from that of a raging tiger to one of a love-struck puppy. Although Maria was a singer with a passionate, highly trained voice, that voice was not a sexy one. Jackie's voice, while often a mere whisper, could move her husband as much as Maria's voice moved those in her audience who had sat mesmerized. Mr. Onassis was not a man of many words, and the tone of his words was relatively unremarkable, but he obviously spoke enough of them to his wife to convince her he desired her often and greatly.

Sometimes, when they were in public, Aristo would kiss his wife passionately on her lips, oblivious to whoever was watching him. At those times, the two of them were teenagers, unable to keep their hands and lips from each other's bodies. Artemis would smile at me when they acted like that in front of us, appearing almost as content as her brother and sister-in-law.

Certainly, however, not everything Mrs. Onassis did pleased her husband. One habit of hers that particularly displeased him was her smoking, a habit she shared with Artemis. Mrs. Jackie was particularly careful not to smoke in public but when she was on the outside deck of the *Christina*, or in other places away from the glare of the public eye, she enjoyed smoking her cigarettes. "Please, honey," Mr. Onassis would say to her sweetly, as he playfully tried to grab her package of cigarettes out of her hand as she lit up a cigarette. "I do not want you to smoke now. I am afraid it will hurt your health. Please do me a favor and let me throw this package overboard." Occasionally, Jackie would let him do that, but most of the times she would smile just as sweetly as he spoke and continue to smoke.

As the first few years of their marriage moved along, however, Maria, far more than Jackie's package of cigarettes, was a threat to their marriage. For, no matter how sweet and adoring Aristo appeared to his second wife, it did not appear as if his love and passion for her were enough to satisfy him or that his affair with Maria would ever end. Artemis and I discussed Maria endlessly, more, it seemed, after Aristo married Jackie than before. As much as it disturbed her to admit it, Artemis was certain Maria understood everything her brother said, often before he uttered the words. She was the one woman from whom he could not be separated. If Jackie had not come along, he would have stayed with Maria forever, perhaps, because of Artemis' feelings and his own complexity, not marrying her, but never abandoning her for another woman.

"But why did he marry Jackie when he never married Maria?" we would ask each other, repeating the same question, searching for the perfect answer.

"Because Jackie was different from any other woman he knew," Artemis said. "Because she was the most famous woman in the world and she wanted to marry him," she added a few minutes later. "Because the only way he could have her was to marry her," she concluded.

"Yet he must have known that Maria would never leave him, no matter what he did," I added. "Or else he would never have married Jackie."

Artemis shook her head, still confused as many unspoken thoughts passed between the two of us. We both knew that Aristo had never expected his marriage to Jackie to improve his business relations with America. Personally, I had seen on my desk the often negative results of this marriage. There were some Americans who were angered by Aristo's impudence, his audacity in marrying America's most celebrated woman, and removing this American treasure from their soil. This was too bold a crime to ignore and there would be a price to pay. Perhaps a deal would be ignored or a promise broken. Or an oil refinery removed farther away from his control. Whatever the reason, Aristotle Onassis' relations with American businessmen and government officials did not improve after his marriage to Jackie Kennedy.

The other relations that did not improve in the first few years of his marriage to Jackie were those between her and his children. There was no doubt that Christina was willful and difficult, that she despised Jackie before the woman even became her stepmother. But Jackie was particularly abhorrent to both of Aristo's children. There might not have been much Jackie could have done to make Christina love her, yet she never tried.

One night, after a particularly unpleasant evening with her niece and her sister-in-law, Artemis confided her fears about her brother's wife to me. "I worry that Jackie is too much of an egotist," she told me. "She loves her own children and she loves Aristo, but she also loves herself. Perhaps that self-love is what helped her endure the terrible tragedies that might have shattered a weaker woman. She is so immersed in herself, in her own needs, in her material possessions and her love for Greece that she cannot be bothered making the gargantuan effort it would take to have become a role model or even a friend for Christina. So she simply never tried. Do you think I am right, Kiki?"

As much as it hurt me to do so, I had no choice but to agree with Artemis. We were all so delighted that she had fallen in love with Greece, but Artemis and Aristo would have been a lot happier had she fallen a little bit in love with Christina. But Jackie was too busy taking care of herself to tend to the needy Christina. She never considered

Christina a daughter, for she would never have wanted a daughter as untidy, spoiled, miserable, confused, and often unattractive as Christina. It was much easier to join the ranks of those who could not deal with Christina than to have grown to love or even care for her. I do not think Aristo blamed Jackie for her lack of affection for his daughter, but I do think he was disappointed by it. And Jackie's poor treatment of his daughter came back, not so many years later, to haunt Jackie herself.

Although I was in some respects able to understand Jackie's lack of love for Christina, I was never able to comprehend her inability to develop some sort of a relationship with her stepson. Granted, Alexander also wanted nothing more than for his parents to remarry, but he was an overly sensitive young man who could have been won over by Jackie. But with him, as with Christina, she never even tried. And, through a terrible act of fate over which he had no control, he too made her pay for that failure.

But Jackie's failures with her stepchildren were not the only shadows on the sunny days Aristo and Jackie spent together. One more that came to haunt them arrived in the letters Jackie had written to Roswell Gilpatric, one of her former suitors. In February 1970, some of these letters to Gilpatric ended up in American newspapers and magazines. The last of these letters, sent to Gilpatric from the *Christina* during Jackie's honeymoon on October 13, 1968, included the line, "I hope you know all you were and are and will ever be to me. With my love, Jackie."

Since part of my responsibilities was to receive and translate into Greek whatever newspaper articles the Olympic Airways correspondence staff found concerning the family, I was the first to view these letters. The letters were, of course, a great source of embarrassment to Mr. Onassis and his family. In his typically proud manner, denying that he had been humiliated, Mr. Onassis refused to discuss the letters with his family or with the press. Yet the fact that he appeared in Paris at Maxim's with Maria on May 21, 1970, and willingly posed with her for photographers was perceived by some of the personnel at Olympic Airways as revenge for his wife's indiscreet letters. Naturally, Christina found the incident humorous and encouraging and delighted in talking about it to whoever would listen to her. The person who listened the longest and most happily was, of course, her brother.

Still, despite this embarrassment and the problems with his children, Mr. and Mrs. Aristotle Onassis made a determined effort to make their marriage, as unorthodox as it might appear to others, work. And for many days during their first years together, it did seem that they were succeeding.

Many afternoons, the two of them would take long walks around Skorpios, walking hand in hand, talking contentedly and continuously. Sometimes, he would recite poetry to her in Greek, and even though she could not understand the words he spoke, she cried at the beauty of his recitation. Other times, she read passages to him from a book she adored and he walked slowly and concentrated on her every word, smoking his cigar and nodding his head in agreement. Or they simply laughed and talked about other people and amused each other with their wry senses of humor.

One day, however, they were gone on their walk for a much longer time than usual, so some of the personnel from the *Christina* went looking for them. They finally found the two of them, long after it had turned dark, trapped by heavy foliage, which they needed a hatchet to cut through. Jackie was still distraught when they finally returned to the ship. "I was worried that we would never get out of that forest," she told me. "I was frightened by the lizards and the mice, but mostly, I was terrified that someone would harm the two of us."

"Don't be silly," Mr. Onassis laughed. "I kept telling you there was never any danger for us. I never carry any money. Besides, if someone wants to kill me, he will find me. No matter what I do." Jackie shook her head angrily and walked away from him.

There were other times, however, when Aristo made Jackie laugh with delight. One other day, the two of them were walking alone on Skorpios, just enjoying each other's company. Suddenly, Aristo dropped Jackie's hand and, before her startled eyes, began to climb a tree directly in front of them. "What ever are you doing, Aristo?" she yelled, but he ignored her and continued to climb higher among the branches of the tree. "Come down now!" she urged him when she began to lose sight of him as he disappeared among the higher branches of the tree.

"Okay, my darling," he finally answered her. "I am coming down now."

Then she heard a terrible sound, like that of a breaking limb. "Aristo!" she screamed. "Are you all right?"

There was silence for a while, then she heard her husband's voice, much louder than before now. "Get Yiannis!" he shouted to her. "Go to the *Christina* and get Yiannis! Tell him I need help quickly."

Jackie took right off and ran all the way back to the Christina where she found Yiannis, one of her husband's favorite employees on the Christina, and told him of his boss's problem. Yiannis raced back to the tree with Jackie, expertly climbed up the tree, and carried his boss back down on his strong back. Once Aristo was safely back on the ground, Jackie took a look at him and began to laugh uncontrollably. His pants were ripped on the seat and both legs, and his shirt was covered with dirt, and his head with leaves. "You look like you were in a terrible fight," she said to him when she was able to stop laughing.

"Well, it was a fight I lost," Aristo said softly.

"Oh, Aristo," Jackie said sweetly, as she wrapped his arm in hers and headed back to the *Christina* with him. "You have to remember that we are not as young as we think we are, my darling."

"For once," Yiannis told me as he finished telling the story to me the next day, "Megalos was silent and simply nodded his agreement."

Often, Jackie enjoyed being alone on the island, having massages, reading on the beach, and swimming. Although there was no doubt she was far more protected from the relentless glare of the paparazzi who had hounded her before her marriage to Aristo, she was not immune from their attacks in Greece. Here, she preferred to swim in the nude, and photographers with expensive equipment were often able to take embarrassing pictures of her. Many times I paid large amounts of money to keep those photos out of the newspapers. Yet each time she just shrugged and smiled. "I have to live my life," she told me. "If I think about the photographers all the time, I will not be able to move out of my bed in the morning."

The problems with the photographers, however, grew worse with time. One photographer especially, Nikos Koulouris, did all he could to destroy the peace and pleasure of Jackie's life in Greece. Koulouris was a small, nasty man who dedicated his life to snapping photographs of Jackie. He would swim to shore in Skorpios, or hide behind a clump of bushes, or race a speedboat up to where Jackie sat or lay on the beach just to surprise her and take her picture. And he did not care if Aristo was with her.

One day I was enjoying a quiet lunch with Jackie and Aristo at Nikos Kominatos, one of their favorite spots, a beautiful bar overlooking the ocean in the port of Nydri, on Levkas, the island next to Skorpios. The two of them were in wonderful moods and were laughing and joking with each other. Suddenly, just when we started to eat our lunch, Koulouris leapt out of a group of trees near where we were sitting and began taking pictures of Jackie. Aristo flew out of his chair, his face filled with fury, and began to scream at Koulouris. "Who do you think you are, you stupid man!" he screamed. "Why do you not leave Jackie alone? Are you crazy! Go away!"

When Koulouris refused to move and continued to snap his pictures, Aristo pulled Jackie out of her chair, lifted up her skirt, and shouted, "Here! Are you happy now? Is this the photograph you want? Then take it and get the hell away from us!"

Jackie turned bright red and, for a moment, looked as if she were going to faint. I could barely breathe. But when Koulouris snapped his picture and then vanished from sight, she smoothed her dress back down and sank back into her chair. When Aristo finally sat back down also, she stared silently at him for a few minutes and then slowly began to eat her lunch again.

Koulouris came to my office with the photograph the next day and I paid him a large amount of money for the negative and the pictures. And then I destroyed them. Over the years, I paid him a small fortune for pictures of Jackie and Princess Radziwill swimming nude, or of Aristo and Christina or Alexander and Fiona, pictures that the family did not want to see published. We never knew when he was suddenly going to appear out of the water or the woods and ruin a beautiful day for Jackie or Aristo and their families and guests.

Yet, despite the constant hounding by Koulouris, Jackie continued to pursue the outdoor activities she adored. Often, when she was in Glyfada, she was driven to an area outside of Athens, called Kafissia, where she could ride beautiful horses for hours. The owner of the stables where Jackie rode, however, frequently complained to me that Jackie never tipped him for his services. One day she gave him a bag of pistachio nuts for his two children, for which he thanked her. He did tell me, however. that she could ride for hours and always seemed to find it difficult to conclude her ride. A few times, Mr. Onassis came with her and watched her ride for a few moments before he left. He made it very clear that he did not want a horse to ride, but he enjoyed watching his wife ride. The times he came with his wife, he made certain the owner of the stable was well paid for his services.

Many times when I was working, Jackie would call me and ask if it was all right to bother her husband for a moment. I never hesitated to put her calls through. When she called to ask Aristo to meet her for lunch, he never refused, canceling an appointment if it was necessary. Sometimes, before going out for lunch with Jackie, he would ask to borrow my comb and mirror so that he could fix his thick silver hair before she arrived. I always kept a fresh comb in my purse for such occasions, but once when I was on the phone, he opened my pocketbook, searching for a comb, and pulled out my sanitary napkin. I was so embarrassed I nearly died. But he merely held it up and laughed heartily, before putting it back in my bag and continuing his search for the comb.

There was a period of a few months, however, when Jackie did not appear in Greece at all. We soon learned that she had plastic surgery in New York and stayed there to recover before risking the sunshine and photographers in Skorpios. Apparently, it was a face-lift, and Jackie looked prettier and healthier when she returned to Greece. But none of us talked about it. We just told her she looked wonderful and she smiled her usual enigmatic smile. Many times I discussed my own skin concerns with Jackie, who patiently explained the benefits of several different facial creams, including one of her favorites, Pierre Ange, which I routinely ordered for her from Paris.

Like Maria before her, Jackie spent a considerable amount of her time in Greece entertaining the famous celebrities who visited the *Christina.* Richard Burton, Elizabeth Taylor, Liza Minnelli, Frank Sinatra, Rudolf Nureyev, the Forbes family, the Rothschilds, and Prince Rainier and Princess Grace, along with many well-known heads of oil corporations, such as J. Paul Getty, or prominent socialites, were just some of the famous people who spent time with Mr. Onassis and Jackie during their marriage. Because Mr. Onassis abhorred schedules, it was rare that he would arrange for such company weeks in advance. More often, he and Jackie would decide on the spur of the moment that they desired someone to visit them. Once they had decided who they wanted to visit them, whether it was a friend such as Hakotis, the antiques dealer, or a celebrity such as Frank Sinatra, Mr. Onassis would call me and ask me to make the necessary arrangements for their guest. The first thing I would do would be to call their future guests and inform them that Mr. and Mrs. Onassis would like them to arrive on the *Christina* as soon as possible. Then I would relate the information about the next available Olympic Airways flight and make all the necessary travel arrangements for them. It was extremely rare that a guest would refuse such an invitation.

Mr. Onassis' favorite guests were often the same as his wife's: members of the Kennedy family. Many times he urged her to invite her brother-in-law Ted Kennedy or her mother-in-law, Rose, or other members of the family to Skorpios. He was pleased that Mrs. Jackie maintained close relations with her former in-laws and always welcomed them to his homes. When Ted was a guest on the *Christina*, Mr. Onassis could sit for hours discussing world history and politics with him. Mr. Onassis was also generous to the senator's political campaigns and made liberal contributions to them.

Not all guests, however, were always warmly favored by Mr. Onassis. One particular time, Mr. Onassis told me that he and Mrs. Jackie would like to have Rudolf Nureyev visit them for a week on the *Christina*, as soon as possible. I knew that the celebrated dancer was not one of Mr. Onassis' prized guests but that Jackie enjoyed his company immensely. Often, when Nureyev was in Greece, Jackie would meet him for lunch in Athens and occasionally took Artemis with her. This time, however, I called Mr. Nureyev, extended the invitation, which he graciously and immediately accepted, and scheduled his flights on Olympic Airways. A few hours before Mr. Nureyev was due to arrive in Athens, however, Mr. Onassis called me and informed me that he had changed his mind and did not want Mr. Nureyev on the *Christina*. Instead of arranging for him to come to Skorpios, I was to book him into the Astir Palace Vouliagmeni in Athens for the coming week.

Once Mr. Nureyev was settled in his hotel, he called me. "Miss Feroudi," he greeted me, clearly annoyed, "I do not understand what is happening. I am supposed to be on the *Christina*, but I am in this hotel. What has happened?"

"Oh, Mr. Nureyev," I said as sweetly as I could. "I am so sorry. Mr. Onassis has had an unforeseen problem with one of his tankers. I personally am unable even to locate him at this moment. All I know is that he felt very badly he was going to be tied up with this urgent business matter and he asked me to check you into the hotel until he is free to greet you himself. Please make yourself comfortable and let me know anything I can do to make you happy while you are here."

For the entire week, both Mr. and Mrs. Onassis avoided Mr. Nureyev and kept him in the hotel. The day Nureyev was scheduled to leave Athens, Mr. Onassis had him delivered to the *Christina,* where he spent the day and was flown back to Athens in time to make his evening flight. I felt terrible for Mr. Nureyev, but I knew there was nothing I or Mrs. Onassis could do to make Aristo change his mind. I also knew that Mr. Nureyev, like all of Aristo's guests, would return to Greece the moment he received a call from me, extending my employer's gracious invitation.

When the invited guest did make it to Skorpios, however, the plans were fun-filled and lavish, even though Mr. and Mrs. Onassis did not spend every available second with their guest. While Jackie and Aristo always had appetizers and dinner with their guests, they did not feel obliged to entertain their guests all moments of the day and night. Chris-Crafts were available to ferry the guests to nearby islands for shopping or sightseeing, and the island of Skorpios had many possibilities of activities for all hours of the day. A guest could swim in the ocean or in the pool, take long walks, alone or perhaps with his host or hostess, read, watch a movie or listen to beautiful music. In the evening, the host usually was at his finest, making certain the foods were prepared according to his guest's wishes. Appetizers were served around the pool area, where guests could sit and watch the sunset and talk about politics or literature or merely gossip about those who were absent. After appetizers, dinner was served in the formal dining room, where much attention was paid to the guests' particular tastes and wine preferences. After a long and sumptuous dinner, Mr. Onassis often supplied a bouzoukia band and a singer to entertain his guests on the dance floor, which had replaced the pool, often until the sun rose. The next day, however, it was not unusual for Mr. Onassis to have disappeared to London or Rome on business before his guest awoke, yet he could return as soon as in eighteen hours or perhaps not for a week.

One guest whom both Mr. and Mrs. Onassis always enjoyed was Frank Sinatra. Mr. Sinatra was polite and pleased when I called to extend the invitation to come to the *Christina*. When he arrived on the boat, he was always making jokes and laughing. Sometimes, especially when Jackie asked him, he would sing a song for them. Alexander and Christina also enjoyed Mr. Sinatra's visits and liked to be in attendance when he arrived on the *Christina*.

There were few guests whom Aristo invited to Skorpios whose company Jackie did not appear to enjoy. Most times, she was relaxed on the *Christina*, and content to let Aristo smoke his Havana cigars, savor his ouzo from Mytilene, and enjoy his guests. I was amazed at the way he would just sit there, either in one of his favorite chairs in the main living room or out on the deck, smoke his cigar, and stare out at the sea, sometimes even fingering his fourteen orange and green rosary beads, while the most fascinating conversations were taking place around him. It would seem as if he were far away from the group gathered around him, not hearing the words that were being spoken. Yet, suddenly, after the conversation was over, he would add something that was very intelligent and thought-provoking and showed that he had indeed heard every word. Jackie seemed proud of her husband's intelligence and would smile broadly as he spoke.

However, not every evening on the *Christina* was pure bliss. Not even when the two of them were all alone enjoying a specially prepared romantic dinner. One of the waiters told me that one evening while he was serving dinner to the two of them, Mr. Onassis had told him it was all right for him to clear the table. Suddenly, however, Jackie declared, "It is not time to clear the table. I will tell you when it is."

The busboy stared at Mr. Onassis, who shrugged and told him to listen to his wife. Jackie smiled and a few minutes later, she called him back and told him it was time to clear the dishes. This time, Mr. Onassis said nothing, but he did not look unhappy at all. That happened often, the busboy told me. He considered it examples of Mrs. Jackie just wanting to get the last word.

But there were other examples of her getting the last word. One day, she appeared at lunch a few minutes late and found that Mr. Onassis was already halfway through his lunch. She sat down for a moment, spoke to her husband, and then waited silently as the waiter was summoned to their table, and then removed all the dishes and began to serve the two of them the first course of their meal. Mr. Onassis did not complain, and finished every morsel of food that was served to him that afternoon.

At other times, when she was late for a meal or an appointment, however, Mr. Onassis was not as considerate to his wife. Like most Greek men, when Mr. Onassis was on time for social functions, he could not tolerate his wife being late. If he had been out partying the night before, he might be late for an important meeting at his office the next morning, but for the most part, he was ready to leave his home for a social engagement at close to the appointed time. Mrs. Jackie, however, was notoriously and significantly late. "If you are late tonight, honey," he told her one day before they left to get ready for a dinner party, "I will leave without you." When she was an hour late, he left without her. That night, Mrs. Jackie remained by herself on the *Christina* after her husband had been sped away alone for an evening in Athens. The employees on the boat told me she looked furious when she was told her husband had departed and would not return until well after midnight. She retired to the suite she shared with him, angrily slamming the door behind her.

If that scene had happened with Maria, she would have been screaming and yelling for hours; however, Jackie would never publicly display such hysteria, for she was always, above all else, a lady who knew how to handle her husband. She might slam a door, but most times she held her tongue and remained perfectly calm. "Do not worry," she would say to him when she saw him becoming upset and angry over something. "It will be all right, Ari." She would compliment him on his suit or tell him how handsome he looked that day, and keep flattering him until she saw a change in his face and mood. He was a smart and sensitive man, and he had to know that she was manipulating him. Yet if he did, he never seemed to mind.

She also knew that when he was upset or in trouble, he tended to eat lightly, only bread and cheese, and go to bed early and sleep for many hours. When she saw him acting like that, she did not argue with him. Instead, she allowed him the peace and quiet he needed and waited patiently for him to return to his normal lifestyle. And when he did return, he could be utterly charming. And generous. And adoring of his wife. So many evenings when she would walk into the main dining room of the ship, he would stand up and make certain every guest noticed her. As she laughed softly, he would hold her hand and draw her closer to him. "Look at my angel," he would urge his guests as he kissed her in front of everyone. "Has anyone ever seen a more beautiful angel than my Jackie?" And she would smile and squeeze his hand as he led her to her seat, basking in his outspoken affection.

There were also many times when I personally witnessed the adoration she held for her husband. One day when I went to visit Jackie in the pink house, she was writing in her journal, something she did nearly every day. That day, however, surrounded by the luscious wildflowers in her garden, she was so absorbed in her writing that she scarcely noticed my approach. "Oh, I would love to know the secrets that you write there," I told her when she finally looked up and motioned for me to join her. "How much will you charge me for a small glimpse into your journal?"

"Oh, Kiki," she laughed. "I will tell you all the secrets you want to know for no money." And then her face turned more serious. "But the first secret you have to know is that my journal is my *Odyssey* and Aristo is my Odysseus. Surely, you can understand why I feel that way, can you not?"

I was astonished by her passion and her earnestness. Rarely did she exhibit such emotions in front of me. "Oh, yes, I can," I agreed.

Jackie closed her journal and put down her pen. She spoke slowly and softly, and I strained to listen to her words. "Like Odysseus, Aristo is shrewd and clever, generous and noble. Even when the sea nymph Calypso offers Odysseus immortality to stay with her, he refuses, desiring only to return to his wife Penelopi in Ithaki, and remains imprisoned on her island of Ogygia for seven years. Can you imagine foregoing eternal life to return to the woman you love?

"And when he is finally released from Calypso's clutches, he endures overwhelming hardships in his determination to return to his beloved Penelopi and Ithaki. He survives the attacks of the lotus eaters and blinds the Cyclops, winning the hatred of Poseidon. The unfavorable winds blow him back into the hands of his enemies. All but one of his ships are destroyed by the cannibal Laestrygonians, and the enchantress Circe turns his men into swine. He descends into Hades, avoids Scylla and Charybdis, and sails past the Sirens with wax in his men's ears, but ties himself to the mast so he can enjoy their song. Even when he finally reaches his precious Ithaki, disguised as a beggar, he remains in the hut of the his faithful swineherd while he plots to remove his wife's relentless suitors from his house. Finally, with the help of his son Telemachus, he shoots down the suitors with his bow and is, at long last, united with his wife and aged father and mother and reestablished as king of Ithaki.

"Aristo has fought so many wars to reach the success he now has, and every day I feel as if he goes out to fight yet another battle to return to his beloved Ithaki. And I, like Penelopi, will be waiting for his triumphant return to his glorious kingdom."

I was not certain whether I should smile or cry when she finished her story. She was so serious and so intense with each word that she spoke. I knew at that moment that I would never forget one word that she had spoken to me. I was not surprised that she knew all the details of this famous epic poem by Homer. I had seen her reading it many times. "But where is the shroud you had to weave to hold off your suitors, Penelopi?" I finally asked, keeping my face as serious as hers.

"Ah, yes," she said, smiling now. "My shroud for my father-in-law. I unraveled it every night so that I could stall them one more day. But, seriously, Kiki, do you not think Aristo would have made a perfect Odysseus? He has such strength and brilliance. No matter where he was taken, he would somehow manage to return to his cherished Ithaki. No one could keep him away from his kingdom."

"Or from his Penelopi," I added, and she shook her head.

"He told me that Tina was not a good Penelopi," she said. "She did not wait faithfully for him, ignoring all the suitors who only wanted his kingdom and his riches. But I will wait faithfully."

I could not tell for certain if she was joking with me, the way she often did. So I nodded and let her go back to her writing. That day, as I watched her writing in her journal, I would have given anything to have a quick glimpse into its pages so that I could see for myself the journey on which her Odysseus traveled. I knew how much he loved the island of Ithaki, where Odysseus was born, how much he appreciated the physical beauty of the island, with its luscious green plants and its history of inspiration for poets and artists throughout the ages. So often he and Jackie would travel to Ithaki, which was close to Skorpios, for the day and walk slowly through the archaeological treasures of the island, seemingly almost as comfortable on that island as they were on the island he owned.

That afternoon, however, I sat quietly in my chair and occupied myself with my own thoughts as Aristo's Penelopi reclaimed her pen and lost herself in the mythical but glorious world of love and war. I had heard the tales of Camelot and King Arthur and knew, despite the books that had been written to deflate that legend, about the other mythical world Jackie Kennedy had inhabited with her first husband. Arthur might have been neither loyal nor perfect, yet she had been his beautiful Guinevere.

Still, try as I could to stay in that romantic moment, I could not ignore the sad thoughts that filled my mind. Jackie could create whatever fictional works she desired and people it with heroes like Odysseus and heroines like Penelopi. Yet in the real world there were people like Maria and Christina and Alexander and Roswell Gilpatric. And, like the assassin's bullets and the tales of indiscretion, they would never leave the king and queen alone to live happily forever after in the legendary worlds of Camelot or Ithaki. Instead, they were destined to spend their days on a glorious ship that sailed from port to port in search of elusive happiness, or in a villa beneath the bellies of the planes that roared off into the sky above them, leaving behind the smoke and flames that would inevitably consume them and their audacious dreams.

Chapter Ten

Visiting New York with Jackie

RARELY A day went by when Artemis did not discuss with me some issue concerning her brother and his second wife. I listened as attentively as I could and offered whatever advice I thought might be helpful.

"Jackie is very happy here," Artemis would usually begin a discussion about her American sister-in-law. "Don't you think she is very happy here? Don't you think she is very happy being Aristo's wife?" I understood from the beginning of that marriage that an important part of my responsibility as Mr. Onassis' secretary and Mrs. Artemis' confidante was to ensure that everything be done to make the new Mrs. Onassis as secure and comfortable as possible in her new role. While there was no way I could make her husband surrender his mistress or force his children to adore her, I could make her daily life as pleasant and uncomplicated as possible. Strangely enough, although Mrs. Jackie was twenty years older than I, and led a life I could only imagine, as I performed this job, the two of us became good friends. I know I should have been intimidated by her, but from the first moment I met her at Mrs. Artemis' home, I never was.

The truth was that Mrs. Jackie and I had fun together. Often. When she was in Greece, we spoke nearly every day as I made her travel arrangements, paid her bills, or advised her on her husband's business plans or daily moods. I never expected that our relationship would continue when I traveled to New York on business, but almost from the beginning of her marriage to my employer, it did. Whenever she heard that I would be in New York for business with Mr. Costas Konialidis or just for shopping or fun, she insisted that I stay in her apartment at 1040 Fifth Avenue, rather than in the company suite at the Pierre Hotel. "It is the least I can do for you, Kiki," she would say, sounding pleased that we would both be in the city at the same time. "You take care of me in Greece. Let me take care of you in New York."

Although I was flattered by her invitation, I did not accept every time I visited New York. Many of the times I came to New York either on business or pleasure, I traveled with Costas and Ritsa Konialidis, and stayed with them at the Pierre Hotel. Other times, I enjoyed staying by myself, so I could devote my free time to one of the great joys of my life: shopping. I adore wandering from store to store and shopping on my own schedule, not worrying about meeting someone for dinner or fulfilling any social obligations.

Each time I did accept Jackie's invitation, however, she would send a driver for me at the airport and was often waiting to greet me at her apartment when I arrived. "Welcome, Kiki," she would say as she kissed me in the traditional Greek way. "I am so glad you could come here for a little visit." She always looked different in New York than she did in Greece, since she did dress more formally in New York, favoring suits and short dresses, and dressier shoes. I knew from the bills I paid for her clothes that she bought many of them from Cardin, St. Laurent, and Courreges, and I noticed that she wore more of these designers' apparel in New York than she did in Greece, where her clothing was less formal and more free-spirited. I saw more of her long skirts, peasant blouses, expensive belts, and pastel-colored short sleeveless dresses with matching jackets, along with the perfunctory white pants, shirts, sandals, and T-shirts, in Greece than I did in New York. In New York, also, her hair was rarely covered with a white scarf the way it was so often in Greece. I did notice that she walked faster in New York than she did in Greece, but everyone else did, too. Yet, other than that, she didn't look that different walking out of her Fifth Avenue apartment than she did leaving the pink house in Skorpios or the villa in Glyfada. Most important, always, she wore her big sunglasses and her mysterious smile.

The Fifth Avenue apartment was very spacious, with an abundance of windows and five bedrooms. Each room in the apartment on the fifteenth floor, overlooking Central Park, was filled with lovely antiques and beautiful paintings. As she did with her decorations in Greece, Jackie favored light colors in her New York apartment. The overriding colors in the apartment were white and light pink, creating an aura of warmth and beauty. I could feel her presence in each room, just the way I did in the pink house in Skorpios. She had a wonderful talent for selecting furniture and accessories that created a glamorous yet comfortable setting. In New York, more than in Greece, her home was filled with mementos and photographs of her handsome Kennedy family, each picture worth staring at for long periods of time. I was amazed at how in each photograph Jackie and her late husband were always smiling, looking not just handsome or healthy, but perpetually happy. It seemed impossible that horrible things, like assassinations and flagrant infidelity, could happen to members of this beautiful family.

I was always delighted to see that her New York apartment also contained many photographs of her present life in Greece. Pictures of her and Aristo, usually in a boat in Skorpios or sitting together on the *Christina,* were in lovely silver frames, positioned beside photographs of Jackie and Artemis walking along the beach in Glyfada or sitting on the *Christina.* Small Greek statues and other antiques she bought in Greece looked natural and perfectly in place on her tables or shelves.

Whenever I visited her, Jackie asked many questions about her Greek sisters-in-law, and I would fill her in on their activities. Even though she kept in touch with Artemis almost every day, she still wanted to hear particulars about her and Kalliroi and Merope from me. Yet when I returned to the apartment after a day of shopping, she was equally as interested in my every purchase. "Oh, my," she would say as I walked in with my driver for the day, the two of us laden with all my bundles, "I can see you have had a most successful day. Come show me exactly what you have bought." After my driver left, I would open every box or bag and tell her where I had bought each item and how much I had paid for it. She was one of the few people in my life who understood how I could not buy just one pair of eyeglasses or one sweater, and she would praise every one of the ten pairs of glasses and each of the five black sweaters that I had bought that day.

"You like this sweater, Mrs. Jackie?" I would ask as I held up yet one more sweater to my chest.

"Oh, yes, Kiki," she would say sincerely. "It is the prettiest black sweater I have ever seen. And the price you paid was wonderful."

The views from her apartment were spectacular as I gazed down at Central Park. One window captured the tennis court in the park, and sometimes I would sit there and stare at the players beneath me, intrigued by their stamina and energy.

One day, the children's governess, Martha Sgubin, showed me Jackie's bedroom. Although I was a bit ashamed to be staring at Mrs. Onassis' personal room, I could not help glancing appreciatively at her beautiful handmade bedspread. The books and pictures in the room, along with the charming lamps and interesting antiques, all reminded me of Jackie. I knew how on a rainy day in Greece, she loved to stay in her bedroom at the pink house and read all day long. I could easily imagine her doing the same thing here on a cold, snowy day. All the pieces of furniture, as well as the accessories, were elegant, yet warm; originals, yet comforting. The room, I told myself, as I tried quickly to absorb each small, delightful detail, was pure Jackie.

One of my favorite rooms in the apartment was the library. I knew how much Mrs. Jackie loved books, so I was not surprised that this room was an especially comfortable and beautifully appointed spot. The chairs in the room had deep cushions, as did the elegant bench between them. Eighteenth-century tables were positioned beside the chairs, their surfaces covered with blue glass, Greek worry beads, and baskets of flowers and fruit. Books on art and history competed with books of fiction, on the shelves and on the tables, more books than I could ever imagine one woman reading in a lifetime. But Mrs. Onassis was a voracious reader, and the one person who probably had read all these books. The walls of the room were covered with paintings of horses and photographs of Greece. One particular photograph that I adored was of Skorpios, and I studied it carefully. When Jackie was home, she often lit candles in this room and the sweet and varied scents of the candles filled the library, propelling a visitor to settle into the overstuffed chair, pull any book at all from the shelves of the library, and remain there, perfectly contented, for at least twenty-four hours. This room, more than any other room in the apartment, had a strong Greek flavor. "I want Aristo to be comfortable here," she told me one day. "As comfortable as I am in all his homes."

The first time I stayed in Jackie's apartment, however, I was, regrettably, not the least bit comfortable. "You must sleep in this room, Kiki," Jackie told me when she showed me around the apartment. "It is a very special room and I think you will like it very much."

It was a large room, the biggest one in the house, with a perfect view of Central Park. But one wall was filled by a large portrait of her late husband, President John F. Kennedy. Everywhere I looked, all I could see was that picture. It seemed as if his eyes were following me everywhere I went, almost as if they were moving within his face. For a while, I stared at the picture and gratefully accepted this unique opportunity to view this most famous of men. I studied his half-smiling mouth, his thick reddish hair, his firm jaw, his aquiline nose. He was not merely handsome, I decided; he was almost godlike. Finally, after a long while, I pulled my eyes away from that face and tried to be comfortable in that room. I changed into my nightgown, brushed my hair, and unmade the bed. However, as soon as I lay down on the bed, I knew I could not spend the night there. An hour after I had struggled unsuccessfully to fall sleep, I finally came out of the room and told Jackie, who was still awake in her own room, reading a book, that I could not sleep there.

"I am so sorry," I told her, as I tried to express my feelings to her. The last thing I wanted to do was to hurt her feelings, but I knew I could not survive one more second in that room. "But I feel as if I am in a room where I should not be. The picture of your late husband makes me feel uneasy, as if his spirit is still there. I just don't belong there, Mrs. Onassis."

Jackie closed her book and studied my face for a long time. She looked so sad I was certain she would cry, but even though her eyes were moist, there were no tears. "I know what you are saying, Kiki," she told me. "I sometimes feel the same way. But I was wrong to put you in there. The room is too overpowering for you. Let us find a nice peaceful room where you can get a good night's sleep." And she led me to a guest room, next to Martha Sgubin's room, where I promptly fell asleep. From that night on, every time I came to Fifth Avenue, I slept in that pretty guest room, where I was indeed very comfortable. But I always walked into the room with the late president's remarkable portrait and spent a few minutes gazing affectionately at it.

Some people have written that Jackie did not like Mr. Onassis to be in her Fifth Avenue apartment. That is a terrible lie. Many times when I was in the apartment, he, too, was there. There were nights when he was involved in a late business meeting and he would sleep at his suite in the Pierre Hotel rather than come back to Fifth Avenue very late and awaken Jackie. Yet, so often, when I called him in New York from Greece concerning business or spoke to his New York secretary Georgette Mitzakos, he was staying at Jackie's apartment. When I was there with the two of them, I saw that Jackie did everything she could to make him comfortable. Including making certain they slept together in one bedroom.

As in Greece, however, when Mr. and Mrs. Onassis were in New York together, their schedules, like their interests, were quite different. Mr. Onassis did not enjoy sports, either as a spectator or as a participant, and was eager to spend his days doing business. Sometimes, he attended services in a Greek Orthodox church in New York. In the evenings, he enjoyed dining in fine restaurants with his wife and friends. When he was in the apartment, he loved to listen to beautiful music in the living room, a room decorated primarily in whites, sitting in a comfortable chair beside the piano, his eyes closed with pleasure from the sounds of the classical music he adored. His sleeping hours were always unconventional. He would stay up until four or five in the morning, and unless he had a business appointment in the morning, he might sleep until noon.

Mrs. Onassis, on the other hand, loved to run in Central Park or take long walks there. She adored the theater and could attend a performance every night or afternoon, if possible. When she was home in the apartment, she would read or write for hours at a time. Her sleep habits were more typical than those of her husband. She preferred to go to sleep before midnight and to rise at a normal hour in the morning so that she could see her children off to school or go for a morning run in the park. Both of them spent time talking on the telephone; however, Mr. Onassis could speak to a business associate for several hours at a time, while Jackie's conversations were usually more brief.

One interest they shared, however, was Jackie's children. Even when Mr. Onassis was in New York on important business, he managed to spend time with Caroline and John. As he did in Greece, he devoted whatever spare time he could find to speaking to them, answering their questions and buying them presents. Often, he took them out with him and Jackie for lunch or ice cream or just for a walk in Central Park. When they were outside the apartment, even if Secret Service agents were with them, he always held their hands tightly and protected them.

One afternoon when I was at the New York apartment with Mrs. Jackie, Mr. Onassis decided to take John, who was eight or nine at the time, out for a walk. Jackie and I were looking out the window after they left, watching the two of them head down the street. It was obvious, even from our view, fifteen stories up, that they were involved in a serious conversation. We could see that Aristo was talking to John about something important, gesturing with his free hand that was not holding John's hand, and bending down a bit so that his young friend could hear him easily. It wasn't difficult for us to see also that John was listening carefully to every word his stepfather was speaking to him.

"I used to wonder what they were talking about," Mrs. Onassis said to me when they had disappeared from our view. "One day, I asked Aristo and he told me that he was teaching John how to be a successful man."

"That is a good thing," I said.

"Yes," Mrs. Onassis agreed, looking very serious for a moment. Then she added, "But I have to wonder exactly what he meant."

"Oh, I am sure he is teaching him how to act grown up and serious," I suggested. "Like a grown-up person, not a little boy."

"Oh, dear," Mrs. Onassis said, laughing now. "I just hope he isn't spending all their time together telling John how to get a woman." The two of us laughed for a long time as we imagined such a conversation between the two of them.

There was always a relaxed, comfortable feeling in Jackie's Fifth Avenue apartment. When she was not busy with the children, Martha Sgubin did some cooking for Mrs. Onassis and her children. When Mr. Onassis was there, she even prepared some Greek specialties for him, including a few dishes from his native Smyrna. Mr. Onassis was particularly fond of Martha, who was originally from Spain, and was especially delighted when she surprised him with a Greek dish. The New York apartment, as with all of Mr. Onassis' residences, was well stocked with his favorite cheeses and breads and water and ouzo, which were always flown in for him before he arrived there.

Martha Sgubin, who was around thirty-five or forty when I first met her, was also gracious to me. A kind, rather shy woman with no pretenses, she wore few cosmetics, dressed in a black skirt and simple white blouse, and always looked refreshed and natural when she greeted me in the kitchen. Since I did not like to disturb anyone or have anyone wait on me, I preferred to fix my own breakfast, usually just a slice of toast and a cup of tea. Often Martha and I met early in the morning in the kitchen and relaxed over our tea before the others in the apartment awoke. When she did not get up with her children, Mrs. Onassis often preferred to have her breakfast in her bedroom, where she could relax with her coffee while reading a book or the morning newspaper. Although John was there when I visited Jackie, sometimes Caroline was not present. Jackie explained to me that she was spending time with one of her grandmothers and would return shortly. Other times, John and Caroline were busy with their sporting activities or off with their friends, and I saw little of them.

One of the nicest days Mr. Onassis, Jackie, and I spent together in New York was on a hot summer day in August 1970, when Mr. Onassis decided his driver would take us to someplace in Connecticut for a cool and leisurely lunch. I had finished my work for Mr. Costas Konialidis and was planning to relax that day. I did not want to interfere with whatever plans Mr. and Mrs. Onassis had made and assured them I would be content to spend the day shopping or visiting friends. But, as always, they insisted that I was their guest and I would spend the day with the two of them.

That summer day, Jackie wore, as she did so often, a pastel-colored summer dress, stylish but simple. One of her favorite colors was pink, and that day she looked especially youthful and lovely in her pink dress with its matching jacket and set of beautiful pearls. Her hair was pulled back, and, of course, she wore her big black sunglasses. Mr. Onassis wore, as he so often did in New York, a dark suit and a silk shirt and tie. Two hours later, when we arrived at the restaurant, which was very old, maybe 200 or 300 years old, it was after noon, and there were few people there. It was a charming restaurant, with big wooden tables and comfortable armchairs and pretty bright red, white, and blue tablecloths. Jackie and Mr. Onassis were in wonderful moods and the three of us joked and laughed during the whole meal.

After Mr. Onassis took charge of the ordering, the waiter brought us a tray filled with bright red lobsters, all cooked and warm. While Jackie and I watched and giggled, a waiter put a big red-and-white plastic bib across Mr. Onassis' shirt. Then Mr. Onassis used special metal utensils to break apart the lobsters and serve us delicious lobster meat. Mr. Onassis was very careful to do his work neatly, and Jackie and I praised him many times. I had never before eaten a lobster cooked in such a manner and I was amazed at how much time and effort it took for Mr. Onassis to get us our lobster meat. "Well, what do you think of this New England lobster?" he asked, watching me earnestly as I took my first bite.

"It is delicious," I told him as I chewed the sweet, warm fish. "Much better than any other lobster meat I have ever eaten. You have done a wonderful job of preparing my meal."

Mr. Onassis beamed at my compliment. "It was my pleasure to serve my lovely two companions," he said formally, as he finished serving Mrs. Onassis and me our lunch and poured us some more wine. The waiter brought us big plates of warm sweet corn and crisp french fries and fresh melted butter to eat with our lobsters.

I was surprised to see Mrs. Jackie eat her french fries with her hands. When I hesitated before eating any of my fries, she smiled at me. "It is perfectly acceptable to eat french fries with your hands in America," she informed me as she placed a large fry in some ketchup and ate it hungrily. "It tastes much better that way." And she was right. I watched the way she ate the buttered corn in her hands also, and imitated her manners, instead of using my knife to remove the sweet corn from the cob. It took us a long time to finish that lunch, at least two hours, but every minute of it was wonderful.

As always, there were people eating in the restaurant who recognized Mr. and Mrs. Onassis and were excited to see the two of them eating there. It was so pleasant that there were no photographers to bother us. A couple of the other diners in the restaurant came over to talk to us, and Mr. Onassis was friendly and talkative to them. He had an amazing way of talking to strangers, making them feel as if they were good friends after just a few minutes' discussion. Sometimes, in a restaurant, he would get up in the middle of the meal and walk over to complete strangers. Within minutes, he would be conversing naturally with them, as if they were old friends. Many times, in fancy restaurants, he would end up talking to celebrities he'd never met before but would soon invite to Skorpios as his guests. That day in Connecticut, during our lobster dinner, Jackie did not mind the visitors who came to our table. She was just so happy and free that day.

When we finally left the restaurant after our wonderful lunch and had the driver take us back to New York, Mr. Onassis said we would do this again. Jackie agreed completely. Although we had some wonderful dinners at lovely New York restaurants, such as the Twenty One Club and Cabaret Clark, I do not remember our ever returning to Connecticut for a second meal at that wonderful restaurant.

One other special day the three of us spent together was when we went on an excursion to Hyannisport. We knew that none of Jackie's famous Kennedy relatives would be there, that they were all in Palm Beach for the winter season, but Jackie decided it would be fun for us to take a look at her late husband's home in Cape Cod. I was surprised to see Mr. Onassis dressed in a formal suit, since we were going near the ocean, but Mrs. Jackie was pleased with the way he looked as we got into the car. "Doesn't he look handsome, Kiki?" she asked me as she straightened the red handkerchief in his pocket.

"Oh, yes," I agreed. "But he always looks handsome."

Mr. Onassis was smiling broadly as his driver opened the back door of the Cadillac and let him in. We left early in the morning, before nine, since we had a long ride from New York City to Hyannisport. I sat in the front seat with George so I could see all the lovely sights Jackie pointed out as we drove the five hours to Hyannisport. The day was especially beautiful, not too cold and with lots of bright sunshine.

Jackie was in a wonderful mood during our ride to Hyannisport, joking with Aristo and explaining each town we drove through when we entered Massachusetts. She explained that the highway was always crowded during the summer, but she loved the feel of Cape Cod in the winter, when the tourists were no longer there. Before we got to the Kennedy house, we stopped not too far from Hyannisport in an Italian restaurant that Jackie liked a great deal.

"Well, what do you think of this restaurant, Kiki?" Mr. Onassis asked me after we sat down and ordered our lunch. I never ordered for myself when I was with the two of them. Usually Mr. Onassis ordered for me, since he knew I disliked red meat and preferred fish and pasta. In the United States, he was often partial to spaghetti and frequently ordered that for himself. This day, however, Jackie ordered a flavorful chicken dish for me, which had lots of vegetables and a zesty red sauce. She also ordered dishes of pasta for the three of us.

"I can tell already that it is very special," I answered Mr. Onassis. There was a fire roaring in the fireplace in the cozy dining room, and unusual antiques and memorabilia, some hanging from the ceiling and others resting on the wide-planked wooden floor, filled the room. "The smells coming out of the kitchen are delicious. I know this is going to be a perfect lunch."

"Well, of course, it will be perfect," he said. "My wife selected it."

Jackie loved it when I complimented her in front of her husband. I would always tell him what a fabulous job she was doing decorating the pink house in Skorpios or what a stunning dress she was wearing or how lovely her hair looked. You would think that a beautiful, famous woman like Jackie would be tired of hearing compliments from people, but she was always delighted when I praised her in the presence of Mr. Onassis. If I was ever there when the two of them were disagreeing over something minor, Jackie would ask my opinion. Without hesitation, I took her part and told Aristo his wife was right. He was never angry with me for taking her side, and she offered me one of her beautiful grateful smiles. If it was a serious argument, which did not happen often, however, I knew not to open my mouth.

"Oh, we are going to get fat today, Kiki," Jackie told me when our the large dishes of our food arrived at our table.

"Oh, not you, Mrs. Jackie," I answered her. "You have nothing to worry about. It is me who has to worry about getting fat."

She laughed and ate, as she always did, more than me. Yet I was the one who gained weight, not Mrs. Jackie.

That day, I praised her continually during our lunch, because, as always, her choice of a restaurant or a dish was flawless. Mr. Onassis relaxed during the meal and let his wife assume complete control. It was amazing the way she knew how to behave around her husband. She treated him with so much respect and admiration when he was in charge. Yet when it was her turn to be in control, she fussed over him and cared about nothing except his pleasure. I was always impressed with how clever she was in regard to handling her often moody husband. If he was angry, she let him yell for a minute or two and waited patiently for him to calm down. If he was quiet and didn't want to talk, she would leave him alone and remain silent until that mood too had passed. I never saw his sisters or his daughter master the art of handling his moods quite the way Jackie did. There were, of course, exceptions, but the instances when he exploded viciously with her were rare.

Later that day, as we approached Hyannisport, it did begin to get a bit darker, and Mr. Onassis' driver was worried that it might snow. When he heard on the car radio that an unexpected storm was heading up the coast, we stayed in Hyannisport for only a short time, gazing at the gates surrounding the Kennedy compound, listening to Jackie describe the house where she and her family stayed and all the activities, such as sailing and swimming, that they enjoyed on the ocean during the summer time. I knew that Mr. Onassis had previously been there several times with Mrs. Jackie and had enjoyed his time there very much, but he was silent as she described the estate. We were all a bit subdued during the ride back to New York City, perhaps because we were concerned about the approaching storm or perhaps because we were still full from our heavy lunch or perhaps because we were leaving Jackie some space to be with her sad but beautiful memories.

Another opportunity I had to meet some other members of the Kennedy family happened one summer day when I was staying in New York with Jackie. One of Mr. Onassis' drivers had to drive to Washington on business for him, and Jackie suggested that I accompany him and enjoy a day in the nation's capital. She also promised to make the arrangements for us to visit Ethel early the next morning on our return to New York. I do not remember Mrs. Ethel Kennedy's ever coming to Skorpios to visit Mrs. Onassis, but I had heard many nice things about this widow with the large family, and Mrs. Jackie knew I was anxious to see her and her children.

When the driver and I arrived at Ethel's house, it was barely seven o'clock in the morning, and all the children were sleeping. Ethel was a plain-looking, friendly woman and she seemed delighted to have us visit her, even at such an early hour. She said it was most unusual all her children were still asleep, but I insisted that she not wake them for us. Instead, she took the time to show me each one of her small horde of children. As she led me to each room and told me which child I was looking at, I kept exclaiming, "How many more children do you have, Mrs. Kennedy?"

"Just one more," she would tell me and usher me into the next bedroom. The house itself was large and beautiful, although not as neat as Mrs. Jackie's Fifth Avenue apartment, but Mrs. Ethel was warm and friendly as she served the driver and me coffee in her big kitchen and chattered away with us. I only regret that we did not have more than an hour to spend with this outgoing, pleasant woman.

Jackie and I spent many afternoons together in New York, shopping and visiting museums and having lunch and going to the theater. One afternoon, she took me and Caroline to a musical where there were at least a hundred people dancing on the stage. Again, people stared at Mrs. Jackie, but she concentrated on the play and on Caroline and me.

Shopping with Jackie in New York could be quite an experience.

While I have my sunglasses and black sweater fetishes, Jackie was that way with many different articles of clothing. Once I watched as she ordered ten blouses in the same style and color in Saks Fifth Avenue as well as fifteen sweaters, all black. Jackie performed her shopping exercise in a remarkably short period of time, but by the time she was through, the entire department was a mess and the saleswomen seemed exhausted. I did notice that other shoppers were ignored while all the available saleswomen showered their attention on Mrs. Onassis. Also, none of the saleswomen appeared surprised at Mrs. Jackie's routine, almost as if they'd all done similar transactions for her in the past. We concluded our day with a visit to Lord & Taylor, where she did the same thing with ten pairs of the same black wool pants, all of which she had returned to the store by her driver the next day, and a last-minute run into Bergdorf Goodman's, where she bought two dozen pairs of shoes in under an hour. I was as exhausted as the saleswomen in Saks Fifth Avenue when we finally returned to her apartment.

One other time when Jackie and I went shopping together in New York, I picked out a beautiful thick silver bracelet in a jewelry store called Van Cleef & Arpels. When I went to pay for it, the man told me that Mrs. Onassis had already taken care of it. I was embarrassed, but Jackie was delighted to surprise me that way. To this day, I treasure that wide silver bracelet and wear it often.

During yet another one of our shopping sprees in New York, Jackie bought me a necklace in Tiffany's that was filled with many different stones. It was very beautiful, but too fancy and too heavy for me to wear often. After a few weeks, I returned it to a different jeweler in Athens, and he gave me two smaller pins to wear instead. Another time, however, Jackie gave me a different necklace, not such an expensive one, with gold and blue stones in it. That one I did not even think of exchanging. Several times, Jackie commented on how pretty the silver bracelet or gold-and-blue necklace looked on me, but I am grateful she never asked me one question about the special necklace with all the precious stones that I thoughtlessly returned.

One day, in the summer of 1971, Jackie and I went to lunch with Asta, who was having a long-term relationship with Mr. Onassis' close friend, Costas Gratsos. Asta, who I always thought resembled Doris Day, with her pretty, round face and blond hair and thick bangs, had an apartment in New York and frequently met me when I was in the city. Jackie also enjoyed Asta's company when she and Aristo went out for dinner with her and Costas. After we had our lunch, Jackie said the three of us must order dessert. I was so full, I did not think I could eat another thing. "Oh, we must eat dessert," Jackie told me and Asta. "It's a very hot day, so let's order a little ice cream."

Asta was happy to eat the ice cream, but I was too full. "I will just have some more iced tea," I said, but Jackie insisted that I have the ice cream, too. When the three dishes of ice cream arrived, they were three giant mountains of ice cream, surrounded by bananas. "Oh, my goodness," I said when I saw the waitress carrying the huge dishes to our table. "That must be a mistake. How can we ever finish all that ice cream?"

"That will be no problem," Jackie insisted. "It will be gone in no time." Indeed, both she Asta did not stop eating until all the ice cream was gone from their plates. And the two of them laughed almost the whole time they were eating. No matter how hard I tried, I could not eat more than a few spoonfuls of my rich ice cream. I just let it melt in front of me while my companions savored their huge desserts. When we got up from the table, I wondered if either Jackie or Asta would feel ill, but they both looked full of energy and were anxious to get out of the restaurant and do some shopping. That day, I bought a radio and both Jackie and Asta bought some clothes. Neither one of them tried anything on. Maybe they just didn't want to waste their time. Or maybe they were feeling too full.

One of my visits to Jackie's Fifth Avenue apartment, however, was not such a happy time. It was a winter day and George had dropped me off to do some shopping by myself, promising to meet me two hours later in front of Alexander's department store. Unfortunately, whenever I go shopping I lose track of the time and I am usually late for whomever I am supposed to meet. When I finally got to Alexander's, I was over an hour late, and George was nowhere to be seen. I was certain he had been forced to drive around the block and would return in a few minutes. While I waited for him, I opened my wallet to see how much money I had left. I was holding one hundred dollars when a man came out of nowhere, hit me in the face with his fist, and grabbed the bills out of my hand. I was lying on the sidewalk when George and the black Cadillac came racing up to the sidewalk. George, who is a very big man, jumped out of the car and carried me into it. I was hysterical, crying and screaming. There was a lot of blood coming out of my nose and I was so confused in my head that I could not calm down.

When George carried me into Jackie's apartment, she too started to scream. She wanted to take me to the hospital, but I was too frightened to go. "Please, Kiki," she told me. "Let me take you to the emergency room, where a doctor can look at you and make you feel better."

"Oh, no," I cried even louder now. "I cannot bear to go to a hospital. Please do not make me go." Finally she gave up trying to convince me to go the hospital and made me lie down on the couch while she gently and thoroughly cleaned up my nose and face. My nose hurt terribly, but she was hopeful only the inside had been damaged. Every time she touched my nose with her finger, I wanted to cry out in pain but I kept myself quiet. When she put cold compresses on my nose, the pain lessened a bit. All night long, Jackie sat by my side and took care of me, applying fresh ice on my nose and under my eyes.

When I remembered that she had theater tickets for that night, I begged her to go. "Have you lost your mind?" she asked me. "Do you think I would go out and leave you alone tonight?" I tried to convince her that I was feeling better but she would not move from my side.

Caroline was visiting her grandmother that night, but John was home and was every bit as kind to me as his mother was. He insisted on feeding me strawberries, which he was certain would make me feel better. He worked so hard to get me the biggest strawberries he could find in the kitchen and would cut them up into small pieces for me to eat. I wasn't the least bit hungry, but I would never have refused one bite of his beautiful strawberries.

Even when I finally fell asleep, Jackie remained by my bed all night long. Every time I opened my eyes, she was beside me, applying fresh ice to my face and looking terribly worried. I felt so bad that I had caused her such pain that I tried to act as if I were fine. But I knew she did not believe me when I told her my nose was no longer aching.

After that day, I tried to be much more careful whenever I was in New York. I was very frightened of being mugged again and I became much more suspicious of people on the streets. I just couldn't feel safe there again. One night when I was visiting Jackie and Mr. Onassis, Mr.

Onassis proposed that the three of us go out for dinner in Connecticut. But this time, he wanted us to take a slow trip and do some sightseeing in the car. He especially wanted me to see some of the sights in New York and Connecticut that I had never seen. I sat in the front seat of the black Cadillac with the driver, and Mr. and Mrs. Onassis were sitting behind us. When we were driving through one section of New York, Mr. Onassis yelled to his driver to slow down. "You are driving way too fast here," he told him. "Kiki can not see anything this way."

The driver seemed upset with Mr. Onassis' order to slow down, but he obeyed and began to drive slowly. "This is Harlem," Mr. Onassis said, and I started to open my window to look outside a bit more clearly. At that exact moment, a large man plunged his fist onto the front of our car and glared menacingly at us. In his hand was a big knife. Jackie screamed in fright and Mr. Onassis yelled, "Kiki, do not open the window! This man could kill us." I was so terrified I could barely move, but I was somehow able to close the window the small amount I had opened it.

"Didn't you hear about Nancy Lincoln?" Mr. Onassis asked me when his driver had safely gotten our car out of Harlem and we could all speak again. I shook my head. Nancy was a warm and outgoing woman, the wife of Mr. Onassis' personal lawyer, Tom Lincoln, and the two of us were good friends. Often, when I was in New York together, I had dinner with her and Tom, and I always saw Nancy when she came to Greece. But I had not heard about anything bad happening to her. "She was robbed twice in New York," Mr. Onassis continued. "One time she was in her car, waiting for the light to change to green. Somebody broke open her window and stole her pocketbook with all her money. It took about ten seconds for the man to rob her. She was very lucky she was not hurt, but she was shaken up for weeks afterward."

Jackie looked as pale and frightened as I after Mr. Onassis told his story. Obviously, she had not heard the story about Nancy Lincoln, either. "You always have to be careful in New York, Kiki," she told me, moving forward and touching my shoulder gently. "You can never forget what happened to you outside Alexander's. Promise me you will never take any chances in this city." And I did. The three of us ended up having dinner in New York that night, at the Waldorf-Astoria, rather than heading into Connecticut. I do not remember what I had for dinner, but I do remember that I was trembling all during the meal and that neither Jackie nor I ate very much. Mr. Onassis, however, ate a huge meal and entertained us with jokes and stories all night long.

Mrs. Onassis had a much easier time protecting me than she did her husband. "Look at him," she would remark unhappily to me when the three of us were leaving the apartment. "He is not even wearing a coat. You tell him how cold it is outside, Kiki, and that he should dress more warmly. After all, New York is much colder now than Greece. He will get a terrible cold here and will be very sick."

"She s right, Mr. Onassis," I would say. "You should be dressing better." But he ignored both of us and strode out into the brisk New York air without even his overcoat.

Mrs. Onassis could no more get her husband to protect his life than she could get him to take care of his health. "You should have a bodyguard here in New York, Ari," she told him all the time. "This is a dangerous city and you need protection."

"Why do I need protection, honey?" he would ask her. "I am a poor man. My pockets are empty and I have no money. Who will rob me here?"

"He is impossible, Kiki," she would then say to me. "You talk to him. He will not listen to me."

"You are a famous man, Mr. Onassis," I would say. "You have to be very careful here. Everybody here is jealous of you."

But, again, he ignored us, convinced that everyone liked him and he was in no danger. So often, in places other than New York, it seemed as if Mr. Onassis was afraid of no one. In 1970, shortly after Mr. Onassis' return to Greece from a trip to New York, one of his Olympic Airways planes, en route from London to Greece, was highjacked. A group of Palestinians insisted that when their plane landed in Greece, Mr. Onassis would personally meet with them to discuss their demands. "You must refuse to go, Mr. Onassis," Miltos Yiannacopoulos told him. "There is no way we can protect you so that you can go onto the plane with those terrorists."

However, Mr. Onassis refused to take Miltos' advice and agreed that the Palestinians could land their plane in Athens and he would meet with them. No one, not even Jackie, could convince him otherwise. When the plane landed in Athens, Mr. Onassis was there to meet them. At the highjackers' request, he removed his jacket and shirt and tie and, wearing only his pants and an undershirt, walked onto the plane to talk to the Palestinians. The airport was filled with junta government troops, who were ready to storm the plane if such action became necessary. However, less than an hour after he boarded the plane, Mr. Onassis walked off. "The matter has been solved," he said calmly. An hour later, the Palestinians were allowed to leave the airplane and return to their homeland without any further confrontation. No one ever knew what he said to that group of Palestinians or what they said to him. Miltos Yiannacopoulos was furious with Mr. Onassis for the way he had handled the situation, but he did not say one more word to him about it. Jackie had a great deal to say to him, but he paid as little attention to her concern for his welfare as he did to Mr. Yiannacopoulos'.

Fortunately, Mrs. Onassis' children paid more attention to her orders than her husband did. No matter where we went in New York or what we were doing, I was always impressed with the attention Mrs. Onassis paid to her children. It seemed as if Caroline or John were always asking her a long question, but no matter what she was doing, she took the time to answer it as completely as she could. She never appeared too busy to talk to her children. When they would argue with her over something, she remained calm and kept repeating what she wanted them to do, her voice never rising or getting angry. Whenever she was going out, she made sure they knew where she was going and what she was doing and when she would be back. I also noticed that in Greece, Mrs. Onassis slept later, usually until around nine-thirty, but in New York she was usually out of bed before eight to give her children breakfast and see them off to school. Both the children could be noisy and high-spirited, but above all else, they were polite and respectful children. Even when they were young. John was an especially beautiful little boy, and a very clever one as well. Caroline was every bit as clever as her brother and very close with her mother. I knew they were indulged and that Mr. Onassis, especially, would buy them anything they wanted, but they never seemed spoiled or obnoxious.

One of the reasons that the children were so delightful was the expert attention given to them by Martha Sgubin, their governess both in Greece and in New York. I was always impressed with Martha's complete devotion to Caroline and John, no matter where they were. An attractive woman with long, thick brown hair, which she wore gathered in a bun behind her ears, Martha was also a religious woman. There was no doubt she was the main reason Mrs. Onassis was able to leave her children in New York and spend time in Greece without them. No one ever had to worry about the children when they were with Martha.

In New York, I often heard Martha telling Caroline and John to study, helping them with Latin or math, and reprimanding them when they did not do their schoolwork. A second mother to them, she lectured them about how they should behave, both at home and in the outside world. Jackie trusted her judgment and listened to everything Martha told her about the children. Fluent in many different languages, Martha knew just as much about raising children, and devoted all her life, including her personal life, to Caroline and John. Both children appeared to adore her and knew she cared deeply about them. There was not a moment in the children's daily lives when Martha did not know where they were and with whom.

Mr. Onassis was very fond of Martha and frequently praised her work with the children to me. "Jackie is lucky to have her," he told me several times. "She is a completely trustworthy and most intelligent woman." The two of them would often talk for long periods of time, and he went out of his way to make sure she was comfortable and happy whenever she was in his country. It was evident that Martha also liked the Onassis family very much and was pleased when she and the children came to Greece. Yet whenever she was with Mr. Onassis and his sisters, she was respectful, always keeping her eyes down when she was with them, rather than looking directly at them. She never spoke unless they spoke to her. Yet when I saw Martha and the children in New York, she was even more serious than when she accompanied them to Greece. I noticed how, like her employer, she smiled more when she was in Skorpios and seemed more relaxed on the *Christina* than in the Fifth Avenue apartment. But wherever she was, she was aware that, to Mrs. Onassis, she had the most important job in the world.

New York was not the only place where I was able to share special moments alone with Mrs. Jackie. Although in Greece I saw a great deal of her, one particular trip that we took together in my country was very special. It all began one afternoon when Jackie called me at my office to inquire about a telex I had sent for her to New York. When we had finished discussing that matter, she said, "Kiki, you have been sounding very tired lately. I mentioned that to Artemis last night and she suggested I take you away for a few days. Where can we go, just the two of us, where it will be quiet and where there will be no paparazzi and just beautiful scenery and good food?"

When I suggested the island of Hydra, a small island not far from Piraeus, she became excited. "It sounds like the perfect place for us," she decided immediately. "Would you please make plans for us to go there for three days? Just to relax and have fun."

I was delighted to do exactly as she asked. As it turned out, an American friend of Jackie's also came with us, and the three of us had a wonderful time together. Jackie wanted to go on the common boat that carried fifty people from Piraeus to Hydra, rather than fly on a private plane. The boat ride was delightful and uncomplicated and lasted about an hour and a half. All during the trip, Jackie sat in a chair, facing the ocean, happily engrossed in a book, unnoticed by any of the other tourists.

Once we arrived on the small island, the three of us spent two nights in the Hotel Hydra, an old but charming island hotel, had lunch and dinners there, and spent the rest of our days and nights walking, seeing the sights of the lovely island that Professor Georgakis had described, and shopping in the little stores. Although some people in the hotel recognized Jackie, she was friendly and desired no special treatment. Each day, she wore white pants and simple short-sleeved shirts. Her hair was covered with a white scarf and her eyes with her traditional oversized sunglasses. She wore comfortable flats and had lots of energy for our walking expeditions. When we went into the little *kafenios*, no one recognized us. We had no guard with us and Jackie kept telling me how free she felt. Even though she was thin, I did notice that her legs were a little bit heavy. Still, she ate most foods without hesitation during those days, always ordering Greek specialties.

Our nights were very quiet, since none of us had any desire to go to the nightclubs after our dinner. We simply took a long walk and then returned to our three separate rooms, where Jackie told me she loved having the time to read the books she had brought with her. When we returned to Athens on the common ferry, Jackie hugged me and told me I had planned the most perfect trip. "I feel completely refreshed," she told me, "and you look absolutely wonderful. We will have to do this again soon, just us women, but to another island." I assured her I would be ready whenever she was.

Skorpios, and all the other Greek islands, including Hydra, provided their share of pleasure to Mrs. Onassis, but there was an excitement to New York City that could not be felt in any other place in the world. I saw firsthand how comfortable and confident she and her children were there. Here, Mrs. Jackie, rather than Mr. Onassis, appeared in charge of their lives. It was not as luxurious or romantic a life as the one she lived in Skorpios, yet the flavors and thrills of the city provided an incomparable world of their own. In New York City, she was Jackie Kennedy Onassis, widow of President John F. Kennedy, mother of Caroline and John; in Glyfada and on Skorpios, she was Mrs. Aristotle Onassis. It was part of her mystique that she was able to lead both lives and perform each role so effectively. Yet I understood each time I left New York and flew back to Athens that it could not be easy for her to do what I was doing. I was a Greek woman returning home. She, on the other hand, was an American woman returning to her husband's home, a luxurious home she shared with him, despite the hostility of his two children and his love for his mistress. If it was a game we were all playing and she was the trophy, then Mr. Onassis had to supply a lot of prizes to remain the winner.

Chapter Eleven

Jackie and the Three Sisters

I H A D sensed from the first time I met Jackie that she and Mrs. Artemis would become even more than dear friends. I was not surprised to see that as the years of the marriage moved on, there was nothing Mrs. Artemis would not do to make her only sister-in-law happy in Greece. If Mrs. Artemis Garofalidis ever felt displaced by the new queen in her brother's life, she hid it well. She was determined to do everything within her power to make certain both that this marriage was a successful one and that she had a strong and meaningful relationship with the new Mrs. Aristotle Onassis. With Jackie, the aristocratic widow of the slain American president, beside her beloved brother, Mrs. Artemis no longer needed to fear that Maria, the peasant woman with the famous voice, would become his wife.

Mrs. Artemis was convinced, even before the wedding, that Jackie was looking for more than just a wealthy new husband. "She wants a new family," she told me the day before the wedding. "And we must all work very hard to give that to her."

A bossy woman by nature, Mrs. Artemis was happiest when she was in control and teaching someone. Although she was twenty-five years older than her brother's new wife, Mrs. Artemis felt an immediate and strong affinity with Jackie. For her part, Jackie seemed to understand from the beginning that Mrs. Artemis had something important to teach her and that it was to her advantage to learn it quickly. And it didn't take long for the two of them to learn that not only did they love the same man, they genuinely cared for each other. Although Jackie always wore a smile on her face, it wasn't difficult to see that some of the new people in her life in Greece made her uncomfortable or confused. But that was rarely the case with Artemis. There were many moments during her six-and-a-half-year marriage when Jackie was frustrated and unhappy with the behavior of her husband, but almost none when she was unhappy with the way Artemis treated her. It was Jackie's nature, I learned early in my relationship with her, to offer everything she could to those she loved. And Artemis was one of those. To those she did not love, like her new husband's two children, there were no gifts of herself. A phony smile or an indifferent remark or a thoughtless gift might be offered to her husband's children, but for all three of his sisters, her generosity was limitless.

Mrs. Artemis was quite specific in telling Jackie how she should handle her new husband, explaining that she should ask him for expensive items when he was busy and unable to concentrate on what she was asking for. She urged Jackie to show him great affection and not to be afraid to kiss him in public. When Jackie was upset with her husband, she visited or called Mrs. Artemis, who soothed her and provided specific instructions on how to deal with Mr. Onassis' fiery temper. When Aristo refused to wait a few minutes and left Skorpios for an engagement without Jackie, Artemis calmed Jackie down. "All Greek men are like that," she told her when Jackie walked into the house in Glyfada the next day. "They have no patience. When they are ready to leave, they leave. Next time, you be ready an hour ahead of time and keep calling Aristo and making him nervous." I do not know if Jackie took her exact advice, but Artemis did tell me that Jackie was working very hard to be on time.

When Jackie saw pictures in the newspapers of Mr. Onassis and Maria together on some remote beach, it was Mrs. Artemis who soothed her. "Those photographs mean nothing," Mrs. Artemis told her. "You are the one he made his wife." When Jackie's letters from Roswell Gilpatric became public and Aristo went to Paris and was photographed at Maxim's with Maria, it was Mrs. Artemis who urged Jackie to go to Paris and be photographed in Maxim's with her husband, advice Jackie followed.

Many times, I would see the two sisters-in-law sitting next to each other on the pink couch in Mrs. Artemis' Glyfada home, lost in conversation about Mr. Onassis and how he needed to be handled. Jackie was listening intently while Mrs. Artemis told stories about her brother and his moods and his eccentricity.

Mrs. Artemis also encouraged Jackie to do whatever she wanted to redecorate the pink house or Aristo's house in Glyfada. She urged her to take as long as she needed to complete the project in Skorpios. "It will be your special place," she told Jackie one night when Jackie was describing the changes she planned to make in the pink house. "You need to do everything you can to make it perfect so that you and Aristo will be comfortable there for a very long time." Every time Jackie showed her something she bought for the house or some fabric she would be using there, Artemis applauded her excellent taste. "I never saw her so happy as when she is decorating," Artemis told me. "I wish we could find many other houses for her to work on as well."

One day when Jackie was in the midst of her decorations, I met her at the Athens airport, where she had just flown in from New York, en route to Skorpios. We had barely had time to say two words to each other when she was besieged by Greek journalists, who began asking her far too many questions. I was impressed with how calmly Mrs. Onassis handled the onslaught of the press. "Don't worry, Kiki," she told me as we became more and more surrounded by an ever-growing group of reporters and photographers. "I do not mind talking to them today." I watched, not saying a word as she took the time to answer each question politely and cheerfully.

One night, however, shortly after the wedding, when Mr. Onassis had gone back to work in Athens, Mrs. Artemis came to keep Jackie company on the *Christina*. Jackie was quiet and sad all day long. Finally, when Artemis asked her what was wrong, Jackie began to cry. "I am having a very bad day," she explained to her new sister-in-law when her tears finally stopped. "I know I should be happy now, but all I can think about today is my first husband and what happened to him in Texas. Sometimes I think I will never be able to be truly happy again. I try but I cannot forget the pain. And when I am feeling happy, I am just waiting for it to return."

Mrs. Artemis hugged her and assured her that life would get better. She told her how she had felt when she lost her daughter, Popi, and how she thought she would never recover, but she did. Mrs. Artemis told me that the two of them stayed in Mrs. Artemis' suite and talked all through the night, and in the morning, Jackie seemed happier and more at peace with herself.

Whenever they were together, either in Glyfada or in Skorpios, Mrs. Artemis and Jackie would take long walks together. Mrs. Artemis insisted that the best time for a walk was at seven o'clock in the evening, before dinner, so the two of them would take off, arm in arm, and walk, often for an hour. When I watched them, I thought they looked like two sisters, even though Jackie was taller and younger, with their long hair covered with white scarves, and oversize sunglasses covering their eyes, even when the sun was down. "We talk about everything," Mrs. Artemis told me. "About her children and her family and friends. About places we have both been and sights we have seen. About Greece and America. But mostly we talk about Aristo." That was why, I was certain, they never ran out of things to talk about.

I also used to enjoy seeing the two of them sitting in the shaded gardens at the villa at Glyfada, reading or talking, their long black hairdos pulled into big rollers. I was relieved that no photographer ever caught that picture. Sometimes, they even put rollers in each other's hair, laughing like schoolgirls as they did. Both of them went to the same hairdresser in Athens, Angelos, sometimes as often as twice a week. But when they were too lazy to do that or when Angelos was not available to come to their homes to fix their hair, they acted as each other's hairdresser.

When the renovations on the pink house were completed, Mrs. Jackie urged Artemis to come to Skorpios and spend the night there with her. Mrs. Artemis, however, refused. She was always more comfortable in her own house, surrounded by her own foods, the cheese and bread and vodka she preferred right in her own kitchen. However, she rarely turned down an invitation to go on a cruise on the *Christina* with Jackie and Aristo. Even though she trusted her brother would have a full supply of her favorite foods and drinks in her own suite, she still carried enough of her special foods to last throughout the trip.

When they were not on the *Christina,* Jackie and Mrs. Artemis spent many afternoons shopping together in their favorite shops in downtown Athens. They often went to the stores in Panepistimiou and Voukourostiou Streets, spending much time in Costas Haritakis' store. Costas Haritakis was a close friend of the family who had taught Jackie the *syrtaki,* the Greek dance with the complicated steps made popular in *Zorba the Greek.* Not only was Haritakis an excellent dancer, but he owned one of the finest antique stores in Athens. In this store, Artemis and Jackie could spend hours poring over old silver lamps, dishes, and bowls that Costas would help them select.

Mrs. Artemis also introduced Jackie to Zamit, one of her favorite shops in Athens. In this small store on the Plaka, Jackie found other silver items she loved. Many times, I would call the owner and ask him to bring to my office some silver bowls, large dishes, lamps, or candlesticks that Jackie wanted to examine. Then Jackie would come into my office and choose which ones she wanted to purchase. Other times, I would have Zamit send them to her house in Glyfada, where she would select the silver items she wanted. Once her decisions were made, I would tell Zamit to come to my office or to Glyfada to pick up whatever items Jackie did not want. Then he would bring me a bill, which I would sign so he could go to the financial building, which was next to our main headquarters on Syngrou Avenue, and be paid for Mrs. Jackie's purchases.

Sometimes, however, Jackie had other ways of buying items for herself or for her Greek homes. In particular, one day when she was shopping with Artemis, she purchased ten pillows for the pink house in Skorpios, each of which cost more than 500 drachma. That time, she decided she did not want to have her husband see the excessive bill, so she asked me to have Miltos Yiannacopoulos sign for the bills. Since Miltos always had the authority to sign for any bills concerning Mr. Onassis, that was not a problem. It was unlikely that Mr. Onassis would have objected to the bill, yet since it made Jackie happy to take care of the bill in that manner, Miltos and I were happy to indulge her.

On other shopping expeditions, Jackie and Artemis concentrated on jewelry, both new and antique pieces. Often, Jackie went back to her favorite jewelry stores alone and purchased items, such as gold and silver necklaces, rings, earrings, and bracelets that Artemis had previously admired. Later, she would give them to her sister-in-law as gifts, always delighting Artemis with her thoughtfulness and generosity.

Jackie's generosity to Artemis often knew no bounds, as it went well beyond the stores of Greece. One day, Artemis complimented Jackie on the shoes she was wearing. Jackie thanked her for the compliment, and when she returned to New York, she searched several stores until she found the same shoe in Artemis' size. I was in Glyfada the day the shoes arrived from New York for Artemis. The usually composed Artemis squealed with delight when she opened her package.

Yet another time, Artemis asked Jackie where she had bought the pants she was wearing. Jackie told her, and this time, when she returned to New York, she sent Artemis twenty-four pairs of the same pants in her size in an assortment of different colors. "Oh, my God, Kiki," Artemis told me when she received the huge box filled with pants. "I am afraid to open my mouth around her again. Next time, she might send me an entire store."

Although Mrs. Artemis would accompany Jackie on many shopping expeditions in Athens, she preferred to have her own dresses created by her personal designer, Roula Strathis, who also designed blouses or skirts for Jackie. Roula was a talented, charming woman who owned an exclusive boutique on Amalia Avenue next to Syngrou Avenue in Athens, with at least fifty seamstresses who worked for her. Not only did Roula design clothes for many of the wealthiest women in Athens, she also created new uniforms for the stewardesses at Olympic Airways. A stunning redhead with expressive green eyes, Roula could have been a model herself had she desired such a career. Model-thin and delicate, she had a quick mind and an unusually soothing voice. Roula's clothes were quite expensive and carried by many stores in the United States, including Saks Fifth Avenue in New York.

A popular dressmaker among the high society women of Athens, Roula had a full schedule of clients each day, and I had to call her at least a day or so before Artemis and Jackie went to see her or to arrange for her to come to Glyfada for a special fitting. Although Roula made almost all of Artemis' clothes, she also designed some unique dresses and skirts and blouses for Jackie. Roula found Jackie easy to fit and Jackie was always correct with her, showing her the proper respect by the way she addressed her, never treating her like an employee but rather as a close friend. Often, Jackie ordered the same outfit or jacket or blouse in two or three different colors. Although she preferred simple clothes in solid colors, occasionally she had Roula design her a dress in a printed design. One dress that Roula made for her which I particularly admired was a short dress, pale pink with flowers which were a darker shade of pink running through the light cotton fabric. I remember paying the bill for that dress, which converted to approximately $300 in American money in 1970.

One particular day when Roula was making alterations for a different dress on Jackie, Jackie turned to Artemis and said, "Look at Roula. Her face is so beautiful and her figure is like a young girl's. And look at her lovely long red hair." At that moment, Jackie leaned forward to embrace Roula, but a large bunch of the pins Roula was using to make the dress began to stick into Jackie's flesh. Jackie let out a loud cry.

Alarmed by Jackie's piercing scream, Artemis began to yell at Roula. "Oh, my goodness, Roula," she said when she realized what had happened, "I thought you were killing my precious sister-in-law! But now that I see that you are just sticking pins in the skin of Aristo's wife,

I am not upset." Then all three women started laughing, and Jackie stood as still as she could until Roula finished her fitting.

One afternoon, Jackie visited Zolotas jewelers and returned to Glyfada with a pair of large, expensive gold earrings. They were copies of the ancient earrings that Ericos Sleaman had discovered in the Peloponnesus when he unearthed the ancient city of Mycenae. Ericos uncovered five graves inside of which were the twenty-four-karat gold jewels that resembled those worn by Klytemnestra. The original jewels are kept in the Museum of Athens, but Zolotas sold some exquisite reproductions. Roula had just delivered a new gown to Artemis and was having a glass of wine with her when Jackie returned from Zolotas. When Jackie asked Artemis if she liked her new earrings, Artemis looked at them for a long time before finally answering her. "Jackie," she said authoritatively, "those earrings suit Roula more than you. They will look much better with her long red hair than they do on you. I just don't think they are pretty on you. You are too modern-style for them." As always, Jackie listened to everything her sister-in-law told her, took off the expensive earrings, and put them in Roula's ears. To this day, those earrings are Roula's favorite piece of jewelry.

Many other members of the Onassis family had Roula design their clothes, including Tina, Merope, Ritsa Konialidis, and Christina. Christina was one of Roula's most difficult clients. Roula did not like Christina's taste and was always working hard to convince Christina to let her make more fashionable clothes for her than the ones she desired. Also, Christina's weight was such a problem that many times Roula threatened not to make her clothes any longer if Christina gained any more weight. It was a threat Roula never carried out, but she did speak to Christina often about how bad it was for her health to gain so much weight and then starve herself to lose those extra pounds. Once when I went to Roula's boutique with Christina for her fitting, she kept telling Roula how beautiful she looked. "If I could have eyes and hair and a face like yours, I would never have to worry about my body," Christina told Roula.

"Your face is far more beautiful than mine," Roula insisted. "You are much younger than I and the beauty of youth is still yours." But Christina kept shaking her head and did not believe one word Roula told her that day.

Ironically, if life had been different for Roula and me, we would have been sisters-in-law. When I was engaged to Mr. Onassis' pilot, George Kouris, Roula was romantically involved with Dimitris Kouris. Had the two brothers not been killed in the plane crash in Monte Carlo, Roula and Dimitris were planning to become engaged the next week. Both of us married different men, but whenever we see one another, we remember what might have been, and hug each other for a long moment.

Even when she was married, however, the beautiful Roula was never without male adoration. Late one evening, at around two o'clock in the morning, Artemis and Roula had changed into their nightclothes and were lying on the bamboo couches on the patio in Glyfada, sipping glasses of wine and enjoying the gentle breezes of the night. Suddenly Panagiotis came running onto the patio. "Madame," he told Artemis, "you must go into the house right away. Prince Radziwill is coming up the front walk, holding on to two beautiful young women. Please come into the house immediately before he sees you."

Unfortunately, before the two women could move, the prince had staggered onto the patio, drunk as could be, held up by two blondes, neither one of whom was more than twenty years old. "My wife is not here, is she?" he greeted Artemis.

"No, she is not," Artemis answered him. She had barely spoken those words when the prince noticed Roula lying on the couch, pretending to be asleep. Suddenly, he pried himself loose from his two companions and was squatting on the floor beside Roula. "Who is this beautiful creature?" he asked Artemis as he gazed lovingly at the supposedly sleeping Roula.

"She is my dear friend Roula Strathis," Artemis told him. "And she is exhausted and sound asleep."

Ignoring Artemis, he spoke directly to Roula. "Oh, my sweet beauty," he told her in French, "you are the most gorgeous woman I have ever met. Please, come with me. I will give you the stars and the moon and anything you desire. We will share an evening you will never forget."

"She does not speak French," Artemis informed him, so he repeated his plea in English. "She does not speak English either," Artemis said. "She speaks only Greek, which you do not understand."

At that moment, Roula opened her eyes and said to Artemis in Greek, in her beautiful, lilting voice, "Tell the stupid prince that he should come to see me tomorrow morning when he is not so drunk. Right now he is with two beautiful young girls who are twenty years old and he is asking a forty-year-old woman to follow him to the stars and the moon. Is he crazy or drunk or just stupid?"

At that moment, a loud laugh was heard in the bushes in front of the patio and Mr. Onassis emerged. "Oh, Strathis," he said in Greek as he walked over to the couch where Roula was now sitting up, "I have never laughed so much as I have just now, thanks to watching and listening to you."

"Come, my friend," he then addressed the prince in English. "Say good night to all these lovely ladies, and you and I will have one last drink together."

When Jackie heard the story the next day from Artemis, she laughed almost as loud as her husband. The next time she saw Roula in her boutique, she asked her, in French, "Tonight, beautiful lady, can I give you the stars and the moon and everything else you could desire?" The three women laughed together, at the expense of Jackie's brother-in-law, for a long time that afternoon.

Although Artemis could laugh about the sexual escapades of Jackie's brother-in-law, she did not find stories about Jackie's sister amusing. Artemis knew that Aristo and Lee had been romantically involved, and she always worried about the two of them spending time together now that they were related. Although Artemis liked Lee and complimented her when they were together, she did not feel comfortable when Aristo and Jackie spent time with Lee. "I cannot help how I feel," she told me. "Lee just worries me. What do you think of her?"

Personally, I always found Mrs. Radziwill pleasant and easy to be with. Shorter than her sister, she was also thinner, but not as beautiful. Artemis always called Jackie's sister a Paris woman, meaning that she had an enviable French sophistication. Mrs. Radziwill seemed to be a happy woman and I had noticed that she looked at Jackie with sort of a satisfied smile, almost as if she were proud of herself for having helped arrange her sister's second marriage. "I think she is happy her sister is married to Aristo," I tried to convince Mrs. Artemis. "There is nothing for you to worry about here." Still, I could tell that Artemis did not believe me.

Artemis assured me, however, that she never brought up her worries about the princess to Jackie. Nor did the three of them spend too much time together. As always, Artemis was never happy sharing Jackie with other women. Certainly not when the two of them would stop for a long, leisurely lunch at Dionysus, one of their favorite restaurants near the Akropoli. I considered myself lucky that I was asked to join the two sisters-in-law for lunch at Antonopoulos in Glyfada after they spent the day together there. Always, when I went with them, each of them ordered steak and a salad or fish and a salad. Although Artemis was perpetually on a diet and everybody told her she ate like a bird, occasionally she indulged in a chocolate mousse dessert when she and Jackie had lunch together. Jackie would usually finish her dessert, but Artemis barely tasted more than a few bites of hers. Throughout the entire meal, however, Mrs. Artemis was smoking her favorite Cartier cigarettes.

When Jackie was in New York or Europe, or even in Skorpios, she would call Artemis at least once a day, sometimes twice. Whatever Artemis was doing, the minute she heard about Jackie's call, she would stop what she was doing and answer the phone, greeting Jackie in Greek and smiling and laughing during most of the conversation. Although Artemis was deathly afraid of horses and would never accompany Jackie to her horseback riding sessions, she was delighted to prepare a lovely lunch or dinner in Glyfada, which would be waiting for Jackie when she was through riding in Gafissia.

One morning when Mrs. Artemis was not feeling well, I stopped in Glyfada on my way to work, at around eight o'clock, to see how she was doing. She was upstairs in her bed, much of her jewelry lying at the end of the bed, where she could look at it. She was wearing a long blue silk robe tied at her narrow waist with a wide sash, awaiting her breakfast. I was quite surprised when, instead of Panagiotis, the butler, carrying Mrs. Artemis' breakfast, Jackie walked in, holding a tray filled with Mrs. Artemis' breakfast and a beautiful arrangement of flowers. "Oh, Jackie!" Mrs. Artemis said, obviously delighted with Jackie's presentation. "You did not need to do this for me."

"It's my pleasure," Jackie insisted as she arranged the tray on a table in Artemis' sitting room. "Also, I wanted to keep you company while you ate."

"But you're going to get so tired walking up and down the stairs carrying trays," Artemis chided her as she took a roll baked with cheese off the plate and began to munch it slowly. "Then you will be too tired to go for a walk with me when I feel better."

Jackie smiled and poured three cups of coffee, for Artemis, herself, and me. "Don't worry about that," she said. "I promise I will be ready for a long walk the minute you're out of this bed." The next night, when I appeared for dinner in Glyfada, Jackie and Mrs. Artemis were outside walking together.

Another time when Jackie was in New York and had been married to Mr. Onassis for several years, Mrs. Artemis had a bad accident. In the middle of the night, she had gone to the bathroom and slipped and hit her head. She suffered a concussion and for more than a week was unwell. As soon as Jackie heard about the accident, she flew back to Athens and went immediately to Glyfada. She stayed with Mrs. Artemis for the rest of the week, sleeping only for an hour or two for three nights, so that she could tend to her ailing sister-in-law all night long. When I visited Mrs. Artemis each day after work, she looked better, but Jackie looked terrible. "I am so worried about her," Jackie told me. "I just hope she is going to be all right."

"I am so worried about Jackie," Mrs. Artemis told me that same day when Jackie left the room. "You must tell her to get some rest herself, or she will be the one lying here in bed and I will be taking care of her." Mrs. Artemis, at age sixty-eight, made a complete recovery and was soon walking the beaches again with Jackie, but Jackie held her sister-in-law's arm even more firmly after that accident.

Mrs. Artemis was never good about sharing Jackie with her younger sisters, Merope and Kalliroi. She made it clear to both of them that Jackie would stay with her and would not travel to Lagonissi to Kalliroi's ocean-front home or to Merope's luxurious home in Monte Carlo. Occasionally Jackie did visit her other two sisters-in-law, but she made her visits short and always returned to Glyfada to tell Mrs. Artemis every little detail of her visit. A successful businesswoman in her own right, Merope was usually too busy to spend much time with Jackie, yet Kalliroi was always hoping that her sister Artemis would include her on some of the lunches or dinners she shared with Jackie.

Two people who did not object to Artemis' possessiveness toward her sister-in-law were Christina and Alexander. Unfortunately, they were one topic concerning which Mrs. Artemis did not seem to be able to teach Jackie very much. Often, she urged Jackie to try to become friends with her stepchildren, but Jackie never followed that advice. Although Artemis never found any fault with Alexander, there were times she confessed to Jackie that she was worried that Christina was acting crazy and that she understood how hard it would be for Jackie to win her niece's affections. If Mrs. Artemis had been more insistent, however, or had spent more time on that issue, I do think Jackie might have had some success in that area. Artemis could have provided Jackie with more occasions when the three of them would be together, as well as with more advice on how to handle the difficult Christina.

Mrs. Artemis was one of my closest friends, and I loved her as if she were my mother. She was the *koumbara* at my wedding, for which she gave me an exquisite large gold cross, studded with diamonds, which I proudly wore with my wedding gown that day. She was also the godmother of my first son, Alexander, named for Alexander Onassis, and held him tightly and lovingly at his baptism. She knew my innermost dreams and fears; there was nothing about me she did not understand. Yet there was one side of her that caused me much anguish. Whenever Mrs. Artemis drank vodka, often no more than one or two glasses lined with ice, she became a much different woman than the one I knew and adored. It would happen when Panagiotis was serving us special appetizers, carrots slices in an orange sauce, fried zucchini, garlic salad, Gruyère cheese, baked rolls with cheese, miniature pizzas, and red caviar. She would insist that everybody join her in drinking vodka on ice, arguing with any of her friends who requested another type of drink. Once even the small amount of vodka overtook her mind, she could suddenly turn nasty or even vicious. The smile on her face became cruel and unloving, and her voice turned shrill. She would misunderstand the words of her friends and argue with them over the slightest point. At those moments, I would die inside, as I listened to her berate me or reveal a private secret I had confided to her. Those moments passed quickly and were never remembered or discussed the next day, yet the memory of the pain and embarrassment I suffered at those times never faded from my mind.

Despite her problems with vodka, Mrs. Artemis usually managed to control herself when she was around either Aristo and Jackie. It had to have been a giant effort to have prevented herself from attacking either one of them, but I was certain that she would rather die than allow that to happen often. However, the few times that Jackie did witness Artemis losing control of herself because of the vodka, Jackie looked very sad. Jackie and I would glance at each other with sadness, both of us unable to do or say anything to end the unpleasant scene around us. Even though Mrs. Artemis' nastiness was never directed at Jackie, Jackie looked deeply disturbed when those incidents occurred. Once when Mrs. Artemis was being especially cruel to me, relating a secret I had told to her about a man I was dating, I could not stop myself from crying. In a very discreet manner, so that Mrs. Artemis could not see what she was doing, Jackie squeezed my hand warmly.

One especially painful time for me occurred the first time I introduced a man with whom I was considering marriage to Mrs. Artemis. Mrs. Artemis' first cousin Tiamkari, Letta, and Jackie all were in Glyfada that evening, and I was both nervous and excited about their meeting my suitor. Unfortunately, by the time I arrived at Glyfada, Artemis had already had too much vodka. To my gentleman friend, she was the perfect hostess, complimenting him on his appearance and fine manners, flirting with him, and winning his admiration.

When it was my turn, however, the vodka spoke. "You must be feeling much shame to be wearing such a dress," she said to me, pointing to the small spot where my long white dress opened above my bust. "How can you go out with someone with such a terrible appearance?" she asked my date while I stood there, unable to speak a word as our hostess continued to insult me. "She should never have left her house looking so ugly. She is a disgrace to all of us." By then, everyone, including Merope's husband, Nikos, and Mr. Onassis, was staring at me.

I am certain that Mrs. Artemis would have continued to insult me for a much longer period of time had Jackie not rescued me. "You must try some of our hostess's excellent meatballs before everyone else finishes them," she told my escort, managing to bring Panagiotis and his tray of delicious appetizers over to the two of us. In the same quick but graceful manner, she began to talk to Artemis about the food, distracting her from my appearance. My eyes were filled with tears and I could not eat one bite of food, but Jackie's eyes met mine and I knew that she was telling me with her eyes what she always said with her voice: "Do not be sad. Artemis loves you and she does not know or mean what she is saying."

Later that evening, when we were alone, Jackie told me that, next to Aristo, Artemis loved me more than any other person in the world and that I should never forget that. "They can both be difficult people, Aristo and Artemis," she explained to me. "But they are not bad people. We must always remember that." Despite the pain Mrs. Artemis might have caused me, I believed Jackie's words, for Artemis could also be my kindest, most generous friend.

Although Mrs. Artemis was constantly giving Jackie excellent advice on how to handle an occasionally difficult husband, she could have used a little bit of that advice for herself. Even though her husband, Professor Theodoros Garofalidis, was one of the most respected men in Greece, he could be a bit strict with her and would shout at her if she angered him. As a result, she rarely allowed the vodka to make her nasty or difficult when he was around. Mrs. Artemis was very proud that her husband was well known for his generosity and thoughtfulness. An orthopedic surgeon with an excellent reputation, Dr. Garofalidis rarely received money for the operations he performed. Not only was he charitable to his patients, but he was constantly urging me to find employment at Olympic Airways for dozens of people he met. Sometimes the people he suggested worked out very well at the company, but many times I was unable to find them positions. Luckily, there were so many unemployed people that he recommended that he did not remember all of them.

A tall, heavy, handsome man with a distinctive mustache and thick glasses, Dr. Garofalidis always appeared serious and solemn. Yet he was an exceptionally warm man, who managed to make others feel safe and secure. A few years older than Aristo, he urged his brother-in-law to take better care of himself. "You must not work so hard," he told Aristo frequently. "You must go to bed early and get up early. You must get rid of some of the stress in your life, and you must eat only the right foods."

Aristo listened to him patiently, but always said, "Don't worry about me, Theodore. I am very strong."

Yet it was Dr. Garofalidis' relationship with Jackie that offered the best view into his character. As close as she was with his wife, she adored Dr. Garofalidis and he returned her admiration. An avid huntsman, Professor Garofalidis went to the north of Greece at least four times a year on hunting expeditions. Mrs. Artemis complained about his lengthy hunting trips, frequently causing a scene when he was preparing to leave. Yet her childish behavior never prevented him from traveling to Alexandroupoli and Halkidiki, returning most times with a bag filled with the results of his labors. Frequently, he brought home bags of *bekatsa*, or small birds such as *trigonia*, and had the cooks in Glyfada prepare the birds for Artemis' dinner parties.

Although Jackie was deeply fond of the Dr. Garofalidis, like me, she found it almost impossible to eat the birds he killed. They were always greasy and unappetizing to both of us, and the thought of them flying around free and happy hours before we ate them did little to help us overcome our distaste. Mrs. Artemis worked hard to instruct Panagiotis in a creative way to cook the birds with a delicious sauce and many of the guests, especially Mr. Onassis, were delighted to eat them. Yet I always noticed that Mrs. Artemis rarely ate one bite of the birds herself. Still, there was no way that Jackie would insult Dr. Garofalidis by telling him she did not enjoy the *bekatsa*, so she would force herself to taste the birds and pretend she was enjoying the meal. I was probably the only one at the table who knew how hard it was for her to carry out such a game. During the dinner, our eyes would always meet as we both struggled to act as if the *bekatsa* were delicious, but sometimes we couldn't control ourselves and we would start giggling. We would try to pretend that we were laughing about something other than the birds, but luckily our host enjoyed eating the foods he caught so much that he did not pay too much attention to what was left on our plates. No matter how much we ate, anyhow, we could never keep up with his large appetite. He was always telling Jackie and Artemis they ate too little. "You are both too thin," he said many times. "If a strong wind comes by, it will blow both of you away."

For some strange reason, Jackie had difficulty pronouncing Theodore's name. As a result, she avoided calling him by his first name, an omission that was not missed by Professor Garofalidis. He would wink at me when she called him Professor, but he would never do anything to make her feel uncomfortable. Truthfully, it was amazing that he heard what she called him since his hearing was so poor. Most often we would have to shout to make certain he heard what we were saying. Once Jackie commented to me about his hearing problem, telling me, "If I ever had a secret, I would never be able to tell it to Dr. Garofalidis. For I'd have to shout it to make sure he heard it."

Yet, Jackie, who was always seated to his right, never hesitated to lean over toward him and speak loudly into his ear so that he never missed a word she said. It was often embarrassing when he came into the Olympic Airways office and I would have to tell him to stop shouting because there was a meeting going on and he was disturbing everyone there. As a result of his deafness, he had no idea his voice was so loud. If everyone could have talked to him as carefully as Jackie did, it would have made his life easier.

A meticulous dresser who favored white suits, Dr. Garofalidis was never without a red rose in the lapel of his jacket. One of the first times he had dinner with Jackie, he handed the beautiful flower to her. She kept the rose in her hands all night long and drew a lovely picture of it the next morning, which she proudly gave to him.

One especially memorable night at Glyfada, after we finished dining, Artemis put some beautiful music on the phonograph and we all started to dance the waltz. After Artemis danced with her husband, Dr. Garofalidis asked Jackie to dance. It was delightful to watch the large yet graceful man waltz such a slender and elegant woman around the room. Jackie laughed and chatted happily with her partner while she waltzed and looked perfectly comfortable in his thick arms. Mr. Onassis stood in a corner of the room, smoking his cigar, looking proud and happy as he watched his wife waltz effortlessly with his brother-in-law.

Another night, Jackie, Artemis, and I were having a relaxing dinner, just the three of us, in Glyfada. Mrs. Artemis had only a few sips of her vodka that night and was the perfect elegant hostess. However, Jackie was unusually quiet all night long and Mrs. Artemis looked very concerned about her. Finally, when we were finishing our coffee, Mrs. Artemis asked Jackie what was wrong. "You do not seem yourself tonight, my dear," she said gently. "Is there something I have done to upset you?"

Jackie looked stricken. "Oh, no, of course not," she answered immediately. "It has nothing to do with you. You must forgive me. I do not feel well."

Mrs. Artemis looked both relieved and concerned at the same time. "Oh, what is wrong?" she asked, moving closer to Jackie on the couch. "What can I do to make you feel better?"

"Nothing," Jackie said, slowly and painfully shaking her head. "It is my neck. And my arm. I hate to complain but sometimes the pains in my neck are so bad that I can barely stand it."

"Have you been to the right doctors?" Mrs. Artemis asked.

"Oh, I have been to many different doctors," Jackie answered her. "But there is nothing any of them can do." She hesitated for a long few minutes before she continued. "It has to do with the night my husband was killed. I was holding his head so tightly in my arms that I must have damaged a nerve in my neck. Most of the time, it is fine. But other times, like tonight, it is not. But please do not worry. I will be fine in the morning, I promise you."

Jackie left us a few minutes later to retire for the evening, but Mrs. Artemis and I sat in her living room for a while longer. We said very little to one another after Jackie left us, but I am sure that, like me, Mrs. Artemis could not wipe the image of Jackie and her husband in that limousine in Texas out of her mind.

There are, unfortunately, other memories of unpleasant evenings spent in Artemis' living room. One rainy, stormy evening, Mrs. Artemis was feeling very tired and had gone upstairs to retire for the evening. Mrs. Jackie and I were sitting beside each other on one of Artemis' large sofas. Facing us on the other sofa were Mr. Onassis, Miltos Yiannacopoulos, and Professor Georgakis, who had been talking to one another most of the evening. Jackie had been reading a book about Socrates all evening and had barely spoken a word to anyone. Finally, she put down the book and asked the professor thoughtfully, "Do you honestly think that Socrates really existed or might there have been many philosophers who resembled such a man? Perhaps Plato simply invented Socrates to represent this large group of philosophers. "

"I certainly do not know for sure," the professor answered her.

"Perhaps it is like with Jesus Christ and the *Apostolus*. Perhaps Jesus Christ was really the *Apostole* Pablo, or Paul. Perhaps . . ."

Suddenly, before the professor could finish his discussion, Aristo jumped up from the couch and began to scream at Jackie. "What is the matter with you?!" he shouted at her. "Why do you have to talk about such stupid things? Don't you ever stop and think before you open your mouth?"

Mr. Onassis continued to rant and rave, swearing at the professor and yelling at Jackie. "Have you ever noticed the statue of the man with the mustache that is in the center of Athens?" he shouted at her. "Are you too stupid to know that is a statue of Socrates?"

I was so embarrassed for Mrs. Jackie that I nearly died. I knew that Mr. Onassis was a deeply religious man and that such a discussion about Jesus Christ would seem blasphemous and offensive to him. Still, I had never seen him treat his wife in such a disrespectful manner. Before I knew what was happening, Jackie had left her spot on the couch, crying and whispering to herself in French, and was heading upstairs. While the four of us sat there in a terrible silence, she retrieved her raincoat, came back downstairs, and began to walk out of the door without so much as a glance at the rest of us in the room.

"Mr. Onassis," Miltos said as Jackie headed into the storm, "you must stop her. It is a terrible night. She will get soaking wet."

"You go get her," Mr. Onassis told Miltos flatly.

Miltos did not wait one more moment. He ran to the door, grabbed Jackie by her waist and her arm, and hauled her back into the house. Her face was expressionless as she walked back upstairs, her raincoat and hair both slightly wet.

As I would have expected, Mr. Onassis did not apologize to his wife when she came back into the living room a few minutes later without her raincoat and quietly sat back down beside the professor. He continued to rant for a few more minutes about "idiotic conversations," and then closed his eyes and lost himself in the music and his own thoughts. He was through now. He had acted like a true Greek man who liked to scream and say whatever he wanted. For her part, Mrs. Onassis acted like a true Greek wife, and she did not say anything else to her husband to continue their fight. A German woman, I thought that night, would never put up with such behavior from her husband, but Jackie, like the rest of us Greek women, did.

The next day Artemis was very upset when I told her about that scene she had missed in her living room. But she agreed that Jackie had handled her brother in the only way she could. "Maria would have carried on like a crazy woman if he had done that to her," she said. "They would have had a terrible fight and they might even have thrown things at each other."

As for Jackie, however, Mrs. Artemis admired her sister-in-law's civility. "He will send her some piece of jewelry today," she explained to me. "That will be his way of apologizing to her for his behavior." Mrs. Artemis, as always in regard to her brother, was correct. I got the bill from Zolotas for the very expensive gold bracelet several days later.

Jackie also bought Mrs. Artemis many presents of jewelry when she returned to Greece from New York or Paris, often calling me from New York and asking my advice about a particular piece of jewelry. Sometimes, she selected books or small paintings that Mrs. Artemis appreciated. Several times, Mrs. Artemis visited Jackie in New York, but as she grew older, she preferred to spend her time in Greece. Unquestionably, her favorite pupil and visitor was Jackie, and, no matter what she was doing, when Jackie called to say she was coming to visit her, Artemis made sure she was available to receive her.

Even if Artemis had plans to be with Merope or Kalliroi, she canceled them if Jackie was coming to visit. Rarely would she include her two younger sisters in any activities she had planned with Jackie. Still, Merope and Kalliroi called Artemis frequently and tried to stay in touch with all the happenings in Glyfada. When Jackie was staying in Glyfada and one of her sisters called, Artemis would speak to her for less time than usual, explaining that she needed to spend all her time with Jackie. Merope and Kalliroi understood that Artemis preferred to keep Jackie and all the details about her marriage to their brother to herself and never created a problem over their sister's selfish behavior. It was not difficult for Jackie to see that Artemis was unhappy when she spent time talking to her other sisters-in-law on the telephone, so Jackie also kept her phone calls to them from Glyfada as short as possible.

Merope's husband, Nicholas Konialidas, who was also a first

cousin to Aristo and Merope, was a shipowner who traveled a great deal on business and spent little time in Greece or New York. However, he and Merope found time to visit Skorpios at least twice a year, making certain they were not there when Artemis was visiting Jackie. When they visited Skorpios, Nikos always planned a fishing trip. For those trips, Jackie and Aristo awoke by four-thirty A.M. to join Nikos and Merope on the fishing boat that he had stocked for their trip. Although Aristo was dressed like a sailor for those occasions, wearing a cap with an anchor on its brim, a blue-and-white striped T-shirt and white trousers, he was sleepy and cranky and grumbling about the early hour when he got on the boat. Sometimes he had been sleeping only an hour or two when Jackie woke him at four-thirty. His brother-in-law laughed and insisted that the only way to catch anything was to head out before the sun rose. Jackie never seemed to mind rising that early and looked cheerful and excited when she boarded the fishing boat, dressed in white pants and a white jersey, her hair covered with a white scarf, and her large black sunglasses shielding her eyes even before the sun was up. Nikos was an outgoing, fun-loving man with a warm, generous spirit and Jackie enjoyed his company. In addition, she liked the fishing and was not the least bit squeamish about the sport.

It was delightful to watch the way Jackie got along with her brother-in-law Nikos Konialidis. A small man, who physically resembled his cousin Aristo, Mr. Konialidis was an excellent businessman, but above all else he was a very honest man. If he liked you, he would be excessively generous, giving you money and anything he could to let you know how he felt about you. However, if he disliked you, then he would let you know that immediately and would not waste one minute of his time talking to you. Both Nikos and Merope were never pretentious. They were two of the most original people I have ever met.

One thing that irked Mr. Konialidis was when someone tried to act as if he was more important than he was. For instance, one time when I was flying into Paris with Mr. Konialidis, we were met at the airport by a man who immediately announced that he was the director of the Olympic Airways office in Paris. There was something haughty about the man, which I could easily see annoyed Mr. Konialidis.

"I don't know or care who you are," he responded to the director. "Just let me go about my business without your unnecessary interference." Before the poor man had left our side, Mr. Konialidis said to me, perhaps too loudly, "What a stupid, self-important man he is, Kiki. I only hope he stays out of our way." It is very possible the man heard those words, for I never saw him again during any of our trips to Paris.

Although Mr. Onassis respected his brother-in-law and frequently discussed important business decisions with him, the two men could quarrel often and loudly about these matters. But they were connected by both blood and marriage, and their genuine love for each other would never be broken. Even when they disagreed about a business deal.

I was very fortunate to be one of the people whom Mr. Nikos Konialidis liked. Many times, he and Merope invited me to their elegant home in Monte Carlo, where I was treated with great hospitality and generosity. Once Kalliroi and I spent fifteen days in Monte Carlo at Merope's lavish home. Despite our age difference, Kalliroi and I enjoyed our time together, shopping, visiting Prince Rainier's palace and the famous sea creature museum, and even took bus excursions to the nearby villages surrounding Monte Carlo. One day Nikos took us to the charming Italian town of San Remo, which borders Monte Carlo.

Every morning when I woke up, I would find money under my pillow. Each evening, when Merope and Nikos would take Kalliroi and me to the casino, they would insist that I walk between the two of them and they would ask, laughing, if I had any money I could spend that night. I used the money they had given me to play the slot machines for, like Mr. Onassis, in the casinos, I was not much of a gambler.

Many people at the casino thought that I was Merope and Nikos' daughter. "We only wish she were," Mr. Konialidis told one gentleman who asked that question one evening. "But sadly we have only our two sons, George and Marios." And then he smiled and added, "But Kiki is like our daughter. In every way possible."

Jackie enjoyed her conversations with Nikos and she sought his opinion on many subjects, ranging from politics to the theater. She, too, was one of the small group of people he genuinely admired, and if there was anything she ever needed, he considered it an honor to give it to her.

Jackie's relationship with Merope was equally cordial and warm.

A small, beautiful woman with a calm sweet manner most unlike the often gruff personality of her husband, Merope was a delight to spend time with. I did notice that when people met her for the first time, Merope could appear a bit distant, and she, too, did not like everybody she met, yet those who were her friends were most fortunate. Like everyone who knew Merope, Jackie admired her sister-in-law's superb taste, especially in jewelry and furniture. In regard to her clothing, Merope always favored strong colors, yet it was her the jewels that adorned these dresses that caught one's eye. No matter what the occasion, Merope was always wearing exquisite and expensive jewelry. Jackie once commented to me that she was not surprised that Merope was wearing a large diamond necklace the first time they went fishing together. I think Jackie was joking, but I am not certain.

It was not a joke that everything Merope bought was of the best possible quality. Whenever Artemis, Jackie, Merope, Kalliroi, and I had dinner together before Christmas or Easter or for each other's birthdays, we gave each other presents. At those times, Merope's presents were the most desirable and I held my breath when I opened the box she handed me. Today, I still treasure each piece of jewelry she gave me, including an antique gold watch and a gold ring, but I especially adore the gold necklace and matching bracelet covered with stunning lapis blue stones, which she gave me one Christmas. On another holiday, she gave Jackie a most unusual necklace and bracelet adorned with several different stones. "Do you like it, Jackie?" Merope kept asking even before Jackie had unwrapped the second box.

"Oh, yes, I do," Jackie whispered excitedly as she held up the two ravishing pieces of jewelry. "I will treasure them always." It was interesting to watch Jackie open her presents. Certainly, all of us enjoyed receiving lovely presents from one another, yet Jackie's pleasure was the greatest. It was as if every time she received a beautiful present, she was being shown that she was loved. With each gift that she opened from her sisters-in-law, she seemed more comfortable, proud, and secure. The look of joy on her face as she unwrapped each gift seemed to be in appreciation of more than a mere piece of jewelry or clothing that she could have purchased for herself. Even when she received my far more inexpensive presents, which were usually just baskets of her favorite flowers, she looked ready to cry with her happiness. "You make me so happy, Kiki," she would say as she carefully examined each flower. "How can I ever thank you?" Of course, I wished I had enough money to buy Jackie and her sisters-in-law expensive pieces of jewelry for their special occasions, but the look on Jackie's face when she held my flowers convinced me that it was the idea that I cared enough about her to give her a gift that mattered far more than the gift itself.

Artemis might have hosted the best dinner parties, but when it came to giving presents, Merope was the winner. Yet Merope did not just purchase the most expensive items she could find. She was an excellent shopper and knew where to go for the best prices on many items. Jackie loved to go shopping with Merope and trusted her judgment completely. When Jackie was buying furniture for the pink house, she spoke to Merope frequently, asking her opinion about each piece she was considering purchasing.

Yet Merope and Nikos did not merely dedicate their lives to shopping for beautiful items. Like both Aristo and Professor Garofalidis, they were concerned about those who had far less than they. As a result, they invested a substantial amount of their money in the previously undeveloped and poor island of Skiathos. The first thing they did was to build an adequate hospital on the island and provide decent heath care to its residents. To improve the economy on Skiathos, they gave me instructions on how to import over one hundred cows from Switzerland. These cows were the beginning of an ultimately successful dairy business for the villagers. They also erected churches on the island, as well as a luxury villa. The villa employed many of the villagers and was the place where Merope and Nikos entertained their own friends, urging them to return and vacation at a later time. Although Nikos and Merope did not own Skiathos the way Aristo owned Skorpios, all the inhabitants of the island, revered them as if they were the island's king and queen.

When Kalliroi and her husband, Gerassimos Patronikolas, divorced in 1972, her relationship with the rest of the family changed somewhat. Jackie was especially surprised when Kalliroi and Gerassimos announced their divorce. One evening when we were having dinner in Glyfada, she said to me and Artemis, "I do not understand what happened. Gerassimos is so sweet and so educated and so good looking. And they always seemed like such a happy couple."

"That often happens," I answered her. "Some couples appear so happy, but inside their own homes they are not what they appear."

Artemis shook her head and agreed with Jackie. "He is such a wonderful man," she said. "I will always admire him."

Kalliroi's husband, Gerassimos Patronikolas, was, like Artemis' husband, an orthopedic surgeon. Handsome and tall, Gerassimos was a wealthy man with a warm, outgoing manner. Not only did he maintain his medical career, but he also owned luxury hotels in Miramare, Corfu, Rhodes, and Olympia. After I had been working for Mr. Onassis for two years, Dr. Patronikolas, who was on the board of directors at Olympic Airways, decided that I looked tired and needed a vacation. Before he discussed the matter with me, he spoke to Mr. Onassis and made the arrangements for me, my mother, and my twelve-year-old brother, John, to spend fifteen days in one of his resorts. During our luxurious family vacation, Gerassimos Patronikolas did not come to the hotel where we were staying, but he made certain that the three of us were given every possible amenity. It was a vacation my mother, my brother, and I will never forget.

Even after the divorce, Mr. Onassis kept in close contact with his ex-brother-in-law and made certain he remained on the board of directors for Olympic Airways. Unlike his sisters, he did not openly state his disapproval of his younger sister's new friends, but he, like Jackie, hoped that she would find a new husband. He was disappointed that such a marriage never occurred.

Kalliroi physically resembled her sister Merope more strongly than she did Artemis, yet she was even more beautiful than Merope. She was also the most fun-loving of the three sisters. Unlike Artemis, she was never bossy; unlike Merope, she was sensitive and easily brought to tears. Still, Kalliroi was a clever, intelligent woman who was very much her own person. Although Jackie went on cruises and shared fun times with Merope and her husband, she was closer with Kalliroi. Even though Kalliroi was only six years younger than Artemis, she appeared even younger than her age. She had a great deal of energy, and unlike her oldest sister, she could spend endless hours combing the stores with Jackie. Her physical beauty grew even stronger with age, and Jackie always commented on how beautiful she looked whenever they greeted one another. Although Jackie relied on Artemis for motherly advice and help, and Merope for shopping advice, Kalliroi brought fun and laughter into her Greek life.

Whenever Artemis was busy or distracted or feeling generous toward her sister, she allowed Kalliroi to entertain Jackie at her seaside villa in Lagonissi, where Kalliroi loved to have large parties around her beautiful pool. Kalliroi especially enjoyed sweets, such as halvah, and always served fattening desserts. "We will diet tomorrow," she would promise Jackie as she tempted her with a tray full of rich sweets. Artemis would never touch the rich desserts, but Jackie always took a few tastes of most of them. Somehow, Jackie seemed younger and more relaxed at Lagonissi than she did in Glyfada, but of course I would never repeat such a disloyal thought to Mrs. Artemis. When Artemis was her usual jealous self, however, Jackie would never travel to Lagonissi or meet Kalliroi for lunch or shopping, but she did find time to speak to Kalliroi on the telephone every day, even if only for a few minutes.

Kalliroi loved to dance and visit the Neraida taverna to listen to the live music and dance. When Jackie and Aristo would accompany Kalliroi there, Jackie delighted in watching her sister-in-law dance all the Greek dances, drop baskets full of flowers, and eat delicious Greek specialties until the early hours of the morning. Sometimes Kalliroi would convince Jackie to join her on the floor, where she would patiently explain the complicated steps of some of the dances. Jackie was much taller than her small sister-in-law, yet it was a delight to watch the two beautiful women, hand in hand, moving across the floor, one Greek woman surefooted and vibrant, totally uninhibited as the music moved her legs to perform complicated dance steps, the other dancer, taller, more slender, more reserved, yet obviously anxious to emulate the smaller woman's exuberance. Once, after a long dance ended, both women returned to our table at the Neraida, out of breath and sweating, excitedly hugging each other. "You were wonderful, Jackie," Kalliroi insisted. Jackie blushed and shook her head, but I could see the smile that crossed her face and lit up her eyes.

Kalliroi often seemed in awe of Jackie and would never criticize her, not even when Jackie was less than loving to Kalliroi's niece and nephew. Artemis was always free with her advice to Jackie about how to treat her brother, but on the subject of Jackie's frequent trips to New

York or Paris, Artemis remained uncharacteristically quiet. It was as if she understood that this was the one area in which Jackie would not easily change her behavior. However, Artemis would never hesitate to complain to me about Jackie's frequent absences from Greece, which began to occur more often after she completed her renovations on Skorpios. When Jackie was busy redecorating the pink house, she was spending most of her time in Greece. She would fly over to Skorpios in the morning and spend the entire day there, supervising the restorations. Many nights she spent on the *Christina*, but often she returned to Glyfada, exhausted but excited over her projects, and anxious to discuss each detail with Artemis. It took several years for everything she planned to be completed; however, when it was all through, Jackie began to spend more time in New York than she had done previously.

"I wish she would be more of a Greek wife," Artemis told me several times when Jackie had been gone for more than week at a time. "Jackie is not doing so well to leave Aristo and go to New York for weeks at a time. It is not good for the Greek family to be separated like that. One should not go one place and the other one to somewhere different. A Greek man and wife should stay together as much as is possible."

I tried to remind Artemis how difficult it was for Jackie to leave her children alone in New York. "They are growing older and they need more attention now," I tried to explain to her.

"They have Martha Sgubin," Artemis answered me. "She is wonderful with the children. She is never leaving them alone. Besides, we have schools here in Greece, do we not?"

But Artemis would eventually agree with me that it was not a good idea for Jackie's children to leave their family and friends and come to live permanently in a strange country so far away from all of them. It was enough, she agreed, that the children came to Greece for all their holidays and school vacations. Still, when she heard her brother ask Jackie to please change her plans to go to New York so that she could go somewhere in Greece with him, Artemis was very disturbed when Jackie answered that she could not do that. "It is not good for a wife to be so far away from her husband," she complained to me, although she did not repeat her thoughts to her brother or sister-in-law . "There are other women who will come to his side when she is not there."

I knew exactly who she meant, and I also understood that

Jackie's habit of spending two weeks in Greece and the next week or ten days in New York and a few days in Paris or Switzerland made it easier for Maria to remain at her lover's side.

Artemis worried that, with his wife away, her brother might become even closer to his mistress. Artemis was a strong, highly motivated woman who dedicated herself to keeping her brother and his second wife happy and in love with each other. But even she had her limitations.

Chapter Twelve

The End of His Dream

D

ESPITE ARISTO'S ongoing affair with Maria, his marriage to Jackie might have continued had life not dealt him a devastating blow from which he could never recover. On the occasion of the fourth anniversary of that marriage, Miltos Yiannacopoulos commented to me, "My friend is indeed an amazing man. I believe he can go on forever with both Jackie and Maria in his life. They both know what's going on with the other woman, and seem capable of living with the reality of the situation."

Miltos knew, however, as we all did, that the marriage, as it moved into its fifth year, was not one made in heaven. We could all see that it had been stronger and more loving when it had begun than it was now. Yet, it was far from over. Aristo and Jackie still spent wonderful moments together and frequently looked as if they loved each other. They enjoyed fun-filled days and evenings aboard the *Christina*, both in Skorpios and on cruises to exciting locales. I often saw them walking along the beach near Glyfada, arm in arm, talking earnestly to one another. There were romantic dinners in tavernas in Greece and in fine restaurants in Paris and London and Rome. Jackie did seem to be spending less time in Greece, but when she was there, she and Aristo appeared happy to be together.

But when the accident happened, when Alexander was lost forever, everything that mattered to Aristo was gone. Unlike a woman, a ship, or an airplane, Alexander, his one and only son, could not be replaced. For Alexander was his future, his reason to live. And so it was Alexander's death that shattered the world of every member of the Onassis family.

What might have happened to Jackie's and Aristo's lives had that accident never happened, no one will ever know. Perhaps they would have defied their critics and the gods and continued living together as man and wife, building a stronger marriage every year they were together. Or perhaps they would have gone their separate ways. All I do know for certain is that the plane crash that took Alexander's life in 1973 destroyed not only his father's marriage, but Mr. Onassis' life as well.

The day of that plane crash remains as firmly etched in my mind as I am certain the day of President Kennedy's assassination is imprinted in the mind of every American citizen who was alive on Friday, November 22, 1963. It was a Monday, January 22, 1973, a cool but unremarkable winter day, and Alexander and I were alone in our Olympic Airways offices. We had planned to have lunch in Athens that day at Antonopoulos, Alexander's favorite fish taverna, with two German friends to discuss business. But two hours before the lunch, one of the men called the office to report that he had a bad stomach problem and asked if we could postpone our lunch until the next day.

Alexander was in a quiet, somber mood that day. He was like that sometimes and for no apparent reason. Since his mother, Tina, had married her former brother-in-law Stavros Niarchos fourteen months earlier, Alexander had been having more blue days than usual. Even though over a year had passed, he could not accept the reality that his mother had married the husband of her sister Eugenie, eighteen months after Eugenie died a suspicious death. After Tina had divorced Sonny Blandford a year before that marriage, Alexander had been full of hope that one day his father would divorce Jackie and his parents would remarry. We had discussed such a possibility many times and each time I had tried to convince him how senseless such hopes were. He'd listen to me politely, but I knew he wasn't accepting my advice. "You need to think about your own life, Mr. Alexandros," I told him. "You must stop thinking about your parents' happiness and concentrate on your own." Again he would shake his head in agreement and politely thank me for listening to his problems, but my words never dispersed his black moods. He spoke to his mother when she called the office, but his words were cool and his face sad.

The more unhappy Alexandros became over his mother's third marriage, the more he resented his father's second marriage. During one of Jackie's recent trips to Greece, Alexander had been even nastier to her than usual. "I am counting the seconds until she goes back to New York," he told me one morning.

A few weeks later, when I heard him talking to his father in New York just before Jackie was due to return to Athens, I knew that there would be a message for me about her travel plans. "When is Mrs. Jackie arriving?" I asked him nonchalantly when he came into my office after his phone call.

"I do not know and I do not care," he said curtly as he walked by my desk. "Let us hope she changes her mind and does not return."

"But I need to know what flight to book her on and when the car should pick her up at the airport," I told him. "Can you just tell me the day she intends to arrive?"

"I told you," he repeated even more curtly than before. "I do not know and I do not care." And he left the office. I was just about to call

New York and speak to Jackie directly, which of course would be embarrassing, since she had given the information to Mr. Onassis to give to Alexander and me, when Alexander called me, informed me the date she was arriving, and hung up. The hate in his voice, even with those few words, was palpable.

The day of his accident, Jackie was again in New York with his father, but Alexander was still dark and morose. "Don't put any calls through to my office, Kiki," he told me when he informed me that our luncheon plans with the Germans had been canceled. "I don't want to talk to anybody today."

"Not even Fiona?" I asked him.

"Nobody," he repeated, and returned to his office, where he began to read some letters.

I did not say another word to him, but I knew that if Fiona called, I would put through her call immediately. A few days earlier, Alexander had informed me that in February he would be out of the country for a month. I had promised to make any necessary changes in his schedule, but had not questioned him about his plans. For I strongly suspected he would be on his honeymoon with Fiona. Artemis had spent many hours telling me what she thought was happening with Alexander and Fiona based on her own observations and the talk of the employees. She believed Fiona had become pregnant and Alexander was adamant about marrying her. It would be an act of supreme defiance to his father, but his mind was made up. As Artemis understood it, both Fiona and Alexander were serious people who had not planned to have this baby and were not anxious to become parents at that time in their lives. Yet, if the pregnancy had happened, they would handle it in their own way. That Fiona was forty concerned them the most. That she was sixteen years older than Alexander seemed to matter not at all. They loved each other regardless of their age difference, and whatever they decided about having a baby would not change that love.

One evening, however, Mrs. Artemis greeted me at the door with word that Fiona had lost the baby. Yet, she was convinced that Alexander and Fiona would still marry. For the past week, it had been difficult to talk to Alexander without thinking about what Artemis said was happening between him and Fiona, but I would never break my pledge of secrecy to Artemis. My greatest fear was that, even though Artemis was loyal to her niece and nephew and had previously held many secrets about them from her brother, the vodka would overtake her mind and she would reveal her suspicions to her brother, who had no thought of such matters.

I was also worried about Artemis' revealing her suspicions to Jackie. Artemis was unhappy with the idea of her nephew's marrying Fiona. She disapproved of Fiona and, because she was a religious woman, she had been both saddened and relieved when she heard Fiona had lost the baby. After all, Fiona was forty, and Artemis felt that she was too old to have a child. Fiona had been a frequent subject discussed passionately between Artemis and Jackie, and I had heard their discussions many times. Jackie readily agreed with Artemis that Fiona would not make a proper wife for Alexander. Sometimes, when Jackie was expressing her opinion and stressing all the negative aspects of Alexander and Fiona's relationship, how Fiona was too old for Alexander and how little appreciation she had for Greece and the family, I sensed a streak of jealousy in Jackie's words. Christina, who liked and admired Fiona, was always anxious to point out to me that Fiona was wealthier, as well as more beautiful, intelligent, and independent than her stepmother. "Jackie can't help but be jealous of a real woman like Fiona," Christina told me many times.

Artemis and I had often talked about how Aristo adored strong, independent, beautiful women. Fiona certainly fit that description. Although I hated to agree with Christina in regard to any matter concerning her stepmother, I had to admit that Jackie had no desire for such a rival for attention in the Onassis family.

Fiona could make any woman jealous. If the day came when Alexander brought Fiona into his family and his father was forced to accept this woman as his daughter-in-law, Jackie might well be shaken in her position as the most unique wife of a Onassis man. Perhaps Jackie also worried that if Fiona ever became the mother of Aristo's grandchildren and heirs, Jackie and her own children might suffer financially. Fiona was three years younger than Jackie, was the daughter of a British rear admiral, had achieved international fame as a model before her marriage to a baron, and was a distinct and attractive presence in any gathering. Regardless of whether Fiona became an Onassis wife or mother, I was certain Fiona von Thyssen was not the type of woman Jackie would want sitting opposite her at a dinner party in Glyfada or on the *Christina*.

Although Fiona and Jackie saw little of each other, one day on the *Christina* they were thrown together. Although Mr. Onassis forbade his son to marry Fiona, occasionally he had told him to do whatever he wanted with her, so long as it did not embarrass his family. One afternoon, Aristo invited his son and Fiona to spend the day with him and Jackie and her children on the *Christina*. Unfortunately, he apparently did not inform Jackie of his invitation, for when Fiona and Alexander approached the *Christina* on a Chris-Craft, Jackie was shocked to see them. Jackie had barely greeted Fiona and Alexander when she announced that she had to do some shopping and would be leaving for the nearby Nydri. Before Aristo had a chance to say a word, she arranged for her own Chris-Craft and disappeared for the day.

While Jackie was gone, Fiona and Alexandros spent a wonderful day swimming in the pool and ocean and playing games with John and Caroline. Strangely, that was the first day that Alexandros ever smoked in front of his father, asking permission from Aristo before he lit his cigarette. The day passed quite smoothly, and all five of them appeared happy and relaxed in one another's company. When Jackie arrived back on the *Christina*, loaded with packages from her shopping expedition, she was surprised to find everyone still in the pool, swimming and laughing.

One of the employees of the *Christina* told me that when Fiona came out of the water, she and Jackie ended up sitting in the same chairs that Aristo and Maria always used when they were at the pool. "The two women barely spoke to each other," the employee told me. "The two people in those chairs that day acted nothing like the two who had formerly occupied them."

Often, I had heard other employees on the *Christina* talk about Fiona after she and Alexandros had spent time alone on the boat. Whenever Alexandros and Fiona arrived, the staff on the *Christina* were delighted to have her as a guest on the boat. Her warmth and kindness had made them all adore her. "She is so beautiful," more than one of the employees had remarked to me after her visit to Skorpios. "She would be the perfect first lady of this ship and the entire island." I knew that their unspoken words were insinuating that the current first lady of the island would face stiff competition had Alexandros ever found the courage to marry Fiona.

Ironically, several months before the day of the accident, Artemis had come up with an idea which, if it could have been brought to reality, might have drastically changed the lives of all the members of the Onassis family. An unstoppable matchmaker, Artemis dreamed up the most surprising match of her life: Alexander Onassis and Caroline Kennedy. Such a match had been mentioned before, almost in a joking manner, but this time Artemis was deadly serious.

I was in Glyfada the night she mentioned her plan to Aristo and Jackie. Aristo had been complaining angrily about Fiona and was worried that his son would do something impulsive like marry her. "I do not know what else I can do to make him stop seeing her," he said. "Nothing I say makes that stupid boy realize what a terrible marriage that would be."

"Well, I have one suggestion," Artemis said, and she presented her idea. She had discussed it with me earlier, and I was not at all certain how Mrs. Jackie would react. Her reaction surprised me. She listened carefully to every word Artemis said, as her sister-in-law explained her feelings that it would be good for Caroline to marry an older man. After all, Aristo was twenty-eight years older than Jackie, and look how well their marriage was working. The difference in age between Alexander and Caroline wasn't even nine years. She was sixteen and he was twenty-four. Certainly, she was too young to marry now, but if they could be encouraged to become good friends and spend more time together, then maybe later, when she was ready to marry, they could fall in love.

"Bravo, Artemis," Aristo said, clapping his hands when his sister finished her presentation. "You have come up with a very interesting idea for us to consider. We must plant the seeds for a second marriage between an Onassis man and a Kennedy woman."

Although Jackie was not quite as enthusiastic as her husband, she did smile and said it all sounded like something to consider in the future. She agreed that Caroline and Alexander seemed to enjoy each other's company and that it would be a good idea to try and plan a few more family functions where they would have a chance to be together in Skorpios. Maybe even a family cruise for all of them on the *Chris-*

tina. As I watched her smile and praise Artemis for her clever idea, I could not help thinking that such a marriage, if it ever happened, would please Jackie more than a marriage between Alexander and Fiona. Any worries Jackie might have about Fiona or her child with Alexander receiving a large portion of the Onassis fortune would be dissolved. Instead, it would be Jackie's own daughter who would inherit the millions that would inevitably go to an Onassis heir. I do not know how much Jackie was motivated by considerations of money, but Artemis and I often wondered about the reason for her strong dislike of her stepson's mistress.

Still, we all knew that Caroline was a sweet young girl, but that was all she was, and such a marriage was many years off. I knew how seriously Jackie took her role as a mother, and I understood that she would never consider anything that was not in her children's best interests. In addition, I knew how much Alexander needed to be with an older woman and I doubted that an innocent teenager like Caroline would hold the attraction for him that the experienced, worldly Fiona did. Still, it was obvious that Artemis had given both Aristo and Jackie a great deal to think about, and the match she had suggested was not totally out of the question for either the father of the future groom or the mother of the future bride. For a moment that night, I thought about how the American press had reacted to the marriage of the wife of their former First Lady to Aristotle Onassis. How on earth would they respond, perhaps ten years later, to a marriage between the daughter of the slain president and the son of Aristotle Onassis? Not with unequivocal approval, I was certain.

As I was remembering that fascinating evening in Glyfada, Fiona called the office and I forgot all about Caroline Kennedy and Alexander Onassis, and I put her call through to Alexander immediately. He picked up the phone on the first ring and began to talk to her. For over an hour, the two of them talked. During their telephone call, Koulouris, the offensive photographer, walked into my office, smiling, and holding a package of photographs. Without a word, he placed the package on my desk. I glanced at them quickly, and saw they were all pictures of Alexander and Fiona. I asked him how much he wanted and he told me a hefty sum, which I paid him immediately. As always, I just wanted him out of my office as quickly as possible.

Once Koulouris had left, I opened the package of photographs again and studied each one carefully. They were so beautiful that they almost took my breath away. They had been shot during a recent trip that Alexander and Fiona had taken to Porto-Heli, an island near Piraeus. The two of them looked like children, running uninhibited across the beach, swimming and playing in the ocean, kissing by the edge of the water. Alexander looked so handsome, so dark and athletic, his face filled with smiles I rarely witnessed. And Fiona was stunning and slender, looking years younger than her age of forty, her long, light brown hair blowing in the wind as the two of them raced across the beach. I wondered if she had already lost the baby when the pictures were taken or if she was still or ever really had been pregnant. I wondered if they had already decided to get married when they got to Porto-Heli or if they had just made up their minds that day. I wondered how two people could look so happy and so perfect for each other and still face such overwhelming problems from the Onassis family. And, lastly, I wondered where the photographer had been hiding when he took these glorious photographs.

When Alexander came out of his office, I was still studying the photographs. I was shocked to see that an hour had passed since Koulouris had left. "What are you looking at, Kiki?" Alexander asked me and I looked up to see his serious, unsmiling face.

I handed him the large pile of photographs, but he barely glanced at them. "Did you pay a lot of money for these?" he asked me.

"The usual," I said as he nodded and handed them back to me.

"I'll look at these when I come back," he told me. "I'm going to the airport now."

"But you haven't eaten any lunch," I reminded him.

"I'm not hungry," he informed me, but I kept nagging him until he allowed me to order him a Coca-Cola and a plate of toast. He sat on the edge of my desk and nibbled at the toast and drank the Coke, but he was in a big hurry to go to the airport. I watched him quietly while he finished his small lunch, dressed, as always, in a dark navy suit with a fashionable silk shirt and tie. He certainly looked different than he had looked in the photographs when he had been wearing only his tiny bathing suit. I blushed, despite myself, when I remembered the stories I had heard about Alexandros' legendary sexual prowess. Fiona was, indeed, a lucky woman. I also considered, as I often had before, that Alexandros did not look that much like his father; he was even more handsome than Mr. Onassis. Several years later, when I was about to marry George Moutsatsos, Artemis, in a loving mood, had told George that I was so nice, so good, so beautiful, and so innocent. "But," she added, "Kiki is not so clever or else she would have married Alexandros." That day, in our office on Syngrou Avenue, I pushed away all of those thoughts. Alexandros was my boss, and only my boss. Most of the times when we were together, he would avert his eyes, too shy to look me directly in the face. I knew I was a capable secretary, and that he was always satisfied with and grateful for everything I did for him. Yes, we were friends, too, but we were not destined to become any more than that to each other.

I am certain that Alexandros was not thinking of me as he prepared to leave our office. His life was complicated enough. The subject of his relationship with Fiona made things uneasy between him and his father. And his marriage plans with Fiona, I knew, would only make them more so. Just the way Mr. Onassis' marriage to Jackie had complicated their lives. I had just about given up any hope that Alexander would ever learn to like, never mind love, his father's second wife.

Alexander's relationship with his father, however, had not changed very much during the four years of his father's marriage to a woman Alexander disliked. Despite the fact that both men loved each other, it had never been a perfect father-son relationship. Mr. Onassis was too busy with his business and his personal life to show his son real affection. He could hug him or smile with pleasure when Alexander walked into a room, but in less than a minute his mood could change and he would be angry with something Alexander had done or not done.

Alexander, however, I was certain, was not thinking about his father either as he finished his small lunch. Even though he was in love with Mrs. Baroness Fiona, and she loved him very much and, they were, as I secretly knew, planning to marry, Alexander was still a sad man. The Alexander in the pictures I still held in my hand was a different man from the one in front of me. Perhaps, I thought, I had been foolish to have paid money for those pictures. Perhaps, I should have let the mean-spirited photographer sell the photographs to the newspaper and let everyone know once and for all that Alexander Onassis was in love with the Baroness Fiona von Thyssen-Bornemisza and was planning to marry her.

When Alexander finally got up to leave, I tried to stall him. I did not know why, but I did not want him to leave. I knew he was meeting an American pilot at the airport to train him to fly the Piaggio, but it was already after two. "Why not train him tomorrow, when you can do it earlier?" I suggested.

But he would not listen to me. "Kiki, I am leaving to the airport to fly," he told me. "And if you need something, after flying I will be at the Hilton. Otherwise, I will see you tomorrow."

After Alexander left, I opened the package of photographs again and reexamined each picture. Never had I seen my friend look so carefree, so handsome, or so happy. I could not put them down. I was surprised when I saw my tears fall onto the pictures. I had not realized, nor did I understand why, I was crying. When the phone rang a few minutes before four o'clock that afternoon, I was still looking at the photographs. It was Miltos Yiannacopoulos. "Kikitsa," he said to me in a barely recognizable voice, "we have lost Alexandros."

I was not sure what I was hearing. "What did you say?" I asked him.

"Alexandros went down with his plane," he told me. "He had a terrible accident. We don't know if he is alive or dead."

I was certain I was dreaming. I tried to stand up from my chair, but my legs would not hold me. For a moment, I lost my senses and could not remember anything. I picked up the phone and heard that Miltos was no longer there. I tried to remember the phone number for the house in Glyfada but my fingers would not move. Finally, they dialed the number. I spoke to Panagiotis, who told me that everyone there had gotten the news a few minutes earlier. I could hear the screaming in the background. Mrs. Artemis was out of her mind.

I had barely hung up the phone when the door to my office opened and Costas Konialidis, Aristo's cousin and closest friend, walked in. "Kiki, what terrible thing has happened?" he asked me. "What destruction has come to us?" Before I could answer one word, he took me in his arms and held me and we were both sobbing against each other. For a long time, we just held each other and wept, and then we stopped because we both knew what had to be done. Without a word, we found the telephone numbers we needed and began the impossible task of informing the other members of the family what we had just learned. Together, we called Aristo and Jackie in New York, Christina in Brazil, Tina in Switzerland, and Fiona in London.

"How can I tell Aristo?" Costas cried to me as he dialed the phone number of the New York office. Aristo barely said a word to Costas Konialidis when he learned the news. It was as if he had lost the ability to speak.

I was dialing Fiona's number but I could not get through. I put the phone down for one minute when she called. "Kiki," she asked in a small voice, "is it true?"

"It is true," I answered, and she hung up the telephone.

The moment Mr. Costas Konialidis left the office to go to the airport to make arrangements to meet the family, a cameraman appeared in front of my desk and insisted that he be allowed to take a video inside Alexander's office. I told him that it was not the right time to do such a thing and, out of respect for Alexander, he must wait. But he would not listen to me and began to force his way into Alexander's office. I thought for sure I would kill this man with my bare hands, but I did not. Instead, I screamed and other men from the company came in and forcibly removed the cameraman from the building. Then I locked up Alexandros' office so that nobody else could go in.

It did not take long for everybody to know about the accident, and the telephones started to ring without any stop. I remember that for some time I had lost all my senses. I was answering the phones and talking to some of the press, but I was not really there. I did not know where I was, but the person who was in my office talking about Alexandros' accident was not me. It could not be.

All I could think about was how many times Mr. Onassis had told Alexander not to get on the airplane before it had been checked. I could hear him standing beside my desk, telling his son to make sure all the instruments had been carefully inspected. And Alexandros had always answered him with a gentle, half-mocking smile. "Yes, Baba," he would say. "I will check everything. There is nothing for you to worry about." And Aristo would half push and half hug him and watch his son walk out of the room. This scene happened so often it was engraved into my mind. But I would never see it happen again. I would never hear those words, "Yes, Baba," again. I would never see that son walk out of my office again. This could not be happening. It had to be a dream.

But it was not a dream. And immediately after the accident I learned that the flaps of the airplane had been put in the wrong places. The left was where the right should be, and the right where the left should have been. That is why the Piaggio plane, at 3:15 that Monday afternoon, with Alexander in the right-hand seat, and the American pilot he was training, Donald McCusker, in the seat to his left, and the experienced Canadian pilot Donald McGregor, in the rear left seat, instead of going up more than one hundred feet, crashed down onto the runway. The two other pilots would both live, but Alexander would die. The doctors at Kat Hospital in Athens would keep him alive with machines until the family arrived, but there was no chance that he would survive the accident involving flaps that must not have been checked.

The next twenty-four hours were a nightmare. Alexander's handsome face had been smashed beyond recognition. Mr. Onassis and Jackie went directly to Kat Hospital, but there was so large a crowd in front of the hospital that their car could not pass through. Jackie tried to get out of the car and walk the few remaining feet to the hospital, but Aristo could not move at all. She came back into the car and sat beside him until the car finally made its way to the door of the hospital. Seconds later, Tina and Stavros Niarchos arrived at the hospital. With faces turned yellow with shock and pain, Tina kissed Aristo, and Aristo kissed Niarchos. For that moment, all their differences were forgotten and only one thing mattered: Alexandros. However, no one, I noticed, kissed Jackie, who stood beside her husband, silent, her eyes looking down.

Despina, the wife of President Papadopoulos, had been at Alexander's side before members of the family arrived, but Fiona came soon and never left. When Aristo got to the hospital, Fiona was already there. For the next twenty hours, she never left Alexandros' side. She never looked at anyone in the room, except for Alexandros, although she did answer Aristo and Tina when they spoke to her. She did not move from Alexandros' side, nor did she eat a morsel of food or take a sip of water. The nurses had given her a white robe, which made her look even taller and paler than usual. With her light brown hair streaked with blond and translucent skin, she looked almost angelic, as if she were a mirage in the midst of the hell into which we all had fallen. But if she were an angel, she was an angel without life. Her eyes, which were locked on Alexander's face, did not seem to see anyone else in the room, just her lover. She held his hand in hers, as if she believed he could feel her touch. Her lips moved in what I thought was silent prayer.

During those final hours of Alexander's life, the room was filled with the members of the family, as Artemis, Tina, Merope, Kalliroi, Christina, Jackie and Aristo came and went, each of them crying, some aloud, some silently, their lips all moving, like Fiona's, in prayer.

In my own private world of grief, I could still see Fiona, and despite the haze in which I stood, I noted the way the family deferred to this woman they had, for the past six years, shunned. Even when Aristo came to touch his son, Fiona barely flinched. Her hand still clutching Alexander's, she assumed the position in his death scene that she had never been allowed in his life, connected to him by a bond no Onassis dared disturb. Occasionally her hand traveled to her lover's face, where his nose, which miraculously did not seem shattered, and his eyes, which never opened, remained unbandaged, or to his motionless body beneath the white sheet, but mostly it was his hand she would not release.

One of the most tragic figures in that room full of tragic figures was unquestionably Christina. Supported by her aunts, she stood beyond the bed, sobbing openly, shaking her head as if to rid herself of a hideous dream, crying out her brother's name, begging him to wake up and speak to her. Even when Christina cried out, Fiona did not flinch. I was certain she heard nothing in the room, except the sounds of the machines keeping Alexandros alive.

Jackie stood beside her husband, her face bare of cosmetics, her lips praying, her skin pale, as if at any moment she might faint. But Fiona did not look as if she might faint. Yet, strangely, although she looked as if she might die, just be blown away by the slightest wind, she also appeared so strong that it seemed to be her breath that was keeping everyone in the room, including the body beneath the sheets, alive. When I closed my eyes I could see that same body running like a young boy across the beach in Porto-Heli, and I thought my heart would break into a million pieces and I would surely die.

Many doctors, neurosurgeons and cardiologists and plastic surgeons, flown in from all over the world, walked in and out of the room, yet not one could offer any hope. Mr. Onassis listened to them all, but spoke finally to the plastic surgeon, who had arrived on Mr. Onassis' special jet from Switzerland. "You must fix his face," he ordered the Swiss surgeon when he arrived in Athens. "You must make him look like Alexander again so that I can remember his face as it was." And the doctor did what Mr. Onassis asked. He performed extensive, highly skilled plastic surgery on the face of a man who would inevitably and soon die.

On Tuesday afternoon when I went to see Alexandros, Fiona was of course standing next to him, holding his hand. Even though the plastic surgeon had spent hours reconstructing his face, it was still crushed badly. There were so many machines attached to Alexander's body that he looked as if he had been swallowed up by an ugly monster armed with plastic tubes. All I could think was that Alexander already looked dead.

A little after six o'clock that afternoon, Mr. Onassis came back to the office. "I have lost my boy," he said to me as he walked to my desk. It was as if his black and silver hair had turned white in one day.

And I lied and said, "No, I do not believe it," but he did not answer me.

Then he came over to my desk and asked me to call the Kat Hospital. I will never forget the words he spoke to the neurosurgeon late that afternoon. "If I give you all my ships, all my property, all my planes, and all the money that I have, would there be any hope to save my boy?" I knew what the answer would be before the doctor told him. "Then leave him be in peace," Mr. Onassis said into the telephone, and he handed it to me.

"It is over," he told me when I put the phone down. "My boy is gone." For a long moment, he stared at me, and then he spoke. "Call Johannesburg for me. You remember someone who was interested in doing business with us. We must call him now."

"No, Mr. Onassis," I said. "I will not make that call for you now. It is not the proper time to do business." He was, I realized, crazy with his grief, and this was the only way he could not lose all his mind. So I waited a few minutes, cleaned my face, and came back and made that one call for him.

While Alexander lay dying in the hospital, the journalists did not let us alone. They forced their way into my office to try to see Mr. Onassis whenever he left the hospital and came into the building. I tried to answer their questions as well as I could, but the sheer effort of putting up with them became too much for me to handle. A few of the journalists were sensitive and tried to consider my feelings, but most of them were callous and unfeeling and just wanted gossip for their papers. After Alexander died, the phone calls and visits became even worse. There seemed nowhere I could hide to avoid the army of the press. Finally, an hour after his son's death, Mr. Onassis decided he would give a press conference. "You do not have to do this, Mr. Onassis," I told him, but he insisted.

"All I ask is that you stand beside me," he said, and then we allowed into the office a group of forty journalists. For ten minutes, Mr. Onassis answered their questions as best he could. And then his voice grew so weak that he could hardly speak. I knew, as I watched him try to conduct himself with some degree of strength, that he was a proud man who would never cry in front of others, who would hold his grief private for as long as possible. In his barely audible voice, he told them how he had offered all his ships and planes and money to save his son's life, but still the doctors had informed him there was no hope. He told them about his plans for Olympic Airways and how he would continue his son's commitments for Olympic Aviation. He told them about the pain of losing his only son. Now tears were streaming down his face, but still they continued to ask him questions.

"It is enough," I finally said, and I beckoned for the security men to come into my office. Without another word, Mr. Onassis sat down at my desk and did not speak another word until the office had been emptied of the press.

The next morning, I had to return to the hospital with the clothes we would put on Alexander's body for his funeral. Panagiotis had no trouble finding me a suitable black suit for Alexandros to wear, but the shoes he brought me would not fit his swollen feet. I stood perfectly still while Fiona tried unsuccessfully to place the shoes on Alexander's feet as he lay on a table in hospital mortuary and the plastic surgeon made more stitches on his face. Suddenly, as I looked at Alexander lying on the table, his face still barely recognizable but with stitches covering the inflamed and distorted skin, I lost consciousness and fell to the floor. A nurse revived me, and Fiona, who had still not left his side, offered me a glass of water.

After that lapse, I forced myself to control my emotions and perform the job I was sent to do. In Alexandros' perfectly neat suite at the Hilton, I searched alone and unsuccessfully for a larger pair of black shoes. So I left the hotel in search of size 48 shoes, which I bought in a shoe store in Athens. This time, when I walked into the hospital mortuary, I did not faint. I handed the shoes to Fiona, ran my fingers across Alexandros' cold, disfigured face one last time, and left the hospital.

Mr. Onassis had finally, after much deliberation, decided that Alexander would be interred in a mausoleum, which would be built as soon as possible in Skorpios. His funeral, however, would be held on Thursday in the Saint Lazare Greek Orthodox Church in downtown Athens, and his coffin would be open. The church was not huge, but the crowd of mourners was. Everyone in the family was in terrible condition, especially Christina. She was unable to stand for a long period of time and could barely move through the crowd. Somehow those who were surrounding Christina moved her from one person's hands to the other, passing her expertly through the crowd so that she did not have to move by herself, until she entered the sanctuary, where the open casket lay. "Why did you want to leave me alone?" she cried to Alexander's body. "I wanted to die, not you. Please come back to me, Alexandros. I beg you to come back to me."

Fiona was positioned between two friends who supported her firmly. She, too, seemed barely able to walk on her own. Yet I saw her stand, her head somehow still held high, beside the casket where Alexandros lay, dressed in his black suit and new shoes, his eyeglasses in place above his straight nose. For a second, I was rendered nearly senseless as I realized for the first time what a miraculous job the plastic surgeon had ultimately performed, restoring all of Alexander's beauty to the rest of his face. Not only was Alexandros recognizable, he was as handsome as I remembered. It was inconceivable that the surgeon could have transformed the disfigured face I had seen a day earlier to its original state of beauty, but that was exactly what the talented doctor had done. I saw Fiona's lips move as she touched his face, but I could not hear one word she spoke. I averted my eyes as she bent down to kiss his near-perfect face and struggled with all my strength to control my sobs for my handsome but lifeless dear, dear friend.

People from all over the world came to the funeral, dignitaries from foreign countries and businesspeople from every major city. Ted Kennedy came, as did all the many friends of the Onassis family and the Olympic Airways directors. Yet Onassis did not seem to notice who was there. He did not take his eyes off his son's casket, nor did he utter one word. Caroline and John were, of course, there, too, seated beside Martha Sgubin, and Jackie's eyes moved back and forth between her husband and her children, but she barely spoke one word to any of them. Before he left the sanctuary, Aristo kneeled in front of the casket and gently kissed his son's face. Fiona, Tina, and Christina did the same. As she kissed her brother's face, Christina fell against the casket and had to be helped up by two of the pallbearers. Jackie never left her husband's side during the service, but when he walked out of the church, he put his arm around Christina, who clung to him desperately. "I have only you now, Baba," I heard her say to him, and he nodded slightly. Jackie let her husband and his daughter pass in front of her, and she and Artemis followed the two of them, their long thin arms tightly wrapped around each other.

After the funeral service was concluded at the church, Alexandros' casket was placed in a closed car and he was secretly brought by plane to Skorpios, avoiding the huge crowd of journalists and photographers who were waiting for the casket to pass them by. Fiona remained at the side of the casket, until it was finally placed on the plane. Then she left for Skorpios on a separate plane. All the other members of the family and close friends also went to the airport, where one large plane and several smaller planes flew them to the airport at Preveza. From Preveza, they were taken by boat to Skorpios. Aristo and Jackie and their families flew on the same plane as Tina and Stavros. Except for occasional quiet weeping, there was a heartbroken silence on that plane.

The weather was even colder and darker than it had been in Athens. The angry sky looked as if it would erupt into rain showers at any moment. As we approached the island on our boat, I could not recognize the beautiful island of Skorpios, where I had previously experienced only joy and pleasure. This could not be the same island, I thought, as the boat was pulled onto the shore by waiting hands. Suddenly I remembered the day, perhaps two years earlier, when I had been standing on the beach watching Alexander approach the waiting Piaggio with several friends. Suddenly there had been a loud burst of laughter and then Alexander was throwing his friend, who was dressed in a business suit, into the ocean. Seconds later, it was Alexander, fully clothed as well, who was being tossed unceremoniously into the ocean by his other friend. "Watch out, Kiki!" Alexander had shouted to me as his head emerged from the water. "Run!" And I had run, as fast as I could, back to the *Christina,* never turning around to see what was now happening at the water's edge. Now, on this cold, black day, there was no Alexander yelling to me, no joy, no laughter. Here the sunshine had been replaced with darkness and the songs of the birds with deathly silence. The *Christina* loomed ahead of us, hushed and dispirited, its flag lowered and barely moving. This was not the magical Skorpios on whose soil I was standing. Instead, it was some cruel land where dreams withered and nightmares came true.

It was on Skorpios, however, that the burial service was held, in the same chapel where Jackie and Aristo had been married four years and three months earlier. This time, the chapel was filled with only white flowers, and all who came wore not bright party dresses but clothes of black. This time Mr. Onassis came not to wed his second wife, but to bury his only son. The casket was carried into the chapel by six pallbearers who were all employees of the *Christina* and had known Alexandros for much of his life. Each one of them was quietly sobbing. Alexandros was buried near the chapel, in a grave that was later covered with a small house or mausoleum. Few photographers and journalists were allowed at the burial service, but hundreds of weeping people from nearby Levkas flooded the island for the service, arriving in an army of small boats. There was so much sobbing and hysterical screaming at the grave that I thought for sure someone would faint, but no one did. Fiona, supported as before by two friends, stood apart from the family. She spoke not a word to anyone during or after the service.

After the service was concluded, Aristo bent to the casket one last time and gently touched his son's handsome face. The rest of the family did the same, dropping wine and soil and flowers into the casket. As Aristo was walking out of the church, his arm tightly entwined with Christina's arm, for one awful minute, it appeared as if he might fall. Christina struggled to hold him up; it seemed as if her father could no longer walk under his own power. At that moment, a simple man from Nydri who was standing nearby, his own face streaked with tears, yelled out, "You must have courage, old man! You must walk by yourself, old man."

I was horror stricken to hear such cruel words, yet Mr. Onassis looked into the face of the peasant who had spoken to him and managed a slight nod. Then, almost as if it were a miracle, Mr. Onassis grew visibly stronger, and with his head held high and his body upright, he moved forward, walking almost jauntily like a young man. It was his intense pride, Artemis explained to me later, that had propelled him forward at that moment. The simple man from Nydri had done him a great favor by reawakening that dormant but never dead Onassis pride.

Finally, that dark winter day, when the burial was concluded, coffee and freshly baked rolls were served in the pink house, but hardly anyone could eat. Slowly, silently, the mourners returned in their boats and planes to Athens or Levkas. Aristo and Jackie and the rest of the Onassis family, but not Fiona, remained on the *Christina* after the island had been emptied of the large throng of mourners.

Forty days after Alexander's death, a memorial service was held in the chapel on Skorpios to mark the end of the mourning period. Again, like the day of the funeral, the weather was cold and cloudy and the skies were ready to rain. This time the mausoleum was complete and I had made certain it would be covered with white flowers before the service. Again, nearly all the islanders from Levkas joined the family and close friends in the chapel. The service was brief, no more than a half hour. Tina and Artemis stood side by side, and Christina remained beside her father and Jackie. Fiona, as always, stood alone. No one talked or wept during the services, and all heads looked down. Unlike the day of the funeral, there was, except for the voice of the priest, complete silence among the mourners.

When the service ended, a simple buffet of bread, wine, and coffee was offered to the mourners in the pink house. Once again, immediately after the buffet, the planes and boats returned the mourners to Athens and to Levkas. Jackie and Aristo, along with Theodore and Artemis, however, again remained in Skorpios for a few days.

Fiona is in her sixties today, and the last time I saw her, she did not look well. I had known that she was very close with two handsome brothers, Dimitris and Michalis Vitos, both of whom had been good friends of Professor Georgakis at Pantios University. The professor had always been very fond of Fiona and had enjoyed whatever time he had spent with her and Alexander. Of course, the three of them were never together with Aristo, but the professor had found time to be with Fiona and Alexander himself.

"Fiona is a wonderful woman, Kiki," he had told me once. "Aristo is very wrong not to encourage her to marry his son." Today Fiona is living with Dimitris Vitos. Roula Strathis told me that Fiona had been planning to buy her house in the Plaka in Greece, but for some unknown reason, that has never happened. Instead, Fiona and Dimitris are living in London, and are supposedly thinking of buying a house in Mykonos. I no longer have the pictures that Koulouris took of her and Alexander in Porto-Heli, but the image of the two of them as they played on the beach will always remain in my mind. I wish Fiona well and only pray that she can find the happiness that eluded her when Alexander died.

There was, of course, an investigation about the plane crash that had killed Alexander. We all knew that something was wrong and strange with the plane, so that instead of going up, it went down. No one had forgotten the crash two years earlier, when the Learjet crashed on its approach to the Monte Carlo airport to pick up Alexander, killing George and Dimitris Kouris, whose bodies were never found. Then, too, there had been an investigation, one led most forcibly by Alexandros, but even he had not been able find out what had caused that plane to explode in the air in 1971.

The investigation of the crash that killed Alexander Onassis in 1973 was as inconclusive as the crash that killed the Kouris brothers. Mr. Onassis offered a reward of $20 million for information about Alexander's crash, but nothing helped him to find the truth. And nothing helped him recover from the death of his son. He tried to go about his business as usual and prove that he was his normal self, but it was a game he could no longer either play or win. The power that had propelled him to build his empire was slowly fading from his grasp.

Yet, far more important, Mr. Onassis was losing not just his power to succeed, but his will to live. For him, there was no longer any reason to continue to exist. Three months earlier, Miltos Yiannacopoulos had been certain that his friend Aristotle Onassis had baffled the world by successfully maintaining both a marriage and an affair, involving two highly desirable and much publicized women, but that feat was no longer of any importance to Aristo. No woman, no matter how much he loved her, could fill the void Alexander's death created. I know how he felt because there were many times I, too, did not want to get up and face the office and the world without Alexander's presence. But I was not Alexander's father, or his mistress, or his sister. To my boss Alexandros, I was just a simple friend. So, even unhappy, I could live. But Mr. Onassis could not.

Chapter Thirteen

Welcome, Thanatos

B EFORE ALEXANDER'S death, Mr. Onassis had lived life like a game he could easily win. In business, he had always told me that the only rule was that there were no rules. With women, we had all seen that he followed the same game plan. For him, the strategy had always worked. But when fate intervened and changed the game, taking away his most precious possession, he could no longer play.

All the women who loved him were still alive and at his side, and each of them struggled to bring him back to life. But no one could. I watched helplessly as Artemis, despite her own broken heart over the loss of her adored nephew, tried to fuss even more than usual over her brother. Yet no matter how she complimented him or what special foods she prepared for him, she could not raise his fallen spirits. Christina struggled to swallow her own grief so that she could help her father deal with his, yet he did not seem able to allow her to perform such a mission. We all noticed that Aristo went even more often to Paris after Alexander's death, seeking solace from his soul mate, the only woman he believed could understand his pain. Yet when he returned to Athens, he was the same sad, defeated man who had left a few days earlier.

As for Jackie, she did all she could to help the husband from whom she had been growing distant. For the traditional Greek forty days of mourning following Alexander's death, Jackie, like his sisters and daughter, wore black dresses, several of which Roula designed for her, and eliminated makeup and jewelry. I sensed a new air of sadness about her, sadness mingled with regret. Perhaps, I often thought, she regretted that she had not loved her stepson more, had not tried to win his affection or, at the very least, his approval. Immediately after the funeral, she talked to me about Alexander, asking me how I was doing and if it was difficult for me to work in the office without him. I was grateful for her concern and kind words and regretted that my tears did not allow me to answer her in a more suitable and proper manner.

Mrs. Jackie was correct, however, in assuming that it would be nearly impossible for me to work in the office without him. For the forty days of mourning, I did not work in the Syngrou Avenue office. As Mrs. Jackie had sensitively assumed, I could not look at my desk or my telephone or Alexander's desk without painful memories. When Costas Konialidis suggested I work in the airport office, I was grateful for the change. However, as soon as the forty days of mourning ended, I was ready to return to Syngrou Avenue. The painful memories were still everywhere, but I felt a bit stronger about facing them. It was then that I began to hear the talk of the curse. "It all started when he married her," employees at the Airways and on Skorpios and in Glyfada began to whisper. "When he was with Maria, there was no tragedy. Only good things happened then. Something caused Alexandros' death. Perhaps it was her."

I ignored all the whispers, but I began to notice that in many places where I went, I heard simple Greek people discussing such a curse. The Greek word *atyhya* ("curse") was mentioned more and more, even once in a small Greek newspaper. Aristo was, I knew personally, a superstitious man, who would wear one particular suit to an important meeting because he had worn it during a successful meeting a week earlier. He hated to fire an employee, fearing that the employee might have been good luck and that firing him would bring bad luck. He had even joked that he stayed with a woman merely because he feared leaving her would disturb his present string of good luck. After all, he had hired me only because the value of the drachma rose the first time I came to his office. But he would never have believed, I was certain, that his marriage to his second wife had caused the death of his son.

Artemis never brought up the subject of a curse herself, but she did not stop her guests from discussing it once one of them mentioned it. "It is just bad kismet," she commented during one such discussion in Glyfada. "Jackie is not responsible for it."

Jackie herself seemed oblivious to the whisperings behind her back. Yet it was apparent to all of us that she was trying to be more loving to her husband. Every day, no matter where she was, Jackie called the office to see how he was doing. And she did appear to be trying to spend more time in Greece. "How is Aristo today, Kiki?" she would ask me, either from Greece or New York. "Does he seem any better than yesterday?"

"A little bit better, Mrs. Jackie," I would answer her, but we both knew I was lying.

"Did he eat much for lunch?" she would ask on her next phone call.

"Oh, yes, Mrs. Jackie," I'd lie again before I put her call through to his line. "He ate a very good lunch today."

Every day, he looked sadder and thinner and more lost. "Why was it not me who died?" he would ask me while I tried to work at my desk.

"Why am I the father still alive and my son is dead?" I had no answers to his questions.

Jackie also called me frequently to make arrangements for trips and dinners and visits that she hoped would restore Aristo's broken spirit. She organized a cruise with Pierre Salinger and his wife from Dakar in West Africa to the Antilles. She cruised with Aristo to Egypt and flew with him to Mexico. But none of these trips held much pleasure for Mr. Onassis. There were times when he appeared to enjoy the dinners Jackie planned or the visits to the tavernas or their quiet walks along the beach in Glyfada, but for the most part, nothing Jackie or anyone did brought him any joy.

So often, on the patio in Glyfada, Artemis and I would watch Aristo and Jackie walking together by the ocean. Jackie tried to encourage her husband to walk every day with her. Some days he agreed, but many he refused. One day, several months after Alexander's death, when I watched the two of them on the beach, Mr. Onassis looked as if he had aged twenty years in these few months. He was bent over and he seemed to have difficulty walking. Mrs. Jackie also looked less strong and she, too, walked cautiously and slowly.

Another day, a couple who lived nearby in Glyfada were out walking when they encountered Mr. and Mrs. Onassis. "They seemed so quiet and sad," the neighbor told me afterward. "My husband and I offered them our arms and we were surprised that they both took them. The four of us continued onward together, but it was obvious that Mr. and Mrs. Onassis were having difficulty walking."

Yet another time, I went for a walk along the ocean in Glyfada with the two of them. My shoes were hurting and Jackie insisted that they wait while I went back to the house and put on a larger, more comfortable pair of shoes. The two of them were walking toward me when I approached the beach, wearing a different pair of shoes. They were walking arm in arm, so lost in a deep conversation that they did not realize I had returned until they reached the spot where I was standing. On that day and so many other times after the death of her stepson, Jackie appeared more human than she had before. Her usual smile was missing and the pain on her face was unmistakable. At those moments, she was sharing her husband's grief.

Still, the talk of the curse continued unabated. Added to this topic was the rumor of a possible divorce between Jackie and Aristo. In January 1974, during a flight returning to Athens from a trip to Acapulco that Jackie had planned for the two of them, Aristo rewrote his will. I have no idea what he was thinking at that time, but he made changes in his will so that Jackie would not receive the one-fourth of the *Christina*, of Skorpios, and all of Aristo's property to which, according to Greek law, she was entitled. But I never personally heard then, or at any other time, any mention of his plans to actually divorce her. Also Miltos Yiannacopoulos, to whom he spoke about all his major decisions, never discussed the subject of a divorce with Mr. Onassis.

Yet there was no denying that life for Mr. and Mrs. Onassis grew more difficult and painful. Especially, of course, for him. Before Alexander's death, Aristo had never had typical sleep habits, but after the accident, he rarely slept at night. Many nights, the personnel on the *Christina* saw him wandering around Skorpios, usually accompanied only by his mongrel dog, Vana. Vana had been found by Achilles, one of the *Christina*'s employees, many years earlier, roaming around the island. Although everybody on the ship fed the dog, she recognized only one person, Aristo, as her master. The dog would pace along the beach of the island, waiting impatiently for her master's Piaggio to return him to Skorpios. It was almost unearthly the way the dog would sense that he was en route to the island. Before his hydroplane could be heard or seen, she would suddenly appear on the beach, and remain frozen in her spot until the Piaggio appeared.

After Alexander's death, Vana became even more important in her master's life and would accompany Mr. Onassis on his midnight walks. The personnel on the *Christina* told me that you could see that Mr. Onassis was talking to his companion during the walk and that the dog's attention was so riveted on Aristo's face that it appeared as if she could understand his every word. With his cigar in his mouth and his dog at his side, and more wine and ouzo than he ever drank before, Mr. Onassis struggled to fight some of the nighttime demons that kept him from his wife and bed.

Many nights, Mr. Onassis and Vana would end up at Alexander's tomb, where Aristo would sit down on the cold evening grass, pull out a bottle of ouzo and two glasses from his jacket pocket, and drink and talk to his son. One of the *Christina* employees who followed him there from a safe distance several times said that Mr. Onassis talked to Alexander about problems at Olympic Airways or Olympic Aviation, his voice calm and clear. Often during the one-sided conversation he would stop talking and concentrate on the silence, as if he were hearing his son's words. "Yes, Alexandros," he would say after a few minutes, "you are right. That is what I should do. Thank you, my boy."

Another time, the same employee told me that Mr. Onassis spent several hours at that spot, weeping openly, telling his son how much he missed him and asking him over and over how such a terrible accident could ever have occurred. He put one glass of ouzo beside the grave and kept lifting his own glass as he repeated, "My son, I want to drink, you and me together. But you don't hear me."

During those late-night excursions, Mr. Onassis was usually wearing only a short-sleeved shirt and pants and seemed oblivious to the chill in the nighttime island air. At my request, the employee went to Alexander's grave every night before Mr. Onassis' visit and spread a wool blanket on the cold grass. Mr. Onassis never questioned how the blanket arrived there and merely sat on it and spread out the wine and bread and cheese for him and his son and dog. Most of these nights, he would remain in that one spot until the sun came up.

Often during the day, Aristo would return to the same spot. Telling everyone that he was going to visit Ithaki, he would head out in a small Chris-Craft, carrying a bag filled with a bottle of ouzo, two glasses, and bread and cheese. We all knew, however, that the boat would never land on Ithaki. Instead, we could hear the noisy motor approach a more remote part of Skorpios, where he would dock the boat and hike slowly to the mausoleum. That seemed to be the only spot where he found any semblance of peace.

One particularly sad Sunday afternoon when I was visiting Jackie and Aristo on Skorpios, he told the two of us to come with him at two o'clock when he visited the mausoleum. When we got there, he had arranged for a table with a white tablecloth and four place settings with napkins, beautiful dishes, and silver and crystal to be set up in front of the grave. A few minutes after we sat down, a servant from the *Christina* arrived, carrying platters filled with a delicious lunch. While he served us lunch, Mr. Onassis filled the four wineglasses and insisted that the food, including the special meatballs that Alexandros

particularly enjoyed, be placed on all four plates. Mr. Onassis was relatively cheerful during the lunch, talking to me and Jackie about
Alexander and some of the warm memories he had of his son. Often,
during the meal, he toasted his son, telling us that there was one place
near where we were sitting where he had heard Alexandros' voice several times. Jackie's eyes met mine during one of these toasts, and she
shook her head briefly and sadly.

After we finished our dessert, however, Aristo's mood darkened
and his eyes filled with tears. "I miss my boy," he said softly as he put
down his empty wineglass. Jackie's eyes were filled with tears as she
reached across the table for her husband's hand. There was, however,
nothing that she could say to ease her husband's pain.

Mrs. Artemis told me of a similar meal she shared with her
brother and her husband and her "nephew." Again, there were the
white tablecloths and the special foods and the toasting and the stories. And, again, at the conclusion of the meal, the heart-wrenching
tears. "Neither Theodore nor I could swallow one morsel of food," Mrs.
Artemis told me. "I thought my heart would break when my beautiful
Popi died, but I survived. My brother, I am so afraid, will not."

Christina was as devastated as her father by the loss of her
brother, but she did attempt to look beyond her own despair over the
loss of her brother and distract her father from his misery. When her
mother suggested the possibility of a match between her and her cousin
Philippe Niarchos, the oldest son of her aunt Eugenie and Stavros Niarchos, Christina listened politely. Philippe was handsome, outgoing,
and fun, and it might interest her father to consider a union with his
rival shipowner. It was against Greek law for first cousins to marry, but
as in most cases, if there was enough money involved, anything could
be done. Philippe's father favored the match and urged the two young
people to try and spend time together and see if they were compatible.
Although Aristo did not actively support the plan, he did not oppose it,
and, considering his depressed state, that was enough to propel Christina to move forward with the match. Philippe, who looked a bit like
Alexander Onassis, was more than willing to follow his own father's
instructions. He and Christina did enjoy each other's company and
indulged their parents' wishes with a weekend away, just the two of
them. During the weekend, however, romance never entered the pic-

ture as the two of them laughed and giggled and behaved just the way two good friends or close cousins would act together. After that weekend, they made certain their parents understood there would never be an Onassis-Niarchos marriage. At least, not between these two relatives.

Once that distraction was over, Christina concentrated much of her energy on finding someone to blame for all the unhappiness that had befallen her family. It didn't take her long to find this person: Jackie. She had never hidden her dislike of Jackie, but now it appeared to overwhelm her. She reveled in all the whispering about the curse and its connection to her stepmother, fanning the flames of a dangerous fire. "I have always known that Jackie was a curse," she told me. "Before she entered our family, we were strong and well. Now the Kouris brothers are dead, my aunt Eugenie is dead, my brother is dead, Olympic Airways is slipping away, and so is my father. Before she came to us, she was by her American husband's side when he died. My unlucky father had to go find her and bring her to our shores. Now the curse is a part of our family, and before long she will kill us all."

No matter how I tried to reason with her, Christina could not listen to me. Everything terrible that had happened was Jackie's fault. I was not the only person to whom Christina offered her theory. Every time she was with her father, she told him her thoughts. Most times, he ordered her to be quiet, but as the weeks and months after Alexander's death moved on, he silenced her less.

To add to Christina's list of catastrophes that had befallen the Onassis family since Aristo married Jackie could be added the failure of Mr. Onassis' New Hampshire refinery plans in 1974. Although the plans for his refinery, carefully orchestrated by Costas Gratsos, appeared to be proceeding successfully and with the encouragement of New Hampshire governor Meldrim Thomson, Jr., when they hit an irreversible snag in March, Costas Gratsos urged Mr. Onassis to stop the negotiations. "Enjoy what you have," Costas urged his dejected friend. "You have enough money to live comfortably for as long as you want. Let things be."

In regard to Olympic Airways, it also became evident that Christina was right. Her father's power was fading quickly. Mr. Onassis had always said that the ships were the heart of his business while the airplanes were for Alexander. Yet Alexander's love for flying had made the Airways all the more important to his father. With Alexander at his side, the Airways had become a powerful challenge, but without Alexander, Aristo no longer had the energy to continue that venture. To make matters worse, the government was constantly challenging him to give up the Airways, so finally, after years of fighting, in January 1975, Mr. Onassis told his lawyer, Tryfon Koutalidis, to make the arrangements to sell it to them. Early one morning, at around one-thirty A.M., after five hours of negotiations, Mr. Onassis came out of a meeting with Koutalidis and the ministers of the government. I saw immediately that he was in a very bad mood. His face was black. He didn't have his jacket on, and the sleeves of his shirt were rolled up.

He looked at me and said, "Kiki, try to prepare the documents we need. Then we will leave." I did as he asked and, after he had signed the papers, the two of us walked to the elevator alone. When we got into the elevator, he started to cry. "You know how it is to give birth to a child?" he asked me as tears fell down his face, and I shook my head no. "Well, I gave birth to Olympic Airways in 1956, and for eighteen years I watched it grow. To see it get so big, then to lose it and let it die, is too awful."

"How did this happen?" I asked him. "I cannot understand it at all."

He told me that he could not avoid what had happened. He said he had to choose between keeping Olympic Airways and giving something else to the government. He was, for the first time in his life, trapped. "But I couldn't believe they would take Olympic," he told me. "It was, you know, all I had left." I knew that was not true, that he still maintained a fleet of at least a hundred tankers, many properties and companies all over the world, and a huge fortune. But I understood what he meant. Again, he had lost his son. Again, his plane had been shot down from the sky.

The terms of the agreement with the government were not perfect, nor were they impossible to live with. Although he asked for $78 million, Mr. Onassis was paid $68,788,312. Frustrated with the way the government was treating him, Mr. Onassis went to court, where a decision was reached ordering the government to compensate him an additional $1.5 million, in four equal payments, to cover the cost of materials for repairs to the planes for which he had already paid. Also, Mr. Onassis was allowed to sell two 707s to Jordan for $9 million and to keep his own Learjet and two helicopters.

Still, that night after the initial portion of the sale had been completed, there was no sense of satisfaction on my employer's face as we got into the car, and George drove to my house. I wanted to say something, but I looked at Mr. Onassis and I saw that there were fresh tears on his face, so I said nothing. But I knew that night that he would not live long. The ships would not be enough to sustain him. He had no reason to live. I wished with all my heart that Jackie could give him a reason to live, but I also knew then that even though she had tried, she had not.

Several months before Mr. Onassis had surrendered Olympic Airways to the government, he had suffered another serious loss: Tina Onassis Niarchos died on September 10, 1974. After Alexander died, she had become ill and Mr. Onassis was very concerned about her health. Many times he had told me that Tina was a child who never grew up. "During our marriage," he said, "I had three children: Alexander, Christina, and Tina."

After the death of their son, Tina became even more childlike. Often she would call him at the office and cry, in her half-Greek and half-English slurred speech, "My baby. My baby. Where is my baby? I want to see my baby." The relationship between Niarchos and Mr. Onassis had deteriorated after Alexander's death, and Aristo knew that Stavros did not want him to call or visit his home. He told Tina that she was welcome to come to Skorpios to visit Alexander's grave anytime she desired, but he also knew that her husband frowned on any trips his wife took to Greece.

Mr. Onassis was, however, delighted when Tina called to tell him that she and Stavros would accept his invitation and come to Skorpios to visit Alexandros' grave. Aristo planned the visit during a week when Jackie was in New York seeing her children. Tina and Stavros arrived on the *Christina* the day after Jackie left for New York and spent two days with Aristo. Mr. Onassis made certain that the beautiful portrait of Tina that Jackie had insisted be removed from the living room of the *Christina* was placed back on the wall where it had previously hung.

Mr. Onassis was deeply distressed to see how worn and tired his first wife looked. The two of them talked about Alexandros every moment they were together. When they were alone, Tina told Aristo she was certain that in the month before Alexandros' death, he had begun to forgive her for what he considered her most serious mistake. Stavros accompanied his wife and Aristo to Alexandros' grave, but it was Aristo who held her in his arms when she nearly collapsed with her sobbing.

Everyone else who saw Tina after Alexander's death also remarked that she looked terrible. Her beauty had disappeared overnight. There were rumors that she was taking too many pills, but never before had she let her looks dissipate. A beautiful woman who had always had ardent male admirers, Tina now, at age forty-five, looked like a tired old woman.

Christina was so unstable herself that Aristo did not feel confident about sending her to care for her depressed and ailing mother. Ironically, shortly before Tina died, Christina had yet one more time attempted suicide. Somehow Tina had managed to go to London and stay at her daughter's side until Christina was completely recovered. However, Aristo knew that asking Christina to help her mother now was a bad idea. Instead, he had asked Roula, Tina's former dressmaker and close confidante, to travel to Paris to stay with her while she was recuperating from yet another illness. Roula went for a short time and stayed in the Hotel Plaza Opéra, close to Tina's house, managing to see Tina every day she was there.

As soon as Roula returned to the hotel each evening, she called Mr. Onassis and reported how Tina was doing. Stavros Niarchos could not understand why Roula came so often, but he paid little attention to her. Many days, Roula convinced Tina to come out of her apartment and walk with her. As the two of them walked slowly beside the Sykouana River, Tina talked endlessly to Roula about her children. "You remember how handsome my son, Alexandros, was, don't you?" she would ask Roula every day, speaking as always in French, Tina's primary language. "No one ever had such a handsome son. And such a good boy. He was such a good boy, wasn't he? And my daughter is so beautiful too, isn't she? She is going to have a fine marriage and a fine life soon. I am certain that will all happen to her now."

Roula agreed with everything Tina said and reminded her how

much her daughter needed and loved her. Roula regretted that she could remain in Paris for only one week and that her brisk business in Athens prevented her from staying for a longer period of time. The last time they were together, Tina was having difficulty walking and the two women could walk for only a few feet before Tina needed to sit down. Her eyes had deep circles under them and her hands shook as she tried to light her cigarette. Her face was heavily lined and her color sallow. It was impossible to believe that the woman was only forty-five. She looked, Roula thought, closer to seventy.

During this time, Mr. Onassis' dislike of Stavros Niarchos grew even more intense and he became desperate to protect his former wife from a man he considered dangerous. When Tina died under conditions similar to those that claimed the life of Niarchos' previous wife, her older sister Eugenie, Mr. Onassis' greatest fear was realized. From the moment he learned of Tina's death, he was convinced that Niarchos, who was in the house at the time of her death, was responsible. Even though no bruises on her body were officially reported, he was certain her husband had beaten her before she died. Tina had been known to abuse pills, but the autopsy report listed acute edema of the lung as her cause of death, without any mention of barbiturates in her bloodstream and without any further explanation. This left much room for speculation.

Tina was buried beside her sister Eugenie in her family's burial plot in Lausanne, Switzerland. Jackie, at Christina's request, did not attend the funeral. Nor did any of her three former sisters-in-law. Christina was, of course, devastated by her mother's death, coming so soon after her brother had died. Again, she blamed Jackie, repeating her belief that Jackie was a curse and pointing to yet another act of destruction that had befallen the Onassis family since the American had become a member. Although there had never been any attempt at reconciliation between her parents, Christina knew that Tina and Aristo had become closer after Alexander's death. Christina had been present when Tina visited Alexander's grave on Skorpios and had witnessed the warm conversations between her father and mother. She was certain that although her parents had been divorced for more than fifteen years, Aristo never stopped caring for Tina and was always concerned about her welfare.

Christina had never stopped hoping that concerns over her own health might reunite her parents and was willing to attempt suicide if it meant providing her parents with a reason to communicate with each other. Once, her suicide attempt did bring both her parents to her bedside at a hospital in Paris, but when she regained consciousness, they were gone. Still, Christina never stopped believing that it was not an impossible task to send Jackie back to the United States, this time as her father's ex-wife, and bring Tina back to Greece as his new wife. Only when Tina died did Christina abandon that belief. And grow to hate Niarchos as much as she despised Jackie.

As for her father, Tina's death nearly drove him to distraction. Those of us who were close to him knew that, in his way, Aristo had never stopped loving Tina. She was his first wife, and the mother of his two children, and no matter what had happened between the two of them since they married in 1946, he had always continued to love that woman.

Mr. Onassis organized an investigation of Tina's death, and spent many long hours talking to her personal physician about it. He was constantly discussing it with me, poring over each detail in the official report and dictating long lists of questions for me to organize and type. It was the first time since Alexander's death that he seemed focused and energized. It was as if all the frustration and heartbreak he had experienced when Alexander died could be thrust into this investigation, riveting all his attention on one important matter, another mysterious death of someone he had loved.

Several weeks after Tina's death, Aristo informed me that the two of us would be going to Paris, along with Miltos Yiannacopoulos, to continue our work on the investigation into Tina's death. For one week, the three of us stayed in the Avenue Foch apartment, and worked all day and all night on the investigation. Mr. Onassis made numerous calls to everyone connected with Tina's life and death, including her physicians, psychiatrists, friends, relatives, and servants. He contacted anyone who had any contact with his ex-wife during the last six months of her life and asked each person involved direct questions about Tina. After each call, he would dictate to me exactly what the person had said to him and I would type up the conversation for him. After he read my typed notes, he would frequently call the doctor again and ask him additional questions. He kept instructing Miltos to obtain and analyze the doctors' words concerning Tina's death, and was impatient with every small delay Miltos encountered. Miltos' calm and sensitive manner, his way of encouraging yet controlling Mr. Onassis, made the week bearable for the three of us.

Repeatedly Aristo explained to me that every detail of our investigation must remain secret and that no one could know what we were doing. People could think he was upset about Tina's death and curious about her last hours, but no one, besides me and Miltos, could know that he was organizing all this material into a full-fledged, official investigation of her death. My notes must be hidden and I needed to have my typewriter with me at my house in Athens when we returned to Greece, so that he could call me at any time and offer me new information. In all the years I had worked with this man, I never saw him so secretive about any important business deal as he was with this investigation.

One evening in Paris, he sat with me, a glass filled with ouzo in his hand, and asked me the same questions over and over. "Why would he kill her, Kiki?" he asked. "She was so frail, so delicate. How could he have beaten her that way? What kind of a husband does that to his wife?"

Most evenings, however, as soon as he decided we had worked long enough on our project, he would leave the Paris apartment and not return until the next morning. I knew, of course, that those evenings he was with Maria. Knowing how close they were and how much he valued her opinion on everything that was happening in his life, I was certain he spent much, although not all, of their time together obsessing over Tina's death.

Then, without an explanation, a few weeks after we returned to Athens, he told me he was stopping his investigation. He had decided that it would never be proven in any court of law that Niarchos had killed Tina, and in fact, there was no official inquiry and Niarchos was never charged with wrongdoing. When I asked him why, he merely shook his head. It was as if he didn't have the strength to think about it any longer. The defeat that had covered his face after Alexander had died returned. This time, for good.

Soon after we returned from Paris, almost as if he had wished it upon himself, Mr. Onassis became ill. Not only did he look pale, but he was constantly tired and was having problems with his eyes. I ordered many special pairs of eyeglasses for him from Switzerland, but when they arrived, he would not wear any of them. It was as if there were nothing he wanted to see. He also refused to wear warm clothes and take any care at all of his health. When he was in New York with Jackie during the wintertime, he would not wear his overcoat, even on brutally cold days. On cool rainy days in Greece, he would walk outside in just his short sleeves, discarding even his suit jacket. Jackie and Artemis both were furious with him, and would chastise him constantly for his neglect. But he was too stubborn and uninterested to listen to either of them.

Finally, in the spring of 1974, Mr. Onassis was diagnosed as having myasthenia gravis, a neuromuscular disorder that is not usually fatal. Initially we were all relieved with the diagnosis, certain that myasthenia gravis, while it might force changes in his lifestyle, would not threaten his life.

Before he became ill, Mr. Onassis and Jackie used many different pills that I had ordered from Switzerland. Some, Mrs. Artemis told me, were geriatric vitamins, like Scriptic, that Mr. Onassis used to keep feeling young and strong, and which he and Jackie took to give them extra energy. Every month, I ordered a large supply of these pills, some of which Artemis liked to give to her friends. She was always giving me boxes of these pills to keep for myself, but I could only take Roche Calc C and Vita, because my doctor told me the other pills were for people over forty. I never discussed any of those pills with Mr. and Mrs. Onassis, but both of them always reminded me to make certain I ordered the pills frequently. However, shortly after Alexander's death, Mr. Onassis instructed me not to order any more pills from Switzerland for him. "But Mrs. Jackie likes these pills," I reminded him. He shrugged and told me to order some for her then, but he wanted no more of them. New pills were prescribed when he was diagnosed with myasthenia gravis, but like his pills from Switzerland, he had no interest in them.

One of the major side effects of Mr. Onassis' disease was his inability to keep his eyes open. No matter how he tried, his eyelids kept closing. One of his doctors ordered a new pair of glasses to help Mr.

Onassis' eyes remain open. While we were waiting for these glasses to be made, I could not stand to see how much he was suffering when his eyes kept closing. One morning, I suggested putting plastic tape on his eyelids and he readily agreed. The two of us walked into the bathroom where there was a large mirror and strong lights. While Mr. Onassis watched through the mirror, I applied several pieces of plastic tape to his eyelids. While I was working on his eyelids, I was struck by the way he stood in front of the mirror, patiently and quietly awaiting the results of my labor. When he realized that the tape would help him with his problem he was very grateful to me. After that, during the week that we were waiting for his glasses to be ready, either he put the plastic on himself or he allowed Christina to do it for him. When the glasses finally arrived they were tortoise color and were able to keep his eyes open without the help of the plastic. For a while, they seemed to help alleviate his problem.

However, it didn't take me long to realize that my boss was becoming less and less interested in finding solutions to his physical problems. Now he had a new goal to achieve. This time, he was not trying to buy a new tanker nor delight a woman. This time his objective was even more personal; this time his prize was his own death. Now all the energy that had been put to sleep by Alexander's death was returning. While some ordinary man might swallow pills or put a gun to his head to end his life, Mr. Onassis could not resort to such methods. For his death, he would assume the role of God, willing himself to become sick and hastening the effects of the disease that would kill his own body. Of course, no one could prevent his death, for there were no pills to remove from his hands or any gun to hide. But he was in charge. And, stronger and more powerful than God, he would succeed and will his body to die. And those of us who loved Mr. Onassis would have no choice but to watch it happen.

Maria Callas was, most certainly, one of those who had a front-row seat for her lover's final performance. During the two years between Alexander's death and his own, Mr. Onassis spent more time with Maria than he had in the previous four years. Although the two of them still relied on Miltos Yiannacopoulos to make the arrangements for their encounters, there were occasional times now when he had me call her directly. He was also photographed several times having dinner with her. Artemis was furious when these pictures would appear, but said little about them. She was so frantic with worry about her brother's deteriorating health that she could speak of nothing else.

As Mr. Onassis grew sicker, however, Maria grew even more important in his life. One morning, on August 15, when he was staying in the Glyfada house with Jackie, he called me at my office and asked me to tell Jean-Pierre de Vitry to prepare the helicopter *Alouette III* for a trip that day. I called Jean-Pierre and gave him the message from Mr. Onassis. "Where will be going, Kiki?" he asked me, but I did not have the answer for him.

When I called Mr. Onassis back and asked him where Jean-Pierre would be flying the helicopter, he said, "I don't know yet. Just tell him I am ready to leave now to come to the airport." I knew that he often did not like for anybody to know where he was going, and that there was nothing I could do about his refusal to give Jean-Pierre his travel plans. Many pilots preferred not to work for Mr. Onassis because of his frequently spontaneous plans and his refusal to release his flying schedule ahead of time. Jean-Pierre was not pleased with my second message, but he, too, knew that when Mr. Onassis refused to provide his destination, it was senseless to argue with him.

When they met at the airport, before Mr. Onassis got on the helicopter, Jean-Pierre was concerned about how pale and sickly his boss appeared. He excused himself for a moment and called me at my office. "I am not sure Mr. Onassis is well enough to be going anywhere," he informed me. "I am uncomfortable about taking him on any trip at all."

I knew exactly how Jean-Pierre was feeling. Every time I saw Mr. Onassis, he looked thinner and more frail than he had the day before. I could not imagine his having the strength to go on any trip. Still, it was not for me to order his pilot not to fly him wherever he wanted to go. When I called Glyfada, Jackie had left to go shopping and Artemis was taking a nap. I asked Panagiotis to wake Artemis. "Let him go," she told me sleepily when I told her of Jean-Pierre's concerns. "There is nowhere he should not be allowed to go to." And then she hung up on me. I called Jean-Pierre at the airport and told him to follow whatever instructions his boss gave him.

Before they took off, Jean-Pierre asked Mr. Onassis one more time where they would be going. "It is very important that I know where we are going before I take the helicopter up."

"Yes, of course, you are right," Mr. Onassis said, and then he began to smile. "We are going to Petalio," he finally told him. And Jean Pierre knew immediately what that meant. Petalio was a private island opposite Evia, which was near Athens. It was owned by a wealthy shipowner, Emberico, and was the island that Maria visited often. "August fifteenth is Maria's name day," Mr. Onassis continued to explain to his pilot. "And I want to give her a special present."

Now Jean-Pierre understood everything. This was the day that Maria celebrated her name with that of the saint for which she was named. It was a special day of the year for Maria, and of course Mr. Onassis would want to be with her on that day. And of course he would not want to tell anyone else, besides his pilot, exactly where he was going. Without another word, Jean-Pierre flew his boss to Petalio.

After the helicopter landed in Petalio, it did not take Mr. Onassis long to find Maria. She was walking alone along the beach and was shocked to see him approach her. For a moment, as his passenger walked across the beach, Jean-Pierre was tempted to follow him closely, so nervous was he that his boss might not be able to walk a long distance in the sand. But Mr. Onassis was moving his painfully thin legs steadily until he was beside his mistress. Jean-Pierre heard her scream delightedly and saw her race into his arms. They embraced for a long time and then they sat down by the water and held each other closely. To Jean-Pierre, it looked as if Maria were supporting Mr. Onassis' weight with her arms. He also saw him hand her a small gift-wrapped box. He was not certain exactly what the gift was but he could hear Maria's excited voice expressing her love and gratitude for him. He could also see, even from a distance, that she quickly put away the box and devoted all her attention to her more important surprise gift.

For the next six hours, while Jean-Pierre sat in an inconspicuous spot where he would not be noticed but where he could see his boss, the two lovers sat beside one another and talked and hugged each other tenderly and lovingly. When the two of them left the beach and walked into a small cottage, Jean-Pierre was happy. His boss, he knew, even though he could not see him at that moment, would be well taken care of now.

When Mr. Onassis emerged from the cottage several hours later, he signaled Jean-Pierre that it was now time to return to Athens. Maria accompanied Aristo to the helicopter and their final embrace was a long and emotional one. Neither one of them seemed concerned with Jean-Pierre's presence, nor did either one want the embrace to end. When it finally did, the pilot noticed tears on both their faces. Jean-Pierre's boss slept for the return journey home and was still sleeping when the helicopter landed in Athens. Jean-Pierre would not disturb him and waited patiently until he awoke an hour later. As he watched Mr. Onassis walk away from the helicopter, Jean-Pierre was again alarmed at how terrible he looked. But he knew for certain that despite the illness that was obviously ravaging his body and his spirit, his boss was, at that particular moment, a satisfied and happy man.

Christina tried to do her part to give her father a reason to live. After her brother died, Christina had begun to see a lot of Peter Goulandris, the son of a wealthy Greek ship-building family. Mr. Onassis was hopeful that she would make him her second husband. It seemed to be the only thing that cheered him up. She had told me that she did not truly love him and could not marry him, but she did not want to disappoint her father with that news. Instead, she pretended to be considering marrying him. I continued the game with Mr. Onassis whenever he brought up Peter Goulandris' name, agreeing with him that his daughter, at long last, was about to marry her perfect mate.

During that time, Mr. Onassis continued to have frequent dinners in Glyfada, often with Jackie and Niki Goulandris, but always with his dear friend Professor Georgakis. He was quieter and more morose during these evenings than he had ever been before and seemed millions of miles away from the conversations at the dinner table. Still, the professor entertained Mr. Onassis with interesting and clever stories, and tried to get his friend to discuss business problems with his companies with him. Yet he knew, like all of us, that none of these tactics did much good. Aristo had lost his will to live, and no one who was around him could restore that will.

Still, for a long time, like all three of his sisters, I never seriously considered the possibility that Mr. Onassis would die. Even in his decline, he was still larger than life. I assumed that he would get tired of being sick and would look at me one day and announce, "Enough of this sickness, Kiki. Call London for me, and let us get back to work." But he did not.

During his last Christmas in Glyfada, Aristo was especially melancholy He insisted that Artemis bring all the servants who worked in Glyfada to the house that day. When each one of them walked into the house, Aristo greeted him or her warmly and handed each person ten thousand drachmas, which at that time was the equivalent of fifty dollars. "This will be my last Christmas with you," he told each servant individually. "I would like for us to pass this day together." As Panagiotis, Argaritis, Kokkalis, Margaritis, Georgia, Magolalini, and Stavro, and all the other servants and drivers who had ever been employed there walked into the house in Glyfada, he hugged them and gave them their gifts. Then he insisted that they all stay and have dinner with him. All the servants tried to encourage him and to convince him that he would get well and that good times would happen to him in the new year. But none of them seemed to believe his own words, and all their eyes were red and full of tears when they left the house that day. The meal that Artemis had arranged for them was a beautiful dinner and we all tried to enjoy the special moment, but it was hard for any of us to eat the delicious food and not choke on our tears. At the end of the day, Mr. Onassis' eyes were red from crying all day long, but he had made sure all the servants knew how much he appreciated them.

Every day after Christmas, he got sicker and sicker, and no matter what Christina or his sisters or Jackie or Professor Georgakis said to him, he refused to go to the hospital. As always, he also refused to take any of his vitamins, or any of the medications prescribed for his myasthenia gravis. One morning when I was in Glyfada with Artemis, she was frantic over her brother's refusal to eat. "He is getting thinner and thinner," she told me. "I am so afraid he will starve himself to death."

In desperation, she prepared a special breakfast for him and carried it up to his room herself. Never had I seen Artemis fuss over a meal as much as she did over this one. She cooked eggs and special cheese rolls for him and decorated the tray with fresh flowers she carefully cut herself from the garden. She refused to allow a servant or me to carry the tray, but she insisted I accompany her into his room. "You and I will convince him to start eating again," she told me. "You will talk business with him and I will tell him gossip and he will begin to get well."

An hour later, the two of us emerged from the room. This time, I carried the tray, which was untouched. The whole time we were in Mr. Onassis' room, he had sat in a chair, staring neither at the newspaper in his lap, nor out the window. Instead, he stared straight ahead, looking at neither Artemis nor me, nor at anything else in the room. He was showered and dressed and looked ready to go to work. But he did not talk, except to answer some of our questions with a simple yes or no. And he did not eat. Not one bite of any of the food on that tray. Artemis tried everything. She begged and pleaded. She cried and moaned. She joked and told stories. And I talked about every business detail I could remember. But nothing we said or did made any difference. Mr. Onassis had decided not to eat, and no one in the world could change his mind. When he finally left his room an hour later, he went for a small drive with Artemis and me, but he did not speak one word to either of us in the car. Again, he just looked straight ahead, his eyes appearing to see nothing.

When he did talk to me, his words were filled with guilt. "I had a chance to love my son," he told me the last time he came to the office and tried to work. "But I was too busy here and I did not use that chance. I never gave him enough love. I was too busy to love my own son."

No matter what I said to him, he would not listen to me. "I do not want to live," he told me over and over until I had no choice but to believe it. "I have lost my son. I have lost everything. It is worthless to be alive."

When Aristo grew sicker and unable to leave the house at all, we knew he would have to be hospitalized. Still, Jackie worried about taking him to a Greek hospital. She insisted that he was suffering from a terrible flu and that complete bed rest would make him well. She convinced Artemis to convert the house in Glyfada into a makeshift hospital, and to equip it with medical supplies and hospital instruments.

When Aristo continued to get sicker despite their efforts in Glyfada, Artemis contacted Christina, who was skiing in Gstaad with Peter Goulandris. One of the few bright spots in Mr. Onassis' life was his daughter's relationship with Peter Goulandris, whom he desired as his son-in-law. When Christina had told him that she was planning a ski trip with Peter, her father had insisted they go, despite his illness. Artemis knew her brother would be upset that she was summoning Christina back to Glyfada, but she felt she had no choice. Both Christina and Peter were at her Aristo's side within hours of the call from her aunt. "We're going to get married as soon as you get better," Christina announced to her father as soon as she saw him. The smile that crossed her father's face convinced her that, whether or not she loved Peter Goulandris, she would marry him.

The brief spurt of energy that Christina's announcement made in her father's condition, however, did not last long. The next day, he appeared even weaker. When the Greek doctor who was summoned to Glyfada did not seem properly concerned about Aristo's condition, Jackie summoned a specialist from Paris. The doctor informed the family that Aristo needed to be hospitalized immediately and convinced them to transfer him to the American Hospital in Paris. At that point, Aristo weighed no more than seventy pounds and was too weak to argue. His friends, such as Professor Georgakis, Costas Gratsos, and Miltos Yiannacopoulos, and several others, visited him every day, and helped persuade him that it was time for him to enter a hospital. At one point, Miltos tried to distract Aristo from his illness by discussing a ship they were considering buying in Singapore. "I will soon go to Singapore to take a look at the ship, Mr. Onassis," Miltos told him.

"You must go now," Aristo instructed him.

"I will prefer to wait until you are stronger," Miltos said.

"Nonsense," Mr. Onassis insisted. "I am okay. You should leave for Singapore on the next flight out of Athens."

Miltos hated to leave his friend in such delicate health and travel so far a distance, but he knew what a proud man Aristo was. He understood that now, as after Alexander's death, Mr. Onassis would never want his friends to see him cry or despair. To refuse to go to Singapore because he was worried about Mr. Onassis' health, Miltos understood, was a cruel thing to do to his proud friend. So Miltos left for Singapore on the next available flight out of Athens.

The day Mr. Onassis left his home for the American Hospital in Paris, he called his dear friend Stelios Papadimitriou to his side and extracted a promise from Stelios that when he died, Stelios would treat

Christina like a sister. Initially, Aristo told Stelios he would give him as much money as he liked so that he could take good care of Christina. Stelios laughed off his friend's irrational suggestion. Instead, he told Mr. Onassis he needed no money to watch over his daughter for the rest of his life, and that he would be honored to be given such an important responsibility.

Shortly after Stelios left Glyfada, Panagiotis carefully prepared Mr. Onassis for the trip to the airport, dressing him and carrying him down the stairs to the waiting Cadillac. In the softest of voices, Aristo whispered to the servants who had gathered by the door, "I am sorry I will not see you again." Each one nodded and wept. As Panagiotis gently handed Mr. Onassis to George Margaritis, who placed him in the black Cadillac, Panagiotis could not hold back his tears. A proud man, Mr. Onassis had wanted to walk to the car, but at that moment he was too weak to do so. Mr. Onassis tried to hug Panagiotis, his most trusted servant, but the effort was too much for him and his arms fell limply to his side. Aristo was almost too weak to speak, but he used all his strength to retain some small measure of his pride and wave to them. Then he stared at Panagiotis for what seemed a long time before he told George to close the door.

Jackie and Christina flew to Paris on February 6 with Aristo and his doctor. Although they were prepared to take him immediately to the American Hospital, Aristo insisted that he spend the night in his Avenue Foch apartment. The two women tried to convince him to go right to the hospital, but he was adamant. He used up whatever remaining strength he had walking into his apartment alone. Aristo was in considerable pain that evening and did not sleep at all. He staggered from room to room in the apartment, moaning softly and trying unsuccessfully to find a spot where he would be comfortable enough to sleep.

When Jackie and Christina arrived with Aristo at the American Hospital the next day, they were surrounded by a small horde of photographers and journalists. More than anything, they wanted to prevent the photographers from taking pictures of Aristo, but they were helpless against the blast of flashbulbs that overwhelmed them. Mr. Onassis was placed in a large private room on the first floor, where a team of specialists began to evaluate his condition. That night, Jackie went back to the Avenue Foch apartment, but Christina checked into the

Hotel Plaza-Athénée. Even though Christina and Jackie spoke to each other when it was absolutely necessary, Christina could not bear to be near her stepmother and was determined never to spend another night under the same roof as the woman she considered more than ever before the curse of her family.

After completing tests on Aristo, the doctors at the American Hospital decided that he needed to have his gallbladder removed. Christina informed her aunt of the decision and Artemis immediately flew to Paris. When the doctors explained to Mr. Onassis that he would never survive without the surgery, he asked to see his doctor alone. "If I give you all of my ships and all of my money, can you make me completely well?" he asked the doctor, repeating many of the same words he had spoke to Alexander's neurosurgeon the night his son died.

When the doctor answered, "I cannot make you such a promise," Aristo nodded in agreement, as if he had already known the answer, and instructed the doctor to let him die in peace. But his physician urged him to have the operation. After the surgery, Mr. Onassis' condition worsened, and for weeks he appeared to be dying. There were, however, brief moments when he rallied for a few hours. During one of those moments, Christina brought Peter Goulandris to his bedside, and Petros asked for Aristo's permission to marry his daughter. Because of the tubes that now reached into his throat, Aristo was unable to speak, yet he used his hands to offer his consent and drifted back to sleep.

Merope and Kalliroi arrived in Paris a few days after Artemis and stayed in the Avenue Foch apartment with Jackie and Artemis. Jackie used the Learjet to fly back and forth between Paris and New York, dividing her time, as she had done over the past six and half years, between her husband and her children. Because her own husband, Dr. Theodore Garofalidis, was ill in Athens, Artemis flew back and forth between Athens and Paris as often as she could manage. When she was at the hospital, Mrs. Artemis would not leave the waiting room beside her brother's room even for a moment, preferring to eat the cheese and bread and whatever else she had brought along for her own meals rather than go to a restaurant. Merope and Kalliroi also flew back and forth regularly from their homes in Monte Carlo and Switzerland and Lagonissi to Paris.

I joined the family several times. Twice I went to the hospital to visit Mr. Onassis, but both times he was barely conscious and unaware of my presence. The family sat in the waiting room, staring at the door leading to Aristo's room, hardly speaking a word to one another. It was as if each one of these women was lost in her own painful thoughts, unable to share them with anyone else. Each time I came, I too stood in the doorway and studied the slight body lying under the white sheets, with tubes connected to its arms. How can you do this to all of us? I asked myself as I watched the fragile body move ever so slightly beneath the sheets.

I wanted to shake him with all my might and scream into his face, "What right do you have to remove yourself from all our lives? You are hurting all those who love you! How can you be so selfish and so cruel?" But I did not say a word. I just stood there and stared, finding it impossible to believe that the insignificant body beneath the blankets belonged to Mr. Aristotle Onassis.

When I returned to Athens, I spoke either to Artemis or to the staff at Glyfada every hour or so, receiving constant updates from Paris about Mr. Onassis. The family explained to me that the doctors offered no hope for his recovery. Still, the hourly calls from Paris continued.

Barely a day went by when Maria did not also call the hospital or the apartment in a desperate attempt to see Aristo just one last time. However, the family's orders were strictly followed and Maria was never permitted to see him or hear personal information about his condition. When I was at the hospital, I asked each sister if she thought perhaps Maria could come to the hospital for one visit when Jackie was in New York, but each one refused, insisting that if a journalist found out she had come, it would be humiliating for Jackie.

Mr. Onassis' sisters and daughter knew that he had managed to keep his wife and his mistress apart for the six and a half years of his marriage. Determined that Jackie would not be embarrassed by the presence of her husband's lover at the hospital, they assumed the responsibility of preventing such a meeting at his bedside. It seemed that as long as he had the strength to walk, nothing could prevent Aristo from making it to Maria's side. But once he became too ill to walk on his own, he would never again see his lover.

One day when I was alone at the hospital with Christina, she left her father's side for a few moments to sit with me in the waiting room.

"Do you also think, Mrs. Christina," I asked her boldly, "that it would be possible for Maria to have one last visit with your father?"

"For heaven's sake, Kiki," she answered me, the hate in her voice unmistakable, "don't you think I would rather have her here than Madame?" I knew it was impossible for her even to speak Jackie's name now.

"If I could live my life over again," she continued, tears running down her face, "I would do everything in my power to help my father to marry Maria. It was the biggest mistake of his life that he didn't marry her. But now I know we were all wrong. Maria was the woman he should have married. If that had happened, we would not all be here today watching him die."

Maria, however, did finally manage, despite Aristo's family, to find a connection to her dying lover. Eleni Syros, who had been Aristo's servant but was now Christina's maid, adored Maria, and often came to her Paris apartment to fix her hair. Whenever she saw Maria, she related every detail she had learned about Mr. Onassis' condition. Bruna, Maria's devoted housemaid, was also Eleni's close friend, and she made numerous calls to Eleni to retrieve information for her desperate employer. Still Eleni had to be cautious, for if Christina overheard her talking to Maria, she would be furious. Eleni told me that Maria was in a terrible state and willing to do anything just for the unlikely opportunity to take one glimpse of her lover. She was barely eating or sleeping and waiting anxiously night and day for Eleni's reports. "It is as if she is barely alive," Eleni told me. "Yet she tells me that when Aristo is in pain, she feels the same pain in her own body. When it is hard for him to breathe, she, too, cannot catch her breath. I believe that when Mr. Onassis dies, so will she."

On March 15, 1975, Mr. Onassis accomplished his final goal and died. Jackie, who had been informed by her husband's doctors that he was relatively stable and would most probably not die in the next forty-eight or ninety-six hours, had taken the Learjet back to New York to be with her children. However, Christina, who had never left her father's side during the six weeks of his hospitalization, was beside him. Christina was so distraught that she attempted suicide within minutes of her father's death. Only the quick action of one of her father's physicians prevented her from following her father on his final journey.

For Aristo's last flight from Paris to Greece, only his daughter was beside him, heavily sedated as she sat beside his casket. The Boeing 727 carrying Mr. Onassis' body and his daughter landed in Aktion, near Skorpios. When the plane landed in Aktion, Jackie, standing beside Edward Kennedy, was waiting, along with Christina's three aunts. As I stood there beside them, my mind racing over every joyful and painful moment I had spent with Mr. Onassis during the past nine years, I watched Christina emerge from the plane. Her skin appeared yellow against her black hair, which was blowing wildly in the wind. Her aunts passed her from one to the next, slowly, as if she were a doll made of glass that could shatter at any moment.

Jackie approached her and hugged her gently and held her hand. I knew how much Christina had resented her stepmother, but at that moment, despite my overwhelming sorrow, I felt a tiny flush of gratification as I thought that these two women might now, after the death of the man they both loved, become friends. Immediately, without allowing Christina and Jackie one moment of privacy, the photographers and journalists descended upon them. For one second, a smile crossed over Jackie's face, a smile I understood was her usual expression, an attempt to mask the pain within. Yet I knew what others would think when they saw the photograph of that famous smile. "What has happened to all of us?" Jackie whispered sorrowfully to me as we walked together, and I shrugged my shoulders sadly in response. As her three sisters-in-law came toward her, Jackie hugged each one, that same sad smile on her lips, and again the photographers leaped out at her.

As Christina approached me, I kissed her and tried to find the words to express my feelings, but when I opened my mouth, not a word would come out. Christina clung to me for a long moment until her aunts gently pulled her away from me. Two cars were waiting to take the six women and Edward Kennedy from Aktion to the port of Nydri, where we would be taken by small boats to Skorpios for the funeral. A special car, transporting Mr. Onassis' body, led the way. Christina was ushered into a car with Jackie and Edward Kennedy, and I traveled with her three aunts. Shortly before we arrived in Nydri, however, Christina's car stopped and she emerged and entered our car. She was deathly silent as she sat between Artemis and Kalliroi, staring straight ahead, tears streaming down her face. "What happened inside that car?" Artemis asked as she touched her niece's hand gently.

Christina shook her head, unable to speak, and no one asked her another question.

When we arrived in Skorpios, again the photographers descended upon us and made it almost impossible to reach the tiny chapel of Panayitsa ("Little Virgin"). Even through the fog in which I felt my mind was enveloped, I could see the small dog Vana standing pitifully on the shore, waiting for her master to come home. The day, as when Alexander had been buried here almost two years earlier, was a gray and rainy winter day. When we arrived in the chapel, the casket, a simple but elegant wooden one with Aristo's name and the face of his patron saint etched on it, adorned with four exquisite silver handles, was already in the chapel. One by one, we approached the casket, kissed the face of the saint, and left a white flower on the closed casket. I watched Christina lean over the casket and my heart broke as she trembled and swayed, and for one awful moment, I was certain she would collapse. Petros Goulandris came forward at that moment and put his arm around her and helped her walk back to her seat in the chapel.

As when Alexander had been buried here two years earlier, all the people on Levkas traveled in small boats to Skorpios to pay their respects to their beloved neighbor. Among the sea of faces outside the chapel where Aristo had married Jackie six and a half years earlier, I recognized so many who had come to my office seeking help for their loved ones. They wept openly when they saw me, each one reminding me of the time my boss had given him money for a doctor or an operation or found him a job. "He was like a father to me," many of them said.

"He was my brother," others told me. Each story brought me yet another painful memory, but I stood as still as I could and listened to every word each man spoke.

During the service, Artemis, Merope, and Kalliroi stood next to one another, sobbing. Artemis moved from Christina, who was still being supported by Peter Goulandris, to Jackie, wrapping her arms around each one. Of the five women, Jackie appeared to be the strongest, as she sat silently and without tears during the service. A thin woman normally, Artemis looked even thinner than usual, so frail and suddenly so old that I feared at any moment she would collapse to the ground. Despite the black sunglasses that each sister wore, the tears could be seen on all their faces. When I embraced Artemis, she whispered to me, "Kiki, I am so afraid for Christina. How can that girl stand so much pain?"

When I saw Stassa Voivoda, the mother-in-law of Tina's brother, George Livanos, embrace Christina, I remembered how much the elderly woman had adored Aristo. "You will stay in our house in Lagonissi as long as you want," Christina told her through her tears, and I knew that she was doing what her father would have wanted her to do. Even in her grief, she was thinking of someone less fortunate than she and doing what she could to help her. Christina adored her uncle George and his wife and mother-in-law. By reaching out to others with acts of kindness, I hoped she would find a reason to live.

All of Aristo's friends and associates wept for their loss. Sadly, his most trusted adviser, Miltos Yiannacopoulos, was still in Singapore on business for Mr. Onassis and was distraught that he could not attend his closest friend's funeral. Costas Gratsos, his childhood friend and business associate, however, stood with Asta, looking dazed and confused. Professor Georgakis, the chairman of the board of directors for Olympic Airways in Athens, appeared just as dazed, all his confidence and good humor gone, as if he, too, could not imagine life without his beloved friend. Costas Konialidis, his cousin and business associate, hugged me, crying openly. I knew how hard Costas had always worked, in his office from early in the morning till late at night, sometimes staying a full twenty-four hours at a time, for Olympic Airways. Yet, no matter how hard he worked, or how tired he was, his face lit up when Aristo walked into our office. They had their problems years earlier, but that was long forgotten. These men were not just cousins, they were brothers. Costas would miss him every day of his life. His wife, Ritsa, whispered to me, "How will we all get along without him?"

Many times during the service, I heard mourners mention the name Maria. "Where is she?" many of them asked. "Where is his beloved Maria?"

"She should be here," I heard them say. "She, of all of us, deserves to be standing here." But she was not there. Eleni had told me that Maria had tried to go to Florida, but she could not stay there.

So she had returned to Paris, where she was flooded with dozens of condolence calls.

"When he was dying, I felt as if I were with him," she had told Eleni. "When they stuck needles into his arms, I felt them. When the machines stopped keeping him alive, I felt my heart stop. But now that he is dead, I feel as if I were his wife. All who call tell me they thought of me as his wife and they are sorry for my loss. Yet when he needed me the most, I was not there for him. How can I forgive myself for not defying all of them and going to his side?"

So often during the service I turned around, certain Maria would simply appear in the chapel, dressed in black, and take her rightful place, a beloved mistress mourning her adored lover. But she never came. Her pride for herself and her respect for her lover's family kept her absent from the one place she yearned to be. It was a noble sacrifice few other women could have made.

At other times during the service, I had heard a few people whisper "*atyhya*," or "curse." I shuddered to hear the dreadful word spoken and knew to whom it was directed. Fortunately, Jackie did not appear to hear the word, nor, I prayed, would she have understood its meaning. It pained me deeply that anyone could speak such a word about or in the presence of the widow of the deceased, yet I knew that his death had strengthened the numbers of those who mistakenly believed that it was Jackie Kennedy who had brought about the fall of the Onassis family.

After the funeral service was over, once again, we all walked in front of the casket, one by one. I waited, barely able to move, as the members of the family passed by the casket for the final time. Finally, when there was no one left but me, I bent down and kissed the saint's face. As I started to walk away, I could feel all my senses begin to leave me. How could I walk away from this man who had been such a major part of my life for the past nine years? How could I just say good-bye and continue to live my life? There were so many things I had yet to speak to him about. I had so many questions for him, so many stories to tell him. Then, despite my tears, my eyes began to see the mausoleum beyond the chapel, and I remembered Alexandros and I knew that now, finally, Aristo was happy. He had done exactly what he had set out to do. So now he was gone from all of us. Now he was with his beloved Alexandros. And so, very slowly, I walked away.

As I walked out of the chapel, I could hear Christina talking to many of the personnel in Skorpios. "Now you are my own people," she wept in front of them. "I have no one else."

In the background, I could see the *Christina,* its flags lowered, its moment of glory concluded. For one moment, I could imagine Aristo standing on the deck of his glorious ship, dressed in his shorts and an open shirt, the wind blowing through his hair, the sun shining on his skin, the cigar in his mouth and a glass of ouzo in his hand. He would be saying nothing, just staring out at the sea, a man mystified and fascinated by the world beyond him, yet enjoying all its pleasures with a rare energy and keen intelligence. He was the captain of his ship, the ruler of his own universe. And now he had left this world he no longer wanted to inhabit, unable to live here without his treasured son. Not one person here had the power to make him change his mind. Not even the woman who could not come to say her final good-bye.

That same day we returned to Athens by plane. Before we boarded the plane, the journalists begged Jackie for a statement. She said a few words. She said that Aristo was a very unique man and that he had taught her much about life. She said she would never stop loving him for all he had done for her. She stayed a few days with Artemis and then she returned to New York. She did return to Skorpios, two more times, once for the memorial service to mark the end of the forty days of mourning.

As our plane departed from Skorpios that chilly, overcast March day, I could no longer believe that Aristotle Onassis was gone. Suddenly, I was certain, he would appear, shake his head in disbelief at what he was seeing, bark out dozens of orders to be followed immediately, and continue to rule the island of Skorpios and the world beyond its luscious shores. But I was wrong.

Chapter Fourteen

The Tragic Onassis

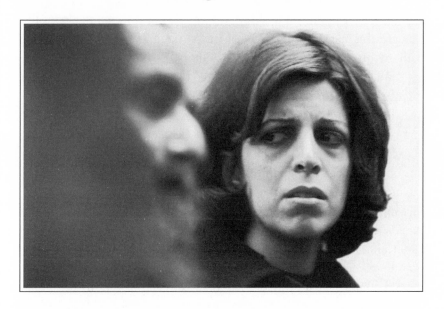

A W O R L D without Aristotle Onassis at the helm of his ship was a difficult one for many of us to imagine, yet for some it would be harder than for others. The person about whom we worried the most was, of course, Christina Onassis. In the brief space of two years, she had suffered the deaths of her brother, her mother, and her father. How could any of us expect such a mentally fragile woman to hold herself together at this time?

Christina's three aunts, Artemis, Merope, and

Kalliroi, spoke to me separately and frequently about their niece. Artemis pleaded with me to spend more time with Christina. "She will listen to you, Kiki," Mrs. Artemis told me many evenings during dinner. "You are so much closer to her age than any of us. You know that she cannot bear to be alone. Promise me that you will pay much attention to her." I promised to do what I could, but my own personal life was growing more involved, and I was struggling to combine that life with my involvement in the Onassis family.

As before, Mrs. Artemis continued to request my presence at her nightly dinners in Glyfada, and I could not refuse her invitations. However, it grew increasingly painful to sit at her table and stare at the empty seats. Alexander, Aristo, and Jackie were no longer there. Dr. Garofalidis was often too sick to join us, and Christina was frequently out of town or partying with friends. Pablo Ioannidis, the captain of Olympic Airways and a president of the Alexander S. Onassis Foundation, which was the official name given to all of Mr. Onassis' companies and properties after his death, remained faithful to his friend's sister and, along with his wife, Katia, and Stelios Papadimitriou, frequently came to the house for dinner.

Artemis grew to rely heavily on Pablo and asked his advice on many matters, especially concerning Christina. Often, during dinner at Glyfada, she would say to him, "Please, Pablo, you must talk to that girl for me and tell her that it is important that she not travel so much and that she spend more time in Athens." Instead of calling Christina herself and telling her what she wanted her niece to do, Artemis relied on Pablo to present the idea to Christina. It was typical of Artemis to ask people to intercede for her in regard to her relations with others, especially with her family members, and Pablo was both capable of and amenable to doing this for her. Since Christina respected Pablo, she often listened to his suggestions and did not fight his interference in her life. Also, whenever Artemis had a problem in her own life, especially a financial question, she would call Pablo and he would offer her solutions quickly and efficiently.

Jackie called Artemis nearly every day from New York, and her phone call was often the highlight of Artemis' day. Kalliroi and Merope tried to come to Glyfada as often as they could, understanding how much their older sister needed their company now. Some nights, the four of us would sit together in the living room in Glyfada and there would be only silence between us. It was as if we had nothing to say to one another, as if our sorrow was too strong to allow words to be spoken. There seemed to be no way we could encourage one another to be strong.

Artemis' friends continued to come and visit her also, but she found she had little to say to any of them. Many evenings, she just sat and stared silently at their faces, too. "From the moment I lost my brother, Kiki," she often told me, "it is like I am dead." She grew even more difficult than she had been before, and all too often she let the vodka speak for her. Those nights, I was the only one who was silent, almost grateful that, even if her words were cruel, at least she was speaking.

Many nights, it was just Artemis and I at the big table in Glyfada. I had started to date a few different men, and Artemis struggled not to make me feel guilty that my life was changing. "It is time for you to have a life of your own," she would say. "I want only for you to meet a wonderful man and get married and have a family. But please do not abandon Christina."

As it turned out, Christina did not need much help from me. Surprising everyone, especially her aunts, she began to assume a strong interest in all her father's properties that he had left to her and in a relatively short period of time developed into a powerful businesswoman. A typical Greek woman, she had always been straight and to the point in her behavior, never hesitating to express her feelings or hide what she was thinking. False compliments annoyed her and she struggled to be as honest as she could in her dealings with others. This personality fit well in the business world into which she now thrust herself. She was a far different person from the seventeen-year-old flighty teenager who had lasted six months in her father's office. Now, seven years later, she was suddenly ready to show that she had learned something from her father, even if she had not worked directly under him. She was conscientious about clearing up any confusion about which properties belonged to her and which were part of the Alexander S. Onassis Foundation. With the help of Stelios Papadimitriou, who fulfilled his promise to her dying father to help her in any way he could and whom Miltos Yiannacopoulos later helped become president of the

Onassis Establishment, she pored over all the legal documents until she was completely clear about the divisions of these two major companies. It was a monumental task, but she proved more than capable of performing it. Costas Gratsos and Professor Georgakis and Miltos Yiannacopoulos were all shocked by Christina's newfound abilities, but like Stelios Papadimitriou and Pablo Ioannidis, they supported her in any way they could.

Christina was adamant about attending all the business meetings with her father's collaborators and many times she was the only one who could produce solutions to pressing problems. Repeatedly, she exhibited strong business sense, which frequently brought to mind her father's abilities. Everyone who was working in the companies vied for her friendship and struggled to be as close to her as possible. She learned quickly whom she could trust and who was an asset for the business, and acted quickly and effectively on her surprisingly competent business instincts. It was a new role for her, but one she assumed naturally and successfully.

Continuing to follow in her father's footsteps, she was a commanding presence at the meetings held in Athens, New York, Monte Carlo, and Geneva. Dressed in smart business suits, looking serious and professional and nothing like the young girl who had sat cross-legged in front of my desk seven years earlier, she was composed and well informed at these meetings. For the first time, she was winning respect from her father's business associates, who conferred with her about important decisions and paid attention to her opinions and suggestions. She was not just the boss's daughter who had inherited his money, but an intelligent businesswoman who was becoming a vigorous new voice for the Onassis Establishment. Often she would call me, her own voice filled with excitement, as she related her latest business success, telling me about a new ship she had bought or a difficult meeting she had chaired successfully.

As Christina was developing her confidence and her business reputation, I was dividing my days between the Olympic Airways offices on Syngrou Avenue, where I worked during the morning hours, and the Springfield offices at 4 Kriezotou Street, where I spent the afternoon working for the shipping companies. In the mornings, I was involved with airplanes, and the afternoons with ships. It was a hectic schedule, but one that both Costas Konialidis and Aristo had suggested for me after Mr. Onassis had sold Olympic Airways to the government in January 1975. Eventually, after Mr. Onassis died, it became too much for me to maintain both jobs, so in 1977 I chose to continue to work for Olympic Airways, where I was the director of Support Divisions at West Airport until 1995. Still, I maintained a close business relationship with Costas Konialidis and frequently handled mail for him and kept him informed as to what was happening at the airlines. As for my personal relationships with other members of the Onassis family, they remained strong, no matter who my employer was. Also, wherever I was, I always made myself available to Christina, in any way that she needed me.

While Christina developed her professional image as a businesswoman, her personal life continued to have its own sets of successes and failures, unfortunately with more defeats than victories. Artemis was pleased and surprised that Christina was exhibiting such strong business capabilities, but she was exasperated over Christina's lack of suitors. "It's good she's become a businesswoman," she said to me. "But she still needs to be married. It is not safe for a woman with so much money to be single. She should not be concentrating only on the business. She needs to have a husband or she will never be safe."

"But she needs to have the right husband," I told her. "Not just any husband."

"That was Peter Goulandris," Artemis insisted. She never got over her disappointment that Christina's romance with Peter Goulandris, which had excited her father as he lay dying, had, for no apparent reason, fizzled. It seemed that the minute her father died, Christina wanted nothing more to do with Peter Goulandris. I knew that Christina had never loved Peter but there was no way I could convince Artemis of that fact.

"He was the perfect man for her," Artemis complained. "Now she will never find such a good match. He was very smart and he did not need her money." But Artemis did not give up easily. Once she was convinced that there was no way Christina and Peter would marry, she threw herself into the role of matchmaker and selected a man she deemed an acceptable suitor for her all-too-available niece. Artemis was deeply worried now that since her brother and nephew were dead, somebody who hated the Onassis family might try to kill Christina. I tried to assure her that she had no reason to fear such a calamity, yet when Christina verbalized the same fears, I, too, became worried. I knew that Christina was carefully watched by security people from her father's companies, but a single woman of her immense wealth and her family's tragic history did seem to be in danger. After all, she had always suspected her brother and mother had died under mysterious circumstances. How safe was she? When Artemis chose Alexander Andreadis, the son of a wealthy shipowner and the owner of the Greek Commercial Bank, as her niece's potential second husband, I was greatly relieved.

The matchmaker's next step was to invite Mr. and Mrs. Stratis Andreadis to Glyfada, where she spoke to them at great length about Christina. Once she was convinced that the Andreadises' were amenable to her plan, she arranged for a meeting between Alexandros and Christina. From the beginning, Christina liked Alexandros and she accepted her aunt's suggestion that the three of them take a cruise together on the *Christina* to get to know one another better. The cruise was a success. Shortly after their return to Athens, Christina and Alexandros became engaged. Artemis was ecstatic. Now, finally, her niece would be safe. Christina was as hopeful as her aunt, convinced that Alexander Andreadis would make her much happier than Peter Goulandris.

The wedding was held on July 22, 1975, just four months after Aristo's death, two months after the end of the mourning period, in the tiny church of Axoni, in Glyfada, less than two miles from Artemis' house. The church was so small that no more than forty people could fit inside.

One of the small group, however, was Jackie, whom Christina invited only because her aunts begged her to do so. Considering her feelings against Jackie, it was a big concession for Christina to give in to her aunts' demand that her former stepmother be present. One of the first things that Christina had done after her father's death had been to make it clear to her aunt Artemis that Jackie was no longer welcome in Glyfada. If she had been able to do so, Christina would have prevented her stepmother from ever receiving any money from Mr. Onassis' estate. However, by Greek law, Jackie was entitled to a certain percentage and there seemed little Christina could do to prevent her from receiving that.

Artemis had been helpless to convince Christina that she should be more gracious to Jackie. No matter what she or Pablo Ioannidis or I said to her, Christina insisted that Jackie was a curse and the downfall of her family. However, Christina eventually did work out a financial agreement with Jackie, which awarded her stepmother $26 million so that her stepmother would not attempt to obtain one-fourth of all of the Onassis properties. Aristo had rewritten his will during a six-hour flight from Acapulco to Athens in January 1975. In that will, Aristo had stipulated that the Alexander S. Onassis Foundation be established, and that a hospital, to be named the Onassium, in memory of his son and father, be built on Syngrou Avenue. In this will, he also limited the amount of money Jackie would inherit. Still, Christina did not want to take any chances that her stepmother would contest the will.

Ironically, Aristo did not leave any money to Maria in this same will. According to Artemis, he had told Maria that she was a wealthy woman and she did not need his money. "Our relationship is stronger than money," he had said to Maria months before he died. "You do not need my money to know I love you."

As for Jackie's share of Aristo's money, Christina told her aunt that she was thrilled to have gotten away with such a small settlement. "I would easily have given her even more if that meant I never had to look at her again," Christina claimed.

Artemis understood how much it infuriated her niece to think that Jackie would be staying in Glyfada when she came to Greece, so with a heavy heart, she gave in to Christina's requests and did not invite Jackie to stay with her during her visits to Greece. Therefore, whenever Jackie visited Greece after Aristo's death, she stayed with her good friend Niki Goulandris. Still, Jackie and Artemis spoke daily and always found a way to meet without Christina's knowing of their plans.

Christina's invitation to Jackie not only to attend her small wedding but also to stay in Glyfada for a few days was proof to Artemis that her niece was at long last growing up into a dignified and self-controlled young woman. "Jackie has so much she could teach Christina," Artemis told me often. "If only Christina would let her." Yet, even though Christina gave in to her aunt concerning Jackie and her wedding, she made it clear that this would be Jackie's last visit to Glyfada.

It seemed that for the day of Christina's wedding, the black cloud that had been hanging over the Onassis family since Aristo's death was temporarily dissolved. Everyone wore brightly colored dresses and smiles, happy not just for Christina but for the memory of her father. Aristo, we were all certain, would have been smiling on that day as he watched his beautiful daughter become the bride of a most acceptable Greek family.

Jackie looked especially lovely the day of the wedding, dressed in a long black skirt and white blouse, and she was delighted for Christina. She understood that the Andreadis family was part of the most prominent Greek society, and she was gracious and charming to all of them. Christina understood that Jackie's refined presence was an asset to her own family that day. When Jackie hugged Christina warmly and told her she looked beautiful, Christina respectfully thanked her for coming. Artemis smiled warmly at the scene between her niece and her sister-in-law. "See, Kiki," she said to me, "I knew it would happen that Christina could accept what Jackie has to teach her."

"Alexander seems like a wonderful man for Christina," Jackie told me before the ceremony. "I cannot tell you how glad I am that finally that girl will have some real happiness. Now, tell me how you and everybody have been since I left." I told her as much as I could, and we joked about the first few years of a marriage always being good, before Artemis joined us. Then Jackie wrapped her arm around Artemis' shoulder and the two women began to talk earnestly and privately. I was delighted to leave the two of them to each other.

Although Christina did not appear to have any problem with Jackie's presence at her wedding, there were other, more painful problems she did have to face that day. The glare of the paparazzi on her wedding day created more discomfort for her than her stepmother's appearance. Although both families had worked hard to keep the Onassis-Andreadis wedding a secret, dozens of journalists and photographers mobbed the bride and groom as they entered the church. Christina was escorted from Glyfada to the church by her uncle, Artemis' husband, Professor Theodore Garofalidis, who was ill but still capable of walking his niece into the church. Christina had always hated the paparazzi, but after the relentless publicity surrounding her father's death, she was developing an even greater fear of them. She was terrified of her wedding's becoming a huge media event with hundreds of journalists lying in wait to catch a glimpse of the bride and groom. She had specifically chosen the small church in Athens, very near the larger church of Saint Nikolas, for the service and had done everything possible to make certain no one but her family would know her plans.

However, on the day of her wedding, a giant throng of spectators, journalists, and photographers filled the area surrounding the tiny church, all straining to get a look at the bride. Christina was terrified and furious that she could not have the privacy she desired and nearly dissolved into tears when she saw them all. Instead of falling apart, as her uncle escorted her into the church, she took a deep breath and fixed a frozen smile on her lips. "I am becoming *Kyria*," she whispered to me before she entered the church. I smiled, despite myself, wondering if it would ever actually happen that Christina could like Jackie, never mind take her advice on any matter. Those who could manage to move through the crowd of paparazzi saw that the small church was overflowing with pink and white roses, and the bride looked slim and beautiful. And smiling.

After the wedding, the family and a small group of intimate friends went to the Andreadis home for a wedding dinner. As I watched Christina at the side of her beaming, handsome husband, I was convinced that she had at long last found true happiness. However, I was wrong.

Almost from the beginning, problems arose between the newlyweds. Christina refused to give up her business interests and continued to work long, stressful days for the company. Alexandros, however, did not possess the same business drive and was far more involved in motorcycles than he was in his wife. Also, at that period in her life, Christina had never looked prettier. She was relatively slim and well groomed, and calmer and steadier in her thinking than she had ever been before. Unfortunately, Alexandros did not maintain the handsome appearance he had presented at their wedding. In a brief period of time, he gained a large amount of weight and Christina told me that she hated having a fat husband. "I have worked so hard to lose weight," she told me. "How could I have married a man who is getting fatter every day that I look at him?"

I tried to make a joke of it and encouraged Christina. I was getting married myself and I told her that I knew it was going to be a lot of hard work to make any marriage work. I also told her to continue to concentrate on her work and be proud of all her accomplishments. Work and her self-esteem, she told me, were no problem. The problem was her choice of husbands.

Yet there were times when Christina and Alexandros were together that she appeared in love with him. Or at least unable to share him with others. During their engagement and the first months of their marriage, she rarely brought him to Glyfada for dinners. Instead, she preferred to dine with him alone, without the presence of her friends or family members. One day, shortly after she was married and when she was in Skorpios with Alexandros, Roula and Artemis were also there. Artemis suggested the four of them have lunch together, but Christina refused. "I like to eat only with Alexandros," she told her aunt. So while her niece and her new husband ate lunch in one room on the *Christina*, Roula and Artemis ate in another. It was a pattern Christina was to maintain during all her relationships with her men. When she was involved with or married to a man, she wanted to be only with him. When she was without a man in her life, she craved the presence of as many friends or family members as she could have near her. The one thing she could never tolerate, even for a brief period of time, was to be alone.

When Alexandros broke his leg in a motorbike accident on Skorpios, there were rumors that Christina left him for a romantic rendezvous with Peter Goulandris in Switzerland, but she swore to me that she went to Switzerland to conduct business, not to meet Peter. It was true, however, that Alexandros and Christina began to quarrel more frequently, often in public.

Artemis became frantic when we heard stories of their quarrels. "What is wrong with the two of them?" she would ask me. "Why do they not get along like all the other couples?"

"It will just take them time to get used to each other," I tried to assure her. "They have both been spoiled and indulged because of their wealth. In time, they will learn how to become a real husband and wife." A mere two years later, however, in July 1977, the marriage was officially dissolved.

During Christina's brief marriage to Alexander Andreadis, I, too, married. I had met George Moutsatsos, a tall, handsome man with thick, blond, curly hair and beautiful green eyes, in 1976 in the office of the Minister of Communications. I was there on official business for Olympic Airways the same day George, a chief engineer for the Latsis petroleum tanker company, was also conducting a transaction in the same office. When he began to talk to me, I could not help but notice how good-looking and intelligent he was. Since I knew a great deal about tankers, we had much in common and conversation was easy and natural between the two of us. As it turned out, George had worked on several of Mr. Onassis' tankers for a short time and knew many of the people in the Onassis shipping companies. Although George was twelve years older than I, it did not take long for the two of us to fall in love, and, within a year of our initial meeting, we were planning our wedding. Now that both Alexandros and Mr. Onassis were dead, it seemed especially important that I marry. I was lonely for both those men, and I wanted someone in my life who would take away some of this loneliness. George Moutsatsos could not have come into my life at a more auspicious time.

Artemis was delighted with my plans to marry George Moutsatsos and was involved with all the preparations of my wedding day. She helped me select my wedding gown and presented me with an exquisite large gold cross filled with multiple diamonds that I wore on my wedding day. It was not unusual for her to shower me with such expensive presents. Her generosity to me often knew no bounds. She accepted gratefully the role of *koumbara* at my wedding and insisted that George and I drive to the small church of Saint Dimitris Loubadiaris, under the Acropolis on the hill of Philopapou, in Jackie and Aristo's black Cadillac, driven, of course, by George Margaritis.

My parents were delighted with my choice of *koumbara* and were especially proud to have so many members of the well-known Onassis family at my wedding. Merope and Kalliroi, of course, attended with their husbands and their families, as did many of Aristo's collaborators and close friends. It seemed, as I looked around the church that beautiful day, as if everyone, including Costas Gratsos, Miltos Yiannacopoulos, Professor Georgakis, Costas Konialidis, and so many others from the Onassis Establishment, were there for me, just as they had been since I had come to work for Olympic Airways ten years earlier. The only men missing were, of course, Aristo and Alexander. My heart ached with sadness over their absence, but I was deeply grateful to all the other men and women who had become such an important part of my life.

From the first moment I began to date George, Mrs. Artemis welcomed him into her home. It was she who asked him when he was going to marry me, explaining to him that I was an innocent, lovely young woman, toward whom she would tolerate no poor behavior. "If your intentions are honorable, then you are to marry her soon," she informed him after the third time she had dinner with him in Glyfada. "If not, then you are to leave her alone now."

George respected Mrs. Artemis' blunt honesty and liked her from the first time they met. He also accepted the fact that she was an important part of my life and willingly accompanied me to Glyfada on a regular basis. Often she asked his advice about a financial matter and grew to rely on him for help in many different ways. No matter what she asked of him, whether it concerned her car, health, house, or finances, he helped her in any way he could. I was especially pleased to see the genuine affection that grew between the two people I loved the most.

On August 7, 1978, my first son was born, and when Artemis tearfully asked me to consider naming him Alexander in memory of her precious nephew, I immediately agreed. To give my son the name of my dear friend Alexander Onassis was a painful but beautiful joy for me. The following February, at the christening in Saint Artemios Church in Pagrati, Artemis was my Alexander's godmother. She bought small gold crosses for everyone, along with an exquisite red velvet dress for the baby. She also handed a great deal of money to the priest who performed the ceremony. A slight woman who seemed even thinner after Aristo died, Artemis was barely able to hold my heavy baby during the service. However, with my husband George behind her and unobtrusively supporting the baby, Artemis put the oil on the baby and wrapped him in the large white towel before dressing him in his red velvet christening gown.

After the ceremony, everyone, including once again Kalliroi and her daughter, Marilena, and her husband, and Merope and her family, along with many of the members of the Onassis Establishment, and, of course Panagiotis, who carried Artemis' special foods, came to my home in Kato Ilioupolis for champagne and dinner. It was a grand day for celebration, and as I watched Artemis kiss my son, Alexander, many times that cold February day, I was filled with hope and love. My son could never bring back the special person for whom he was named, but he would bring love and joy to those of us who had adored his namesake.

Less than a week before my Alexander was born, however, Christina was married again, this time not to an American or to a Greek, but to a Russian. She had met Sergei Kauzov, the thirty-five-year-old head of the Russian maritime department's tanker division, in Moscow in October 1976, when she was trying to conduct a business deal that would allow her to lease some of her smaller dry-cargo vessels to the Russians for a five-year deal. At that time, Kauzov was married to a Russian cellist with whom he had an eight-year-old daughter.

It didn't take Christina, who was still legally married to Andreadis but deciding exactly how to end their marriage, long to fall in love with the warm, outgoing Russian. They met frequently in Paris and also arranged a romantic holiday in Monte Carlo. Still, theirs was an unorthodox alliance. A Russian Communist romancing a wealthy Greek capitalist was startling, but when the capitalist happened to be the Onassis heiress with major shipowning assets, the romance was all the more intriguing. For Christina, the improbability of their relationship made her even more determined that this affair would end in marriage. Even physically, the two of them made an unlikely couple. At five feet four Kauzov was shorter than she, and his rather average blond looks contrasted sharply with her dark skin, thick black hair, and startling black eyes. The fact that one of his blue eyes was glass, a result of a childhood accident, and he often removed it in public, may even have added to the drama of her attraction.

While some members of the Onassis Establishment were skeptical and concerned about such a marriage, Christina remained adamant that Sergei was the one man who could bring her the perfect love that was eluding her.

"He reminds me of my father," Christina told me one day when the two of us were having lunch alone in Glyfada. "Oh, they do not look anything alike, but he is almost as clever and charming as my father. If my father met him, I am certain he would have liked Sergei very much."

I knew that Christina was still mourning her father and brother deeply and went frequently to their graves on Skorpios to offer flowers. She talked about both of them often and dissolved into tears during those conversations. She also talked about her mother and how sorry she was that her mother had never found happiness in either of her last two marriages. "I do not want to make the same mistake my parents made," she told me. "When I meet the one man I can love, I am never going to leave him." The conversation reminded me of the ones we had shared when she was seventeen and working for her father. Then, as now, she desired the perfect love that would fix all the maladies in her life.

When I first met Sergei at a dinner party Kalliroi gave for the couple in Lagonissi, I understood what Christina was saying about Sergei and her father. There was a charisma about this man that did remind me, in a slight manner, of Aristo's unique magnetism. Although Sergei did not talk much that evening and spoke no Greek, whatever he did say, in perfect French, was worth listening to. He had a way, similar to Aristo's, of sitting in a room filled with people and listening to the conversation without adding much. Then, like Mr. Onassis, he would suddenly contribute something thought-provoking, perhaps about politics or religion, that captured everyone's interest.

But, most important, there was no doubt that Sergei Kauzov was very much in love with Christina. Of all the men that I had ever seen her with, he was the most attentive. His eyes followed her wherever she moved that evening and were filled with admiration and adoration for her. Christina was very proud of the new love in her life and seemed to glow with her newfound satisfaction. I found myself believing that Christina had finally found the man who would bring her happiness.

Kalliroi's dinner party was elegant and joyous. Everyone toasted the happy couple all night long as we indulged ourselves in delicious food and especially sweet desserts. Christina looked stunning that night. She had lost all of the weight she had gained when things had begun to deteriorate between her and Andreadis, and her black dress, made by Roula, was elegant. However, she barely ate any of the food put before her, interested, it appeared, only in the blond Russian, who remained attentively at her side all night long.

Artemis was characteristically accepting of her niece's new suitor. "He is a most special young man," she told me as we traveled back to Athens that night. She had been in a good mood all night long, and I was delighted that she had enjoyed herself so much. Of course, she had not eaten any of her sister's delicious foods, having brought her own foods instead, but still it had been a fun-filled evening for all of us. "All I want is for her to be with someone who will make her happy. I believe this charming, intelligent man is going to make my niece very happy."

Costas Gratsos took a little more convincing. He tried to make Christina understand all the ramifications of her marriage to a Russian Communist, how it might affect the Onassis Establishment's business interests in the Middle East and the United States. But, ultimately, he accepted Christina's intended and supported her the way he believed her own father would have, helping to make the arrangements to permit Sergei to marry Christina in a small civil ceremony in Moscow. No members of the Onassis family would attend, and only Sergei's mother, Mariya, would stand beside the couple. The crowd of photographers and journalists besieging the couple ruined any pleasure Christina, wearing a simple white dress and holding a few flowers, and Sergei, dressed in a dark blue suit, might have experienced that afternoon.

One more difficult part of the wedding was that Christina was now separated from her longtime housemaid and confidante, Eleni Syros. Eleni Syros had been her faithful companion and maid since 1973. Before then, Eleni and her husband George had been Aristo's most prized employees in Paris and Skorpios, but, after Alexander's death, he allowed them to work for Christina exclusively. At first, Christina thought that Eleni and George would accompany her to Moscow. However, the Russian bureaucracy made it impossible for even a Greek millionaire to secure housing, and Christina was forced to live in a small, cramped two-bedroom one-bath apartment in Moscow with her husband and mother-in-law. The last time I saw Christina before her wedding, she assured me she would have no trouble living in Russia with her new husband. "If I have to live in a tiny dark house, it will be no problem," she told me. "I will, of course, miss Eleni terribly, but all that matters is that I am together under one roof with Sergei."

I did notice, that day, that Christina had begun to gain back a bit of the weight she had lost when she fell in love with Sergei, but she was certain her new marriage would bring her both happiness and thinness. Unfortunately, it brought her neither. Life in Moscow was cold and difficult and the lack of her diet Coke added pounds to the new bride's quickly expanding body. Still, Christina persevered, bringing Sergei to Skorpios for a celebration and appearing to be very much in love with him during their visit.

During the sadly all-too-brief marriage, Christina continued to work as diligently for the Onassis Establishment as she had before her marriage. Costas Gratsos and many of her other associates at the company were filled with praise for her accomplishments. Even while she was married to a Russian, she received the full support of the Onassis Establishment, attending nearly every meeting, no matter where or when it was held. Few of the members of the Onassis Establishment approved of Sergei and many of them openly hoped that she would divorce him. Still, Costas Gratsos told me that he was convinced that in a short time Christina would no longer need help from any of the other associates and would be able to handle any major problem by herself. For a woman operating in a predominantly male business world, married to a Russian and living in Moscow, she was doing, he admitted, shockingly well.

Shortly after Christina's marriage to Sergei, she received a phone call from her aunt Artemis telling her she was not well and asking Christina to come home to see her as soon as possible. Christina was on the first flight out of Moscow and hurried to Glyfada, where she found her aunt in surprisingly good health. When Artemis saw that her niece was alone, she hoped that meant the marriage was finished and that Christina would return to Greece. Although Artemis had been most supportive of the relationship when she first met Sergei, she changed her mind when she learned that Christina was not happy in Moscow. It didn't take Artemis long to decide that her niece would be less safe with Sergei in Moscow than she would be living alone in Greece. "Forgive me for frightening you," Artemis greeted her confused niece. "I missed you so badly I had to see you. The thought of you so far away in Russia just made me a little crazy, I guess."

Christina smiled immediately and hugged her thin aunt tightly. "I'm not far away at all," she assured her aunt. "And anytime you want to see me, all you have to do is call me and I'll be home as soon as possible." For the first few days of their visit, Artemis was convinced there was a strong chance the marriage was over and that Christina would not return to Moscow. However, by the end of her week in Athens, Christina was ready to return to her husband.

Sadly, despite the fact that Christina's business success soared, Artemis' wish came true and Christina's marriage floundered. The coldness of the Russian winter, the difficulty in finding an appropriate apartment for the two of them, her dislike of Russian food, and their lack of a social life were problems she might have overcome in time. However, the aversion of the Russian people to her was too large a problem for her to defeat. Everywhere she went in Russia, she felt a sense of disapproval. She was a capitalist living in a communist society and there was no feeling of security for her wherever she traveled in her husband's country. The darkness of the Russian winter accentuated her own dark moods and she found herself growing fatter and more depressed. The fact that she had a husband who adored her did not offset the fact that she hated living in his bleak, disapproving country.

Even when Christina and Sergei cut through miles of red tape and received a seven-room apartment on Tyopoly Stan, near the city's botanical gardens, decorating their new home proved an insurmountable task. Buying a refrigerator or paint were impossible tasks and Christina became overwhelmed with frustration and impatience. Still, for a brief period, she persevered and refused to be driven out of the country without a struggle. For her husband's thirty-sixth birthday, she bought him a $3 million tanker, which he used to set up his own company.

Unfortunately, however, the two of them began to quarrel more frequently and Christina again came home to Glyfada alone, this time complaining bitterly about life in Russia. "If Sergei could leave Russia, we would have a chance," Christina told her aunt, who listened sympathetically. "But I don't know if that would ever happen. I don't want to sit around and grow old in Russia."

And she didn't. By November of that year, Christina had asked Kauzov for a divorce. And given him another tanker, the *Olympic Phaethon,* as a farewell present. By December of that same year, she was in St. Moritz for the Christmas season.

At first, Christina seemed ecstatic to be free and home, but when her moods became gloomy, Artemis began to fear that she had made a mistake wishing the marriage would fail. "What is wrong with my niece, Kiki?" she kept asking me, sounding as confused as her niece. "She is twenty-eight and still alone. Why can she not stay with one man for more than a short time? She is never satisfied for a long time with anything. I am so worried that she will always be alone and will never be safe. What am I going to do about her?"

After her divorce from Sergei, Christina stayed in touch with him, calling him often and anxious to remain good friends with him. Often, it appeared as if she were still in love with him. And, from what she told me, it was evident he was still in love with her. Yet her moods grew progressively darker and she spent long hours crying inconsolably. She was bewildered and could never decide what she wanted to do with herself. One minute her hair was shiny and black. Then, to please a man, she became a blonde. She was eating too much, especially her old enemies, Coca-Cola and chocolate.

Many weekends, Christina would pull herself together and arrange elaborate festivities for her friends on Skorpios, wildly drinking and singing and dancing without shoes until all hours of the night. She even built some more small houses on Skorpios so that her friends could use them when she didn't want to put them on the *Christina,* which she gave to the government in 1978. As desperately as Christina wanted friends, it was very hard for her to make or keep them. One of her truest friends was Marina Tchomlekdjoglou Dodero, whom she had known since childhood. As happened with so many people in Christina's life, there came a time when Marina needed something from her friend. That "something" was $4 million for her family's pressing financial problems, which Christina promptly gave her. Yet Marina was a faithful and loyal friend who could not help asking for something which her friend Christina had and which she would have no problem giving to someone who needed it.

Sadly, however, Christina believed that all the people she invited to Skorpios were her friends. She would think nothing of sending the eighteen-seat Learjet to Paris or Geneva or London to pick up a guest or the dozens of other socialites or acquaintances she selected for each gathering, and fly them to the nearby airport of Aktion, where they would be flown by helicopter to Skorpios for their vacation in paradise.

For each hour of her guests' visits, she would have an activity planned, including swimming for extensive periods in the ocean or in the swimming pool on the island, shopping for jewelry on a nearby island, dancing in a disco on yet another island, and eating lavishly prepared meals on the *Christina* or splendid picnic feasts on remote spots of the island. She drove the staff on Skorpios crazy with her special requests for exorbitant banquets or unusual foods, but somehow they all performed their duties perfectly, always anxious above all else to protect and please their employer.

Argentinean polo player Luis Basualdo was one of Christina's most frequent guests. Even though he was always accompanied by his young girlfriend, Clare, he was Christina's most favored paid companion. She paid him an outlandish monthly salary of $30,000 just to have him near her whenever she demanded his company. He kept a close eye on many of her guests, making sure all her demands were followed, but mostly he was available to her twenty-four hours a day. He made sure her demon of loneliness was kept away and those who were interested in her had someone to be jealous of.

Even though Christina's schedule on Skorpios was a frenetically busy one, that did not mean that she ignored her business responsibilities while she was organizing these opulent retreats for her friends. When lawyers or executives, such as Creon Brown, Costas Gratsos, Pablo Ioannidis, Stelios Papadimitriou, or Apostolos Zambelas, called her with business requests, she managed to answer them immediately. She trusted the other employees of the Onassis Establishment to do their jobs when she was not available to them, yet she put large demands upon herself and met them even when she was at play.

At the conclusion of most of these lavish days on Skorpios, she was usually found in a disco on a nearby island with a few of her guests who still had some energy left, dancing wildly on the tables, lost in the music and her own hysteria. Yet the minute each of these capricious adventures ended and her guests departed, her elated mood disappeared, and she became sad and nervous, a grossly overweight woman full of tears and, worst of all, alone.

Artemis was frantic after Christina's third divorce. "She is still so young," she complained to me. "I hear her crying alone all night long. How will she ever find a man who will make her happy when she is either wild or depressed? I am only afraid that I will die before I know my niece is taken care of."

Because of Christina's work and play schedule, however, her aunt saw less and less of her in Glyfada. It was nothing short of miraculous that even when she was miserable or out of control in her personal life, Christina still managed to keep up with her business obligations and work every bit as hard as she had before her most recent divorce. It was important to her that she keep the promise she had made to her father not to lose one piece of his property during her lifetime. Eventually, in 1978, she did give the *Christina* to the Greek government to be used as a museum, in accordance with her father's will, but before then, she kept it running as smoothly and as lavishly as her father had. Between her constant business trips to Paris and Monte Carlo and New York, and her pleasure cruises and escape vacations, there seemed to be months when she was never in Glyfada. "You are away too much," I told her one day. "You are never home and your aunts never get to see you."

"I know, Kiki," she admitted. "You are absolutely right. But I cannot help it. I am confused where my real home is and I hardly understand where I am."

Shortly after our talk, Christina made a concentrated effort to spend more time in Glyfada. However, as her fear of journalists and her weight both continued to grow, she ordered huge trees to be placed around the swimming pool in Glyfada so she could swim with some degree of privacy. Even when her weight was at its heaviest, beyond 200 pounds, Christina was still a strong swimmer, who needed and enjoyed a daily swim to bolster her sagging spirits. Yet each time a photograph of the fat Christina came across my desk, I shuddered as I paid the photographer and threw it away. All too often, these types of pictures were published anyhow, and Christina suffered miserably.

Christina also organized the construction of a small apartment, with its own entrance, on the second floor of Artemis' house in Glyfada, and decorated it to her own personal taste. Considering the luxurious homes she maintained in Paris and St. Moritz, this apartment was a small, unremarkable abode. Yet she cherished it. She was deeply proud of the finished apartment and brought me to look at it the minute her project was completed. "You like it, Kiki?" she kept asking me, and when I praised it, her eyes grew bright. The walls and floors of the apartment were all covered with costly white materials and the entire apartment had a clean, yet simple feel to it. One of the things that Christina loved the most about this apartment was the unrestricted view of the sea from all its rooms. I knew that Christina was not going to spend a great deal of time in this apartment, not with her other more glamorous homes, but there was something warm and special about this place that captured a rarely seen side of this overexposed, over-indulged, overweight, underloved woman.

As Christina and I sat on her chairs, sipping Diet Coke and talking about how she had carefully selected each item in the apartment, I had an unaccustomed vision of this woman. Christina, at that moment, seemed normal. Like a divorced woman reveling in her own private spot, which she could call her own home. But the moment faded quickly. Christina, I knew only too well, was not a normal woman. Still, whenever she walked into that apartment, she wanted to be one.

Shortly after Christina moved into the Glyfada apartment, she also asked me to find a new person to work for her. Except for her brief journey to Moscow as Kausov's wife, Christina was rarely without Eleni Syros at her side. However, Eleni was exhausted with all the demands Christina placed upon her personal handmaid, and Christina wanted another maid to help ease the workload of her cherished Eleni. I searched for the proper woman for such a position and eventually found Patra Argyrou, a retired employee of Olympic Airways. Christina immediately liked Patra and was grateful to me for having found her. A small, thin woman, Patra was a hard worker who adored Christina and worked for her in all of Christina's homes for three years. However, Patra complained to me that Eleni was so devoted to Christina and vice versa that Patra felt unappreciated by both women. Since Patra felt she was not needed, she decided it was time for her to leave.

Yet often during those three years Patra told me how much she worried about her employer. "She is a wonderful girl," Patra told me, "but she is never happy. Even when she is all dressed and ready to go out, she starts to cry. She tells me that everybody approaches her only for her money. She says she spends so much money to make them want to be with her, but they never stay for very long. I feel so sad for her."

In actuality, Christina spent very little time in her Glyfada apartment. Yet she felt more and more need to be with her aunts. Since it seemed to be difficult for her to leave her Paris apartment, she begged both me and her aunts to come spend time with her there. "I am alone so much, Kiki," she told me. "I need you to come back and spend time with me. Remember the fun times we had in Paris before? Please come back and we will have them again." I wanted to be able to do as she asked, but as inviting as Christina made it seem, my work responsibilities with Olympic Airways and my marriage obligations prevented me from simply packing my suitcase and heading to Paris.

Artemis was getting too old and frail to travel as easily as she had before, so Kalliroi headed to Paris to keep her niece company and try to improve her bleak mood. Christina was delighted to have her aunt with her and, at the beginning of Kalliroi's visit, she slept better and ate more sensibly when her aunt was beside her. Christina loved going out to dine or shop with her aunt and asked her opinion on whatever she bought or wherever she was going. Kalliroi offered Christina the same affection she gave her own daughter, Marilena, who was two years younger than Christina. However, within weeks of Kalliroi's arrival in Paris, Christina grew more difficult, flying into rages and exhibiting severe mood swings. For one year, Kalliroi stayed with her, leaving Paris only when Christina headed to her other residences. Finally, however, it became too much for her and she returned to Lagonissi and the calmer life of Marilena and her grandchildren. Christina was heartbroken that her aunt was leaving her, but she understood that Kalliroi had her own family and could not stay with her forever. Before Kalliroi left Paris, Christina presented her with a large and beautiful diamond ring, which Kalliroi proudly showed me when she returned to Athens.

The return of Thierry Roussel to Christina's life in 1983, however, marked the beginning of the worst and most destructive, as well as the last of her four marriages. She had met Thierry ten years earlier on Skorpios when her father had invited a group of Parisians, including Thierry and his pharmaceutical mogul father, Henri, to vacation on the island. Christina and Thierry had experienced a brief affair at that time, which left them with pleasant memories but no strong commitments. When they met again in 1983, Christina had been through two more marriages and two more divorces, and Thierry was continuing his longtime affair with Paris model and translator, Gaby Landhage.

Their reunion, personally engineered by Henri Roussel, sent waves of fear through Artemis. "That playboy does not love my niece," she told me when Christina announced her intention to marry Thierry. "He will never make her feel safe about his love."

I urged Artemis to try to speak to her niece about her fears. "There is no sense," Artemis insisted. "I have tried and she does not listen to me for one second. There is no one in this whole world whom Christina will listen to. She has never before followed my instructions. Why would she start now?"

Blond, tall, strikingly handsome, Thierry tore at Christina's heart in a way no other man ever had. Eleni Syros, Christina's devoted maid, agreed with Artemis. "Christina does not like to believe the truth about Thierry," Eleni told me. "He is the man she has always dreamed of and she will never stop loving him. No matter what he does to her."

What Thierry did to Christina was to continue to love the one woman he had always loved. Gaby Landhage never faded from his life, not even after his March 1984 wedding to Christina in Paris. Those of us who loved Christina worried that this man did not love her. We feared he was still in love with Gaby, but was too much of a playboy to marry her. Artemis asked, "Wasn't it likely that Thierry and his father were more than a little attracted to Christina's massive wealth? If Thierry could marry Christina and at the same time alleviate his family's financial difficulties and continue his relationship with Gaby, why wouldn't he become Christina's fourth husband?"

It was equally simple with Christina. She was in love with Thierry and was used to getting everything she wanted. She wanted him; and even if he didn't love her as much as he loved Gaby, she would still marry him.

Before they married in March 1984, Thierry took charge of what he considered Christina's troubled life and tried to restructure it. First of all, he addressed her deplorable physical condition. Once again, she was grossly overweight and hooked on barbiturates and amphetamines, all of which he insisted she surrender. He knew she was taking pills to quiet her nerves, to help her sleep, and to make her lose weight. And he wanted her off all of them. Considering her dependency on all these drugs, it was an immense task for her to follow his orders, but miraculously or because of her love for him and her desire to please him, she struggled hard to do as he asked.

Thierry's manner of handling Christina's reliance on pills and her weight problem was a particularly severe one. He made it clear to her that if she wanted him in her life, and in her bed, she was going to have to give up all her pills and still lose weight. Chocolate, too, had to disappear from her life. Watching the way Thierry treated Christina often brought Artemis to tears.

"But he is helping her improve her physical condition," I tried to assure Artemis, when she told me how Thierry insulted Christina in front of her. "She needs help and maybe this is the only way she can receive it."

But with Thierry in Christina's life Artemis now worried more than ever about her niece's future. "He doesn't make her feel safe," she told me. "This is one man who doesn't seem to love anything about her."

Another of Thierry's endless list of requests concerned Christina's social life. Like her pills and extra pounds, her friends had to go. He approved of almost none of them and had Christina remove them, along with her bottles of pills, from her life. While some of those friends did seem to offer Christina nothing except an opportunity to throw away her money on their pleasure, some were dear to her. To Thierry, they were all nuisances who needed to be flushed out of her life. Again, with remarkably little complaint, Christina's love for Thierry and her pleasure at seeing him so concerned about what was best for her prevailed, and she dissolved nearly all her relationships with her former friends.

Thierry's dissatisfaction with moving into Christina's Avenue Foch apartment was also dealt with in his unique, albeit self-serving, manner. The couple remained in the luxurious building but in a different apartment on a different floor, which, for a huge price, was rebuilt and decorated according to Thierry's specifications. Christina also replaced her Learjet with a new $15 million Falcon 50 which could seat twenty. Thierry not only found countless ways in which to improve his new bride, but just as many avenues to spend her money.

Yet Christina remained filled with hope that everything Thierry was doing was intended to cement their relationship and provide them with a glorious future. She even took him to New York to meet her former stepmother, anxious to show off her new prize. She was certain that Thierry would be as impressed with her father's sophisticated widow as Jackie would be with her handsome and charming future husband. Jackie, as Christina rightly suspected, was one acquaintance that Thierry would not request his future wife to dismiss. The meeting between the three of them, Christina told Artemis later, was perfect. Jackie was gracious and congenial, obviously impressed with Thierry's charms and good looks. Jackie and Thierry chatted in French about Paris and New York, and both of them were warm and affectionate toward Christina. "I have never seen Jackie act so nice toward me," Christina told Artemis. "If I didn't know better, I would have thought the woman actually liked me." The curse on her life, Christina was certain, was no longer in effect. Thierry had dissolved it.

Their wedding in Paris was a Catholic and Greek Orthodox ceremony, followed by an elegant dinner at Maxim's. Artemis was pleased that her niece looked slimmer and beautiful in her stunning white wedding suit, but she held little hope for Christina's future happiness. "Christina is blind," she told me after her return to Glyfada. "She does not see what everyone else sees. This man will never love her as she loves him. No matter what she does, he will break her heart the way no other man ever did."

But Christina did much to ensure that her aunt's prophecy would not come true. This was one marriage, she was determined, that would not fail. No matter what. When Thierry moved his mistress, Gaby Landhage, into an apartment a mere five hundred meters from Avenue Foch, Christina barely blinked. To Artemis, it seemed a form of kismet that both her brother and his daughter's husband would live in Paris, around the corner from their beloved mistresses. Aristo might have married Jackie, but he never stopped loving Maria. Thierry married Christina, but he never surrendered Gaby. Unlike the son-in-law he never met and would most likely have detested, however, Aristo was discreet about his mistress and never taunted or humiliated his wife with her presence. Aristo, Artemis was convinced, loved his second wife. Perhaps not as much as he adored his mistress, but, for most of the years of his marriage, with a deep affection. Thierry, she was convinced, never loved Christina. Not even for one day.

There was no doubt this was not a conventional marriage, yet Christina was determined to make it work. If it meant including Gaby in her life, then she would do so. After all, she told me proudly, Thierry had married her, not Gaby. "I am the only Mrs. Thierry Roussel," she said. "And I am the only one there will ever be." Gaby was a gentle, lovely lady and Christina wanted her to be her friend. She just didn't want her to be Mrs. Thierry Roussel. She saw no reason for either woman to be jealous of the other. All they had to do was to learn to live with each other.

Thierry's demands for living with him continued to grow. The apartment in Paris did not satisfy his need for a home of his own. So Christina found an eighteen-room villa in the small town of Gingins outside Geneva overlooking Lake Leman. She paid $5 million for the estate and then began to restore it. Her aunts were dismayed when they heard of her latest financial venture. "The house is old and broken down," Artemis told me. "But she is too blind to see that. All she sees is that her husband might like it, so she will buy it and fix it up for him. She is going crazier every day." Artemis swore that she would never go to see that "ugly old house," which Christina named Boislande, and spent $2.5 million to restore; Artemis kept her promise. Christina's aunts complained that Thierry was pressuring their niece to spend all her time in Paris or Switzerland, anywhere except in Greece or with her family. No matter what Christina said to them, none of them felt welcome in Christina's new residences in Paris or Switzerland.

Several months before her wedding to Thierry, Christina had asked me to accompany her to a fertility doctor, Dr. Cohen, in Paris. She had been disappointed that she had not become pregnant as quickly as she had hoped and was certain she had a serious problem. Her impatient nature made it impossible for her to believe that she would get pregnant on her own in time. However, Dr. Cohen assured her that she was fine and that the only thing preventing her from becoming pregnant was the great stress she encountered in her daily life. Christina followed all his instructions about reducing this stress and was ecstatic to learn she was pregnant a mere few months after her marriage to Thierry.

When Christina told Artemis she was pregnant, Artemis cried with happiness. "Now, my niece will find happiness," she told me. "This is my one hope. That motherhood will make her normal and will make this marriage work. Finally, she will never be alone."

Yet, as with everything in her life, Christina could not simply accept her new condition with calm and ease. Her unborn child became her obsession. She was terrified of losing the baby and went through complicated precautions to protect herself during her pregnancy. She was also certain that her newborn baby's safety would take great lengths to ensure and she set about renovating and improving the security systems in all her residences. Thierry seemed thrilled with the pregnancy, even though he had added another woman to his list, this time a beautiful model named Kirsten Gile. Somehow, despite the attentions he showed Gaby and Kirsten, he managed to be at Christina's side more frequently than before. He did seem to become alarmed, however, at how quickly Christina grew fat and warned her repeatedly not to lose all the control she had mastered since he had come into her life.

Just a few months after Christina learned she was to become a mother, Thierry discovered Gaby was also pregnant. In order to keep his mistress's pregnancy away from the eye of the press and his wife, Thierry sent Gaby to her family in Sweden for the final seven months of her pregnancy.

On January 28, 1985, by cesarean section, several weeks ahead of schedule, Christina gave birth to a baby girl, whom she named Athina for her mother, Tina. The baby, as Artemis proudly described her, possessed Christina's large, beautiful black eyes and her father's long, slim body.

The christening, held in Skorpios when Athina was seven months old, was a joyous affair, attended by all the family members and close friends. It was a very hot August day and the island looked beautiful. The ceremony was held in the living room of the hill house, a guest house on Skorpios with a charming roof apartment, where Jackie and Aristo often liked to have a private lunch or dinner together, overlooking the ocean. Since the day of the christening was so hot, all the doors and windows were open, and the party itself was held outdoors. Close to the shore, we could see Thierry Roussel's father's large sailboat moored nearby. It had been years since I had seen the island so filled with excitement and pleasure.

All the servants were dressed in their formal black uniforms, but they were all smiling as they served the caviar, meatballs, shrimp and other kinds of seafood, chicken, fresh fruits, and drinks, delighted to fulfill the requests of any of their guests. After two devastating funerals on the island, it was a sheer joy to celebrate the beginning of a new life.

George Livanos, Tina Onassis' brother and Christina's uncle, was the godfather. In the living room of the hill house, the baby was dunked into the water, and then the priest gave oil to George Livanos to anoint the baby. After the priest and the godfather had placed oil all over the baby, George covered her with a big white towel and helped put the beautiful dress on his godchild. It was a particularly moving ceremony as we all watched the expression of pride on Christina's face. She was as close to happiness as she would ever be.

As I stared at the perfect baby, however, all I could see was the grandfather she would never get to meet. How proud he would have been to have seen his first grandchild, called Athinoula, and named for his first wife, to have known that the bloodline he began was going to be extended long into the future. Suddenly, the baby let out a sharp cry. And I came back to reality. Christina looked radiant but overweight. Thierry was handsome but obviously uncomfortable with Christina's family. I thought of his pregnant mistress and his marriage to Christina and my heart was heavy. I had heard from Christina herself how unhappy she had been during her own childhood, and I had seen firsthand much of the pain of her adult life. For this pretty baby to grow up normal would take, I understood at that moment, a miracle.

For the next three and a half years, Christina threw herself into motherhood with a newfound vitality. Much of her energy was spent protecting and outfitting and adoring her daughter, Athinoula. She installed all sorts of protective instruments in her house in Boislande to protect her daughter. Not only were there massive security precautions to make certain no kidnapper could come near her child, but also provisions so that Christina could hear her daughter crying or breathing, sleeping or coughing. She would personally monitor these programs so that she was aware of her daughter's every move and condition. The constant pressure of photographers, understandably and sadly, increased after Athina's birth, as did Christina's hatred of them. "I am trying not to be too nervous around my daughter," she told me during a visit to Glyfada with Athina. "I know it is not good for her to feel my fears."

Even before Athina was born, Christina was obsessed with her daughter's wardrobe, and had ordered a complete designer wardrobe for her baby. Once Athina was born, Christina changed her daughter's dresses two or three times a day, dressing her in exquisite outfits designed almost exclusively by Dior. She also decided that her daughter would carry the name of Onassis, would be called Athina Onassis-Roussel, and would be proud of her mother's family. "Now that I have a child, my life has a purpose," she told me. "Never can I imagine a life without my Athinoula."

Still, Christina did as much as she was capable of to give her daughter some semblance of a normal life. Almost from the first week of Athina's life, Christina sought out other mothers with children Athina's age and invited them to Boislande. She enjoyed spending hours talking to the other mothers about their children, and as Athina grew older, she loved to see her daughter interact with other little boys and girls. She wanted nothing more for her daughter than to have good friends and loving parents with which to enjoy her childhood.

As for the loving parents, Athina's father divided his time between the sumptuous residences Christina bought for him and their daughter and the smaller home in Switzerland for which Christina had paid. It was in this home near Boislande that Gaby lived with the two children, a son and a daughter, Thierry had fathered during his marriage to Christina.

Shortly after Athinoula's christening, we all began to worry about Artemis' health. She had very little energy and her eyes appeared yellow. She was having difficulty speaking and when she did talk, she spoke so slowly, it was almost impossible to understand what she was saying. Walking was almost impossible for her, and standing up was very difficult. When George and I came to dinner in Glyfada, she appeared to be in pain and could not stay at the table for more than a half hour. Christina was frantic about her aunt's deteriorating condition and admitted her to a private suite at the Igia Hospital in Athens, where the doctors quickly provided the diagnosis of liver cancer. Although we all knew she was sick, it came as a terrible shock that she was so ill. When the doctors told Christina that the cancer was far advanced, she refused to accept their opinion. Every day for two weeks, Christina and I visited Artemis in her hospital suite, where Christina brought dozens of new silk pajamas, always in her aunt's favorite colors of pink and light blue, and bouquets of pink roses. As the doctors administered heavy doses of morphine to dull Mrs. Artemis' pain, she did not recognize either of us.

It was strange, but during those long and painful hours that I spent with Christina during Artemis' hospitalization, I could not help but notice the poor condition of Christina's teeth. It had always been part of Christina's personality that when she was depressed, she cared nothing about her physical appearance. Not only would she gain large amounts of weight, she would forget about washing her hair or brushing her teeth. Her overwhelming sorrow about her beloved aunt's devastating illness erased any thoughts she had about how she looked. I wanted to speak to her about her appearance, but of course I would not utter one critical word.

The only thing that Christina cared about during those long weeks was getting her aunt well. Ignoring the doctors' advice that nothing more could be done for her aunt, Christina had Artemis carried onto her Learjet, which Pablo Ioannidis flew to New York. "I cannot lose my aunt," she sobbed to me before the jet left Athens, as I said what I knew in my heart would be my final farewell to Mrs. Artemis. "She is the only person who really loves me in this whole world. I cannot live without her." Christina and I held each other and cried heartbroken tears until it was time for the flight to depart. It was miraculous that Artemis survived the flight, after which Christina had her admitted to the Memorial Sloan-Kettering Cancer Center in New York City.

As the doctors predicted, Artemis continued to decline and, with Christina at her side, she died a few weeks later. Artemis was buried in Skorpios, beside her brother and her nephew. "So much of what I love is here," Christina wept in her aunt Kalliroi's arms as they prepared to leave the island after the burial service. "My daughter will never have the chance to get to know all these people that I loved so much. When I look at all I have lost, I don't know how I would have the strength to go on if I didn't have my Athinoula."

In 1985, when Artemis died in New York, Jackie also was heartbroken. When Christina brought Artemis to the Memorial Sloan-Kettering Cancer Center in New York, Jackie tried to be considerate of her stepdaughter and keep her visits short. Christina did not say a word to her, but still Jackie continued to visit her sister-in-law at the hospital, always bringing her beautiful pink roses, which she knew were Artemis' favorite flowers.

"You will get well soon," Jackie told Artemis, "and then the two of us will go for a long walk in Glyfada, and we will talk until I am too tired to walk any longer."

The night Artemis died, I was in Greece and Jackie called me from New York. "I cannot believe she is gone," she told me, her voice breaking with emotion. "Now I will miss my sister-in-law, my mother, and my friend every day of my life." She had said farewell to her sister-in-law in the hospital, aware that her presence at Artemis' funeral in Greece would only further upset Christina. Although Artemis' daughter, Popi, was buried in a cemetery in Athens, Artemis was buried in Skorpios, next to her brother.

For me, also, it was a devastating time when Artemis died. I felt as if I had lost my mother and my best friend. There had never been another person in my life with whom I could discuss all my problems and receive such expert advice. Yes, there had been times when the vodka had robbed me of my best friend's kind heart, but those moments were only temporary. What was permanent was her clear and truthful voice, never spoiled by jealousy or insensitivity. Every time I looked at the telephone in my office or in my home, I longed to pick it up, dial, and speak to my dear friend. Each evening when I left work, I wanted to ask the driver to take me to Vassileos Georgiou 35, where I would walk through the front door, either alone or with my mother or husband or brother or friend, and immediately be surrounded by the grace and warmth of this special woman and her inviting home. The thought that I would never again hear her sparkling voice, never argue with her or laugh with her or gossip with her or pour out my heart to her saddened me even more than the deaths of the other members of her family, all of whom I had loved dearly. "Artemis," I cried to myself so many moments of the day or night, "please come back. I miss you so very much."

In 1993, five years after Christina's death, both beautiful villas at Vassileos Georgiou 35 were destroyed. The taxes had become extravagant and it was no longer feasible for the estate to continue paying them. Today, the land where the two houses once stood is flat and empty, with no trace of the extraordinary people who had once lived there.

After Artemis' death Christina and Athinoula did visit Kalliroi in her own villa in Switzerland, but not as often as Kalliroi would have liked. Still, Kalliroi made a special point to send Marilena's daughter, Alexandra, to Geneva on special occasions, including the celebration of Athinoula's birthday. Marilena was anxious to bring Alexandra and her other two children, George and Periklis, to Glyfada or Skorpios when Athinoula and Christina were visiting so that Athina would have the chance to get to know her Greek cousins. However, the increasingly rare times Christina and Thierry came to Greece with Athinoula, he seemed ill at ease with Christina's family and found excuses for them to leave sooner than expected. Watching his wife and daughter interact with Greek people made him particularly uncomfortable. Kalliroi, however, worked hard to make certain that Thierry did not succeed in separating his wife and daughter from their Greek origins. She urged Christina to teach her daughter to speak Greek and never to forget her Greek family. "Athina is an Onassis," Christina assured her aunt. "And she will always know that."

Somehow, despite her husband's objections to all of her Greek friends, Christina did continue her friendship with Marina Tchomlekdjoglou Dodero. Marina's strong personality exerted a positive influence on Christina. She was not wild and, unlike so many of Christina's other friends, she did not like to party excessively. She tried to make herself available to listen to Christina whenever Thierry let her down. Sadly, as Artemis had always known, Thierry would let her niece down often and cruelly. And, ultimately, for good.

On August 8, 1988, after numerous separations and reunions during their five and a half years of marriage, and following an extravagant party at the Villa Trianon on the Riviera, which Christina rented to please her husband, Thierry asked his wife for a divorce so that he could marry Gaby. Although Christina knew that Thierry had never dissolved his affair with Gaby, she had convinced herself that he would never abandon her and Athina and marry Gaby. During Christina's marriage to Thierry, Christina had not only paid the rent for his lover Gaby's residences so Gaby could be near Thierry, Christina had also paid all the expenses for the two children born to Gaby and Thierry. Although she tried to bribe Thierry to stay with her, even offering him $10 million to impregnate her with a second child, she was unable to persuade him to abandon his plan to marry Gaby. It was a crushing blow to Christina, but this time, to everyone's surprise, there was no suicide attempt.

Instead, Christina seemed able to face life, albeit sadly, without Thierry. After Christina's divorce, Marina Dodero was one of the first to rush to her friend's defense and persuaded Christina to spend more time with the Tchomlekdjoglou family in Buenos Aires. Marina's family included her unmarried brother, Jorge, whom Christina had known since she was a teenager. Despite her obsession with Thierry and her intention to win him back, Christina began a romance with Jorge, which miraculously began to have a positive affect on her. Christina seemed calmer and more self-controlled. She concentrated for longer periods of time on important business details and kept in close contact with the other executives at the Onassis Establishment. Although she still discussed Thierry frequently and was not adverse to having her picture taken with a handsome escort in the hopes of making him jealous, she appeared ready to begin a new life without him.

Following Marina's advice, she even put blond streaks in her hair, changing her looks positively. Her weight fell and she was able to wear dresses she had been unable to fit into for years. Although he was very attracted to her, Jorge tried to convince Christina to approach their relationship in a slow, steady manner. Christina tried to listen to him, but her impatient old ways began to surface as she urged him to marry her quickly.

In October 1988, Christina enacted revenge on Thierry by changing her will. In her new will, she left her entire estate to Athina, placing control of the estate in the hands of five trustees: four Greek members of the Onassis Establishment, Stelios Papadimitriou, Pablo Ioannidis, Apostolos Zambelas, and Theodore Gavrilidis, and Roussel. According to this will, a simple majority was all that would be necessary for major decisions. Many years after Christina's death, that stipulation in her will turned out to be a highly debated and controversial aspect of both the Onassis Establishment's and Athina's futures.

However, in October 1988, Christina was still in Argentina, enjoying Buenos Aires and its society more and more, and considering buying a new home there so that she and Athina could move there very soon. The last thing she appeared to have on her mind was the death her will discussed. She returned to Switzerland on October 24, abiding by Jorge Tchomlekdjoglou's decision that they should spend time apart and give their romance a chance to progress slowly and meaningfully. However, by the end of the first week of November, Christina was ready to return to Buenos Aires with Athina. This time, for good. Unfortunately, Athina had become ill with an ear infection and could not travel on November 9. Christina, impatient to see Jorge again, left her with her nurse Monique and Thierry, and made plans for Athina and Monique to join her as soon as her daughter's ear infection cleared. When Christina, accompanied as always by Eleni Syros, arrived in Buenos Aires, she concentrated all her efforts on finding a home for her and Athina and began to make plans for their new life in Argentina. It was a life that tragically was never to happen.

It wasn't until five weeks after Christina's death that Eleni was able to talk to me about what had happened to her beloved mistress. Eleni and my husband, George, and I were in the living room of Kalliroi's suite at the Igia Hospital in Athens, where Kalliroi was recovering from a cerebral hemorrhage. It was December 31, 1988, and Eleni was still wearing black in observance of the forty days of mourning following Christina's death. Differing details had been published in numerous newspaper reports of the event, but Eleni's words were the only ones I would trust.

In order to understand Eleni's story, it is necessary to comprehend that Eleni felt a strong responsibility to protect her mistress at all times, even if that meant listening in secret, whenever possible, to all her conversations. "Christina was a troubled, confusing woman," Eleni explained. "I needed to know as much as I could about what was going on in her life so that I could help her in any way I could. If I knew what people were saying to her, then I could help her deal with the problems that always arose." Standing behind closed doors or outside phone booths where her mistress was talking to others or others were talking about her, therefore, was a necessary part of Eleni's duties. Also, Christina never hesitated to tell Eleni everything that was happening in her life, relying on her maid's good sense to help her make important decisions and cope with her problems. It is safe to say that there were few aspects of Christina's daily life that Eleni did not know about.

According to Eleni, on Thursday, November 17, Christina had visited an Orthodox church in Buenos Aires, where she spoke to the priest about the two miscarriages that she had suffered before she became pregnant with Athina. Many people have written that Christina had abortions, but Eleni swore that was not true, and I have always believed Eleni. Eleni explained that Mrs. Christina was very distressed about these miscarriages and was concerned that she would have difficulty becoming pregnant again. More than anything, she told the priest, she wanted more children and she hoped to have a second child soon. The priest listened to her and promised to pray for her. Christina took the wine that the priest offered her with a small spoon and told him how grateful she was for his prayers. When she asked the priest what she could do for him, he told her that her late father had made a promise to help the poor people of Buenos Aires with a large contribution to the church. However, he had not followed through with his promise and had never sent the church the money he had promised.

Like her father and the other members of her family, Christina was a religious person. She told the priest she was certain her father had intended to give the money to the church, but something must have made him forget his promise. She would rectify that error immediately by giving the church $30,000. The priest thanked her and promised she would be blessed by God for her generous deed.

As soon as Christina left the church, she called Pablo Ioannidis, the chief financial adviser for the Onassis Establishment, and instructed him to send the $30,000 to the church immediately. Ioannidis was upset with her impetuous decision to pledge such a large amount to the church and made her promise that she would check with him before she repeated such an action. Christina was saddened by Ioannidis' words and promised him she would check with him before she made another large donation, but she did not hang up until she was certain the money would be sent to the priest immediately.

That night, according to Eleni, Christina was acting quite strange. She left the Alvear Palace, the hotel in Buenos Aires where the two of them were staying, very late at night and did not return for many hours. Wherever the two of them traveled, even though Christina would never sleep alone, Christina always insisted on two suites for them. At the Alvear Palace, she had arranged for Eleni to be in the suite directly beneath hers. However, whenever she was in the hotel, Christina did not like to be alone in her suite, and was constantly in Eleni's suite, talking to her about Jorge and her plans to move to Argentina, as well as recounting all her problems and concerns. That night, however, when Eleni realized her mistress was wandering around the dangerous city alone, she panicked. She alerted the hotel personnel, and they began a search for Christina. However, many hours later, Christina returned to the hotel, safe, alone, and in seemingly good spirits.

The next day, Marina and her husband, Alberto, arrived at the hotel to pick up Christina and Eleni and drive them to the Tortugas Club, an exclusive country club outside of Buenos Aires where Jorge had his own villa and where they would stay for the weekend. Marina, Alberto, Eleni, and Christina arrived at the Tortugas Club at around five o'clock in the afternoon. Although they always had separate rooms wherever they stayed, this time, Eleni convinced Christina that one suite would do for the two of them.

As always, the minute she arrived anywhere, Christina insisted on speaking with her daughter. Even though she had called her before she left Buenos Aires, she was anxious to hear Athina's voice again. It was extremely difficult to find a phone in this remote area on which to place a call to Geneva, but Christina managed to locate a phone and place a call from Argentina to Switzerland. Thierry answered the phone at Boislande and informed Christina that Athinoula was at Gaby's house, a few miles from their villa. Christina was devastated. "I cannot believe you did that!" she cried to her former husband. "I adopted both your children. I pay for everything they or Gaby need. I accepted Gaby to live next to my children. But I cannot accept my Athinoula to be in Gaby's house when I am not there." Sobbing wildly, utterly crushed that she couldn't hear her daughter's voice, Christina hung up the phone.

For an hour after that phone call, Christina cried to Eleni, complaining about how poorly Thierry treated her and how difficult her life was. Eleni tried to comfort her and urged her to be patient. "You and Athinoula are going to have a wonderful life with Jorge," Eleni promised her. "You just have to be patient and not get so upset when something goes wrong. Tomorrow you will speak to Athina and everything will be fine." Christina finally calmed down and allowed Eleni to prepare her for her dinner plans with Jorge. Eleni remembered how beautiful Christina's hair looked that night and how long she brushed it and arranged it in a flowing feminine style. Christina had added more blond streaks to her hair, and they contrasted brilliantly with the remaining jet black tones. Christina sat perfectly still while Eleni helped her with her makeup and clothes, appearing calm and at ease. When she was finally ready, she hesitated before she left the room and kissed Eleni good night with more emotion than usual.

That entire evening, Christina had never seemed happier. After dinner, Christina and Jorge stayed alone, walking and talking outside Jorge's villa. "I always listened secretly, whenever I could, to her conversations," Eleni explained to me yet one more time at the hospital in Athens. "It was the only way I could know what was happening so I would be prepared to help her. I was able to listen to the conversation she had with Jorge in the terrace outside our rooms. She was telling him that she was ready to marry him and he was telling her that he liked her very much but he wanted to take more time. 'You have already had four marriages,' he told her. 'But I have never had one. This is not a play to me. I want my one marriage to be my one and only marriage. We must both be careful and take our time and not rush into anything that might not work out. I love you and I want to marry you, but I want to move slowly.'

"It was the only evening I let her sleep alone," Eleni told me, her eyes filled with tears. I had heard how confused some family members had been about Eleni's not being with Christina that night and I could see Eleni's own despair over the same issue. "I knew she had been with Jorge and they had seemed so happy. When Christina told me to go to bed, that she did not need me anymore, I thought that she wanted to be alone with Jorge, that the two of them would want to make love. Even Marina had thought the two of them were very happy together and wanted to be alone. So I went to bed and left the two of them alone.

"Around three o'clock in the morning, I got up and I saw that Christina's door was half-open. I looked in just a tiny bit and I could see that a small light was on and that music was playing. I went back to sleep for an hour or so and when I got up, I went back to the room and saw that the light was still on and the music was still playing. I thought Jorge and Christina were together. Three or four times, I did that. Finally, around six o'clock in the morning, I went back again, and this time I thought I would just look in a little bit more to make sure Jorge was still there and that Mrs. Christina didn't need me. I saw that her bed was empty. I thought maybe she had gone to Jorge's room."

But Eleni was mistaken, just as she had been all night long. Christina had taken her sleeping pills and gone to her bed alone. When Eleni went into Christina's bedroom and found it empty, Christina was in the bathroom. Dead.

"I cannot understand what happened," Eleni told me and my husband as the three of us sat outside Kalliroi's hospital room. "Christina had no reason to kill herself. She had stopped taking so many pills. She made a promise to do that. She was so slim. She had lost so many pounds. She was so beautiful, and the most important thing was that she was happy over her diet. She was planning a whole new life for her and Athinoula in Buenos Aires. She was planning to marry Jorge. She had everything to live for. I would have gone into her room earlier, but I didn't want to disturb her and Jorge. If only I had gone into her room before six o'clock. If only she had not drunk some scotch or whiskey that night before she went to bed, for she usually avoided alcohol. If only she had not taken her sleeping pills too soon after she had the unaccustomed alcohol. If only . . ."

The official report on Christina's death listed the cause of her death as pulmonary edema. There were many who thought she killed herself, and others who were certain that the years of dieting and regaining the weight she lost took their toll on her heart. There was no evidence of foul play and no long, drawn-out investigation. Perhaps, I wondered, this was because there was no evidence of foul play.

Or, perhaps, because with this death, there was no heartbroken Aristotle Onassis to rail at the senselessness of his loved one's death.

Even years after Christina's death, however, like Eleni, I am still haunted by the "if onlys" in her life. But I could not erase my own thoughts about what might have happened if Eleni had slept with Christina that November night. Perhaps she could have saved Christina. Perhaps Christina could have married Jorge and bought a beautiful villa in Buenos Aires and raised Athina in Argentina. But, like Eleni and Artemis and Kalliroi, I knew Christina too well to believe that her story would have a happy ending. No matter how hard I tried, I couldn't imagine Christina in one place for very long. Somehow, some way, sometime, she would have gotten tired of Jorge and Buenos Aires and her slimmer body, and the sadness and dissatisfaction and desire for whatever she did not have would have come back into her life. Even with the one person in the world beside her who didn't love her because of her money, her precious Athinoula, she still couldn't find enough happiness in any one place or from any one person to make her happy.

Christina's funeral was held in the church in Nea Smyrni, near Athens. The service took place at almost three o'clock, and the rain was coming down in torrents. At least one thousand people were waiting outside the church, but only relatives and close friends were allowed to enter the church. When I walked into the church, I stood on the left side of the body with Christina's relatives, including Kalliroi, Merope, and Nikos Konialidis. Among the crowd of close friends, I saw Sergei Kauzov. He was sobbing uncontrollably.

Thierry and Gaby were standing opposite me, among the crowd of Christina's friends. I could see the tears rolling down Thierry's cheeks. He was dressed in a long black coat and kept his eyes facing down. For the first time since I had met him, he looked sincere. And deeply grieved. As soon as I entered the church, I could hear the voices taunting Thierry. "He killed her," I heard someone in back of me say.

"He is a murderer," I heard another person whisper loudly. I turned around for just one second to see who was saying such things, but I did not recognize any of these people. They were all strangers to me. Still I understood what they meant. Certainly, no one thought Thierry Roussel had actually murdered his wife. Yet there were many who believed that if Christina had not fallen in love with Thierry and if their marriage had not ended so sadly, perhaps Christina would still be alive. I did not agree that her love for Thierry had killed her. Yes, she had loved him more than she had loved her other three husbands. But it was unfair to blame Thierry for her death. Christina's all-too-short life had been filled with too much pain to blame on just one man.

When I let my eyes rest on the casket, I no longer heard another word being spoken in the church. Never had Christina looked more beautiful. Lying in her casket with its glass cover, Christina was dressed in white, holding a single red rose. The casket was covered with white flowers, including roses and *krinakia*. She was slim and her hair was shiny and lustrous. I could not believe that she was dead, gone forever from our lives. The look on her face was one I could not ever remember seeing there. It was a look of peace. Only in death, I realized at that awful moment, was Christina Onassis peaceful. There was no denying that in her thirty-eight years of life, this woman had seen more pain than joy, more agony than pleasure, more conflict than peace. All the money in the world had not insulated her from the private hell that rarely released its grip on her. Even the love for her three-year-old daughter could not silence the voice of her demons. As I wept at her funeral, I prayed that, as she was laid to rest beside her father, her brother, and her aunt, she might, at long last, find this elusive peace.

The burial on Skorpios was small and private. Unlike with her father's and brother's burial services, boatloads of neighbors from Levkas were not allowed to land at Skorpios. Only the members of the immediate family watched in stunned disbelief as her casket, its glass cover replaced with one of rich wood, took its place in the white mausoleum beside her beloved father and brother and aunt. Athinoula did not attend either the funeral service or the burial. "Mommy has gone away on a long trip," she was told. "A very long trip."

Today Athina Onassis-Roussel lives outside Lausanne with her father and his wife, Gaby, and their three children, her two stepsisters and her stepbrother. It is a surprisingly normal family, where her stepmother loves her and both parents try to shield her from the never-ending glare of publicity. It is, of course, not normal that she must be accompanied by bodyguards wherever she goes, but that is a burden she seems able to accept. She attends a French school and visits Skorpios perhaps once a year with her family and friends. When she is there, she seems happy and relaxed, playing like a typical young girl with whatever Skorpios offers her, seemingly unaware of all the agony that has befallen the former residents of this island. The island is maintained at a cost of over $1 million a year so that she can vacation there the few days her father permits.

Thierry has always maintained a relationship with Kalliroi, who has worked hard not to lose her connection to her grand-niece. Two of Kalliroi's grandchildren, Periklis, who is twenty, and George, who is thirty, often travel to Switzerland to visit their second cousin, Athina. Recently, for Athina's recent thirteenth birthday, both Periklis and George visited her in Switzerland. Athina's father often allowed her to spend time in Kalliroi's home in Switzerland; however, Kalliroi recently suffered another stroke, which has kept her confined to a wheelchair and to Greece.

During one of Athina's last visits to her great aunt's chalet in Switzerland, I saw the young girl play with her aunt's small dog, Delphi, and snap pictures of him as he romped throughout the chalet. It was evident that she adored animals. Although Athina is thinner and taller than her mother was at her age and her nose is straight and pretty, I noticed a resemblance between her and her mother in their large black eyes. That day, Athina was a polite, friendly, eleven-year-old who spoke French but, sadly, no Greek. Yet there was a peace and self-confidence about her that I never noticed in her mother.

It appears, however, that there will always be a controversy concerning Athina's mother's death. Approximately once a year, it seems, a journalist will report that Christina's death was no accident, that she did not kill herself, nor did she die of natural causes. Instead, this writer will insist, both of Aristotle Onassis' children were killed by their father's enemies. Never have any of these journalists been able to exhibit any proof that Christina or Alexander were murdered.

While I, too, have doubts about the official report of Christina's death and do know that there was no evidence that she purposefully took too many sleeping pills or drank too much whiskey, I have seen no evidence that she was indeed murdered. It was, most probably, an accident. Too many pills and too much alcohol. But one never knows.

The most serious battle involving the Onassises today, however, concerns Christina's daughter, and is being fought in Greece between Athina's father and Stelios Papadimitriou, the chief trustee of her estate, over her $3 billion shipping fortune. Stelios is concerned that the heir to the Onassis fortune speaks no Greek, except for, perhaps, *Ti kanis?* ("How are you?"), and will never understand the structure or politics of the companies she will inherit when she is eighteen. While her father has made certain she speaks four languages, Athina has never been taught Greek, and those close to her admit that she has no feeling for or interest in Greece or the Greek people. When asked about her grandfather, she recently replied that all she knew about Aristotle Onassis was that he was a very rich man.

The former playboy Thierry may well lose the legal battle concerning his daughter's right to head the Onassis Establishment, about which he has kept her ignorant. However, his wife, Gaby is doing an excellent job of creating a stable, warm, loving home life for Thierry and Christina's daughter and their own three children. Recently, Thierry accused the Onassis Establishment of hiring Israeli agents to execute a plan to kidnap Athinoula. The agents, according to Thierry, conducted an aerial sweep of the Roussel home in Switzerland to gain information for the kidnapping attempt. The idea that the members of the Onassis Establishment, who were always loyal to the Onassis family and were chosen by Christina to protect her daughter's interests, would harm Athinoula appears ridiculous. Each side accuses the other of lying and caring nothing for Athinoula. I know little about what goes on inside the walls of the Roussel home; however, I have personally witnessed the love and affection Athinoula's Greek aunts and cousins maintain for the daughter and granddaughter of the woman and the man they loved so much. It is my fervent hope that Athinoula will continue to visit Skorpios so that she will be able to pray for her grandfather, Aristotle Onassis, her mother, Christina, her uncle, Alexandros, and her great-aunt Artemis, and that someday she will be capable of managing the property these people would want her to control.

Yet all that is certain today amid this confusion is that in the year 2003, when she is eighteen years old, Athina will inherit her grandfather's $3 billion shipping fortune. The result of the acrimonious legal battle now being fought between her father and the Onassis Establishment will determine whether Athina will spend any of that money or much of her time in her maternal grandfather's country. If she is unable to speak Greek and is uninformed about the businesses she is expected to head, it is possible she may be unable to become president of the Onassis Establishment. Where that will leave Thierry is unclear. Yet regardless of the outcome of that court battle, Athina will never know the mother who loved her more than any other thing she possessed in her thirty-eight years of life, perhaps even more than she adored her father. It seems as if this money, earned by Christina's father and Athina's grandfather, once again manages to do little but cause problems and pain for the Onassis women who were born into the world of wealth and privilege he created for them.

Chapter Fifteen

Farewell, Skorpios

S O M U C H changed after Christina died. For the thirteen years that she lived after her father died, those of us who loved her had concentrated so much energy on her chaotic life that, long after she had gone, a huge void remained. When Kalliroi and I had dinner or lunch together, all we talked about was Christina. "I should have been there for her," Kalliroi would say to me, over and over. "I should never have left her alone,"

"But she wasn't alone," I would remind Kalliroi. "She had Eleni. And she was falling in love with Jorge."

"She was alone," Kalliroi would insist. "No matter what any of us did for her, she was still alone. And no one hated being alone more than Christina."

Sometimes, Kalliroi and I would talk about the good times, how happy Christina had been at the beginning of all four of her marriages. And how much she adored her father and the good moments the two of them shared. And how close she and Alexander had become after the end of her first marriage. But when we talked about Athinoula, and how deeply Christina loved her daughter, Kalliroi shed more tears. "She's all we have left," Kalliroi would insist. "And I am so afraid we will lose her, too."

Jackie sent her sincere condolences to both her former sisters-in-law. Whatever she may have felt toward Christina, she ached for the pain she knew her death would cause her aunts. "You must let me know how Kalliroi is doing," Jackie told me when she called me as soon as she learned of Christina's death. "I know Kalliroi is not well, and I worry about her a great deal." We all understood why Jackie did not return to Greece for Christina's funeral. There had never been any love between those two women. Christina had resented her former step-mother so much that it would have been insensitive for Jackie to have come. And Jackie had paid so little attention to Christina when her stepdaughter had been alive that none of us expected Christina's death to affect her.

Yet Jackie was insistent in her concern for Kalliroi. "I know there is nothing I can do for Kalliroi," Jackie told me. "Promise me you will help her find the strength to handle her terrible loss."

This was not the first time that Jackie had extracted such a promise from me. Thirteen years earlier, in 1975, immediately after Aristo's death, Jackie had taken me aside at Artemis' home in Glyfada. "Kiki, you must promise me that you will watch over Artemis," she had insisted as she held my hand tightly. "And you must promise that whenever you come to New York, you will stay with me. I will send my car to the airport as soon as you arrive to bring you to my apartment. Promise me that you will do both of those things for me." And, of course, I did.

But it had been such a different time then. There had been so many different concerns after Aristo's death than there were when his daughter died thirteen years later. After Aristo's death, I had listened to Jackie's words and promised her I would help Artemis, but I had also worried that I would never see Jackie again after she left Greece. After all, she was young, only forty-six years old, still very beautiful, and an American. And Christina, who was very much alive then, had hated her. It was inevitable, I was certain, that Jackie would marry a fascinating American and forget all about her Greek life.

My fears, I soon learned, were for the most part ungrounded. Jackie did return to New York soon after Aristo's funeral, but she called Artemis nearly every day, and called me often, as well. Although Jackie understood that Mr. Onassis had taken good care of his sisters financially, and that each one of them would each receive $100,000 a year plus cost of living increases for the rest of her life, she was still concerned about Artemis. She knew how dependent Artemis had been on her brother, for far more than merely money, and she worried how Artemis would live her life without him. She also knew how ill Professor Garofalidis was and how agonizing it would be for Artemis to lose both her husband and her brother in a short period of time.

At the end of the forty days of mourning, however, it was Artemis who had called Jackie, apprehensive about her welfare, and told her she must discard her black clothes and begin to wear lipstick and jewelry again. "Jackie, you are so young and beautiful," Artemis told her over the phone as I stood beside her. "It is time for you to live your life again. Now you need to find another man who will give you happiness." Artemis had tears in her eyes as she spoke to Jackie. It was not an easy conversation for her, but I knew how much she loved Jackie and that she could not bear to think of Jackie alone and sad.

Jackie had returned to Greece for the ceremony to mark the end of the forty days of mourning for her husband. She looked drawn and painfully thin as she stepped off the plane, and I worried that she was ill. As we drove together to Glyfada, she insisted that she was well, merely tired from her long flight. Artemis kissed Jackie in the tradi-

tional Greek manner when they greeted each other at Vassileos Georgiou 35. It was the first time since Aristo had died that I saw Artemis
smile. Christina was not in Glyfada when Jackie arrived, purposefully
having left the house before Jackie's flight landed in Athens.

The day of the actual ceremony, when Artemis and Jackie and I
were in the VIP lounge waiting for our flight to Skorpios, many of the
employees of Olympic Airways came into the lounge to greet Jackie personally. She was warm and cordial to each of them, appearing like a simple, unaffected woman as she held their hands and remembered many
of their names. She was touched by their sincere response to her and
thanked them for their sympathetic thoughts. When Christina met
Jackie in Skorpios, the two women were polite to each other, also kissing and inquiring about each other's health. I knew that Christina was
struggling to put aside her dislike for Jackie for the day, and I was grateful that she was pleasing her aunt Artemis with her courteous behavior.

During the ceremony itself, Jackie participated in each aspect of
the service. Although she was Catholic, she was respectful of the Greek
Orthodox ceremony. Accepting the holy water from the priest, she
showed us all that she was still proud to be a Greek woman. As I sat
beside Artemis and Jackie, I noticed how the two sisters-in-law held
hands and frequently whispered to each other. It was obvious that the
warmth and affection they held for each other had not diminished during Jackie's forty-day absence. There have been reports in other books
about Mrs. Jackie that her three sisters-in-law were cold and indifferent to her at Aristo's funeral and at this service. It is obvious to me that
no one who wrote such a thing was ever present to witness the loving
behavior of these four women to one another at these painful events.

Yet no matter how hard we all intended to keep in touch, we
understood that this service also marked the end of Jackie's life in
Greece. Jackie knew that she would always have the love of Aristo's
three sisters and her good friend Niki Goulandris. And she would
never lose the memories of her husband Aristo and their life together.
I saw the way her head turned slightly during the service and she
glanced at the row to her right, where Christina sat, carefully keeping
her eyes averted from Jackie. I touched Jackie's hand lightly. "Do not
worry about Christina today," I whispered softly, and she squeezed my
hand in response.

After the ceremony was over and Christina and most of the other guests had departed the island, Jackie remained. She told me she needed to be alone for a short time while she gathered the rest of her belongings from the pink house and from the *Christina* and prepared them to be sent back to New York. She asked me to join her at the pink house in an hour. When I arrived at the house, she looked even more exhausted than she had when she had arrived in Athens, and I was grateful for the chance to help her. "There is so much to do, Kiki," she told me as she rested for just a few minutes in a comfortable beige chair inside the pink house. "I had not realized how much I had left to do until now." The house looked as beautiful as it had when Jackie and Aristo had been staying in it, but there was no denying that those days were over. I thought of the large, empty bed, with its canopy of gauze, and my own eyes filled with tears.

"You don't have to do everything today," I told her. "After all, you will come back often. All the people in Skorpios like you so much. They will be so sad if you do not return often."

Jackie smiled gratefully as she stood up and got back to work. I knew she was thinking about the words I did not speak. The people in Skorpios would, indeed, be delighted to have her visit, but their new employer, Christina Onassis, would not. Jackie could, of course, return to Skorpios anytime she wanted to visit the grave of her husband. But she would never want to do it when his daughter was on the island. I tried to put those sad thoughts out of my mind and enjoy Jackie's company while she was here.

For the next few hours, I remained with Jackie while she assembled her belongings in the pink house. I helped her decide which items she would leave here and which ones we would put tags on and have sent to New York. I know how many writers have said that all she cared about were money and material possessions. Yet when I watched her sit down and stare at so many of the objects she had bought during her marriage to Aristo, all I saw was a woman alone with her memories. Often, after she put a vase or a statue or a candlestick in a box, she closed her eyes and sat perfectly still, as if remembering some far-off place or some experience from a long time ago.

After the two of us finished organizing her belongings in the pink house, we walked together to the *Christina,* where she gathered the remaining items she would have shipped to New York. The last thing she put aside was the jade statue of the Buddha, the god of the Chinese, accented with rubies, that Aristo had treasured. J. Paul Getty, one of the richest men in the world and Aristo's good friend, owned a similar statue, but Aristo's Buddha had always been the more exquisite one. I remembered that Artemis had told me that Christina had briefly objected to giving that statue to Jackie, but Artemis had convinced her that Jackie should have it. "Oh, let her have whatever she wants," Christina had answered her aunt. "Just so long as I never have to see her miserable face again, I don't care if she takes the whole damned boat."

I was lost in my own thoughts when I suddenly realized that Jackie was standing on the deck of the ship, looking at the ocean, and weeping softly. I was walking away, hoping to allow her a private moment, when she turned around and faced me, her face stained with tears. "Would you mind, Kiki," she asked, her voice breaking with emotion, "if I tell you this one little story?" I stopped and walked over to stand beside her.

"One day, Aristo and I were sitting together outside the pink house and he was feeling very tender," she began, gazing back out at the sea. "'Honey,' he said to me, 'the woman, you know, is like the world.'

"I laughed for I knew he was going to tell me another of his offbeat tales. 'Oh, really, Ari,' I answered him. 'And how is that true?'

"Laughing, he explained it to me. 'At twenty years, she is like Africa. Semi-explored. At thirty years, she is like India. Warm, mature, and mysterious. At forty years, she is like America. Technically perfect. At fifty years, she is like Europe. All in ruins. At sixty years, she is like Siberia. Everyone knows where she is, but no one wants to go to her.'

"When he finished his little tale, I laughed and touched his mouth and said he was a philosopher. 'You must promise to tell me that tale every ten years,' I told him, and he agreed. Then I kissed him and I could tell that he felt very pleased with himself. With his life. And with me. And now I cannot stop thinking about that day."

And then she moved farther away from me, still facing the sea. "My darling," I could hear her say as I stood there, my eyes looking down, "I wish you could repeat that tale to me today. Almost seven years have passed for us and I want to hear it again." Quietly, without another word, I walked away and left her alone.

When the two of us returned to Athens, Jackie stayed with Artemis for a week. We all knew that it would be the last time that Christina would allow such a visit, and it was bittersweet to have Jackie there. Artemis and Jackie spent most of every day together, walking along the beach and sitting beside each other, always talking, always holding hands.

Before Jackie left Athens, Artemis gave a small dinner party for her. Jackie was gracious to Artemis' friends that night and greeted each one with warmth and pleasure. All the help in the house were overjoyed to see her. Panagiotis cooked Greek dishes Jackie had always liked and made certain the bed in the guest room was beautifully appointed for her. He had assumed, correctly, that she would not sleep alone in the huge bed she and Aristo had always shared. All of the employees fussed over her, showing their affection for her. They all adored her, for she was always smiling at them and never talked too much or asked too much of any of them.

During the dinner party, Jackie tried to be gay and take part in the conversations, but everyone could see the pain in her eyes. Artemis talked often of her brother that night, telling stories about the two of them growing up in Smyrna and how strict their father and stepmother had been. She also reminisced about the cruises she and Aristo had taken with high-society people and all the women who had been charmed by her younger brother. "Aristo was indifferent to these women," Artemis said. "The only woman who made him happy was Jackie. He always told me how lucky he was that he found Jackie." Jackie smiled during those stories, but it was her sad smile. I don't know why but I kept thinking of Maria that evening. I knew that she, too, had made Artemis' only brother happy. I hoped Jackie wasn't smiling her sad smile because she shared my unspeakable thought.

That evening, after all the dinner guests had left, Jackie talked to Artemis long into the evening. "I am feeling so fragile," she confided to her sister-in-law. "Sometimes I think that I am responsible for my misfortune. My first husband died in my arms. I was always telling him that he should be protected, but he would not listen to me. Before my second husband died, I begged him to take care of himself, but he wouldn't listen to me. He wouldn't visit the doctor. He wouldn't take his medicines. He would not even use a bodyguard. He could have been killed at any moment during our marriage. No matter what I did, I couldn't save either one of the two men I loved."

"That was God's will," Artemis tried to convince her. "Now, you have your own children to think about, and you have to take care of them and make a new life for yourself." As always, Jackie promised Artemis that she would try to follow her advice. When Artemis told me that story, I could not help thinking that Christina would have agreed with everything Jackie said about herself. But, again, my irreverent thoughts remained, of course, unutterable, hurting only me with their barbs.

One other night during her week in Glyfada, Jackie was especially attentive to my fiancé, George, during dinner, fussing over him, requesting special foods for him and trying to draw him out with her sincere questions. "You will bring Kiki to New York to spend time with me there," she told him as we were preparing to leave, and my husband-to-be promised that he would do just that. But I knew that when I saw Jackie in New York, I would be alone. For, unlike me, my future husband could not relax around this famous woman, or understand that she was no different from any other close friend in our lives.

The day Jackie left Greece, I asked Artemis if George and I could drive her sister-in-law to the airport. As Jackie sat in the back of our car, I stared at her through the rearview mirror and noticed that during the entire ride to the airport, there was no trace of a smile on her face. I thought of all the photographs I had seen of her, during tragic as well as happy times, and how her famous smile had always appeared on her face. If a photographer could have snapped a picture as Jackie sat alone, in the back of George's new white BMW, he would have had a most unusual and one-of-a-kind photograph.

When it was time for her to catch her flight to New York, once again Jackie made me promise that George and I would stay in New York with her for a few days in the near future. "I would love that more than anything else," she told me as she kissed me good-bye on both my cheeks. We both knew that she would never return to Glyfada or Skorpios for more than a quick visit and that her life in Greece was over.

George and I promised that we would come, but in my heart, I doubted that would happen. Jackie needed to begin a new life. She would have her memories of Aristo, but she was a young woman and she had suffered enough. Her future was not Greece. We all knew that.

But the memories of her years with us would remain a part of all of us who had loved the second Mrs. Aristotle Onassis. As I watched Jackie board her plane, a tall, slender woman, I remembered that first day I had met her in Glyfada nearly seven years earlier. She had been so lovely and so gracious, so full of hope, so eager to begin a new life in a new country with a new family. And now it was all over. She was leaving us, with nothing but memories of a marriage filled with promise and love, with pain and sorrow, with extravagant presents and exotic trips, with deception and despair, but most of all with a passion that not even the most persistent of the paparazzi who hounded this extraordinary couple every day of those years could capture on his film.

Although Jackie never brought her children back to Greece after her husband's memorial service, she did return to stay with Niki Goulandris and visit her sisters-in-law. For Christina's wedding to Alexander Andreadis, shortly after the ceremony to mark the end of the mourning period for Aristo, she even managed to stay at Glyfada.

So often, during those years after Aristo died, Jackie called Artemis and the two of them would talk about everything they were doing. One day when I was in Glyfada, Jackie called, and Artemis settled into her favorite chair for a relaxing chat with her sister-in-law. A few minutes into the call, however, I could see that this was not going to be their typical call. "Oh, Jackie," Artemis was saying, "of course, I want you to see him. He is a lovely man and he would be good for you." For nearly an hour the two of them talked, as Artemis kept repeating her plea that Jackie begin a new relationship with another man. Someone Artemis obviously knew.

Finally, when the two women said good-bye to each other, Artemis explained to me that Jackie had met a Greek man in New York, Mihalis Kakoviannis, who had been a business associate of Aristo. Mihalis was also a well-respected producer, in whose films the famous Greek actress Irini Pappa frequently appeared. He even looked a bit like Aristo, was a serious and well-educated man, and had many fascinating stories to share with Jackie about her Greek husband. Jackie had been charmed by Mihalis and was considering dating him. "I hope she does just that," Artemis told me. "Nothing could make me happier."

As it turned out, the relationship between Jackie and Mihalis did not develop into a romantic one. Still, Jackie enjoyed his company and considered Mihalis a good friend. "She is looking for someone like Aristo," Artemis explained to me. "She kept telling me that Aristo made her feel like a real woman and she will never find another man like him. She said that Aristo offered her everything she needed, especially support and security. No one, she insisted, could replace him in her life. But I told her she would find someone who would make her very happy. I do not know if she believes me."

Jackie remained in touch with both Kalliroi and Merope after Artemis' death. However, we all understood that with the loss of Artemis, Jackie's life in Greece was virtually completed. She did occasionally speak to Merope, but since Merope spent her time traveling or in Monte Carlo, and kept busy, both with her husband's business and with her large family of her sons, daughters-in-law and grandchildren, the calls were few. Jackie and Kalliroi spoke to each other more frequently and tried to maintain a long-distance friendship. Jackie worried about Kalliroi's health and would call me, concerned, if she was unable to reach Kalliroi on the telephone.

Once, when I was visiting Kalliroi in Lagonissi, Jackie called and Kalliroi had me pick up the phone to talk to Jackie for a few minutes. I heard the laughter as the two of them talked and was struck by the difference in the two sisters' relationship to their American sister-in-law. With Artemis, Jackie had always been serious, asking advice and discussing important issues. With Kalliroi, she seemed looser, more relaxed and more entertaining. The two women talked about restaurants and clothes and men and gossiped about people they knew. I also knew that when Kalliroi traveled to New York, she would often call Jackie, and occasionally the two of them shopped and went out to dinner together.

A year after Christina died, in 1989, Kalliroi suffered a cerebral hemorrhage, and although she recovered from that stroke, today she can walk little and is confined to a wheelchair. In the winter, she spends her days in her elegant apartment at 12 Rigillis in downtown Athens, the only Onassis who still resides in Greece. During the last few years of Jackie's life, Kalliroi spoke to her sister-in-law occasionally, and she knew when Jackie became very ill. During their final phone call in May 1994, Jackie assured Kalliroi that she was getting better. "I am planning to visit you soon," she told Kalliroi. "I want to spend a few days with you in Lagonissi." But that would never happen. Martha Sgubin told Kalliroi how weak Jackie was, but said that Jackie was adamant about not upsetting Kalliroi with the truth about her condition.

When I learned of Jackie's death on May 19, 1994, I immediately called Kalliroi. The two of us cried over the telephone as we remembered the beautiful woman who had come to Skorpios, full of love and hope for a new life. Later, that same day, Miltos Yiannacopoulos came to see me, and together we mourned this vital and lovely lady. "He loved her very much," Miltos said to me, and I nodded, understanding what he meant. "She wasn't the only woman he loved," he added, "but he did love her very much."

Miltos' words stayed with me as I tried to sleep that evening. But sleep would not come. Instead, I lay there, remembering the employer who had changed my life and who had loved more than one woman. The other woman, Maria Callas, flashed before my eyes many times that night, but the one image that would not quit my mind was of the last time I had seen her. It had been seventeen years before Jackie died, in the summer of 1977, nearly two years after Aristo had died.

I had been shocked, one hot August day, when I picked up the telephone in my office and heard Maria's voice on the other end of the line. "I am so sorry to bother you, Kiki," she had greeted me, her voice soft and tremulous. "But I have a great favor to ask of you." The favor had been for me to make the necessary arrangements for her to visit Aristo's grave in Skorpios. I knew as soon as Maria asked that I would do anything in my power to grant her wish. I had never forgotten what Christina had told me in the hospital in Paris the last time I had visited her father. She had said that she wished with all her heart that Maria had married her father. The callousness of forbidding this woman to visit her lover as he lay dying had never stopped haunting me. Without asking Artemis or Christina for her permission, I promised Maria I would arrange such a visit as soon as possible. She thanked me and hung up.

Two days later, I met Maria's plane from Paris and led her to the

VIP lounge. Here we awaited the Learjet that would fly her to Aktion, where she would catch a ferry to Skorpios. Maria looked thinner and older than I had expected, and overwhelmingly sad. She wore a large black hat and a black dress, flat-heeled shoes, and little makeup. Few people who passed her in the airport appeared to recognize Greece's most famous opera singer. She carried a small pocketbook and a single bouquet of red roses.

"You are so kind to help me," she greeted me. "You were always kind to me when I called to speak to Aristo. I am glad I have a chance to meet you again." The voice was so ordinary that I thought it could not belong to Maria Callas. But when she removed her sunglasses, I saw the large black eyes, red rimmed and filled with sorrow, and unmistakably hers.

"It is my pleasure," I told her, finding it difficult to speak in her presence. "I always admired you. I only wish I could have helped you more."

"There was nothing else you or anyone else could have done," she said sadly. Then she stood up and faced me, her eyes cast downward. She seemed not so much anxious to talk to me, as unable to stop herself from speaking. It was as if the words had been bottled up in her for so long that nothing, not even her exhausted physical condition, could prevent her from releasing them.

"From the moment Aristo married Jackie Kennedy in 1968," she continued, "I have been playing my own tragedy. I can't believe how long my performance has lasted. I never knew exactly how this tragedy would end, but I knew it would be painful. Very painful. Now that Aristo has died, this is my final appearance. The end of my role is here.

"When Aristo lost his son, I understood his pain, for I had lost my self-confidence and could no longer sing in front of others. I tried to sing in London that same year, but I had to cancel my performance because I had lost the strength of my voice. He tried to live without Alexandros, but his confidence and love of life had vanished, too. Both of us lost everything that mattered in our lives. I had no child, but I understood what a great tragedy had happened to him. He did not sing, but he knew that a part of me had died, too. We had nothing but each other. And, for a little while, but just for a little while, that was enough."

I waited, silent, for her to speak more, but that was all she would say. I could not think of a word to speak to her, so the two of us stood in silence, facing each other, until I saw that it was time for her to catch the flight to Aktion. When I walked her to the plane, I asked if she would like me to accompany her to Skorpios, for she seemed so weak and sad that I worried about her health. "It would be no trouble," I assured her. "I can make certain you catch your ferry and that you find the grave."

She did not hesitate. "It is better if I go alone," she assured me. "I know the island well and I know exactly where to find Aristo. I will see you when I return."

I could not head back to my office after her flight left for Aktion. I could not leave the lounge. Instead, I sat in my seat, listening once more to what she had said to me, feeling the pain in her voice as her words replayed in my mind. I regretted that I had not said a word to Maria, that I had not told her how much we all knew Aristo loved her, right up until the day he died. That her face was the only one he wanted to see as he lay dying. That it had been a cruel act to have denied her presence at his deathbed. But, I told myself many times after she left for Skorpios, it had not been my role to have spoken such powerful words to her. Besides, even if it had been right for me to have said such things to her, I understood that she did not want me to speak. She wanted only for me to listen. And that I did.

I made arrangements for an employee from Skorpios to meet Maria's ferry from Aktion and escort her to the mausoleum. He promised that he would be there when she arrived on the island and would watch over her carefully until she left. I knew it was only a half-hour flight, and a brief ferry ride, but I could not stop worrying about Maria. Luckily, I was able to reach the employee at Skorpios, who informed me that Miss Callas had spent almost an hour at the grave by herself, and was presently returning to Athens.

It was less than three hours after she had originally left the airport in Athens when Maria returned there, and I escorted her back to the VIP lounge, where she could await her return flight to Paris. She did not look any weaker than when she'd left for the island, but there was a look in her eyes that told me she had accomplished what she had intended to do. When it was time for her to board her flight to Paris, she shook my hand and kissed me on both cheeks. "You have been so kind to me," she said. "I am very grateful." And then she walked away from me, no longer a celebrated diva, but merely, and at long last, a grief-stricken Greek widow. This time she no longer carried the flowers, and her step was even slower than when she'd arrived. And I knew I had just witnessed the final performance of her life.

I never told Artemis or Christina what I did that day. But the image of Maria Callas, carrying the roses to the grave of the man she loved and who loved her just as passionately until the day he died, will never fade from my memory. Maria died a short time after that visit, at the age of fifty-three, on September 16, 1977. I was not surprised. She had been barely alive the day she went to Skorpios.

The night of Jackie's death, seventeen years after Maria died, my thoughts turned yet once again to the magical island where Aristo had brought both these women whom he had loved. Here, amid the extraordinary beauty and enchantment that defined Skorpios, he loved and was loved by these two extraordinary and enchanting women. Yet, despite the wondrous powers of this island and this man, these loves were not strong enough for them to escape the barbs of fate.

Still, the island's allure continued, long after Aristo had ceased to roam its shores. For it was here, on Skorpios, where Jackie, like Maria, had come, in private, one last time to bid farewell to the man whom she loved and who had loved her. On her last trip to Skorpios, when Christina had been in Switzerland, I spent an afternoon on the island with Jackie. She had been staying in the pink house and, after a quiet lunch in the garden, the two of us went for a walk along the roads she loved so much.

Mrs. Jackie had been quiet and said little as she gathered wildflowers from all over the island, white and yellow and red and violet flowers, to carry to Mr. Onassis' grave. I stayed behind as she approached her late husband's grave, understanding that she needed to be alone there. For so much of her life, she had been besieged by paparazzi who photographed her every move. Yet at that moment, as she slowly and somberly knelt beside her second husband's grave, weeping softly as she gently lay the flowers, taking care to place them elegantly around the headstone, there was no one besides me to record this moment. Quickly I walked away, yet as sad as I was to witness her grief, a part of me found solace in the fact that she had indeed loved this man and would, perhaps for the rest of her life, feel a passion for the love they had once shared. Like Artemis, who was now, like her brother, gone from our world and buried beneath the soil of this island, all I wished was that Jackie Onassis would find new happiness for herself. Soon.

The night Jackie died, I did not sleep at all. Instead, I remained awake, remembering the two women who had loved the same man and who had shared with me their last painful visits to Skorpios. Jackie had surprised no one by continuing to live her life without the man who ruled that magical island. She had been sad and filled with grief, and a part of her continued to love him, but as she had done when she lost her first husband, she had persevered without him. Maria, however, had been unable to live in a world where that indomitable man, the one man she had ever loved, no longer existed. She could no longer stand on the stage and play her role without his scintillating presence. Was Jackie stronger than Maria? Did she love Aristotle Onassis less? Those are questions I would never assume to answer. Both women loved the same man and were loved by him. Of that, and that alone, I am certain.

Jackie's death marked the end of the final chapter in the book of the women who had loved Aristotle Onassis. Yet Maria's chapter, which had ended seventeen years earlier, was so infinitely sad it seemed its own calamitous opera. Who was I, I asked myself as I thought once again about these two celebrated women, to pass judgment on whose love was the more poignant or passionate or tormented? I was not a key player on this stage. But the seat I was given in which to watch this Greek tragedy unfold afforded me a singular view of so many of its acts. Today, the crystal blue sea continues to roll effortlessly against the shores of the island of Skorpios, while so many of its inhabitants whose joys and pains I witnessed have perished, swept away by the waves of disease, despair, and destructive forces beyond their control. But no sea can completely obliterate their stories which, like the hopes and loves of the players of this extraordinary tragic drama, live forever.

Index